Communities
South Carolina

HARCOURT BRACE SOCIAL STUDIES

Series Authors

Dr. Richard G. Boehm

Claudia Hoone

Dr. Thomas M. McGowan

Dr. Mabel C. McKinney-Browning

Dr. Ofelia B. Miramontes

Dr. Priscilla H. Porter

Consultant for South Carolina

Dr. Michael J. Berson

Series Consultants

Dr. Alma Flor Ada

Dr. Phillip Bacon

Dr. W. Dorsey Hammond

Dr. Asa Grant Hilliard, III

HARCOURT BRACE & COMPANY

Orlando Atlanta Austin Boston San Francisco Chicago Dallas

New York Toronto London

 Visit The Learning Site at http://www.hbschool.com

Series Authors

Dr. Richard G. Boehm
Professor and Jessie H. Jones Distinguished
    Chair in Geographic Education
Department of Geography and Planning
Southwest Texas State University
San Marcos, Texas

Claudia Hoone
Teacher
Ralph Waldo Emerson School #58
Indianapolis, Indiana

Dr. Thomas M. McGowan
Associate Professor
Division of Curriculum and Instruction
Arizona State University
Tempe, Arizona

Dr. Mabel C. McKinney-Browning
Director
Division for Public Education
American Bar Association
Chicago, Illinois

Dr. Ofelia B. Miramontes
Associate Professor
School of Education
University of Colorado
Boulder, Colorado

Dr. Priscilla H. Porter
Co-Director
Center for History–Social Science Education
School of Education
California State University, Dominguez Hills
Carson, California

Consultant for South Carolina

Dr. Michael J. Berson
Former President of the South Carolina
    Council for the Social Studies
Assistant Professor
College of Education
University of South Florida
Tampa, Florida

Series Consultants

Dr. Alma Flor Ada
Professor
School of Education
University of San Francisco
San Francisco, California

Dr. Phillip Bacon
Professor Emeritus of Geography
    and Anthropology
University of Houston
Houston, Texas

Dr. W. Dorsey Hammond
Professor of Education
Oakland University
Rochester, Michigan

Dr. Asa Grant Hilliard, III
Fuller E. Callaway Professor of Urban Education
Georgia State University
Atlanta, Georgia

Media, Literature, and Language Specialists

Suzanne C. Baxley
Media Specialist
Brooklyn Springs Elementary School
Lancaster, South Carolina

Dr. Joseph A. Braun, Jr.
Professor of Elementary Social Studies
Department of Curriculum and Instruction
Illinois State University
Normal, Illinois

Meredith McGowan
Youth Services Librarian
Tempe Public Library
Tempe, Arizona

Rebecca Valbuena
Language Development Specialist
Stanton Elementary School
Glendora, California

Grade-Level Consultants and Reviewers

Laura Kaffer Anderson, Teacher
Mertz Elementary School
Mobile, Alabama

Kaffy Babineaux
Thinking Skills/Curriculum Coordinator K–3
A.N. Boucher Elementary School
Lafayette, Louisiana

Della P. Bacote, Teacher
Gold Hill Elementary School
Fort Mill, South Carolina

Carol Brooks, Curator
Arizona Historical Society
Yuma, Arizona

Mary Carl, Teacher
Culver Elementary School
Evansville, Indiana

Monti C. Caughman, Teacher
Gilbert Elementary School
Gilbert, South Carolina

Charlene J. Chapman, Teacher
Meadowfield Elementary School
Columbia, South Carolina

Kathy L. Cook, Teacher
Brushy Creek Elementary School
Taylors, South Carolina

Dr. Debra P. Cox
Curriculum Coordinator
Code Elementary School
Seneca, South Carolina

Dr. Robert P. Green, Jr.
Professor
Department of Education
Clemson University
Clemson, South Carolina

Paulette S. Hallman, Teacher
Oakdale Elementary School
Rock Hill, South Carolina

Alexia Jones Helsley
Education Director
South Carolina Department of Archives
    and History
Columbia, South Carolina

Julie H. Honeycutt, Teacher
Little Creek School
Norfolk, Virginia

Diane Hoyt-Goldsmith
Children's Author
Square Moon Productions
Orinda, California

Dr. Barbara Talbert Jackson
Executive Director
Grants Administration (Retired)
District of Columbia Public Schools
Washington, D.C.

Sherman E. Pyatt, Archivist
Avery Research Center for African American
    History and Culture
Charleston, South Carolina

Gregory S. Soghoian
Learning Director
McCord Elementary School
Orange Cove, California

Margaret Wall, Teacher
Millbrook Elementary School
Aiken, South Carolina

Laura K. White, Teacher
Buena Vista Elementary School
Greer, South Carolina

Shelley S. Winkler, Teacher
Mary H. Wright Elementary School
Spartanburg, South Carolina

Susan S. Wise
Resident Teacher Consultant
South Carolina Geographic Alliance
Columbia, South Carolina

Sandra Wren, Teacher
Pope Elementary School
Arlington, Texas

Printed in the United States of America

ISBN 0-15-314186-7

2 3 4 5 6 7 8 9 10   032   02   01   00

Contents

Unit	What Is a Community?	24

F.Y.I.

Literature, Primary Sources, and Documents

F.Y.I.

Building Basic Study Skills

Building Citizenship

Features

F.Y.I.

Maps

F.Y.I.

Time Lines

Charts, Graphs, Diagrams, and Tables

Atlas

Contents

THE WORLD

WESTERN HEMISPHERE

UNITED STATES

SOUTH CAROLINA

GEOGRAPHY TERMS

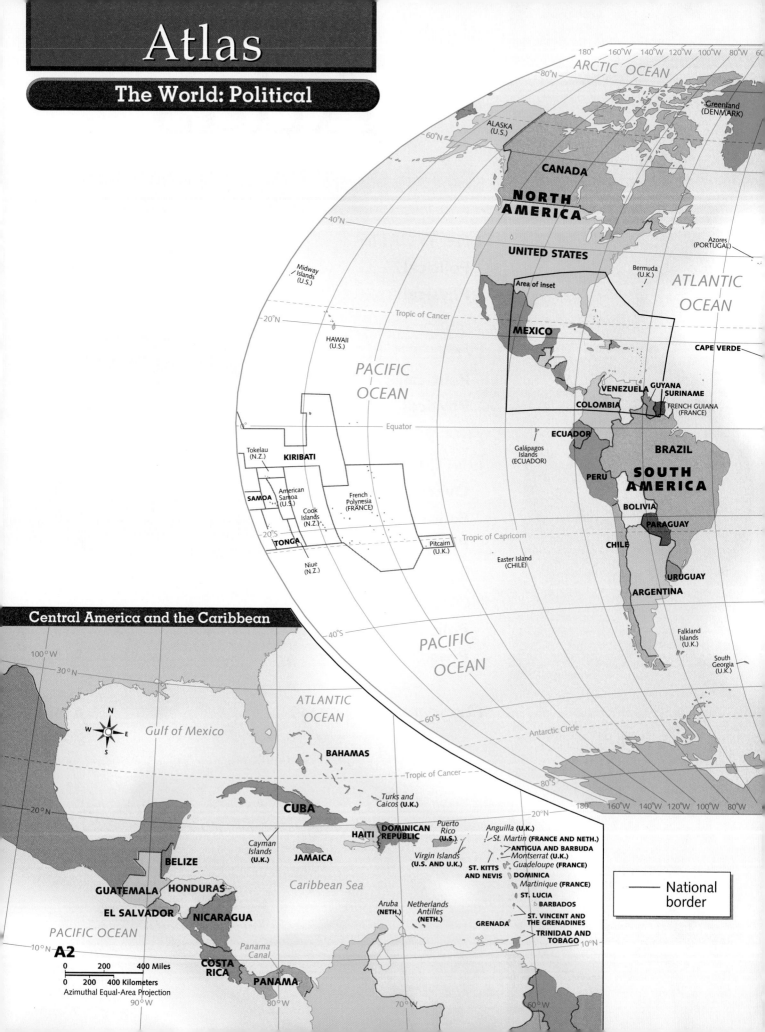

ARCTIC OCEAN

Greenland (DENMARK)

ALASKA (U.S.)

CANADA

NORTH AMERICA

UNITED STATES

Azores (PORTUGAL)

Bermuda (U.K.)

ATLANTIC OCEAN

Midway Islands (U.S.)

Area of inset

Tropic of Cancer

MEXICO

CAPE VERDE

HAWAII (U.S.)

PACIFIC OCEAN

VENEZUELA GUYANA SURINAME

COLOMBIA

FRENCH GUIANA (FRANCE)

Equator

ECUADOR

BRAZIL

Tokelau (N.Z.)

KIRIBATI

Galápagos Islands (ECUADOR)

SOUTH AMERICA

PERU

SAMOA

American Samoa (U.S.)

Cook Islands (N.Z.)

French Polynesia (FRANCE)

BOLIVIA

PARAGUAY

TONGA

20°S

Niue (N.Z.)

Pitcairn (U.K.)

Tropic of Capricorn

Easter Island (CHILE)

CHILE

URUGUAY

ARGENTINA

PACIFIC OCEAN

Falkland Islands (U.K.)

South Georgia (U.K.)

40°S

Antarctic Circle

80°S

180° 160°W 140°W 120°W 100°W 80°W

60°S

Central America and the Caribbean

100°W

30°N

Gulf of Mexico

ATLANTIC OCEAN

BAHAMAS

Tropic of Cancer

20°N

Turks and Caicos (U.K.)

CUBA

DOMINICAN REPUBLIC

Puerto Rico (U.S.)

Anguilla (U.K.)

St. Martin (FRANCE AND NETH.)

ANTIGUA AND BARBUDA

Cayman Islands (U.K.)

HAITI

Virgin Islands (U.S. AND U.K.)

Montserrat (U.K.)

Guadeloupe (FRANCE)

BELIZE

JAMAICA

Caribbean Sea

ST. KITTS AND NEVIS

DOMINICA

GUATEMALA

HONDURAS

Martinique (FRANCE)

ST. LUCIA

EL SALVADOR

NICARAGUA

Aruba (NETH.)

Netherlands Antilles (NETH.)

BARBADOS

PACIFIC OCEAN

GRENADA

ST. VINCENT AND THE GRENADINES

10°N

A2

Panama Canal

TRINIDAD AND TOBAGO

10°N

0   200   400 Miles

0   200   400 Kilometers

COSTA RICA

PANAMA

Azimuthal Equal-Area Projection

90°W

80°W

70°W

60°W

National border

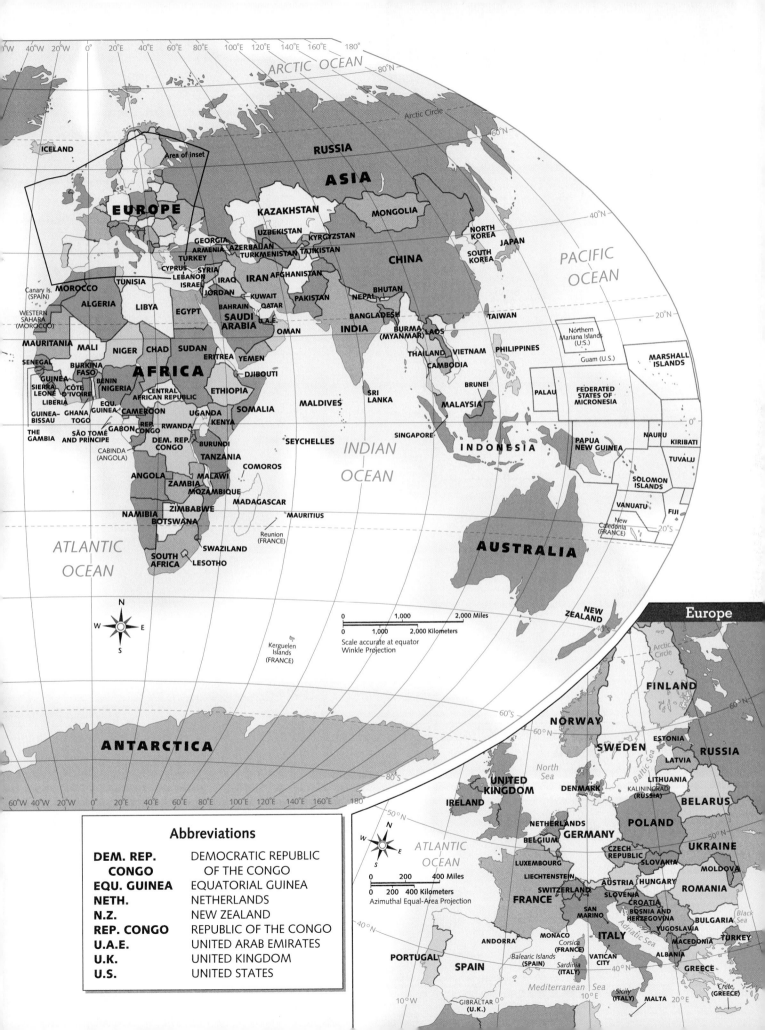

ARCTIC OCEAN

80°N

Arctic Circle

60°N

ICELAND

Area of inset

RUSSIA

ASIA

EUROPE

KAZAKHSTAN

MONGOLIA

40°N

NORTH KOREA

JAPAN

PACIFIC OCEAN

GEORGIA
ARMENIA
AZERBAIJAN
TURKEY
TURKMENISTAN
UZBEKISTAN
TAJIKISTAN
KYRGYZSTAN

CHINA

SOUTH KOREA

CYPRUS
LEBANON
SYRIA
ISRAEL
IRAQ
IRAN
AFGHANISTAN

Canary Is. (SPAIN)

MOROCCO

TUNISIA

JORDAN

KUWAIT

PAKISTAN

NEPAL

BHUTAN

WESTERN SAHARA (MOROCCO)

ALGERIA

LIBYA

EGYPT

BAHRAIN
QATAR
U.A.E.

SAUDI ARABIA

BANGLADESH

BURMA (MYANMAR)

TAIWAN

20°N

MAURITANIA

MALI

NIGER

CHAD

SUDAN

OMAN

INDIA

LAOS

Northern Mariana Islands (U.S.)

ERITREA

YEMEN

THAILAND

VIETNAM

PHILIPPINES

Guam (U.S.)

MARSHALL ISLANDS

SENEGAL

BURKINA FASO

AFRICA

DJIBOUTI

CAMBODIA

GUINEA
SIERRA LEONE
CÔTE D'IVOIRE

BENIN
NIGERIA

CENTRAL AFRICAN REPUBLIC

ETHIOPIA

SRI LANKA

BRUNEI

PALAU

FEDERATED STATES OF MICRONESIA

LIBERIA

EQU. GUINEA

CAMEROON

UGANDA

SOMALIA

MALDIVES

MALAYSIA

0°

GUINEA-BISSAU

GHANA
TOGO

GABON

REP. CONGO

RWANDA

KENYA

THE GAMBIA

SÃO TOMÉ AND PRÍNCIPE

DEM. REP. CONGO

BURUNDI

SEYCHELLES

INDIAN OCEAN

SINGAPORE

INDONESIA

PAPUA NEW GUINEA

NAURU

KIRIBATI

CABINDA (ANGOLA)

TANZANIA

TUVALU

ANGOLA

MALAWI

COMOROS

ZAMBIA

MOZAMBIQUE

SOLOMON ISLANDS

NAMIBIA

ZIMBABWE

MADAGASCAR

MAURITIUS

VANUATU

FIJI

New Caledonia (FRANCE)

20°S

BOTSWANA

Reunion (FRANCE)

ATLANTIC OCEAN

SOUTH AFRICA

SWAZILAND

LESOTHO

AUSTRALIA

N
W E
S

1,000   2,000 Miles
1,000   2,000 Kilometers

Scale accurate at equator
Winkle Projection

Kerguelen Islands (FRANCE)

NEW ZEALAND

40°S

60°S

ANTARCTICA

80°S

60°W 40°W 20°W   0°   20°E 40°E 60°E 80°E 100°E 120°E 140°E 160°E 180°

Abbreviations

DEM. REP. CONGO	DEMOCRATIC REPUBLIC OF THE CONGO
EQU. GUINEA	EQUATORIAL GUINEA
NETH.	NETHERLANDS
N.Z.	NEW ZEALAND
REP. CONGO	REPUBLIC OF THE CONGO
U.A.E.	UNITED ARAB EMIRATES
U.K.	UNITED KINGDOM
U.S.	UNITED STATES

Europe

Arctic Circle

FINLAND

NORWAY

60°N

SWEDEN

ESTONIA

RUSSIA

LATVIA

North Sea

Baltic Sea

LITHUANIA

KALININGRAD (RUSSIA)

UNITED KINGDOM

DENMARK

BELARUS

IRELAND

NETHERLANDS

POLAND

50°N

BELGIUM

GERMANY

ATLANTIC OCEAN

LUXEMBOURG

CZECH REPUBLIC

UKRAINE

SLOVAKIA

N
W E
S

LIECHTENSTEIN

AUSTRIA

HUNGARY

MOLDOVA

200   400 Miles
200   400 Kilometers

SWITZERLAND

SLOVENIA

ROMANIA

Azimuthal Equal-Area Projection

FRANCE

CROATIA

BOSNIA AND HERZEGOVINA

YUGOSLAVIA

BULGARIA

Black Sea

40°N

SAN MARINO

ITALY

Adriatic Sea

MACEDONIA

TURKEY

ANDORRA

MONACO

Corsica (FRANCE)

ALBANIA

PORTUGAL

SPAIN

Balearic Islands (SPAIN)

VATICAN CITY

Sardinia (ITALY)

40°N

GREECE

10°W

GIBRALTAR (U.K.)

0°

Mediterranean Sea

Sicily (ITALY)

MALTA

Crete (GREECE)

10°E   20°E

Atlas

The World: Physical

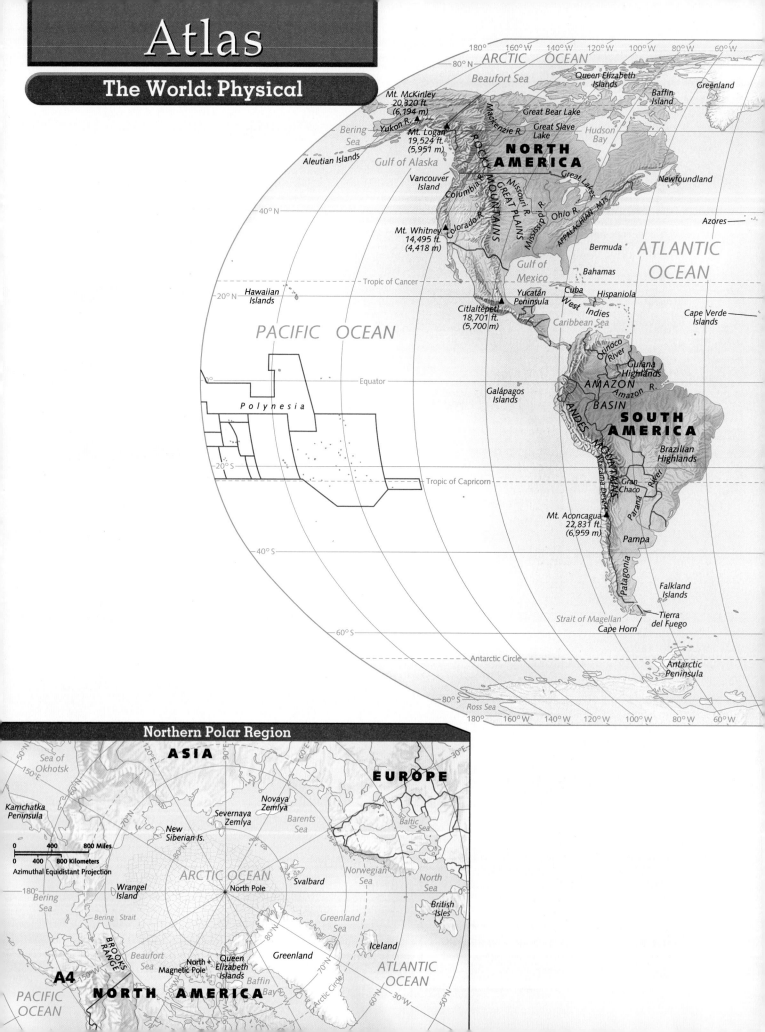

ARCTIC OCEAN
Beaufort Sea
Queen Elizabeth Islands
Greenland
Baffin Island
Mt. McKinley 20,320 ft. (6,194 m)
Great Bear Lake
Bering Sea
Yukon R.
Mt. Logan 19,524 ft. (5,951 m)
Mackenzie R.
Great Slave Lake
Hudson Bay
NORTH AMERICA
Aleutian Islands
Gulf of Alaska
Vancouver Island
Columbia R.
ROCKY MOUNTAINS
GREAT PLAINS
Missouri R.
Great Lakes
Newfoundland
40° N
Mississippi R.
Ohio R.
APPALACHIAN MTS.
Azores
Mt. Whitney 14,495 ft. (4,418 m)
Colorado R.
Bermuda
ATLANTIC OCEAN
Tropic of Cancer
20° N
Gulf of Mexico
Bahamas
Hawaiian Islands
Citlaltépetl 18,701 ft. (5,700 m)
Yucatán Peninsula
Cuba
Hispaniola
West Indies
Cape Verde Islands
PACIFIC OCEAN
Caribbean Sea
Orinoco River
Guiana Highlands
Galápagos Islands
AMAZON
Amazon R.
Equator
BASIN
SOUTH AMERICA
Polynesia
ANDES MOUNTAINS
Brazilian Highlands
20° S
Atacama Desert
Gran Chaco
Paraná River
Tropic of Capricorn
Mt. Aconcagua 22,831 ft. (6,959 m)
Pampa
40° S
Patagonia
Falkland Islands
Strait of Magellan
Tierra del Fuego
Cape Horn
60° S
Antarctic Circle
Antarctic Peninsula
80° S
Ross Sea

Northern Polar Region

Sea of Okhotsk
ASIA
EUROPE
Kamchatka Peninsula
Novaya Zemlya
Severnaya Zemlya
Barents Sea
Baltic
New Siberian Is.
Norwegian Sea
ARCTIC OCEAN
North Pole
Svalbard
North Sea
Wrangel Island
Bering Sea
Bering Strait
Beaufort Sea
North Magnetic Pole
Queen Elizabeth Islands
Greenland
British Isles
Greenland Sea
Iceland
ATLANTIC OCEAN
BROOKS RANGE
Baffin Bay
Arctic Circle
A4
PACIFIC OCEAN
NORTH AMERICA

0   400   800 Miles
0   400   800 Kilometers
Azimuthal Equidistant Projection

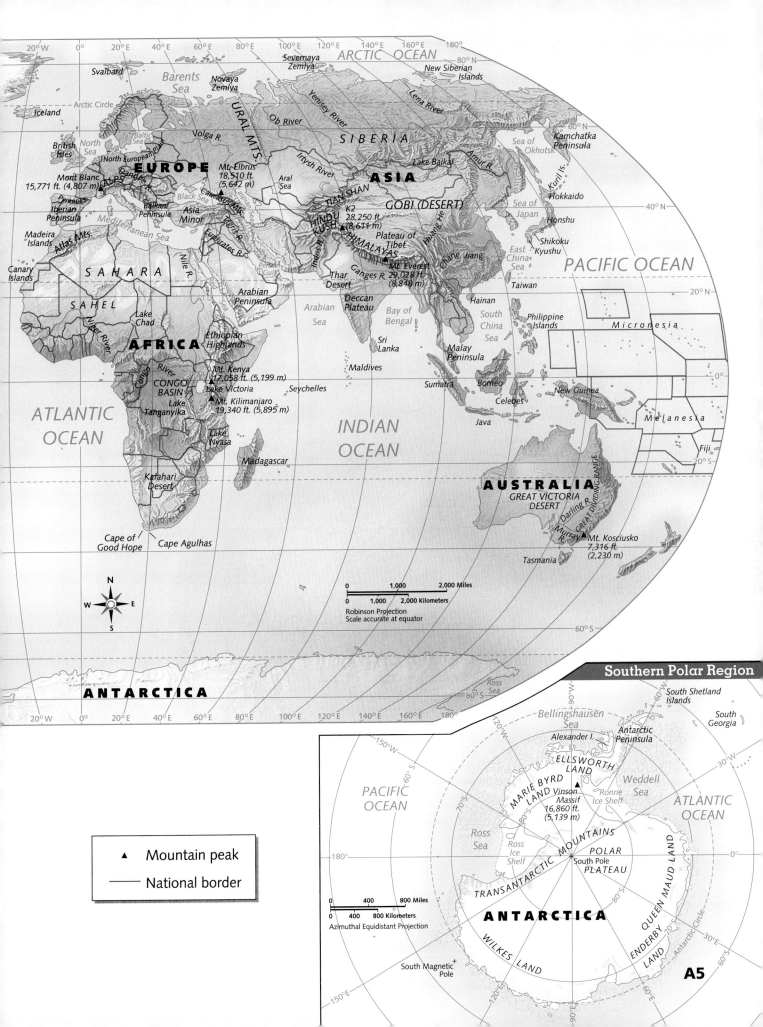

20°W 0° 20°E 40°E 60°E 80°E 100°E 120°E 140°E 160°E 180°

ARCTIC OCEAN

Svalbard
Barents Sea
Novaya Zemlya
Severnaya Zemlya
New Siberian Islands
80° N

Iceland
Arctic Circle
British Isles
North Sea
Baltic Sea
Volga R.
URAL MTS.
Ob River
Yenisey River
Lena River
SIBERIA
Amur R.
Sea of Okhotsk
Kamchatka Peninsula
60° N

EUROPE
North European Plain
Danube R.
Irtysh River
Aral Sea
ASIA
Lake Baikal
Kuril Is.
Hokkaido

Mont Blanc 15,771 ft. (4,807 m)
ALPS
Caucasus Mts.
Black Sea
Balkan Peninsula
Asia Minor
Caspian Sea
TIAN SHAN
K2 28,250 ft. (8,611 m)
HINDU KUSH
GOBI (DESERT)
Huang He
Sea of Japan
Honshu
Shikoku Kyushu
40° N

Iberian Peninsula
Pyrenees
Mediterranean Sea
Tigris R.
Euphrates R.
Plateau of Tibet
HIMALAYAS
Chang Jiang
East China Sea
PACIFIC OCEAN

Madeira Islands
Atlas Mts.
Nile R.
Persian Gulf
Indus R.
Mt. Everest 29,028 ft. (8,848 m)
Ganges R.
Taiwan
20° N

Canary Islands
SAHARA
Arabian Peninsula
Thar Desert
Deccan Plateau
Bay of Bengal
Hainan
South China Sea
Micronesia

SAHEL
Lake Chad
Arabian Sea
Sri Lanka
Philippine Islands
0°

AFRICA
Niger River
Ethiopian Highlands
Maldives
Malay Peninsula
Sumatra
Borneo
Celebes
New Guinea
Melanesia

Congo River
CONGO BASIN
Mt. Kenya 17,058 ft. (5,199 m)
Lake Victoria
Mt. Kilimanjaro 19,340 ft. (5,895 m)
Seychelles
Java
20° S

ATLANTIC OCEAN
Lake Tanganyika
Lake Nyasa
INDIAN OCEAN
Fiji

Madagascar
Kalahari Desert
AUSTRALIA
GREAT VICTORIA DESERT
GREAT DIVIDING RANGE
Darling R.

Cape of Good Hope
Cape Agulhas
Murray R.
Mt. Kosciusko 7,316 ft. (2,230 m)
Tasmania

N W E S

1,000 2,000 Miles
1,000 2,000 Kilometers
Robinson Projection
Scale accurate at equator

60° S

Ross Sea
80° S

ANTARCTICA

20°W 0° 20°E 40°E 60°E 80°E 100°E 120°E 140°E 160°E 180°

▲ Mountain peak
— National border

Southern Polar Region

South Shetland Islands
Bellingshausen Sea
Antarctic Peninsula
South Georgia

Alexander I.
ELLSWORTH LAND
Weddell Sea

PACIFIC OCEAN
MARIE BYRD LAND
Vinson Massif 16,860 ft. (5,139 m)
Ronne Ice Shelf
ATLANTIC OCEAN

Ross Sea
Ross Ice Shelf
TRANSANTARCTIC MOUNTAINS
South Pole
POLAR PLATEAU
QUEEN MAUD LAND

400 800 Miles
400 800 Kilometers
Azimuthal Equidistant Projection
WILKES LAND
ANTARCTICA
ENDERBY LAND
Antarctic Circle

South Magnetic Pole

A5

Atlas

Western Hemisphere: Political

ARCTIC OCEAN

Bering Strait

Beaufort Sea

Viscount Melville Sound

Baffin Bay

Greenland
(DENMARK)

ALASKA
(U.S.)

Yukon River

Fairbanks

Anchorage

Great Bear Lake

Foxe Basin

Arctic Circle

60° N

Mackenzie River

Whitehorse

Juneau

Gulf of Alaska

Bering Sea

Liard River

Yellowknife

Great Slave Lake

CANADA

Peace River

Davis Strait

Hudson Strait

Labrador Sea

Edmonton

Calgary

Vancouver

Athabasca R.

Lake Athabasca

Saskatchewan R.

Saskatoon

Regina

Lake Winnipeg

Winnipeg

Hudson Bay

James Bay

St. John's

Seattle

Portland

Puget Sound

UNITED STATES

Thunder Bay

Great

St. Lawrence River

Ottawa

Quebec

Montreal

St. John

Halifax

Gulf of St. Lawrence

Columbia R.

Boise

Snake R.

Great Salt Lake

Salt Lake City

Reno

San Francisco

Las Vegas

Colorado R.

Denver

Missouri R.

Chicago

Lakes

Toronto

Detroit

Cleveland

Albany

Boston

New York City

Philadelphia

Washington, D.C.

St. Louis

Indianapolis

Richmond

Norfolk

Mississippi R.

Los Angeles

Phoenix

San Diego

El Paso

Tucson

Rio Grande

Memphis

Dallas

Houston

Atlanta

Raleigh

Charleston

Savannah

30° N

Hermosillo

San Antonio

New Orleans

Jacksonville

Tampa

Miami

Gulf of Mexico

BAHAMAS

Nassau

ATLANTIC OCEAN

Honolulu

Tropic of Cancer

MEXICO

Chihuahua

Monterrey

Durango

HAWAII
(U.S.)

Tampico

León

Guadalajara

Mexico City

Puebla

Veracruz

CUBA

Havana

JAMAICA

HAITI

Port-au-Prince

Santo Domingo

PUERTO RICO (U.S.)

DOMINICAN REPUBLIC

PACIFIC OCEAN

Acapulco

BELIZE

Belmopan

GUATEMALA

Guatemala City

HONDURAS

Tegucigalpa

Kingston

EL SALVADOR

San Salvador

Managua

NICARAGUA

San José

COSTA RICA

PANAMA

Panama City

Maracaibo

Caribbean Sea

Caracas

VENEZUELA

GUYANA

SURINAME

Georgetown

Paramaribo

Cayenne

FRENCH GUIANA (FRANCE)

Medellín

Cali

Bogotá

COLOMBIA

Quito

Guayaquil

Manaus

Rio Negro

Amazon R.

Belém

Fortaleza

0° Equator

Galápagos Islands
(ECUADOR)

ECUADOR

Iquitos

Tapajós River

Xingu R.

Tocantins R.

Recife

Trujillo

PERU

Lima

Cuzco

Lake Titicaca

La Paz

BRAZIL

Brasília

São Francisco R.

Salvador

FRENCH POLYNESIA
(FRANCE)

Papeete

Arequipa

Sucre

BOLIVIA

Goiânia

Belo Horizonte

Rio de Janeiro

Tropic of Capricorn

Antofagasta

Paraguay R.

PARAGUAY

Salta

Asunción

Campo Grande

São Paulo

Curitiba

30° S

San Miguel de Tucumán

CHILE

Córdoba

Paraná R.

Pôrto Alegre

Valparaíso

Santiago

Rosario

Buenos Aires

La Plata

Rio de la Plata

URUGUAY

Montevideo

Mar del Plata

Concepción

Bahía Blanca

Valdivia

ARGENTINA

Scale

| 0 | 1,000 | 2,000 Miles |
| 0 | 1,000 | 2,000 Kilometers |

Miller Cylindrical Projection

Legend

— National border

⊛ National capital

• City

Punta Arenas

Falkland Islands
(U.K.)

South Georgia
(U.K.)

N
W E
S

A6

150° W   120° W   90° W   60° W   30° W

Atlas

Western Hemisphere: Physical

North Magnetic Pole +
Queen Elizabeth Islands
Ellesmere Island
Melville Island
Viscount Melville Sound
Devon Island
Banks Island
Baffin Bay
Greenland
Beaufort Sea
Point Barrow
Victoria Island
Baffin Island
Arctic Circle
Brooks Range
Mt. McKinley 20,320 ft. (6,194 m)
Yukon River
Mackenzie Mts.
Great Bear Lake
Foxe Basin
Cape Farewell
60° N
Yukon
Plateau
Mackenzie River
Great Slave Lake
Hudson Strait
Davis Strait
Labrador Sea
Alaska Range
Gulf of Alaska
Mt. Logan 19,524 ft. (5,951 m)
Liard R.
River
Peace River
Athabasca R.
Lake Athabasca
Hudson Bay
James Bay
Labrador
Kodiak Island
Alaska Peninsula
Saskatchewan River
Lake Winnipeg
Aleutian Islands
Queen Charlotte Islands
C A N A D I A N   S H I E L D
NORTH AMERICA
Newfoundland
Vancouver Island
Puget Sound
Coast Mountains
Cascade Range
Snake R.
Sierra Nevada
Great Salt Lake
GREAT BASIN
Columbia R.
Black Hills
Missouri R.
Platte R.
Arkansas R.
Mississippi R.
Ozark Plateau
Ohio R.
Great Lakes
St. Lawrence R.
Gulf of St. Lawrence
Nova Scotia
Bay of Fundy
Cape Cod
Long Island
COASTAL PLAIN
APPALACHIAN MTS.
INTERIOR PLAINS
GREAT PLAINS
ROCKY MOUNTAINS
Coast Ranges
Mt. Whitney 14,495 ft. (4,418 m)
Death Valley (lowest point in N.A.) -282 ft. (-86 m)
Sonora Desert
Sierra Madre Occidental
Sierra Madre Oriental
Baja California
Gulf of California
Rio Grande
Red R.
Cape Hatteras
ATLANTIC OCEAN
30° N
Gulf of Mexico
Bahamas
PACIFIC OCEAN
Hawaiian Islands
Tropic of Cancer
Citlaltépetl 18,701 ft. (5,700 m)
Yucatán Peninsula
Greater Antilles
Cuba
Hispaniola
Puerto Rico
Lesser Antilles
Lake Nicaragua
Caribbean Sea
Isthmus of Panama
Lake Maracaibo
Orinoco R.
Llanos
Guiana Highlands
Line Islands
Equator
Galápagos Islands
Chimborazo 20,561 ft. (6,267 m)
Rio Negro
Amazon R.
Cape São Roque
Marquesas Islands
AMAZON BASIN
Tapajós River
Xingu River
Tocantins R.
São Francisco River
Huascarán 22,205 ft. (6,768 m)
A N D E S
Mato Grosso Plateau
Brazilian Highlands
Cook Islands
Tuamotu Archipelago
Society Islands
Lake Titicaca
Altiplano
Atacama Desert
Paraguay R.
Paraná R.
SOUTH AMERICA
Tropic of Capricorn
Gran Chaco
Paraná R.
Uruguay R.
Iguazú Falls
30° S
Mt. Aconcagua 22,831 ft. (6,959 m)
M O U N T A I N S
Pampa
Rio de la Plata
Valdés Peninsula (lowest point in S.A.) -131 ft. (-40 m)
Patagonia
Falkland Islands
South Georgia

0   1,000   2,000 Miles
0   1,000   2,000 Kilometers
Miller Cylindrical Projection

▲ Mountain peak
▼ Point below sea level
— National border
≈ Waterfall

N
W   E
S

A7

Tierra del Fuego
Cape Horn
Strait of Magellan

150° W   120° W   90° W   60° W   30° W

Atlas

United States: Overview

RUSSIA

60°N

Bering Sea

ALASKA
(AK)

180°

40°N

PACIFIC OCEAN

WASHINGTON
(WA)

OREGON
(OR)

0   250   500 Miles
0   250   500 Kilometers
Modified Azimuthal Equal-Area Projection

NEVADA
(NV)

—— National border
—— State border
⊛ National capital

CALIFORNIA
(CA)

N
W ⊛ E
S

160°W

Tropic of Cancer

HAWAII
(HI)

20°N

140°W

120°W

Atlas

United States: Political

RUSSIA

ARCTIC OCEAN

170°E

ALASKA

Yukon River

Arctic Circle

Fairbanks

CANADA

Bering
Sea

Anchorage

Yukon River

60°N

0   250   500 Miles
0   250   500 Kilometers

Juneau

PACIFIC
OCEAN

180°   170°W   160°W   150°W   140°W   130°W

40°N

50°N

60°N

70°N

120°W

CANADA

120°W   110°W

Seattle
Tacoma
Olympia   Spokane
WASHINGTON

Great Falls

Portland   Columbia   River

Salem   Helena   MONTANA

Eugene   IDAHO

OREGON   Boise

Billings

Yellowstone River

Snake   River

WYOMING

Pocatello   Casper

NEVADA   Great
                    Salt   Ogden
Reno   Lake   Salt Lake City   Cheyenne

Sacramento   Carson City   Provo

San Francisco Oakland   UTAH
               San Jose   Denver

Fresno   Colorado
                                                Springs
CALIFORNIA   Las   COLORADO
              Vegas   Pueblo

Bakersfield

Colorado River

PACIFIC

OCEAN

Flagstaff   Santa Fe

Los Angeles   San Bernardino   Albuquerque

ARIZONA   NEW MEXICO

San Diego   Phoenix

                                Roswell

Tucson

30°N

MEXICO

El Paso

Rio Grande

Legend

Northeast	⊛ National capital
Southeast	★ State capital
Middle West	• Major city
Southwest	— National border
West	— State border

130°W

160°W   PACIFIC   155°W
        OCEAN

Honolulu

HAWAII   20°N

Hilo

0   100   200 Miles
0   100   200 Kilometers

N
W   E
S

0   250   500 Miles
0   250   500 Kilometers
Albers Equal-Area Projection

20°N

120°W   110°W

Atlas

United States: Physical

CANADA

RUSSIA

ARCTIC OCEAN

170° E

Brooks Range

ALASKA

Seward Peninsula

Yukon River

70° N

120° W

Arctic Circle

CANADA

60° N

Bering Strait

St. Lawrence Island

Mt. McKinley
20,320 ft.
(6,194 m)

Alaska Range

Yukon River

60° N

Bering Sea

Gulf of Alaska

Kodiak Island

50° N

0   250   500 Miles

0   250   500 Kilometers

Aleutian Islands

180°   170° W   160° W   150° W   140° W   130° W

40° N

Legend:
- Arid
- Evergreen forest
- Grassland
- Mixed forest
- Mountains
- Tundra
- National border
- State border
- ▲ Mountain peak
- △ Highest point
- ▼ Lowest point

PACIFIC OCEAN

30° N

130° W

Cape Mendocino

Coast Ranges

Point Conception

Channel Islands

120° W

Cascade Range

WA

Mt. Rainier
14,410 ft. (4,392 m)

Mt. St. Helens
8,364 ft. (2,549 m)

Columbia River

Mt. Hood
11,235 ft.
(3,427 m)

OR

Columbia Plateau

Sacramento River

San Joaquin Valley

Sierra Nevada

Pyramid Lake

Donner Pass
Lake Tahoe

NV

Mt. Whitney
14,495 ft.
(4,418 m)

Death Valley
-282 ft.
(-86 m)

CA

Mojave Desert

Salton Sea

Imperial Valley

Sonoran Desert

Bitterroot Range

ID

Salmon River Mountains

Snake River

Central Valley

GREAT BASIN

Great Salt Lake

Wasatch Range

Uinta Mts.

UT

Lake Powell

Colorado River

Lake Mead

Grand Canyon

Colorado Plateau

AZ

Baldy Peak
11,403 ft.
(3,476 m)

Sonoran Desert

ROCKY

Fort Peck Lake

MT

Yellowstone River

Bighorn Mts.

WY

Teton Range

Wind River Range

Great Divide Basin

Mt. Elbert
14,433 ft.
(4,399 m)

San Juan Mts.

CO

Front Range

Sangre de Cristo Mts.

MOUNTAINS

NM

Guadalupe Peak
8,749 ft.
(2,667 m)

Rio Grande

110° W

CANADA

MEXICO

N
W   E
S

160° W   155° W

PACIFIC OCEAN

Kauai

Niihau   Oahu

Molokai

HAWAII   Lanai   Maui

Kahoolawe

20° N

Hawaii   Mauna Kea
13,796 ft.
(4,205 m)

0   100   200 Miles

0   100   200 Kilometers

0   250   500 Miles

0   250   500 Kilometers

Albers Equal-Area Projection

20° N

120° W   110° W

CANADA

ATLANTIC
OCEAN

BAHAMAS

CUBA

Gulf of Mexico

Great Plains · **Interior Plains** · **Central Plains** · **Coastal Plain** · **Appalachian Mountains** · **Piedmont**

ND · SD · MN · WI · MI · ME · VT · NH · NY · MA · RI · CT · NJ · PA · OH · IN · IL · IA · NE · KS · MO · KY · WV · VA · MD · DE · NC · SC · TN · AR · OK · TX · LA · MS · AL · GA · FL

Lake of the Woods · Upper Red Lake · Lower Red Lake · Lake Sakakawea · Leech Lake · Mesabi Range · Mille Lacs Lake · Isle Royale · Keweenaw Peninsula · Lake Superior · Upper Peninsula · Lake Huron · St. Lawrence River · Moosehead Lake · Mt. Katahdin 5,267 ft. (1,605 m)

Lake Oahe · Mississippi River · Wisconsin River · Lake Michigan · Lower Peninsula · Lake St. Clair · Lake Erie · Lake Ontario · Niagara Falls · Lake Champlain · Adirondack Mountains · Green Mts · White Mts · Mt. Washington 6,288 ft. (1,917 m) · Cape Ann · Cape Cod

Black Hills · Lake Winnebago · Finger Lakes · Hudson R. · Connecticut R. · Long Island

Sand Hills · North Platte R. · Platte River · South Platte R. · Illinois River · Wabash River · Allegheny Mts · Potomac R. · Delaware Bay

Smoky Hills · Missouri River · Ohio River · Cape Charles · Chesapeake Bay · Albemarle Sound

Red Hills · Lake of the Ozarks · Harry S. Truman Reservoir · Ozark Plateau · Lake Barkley · Cumberland Gap · Mt. Mitchell 6,684 ft. (2,037 m) · Cape Hatteras

Arkansas River · Canadian River · Ouachita Mountains · Lake Texoma · Mississippi River · Cumberland R. · Cape Fear River · Roanoke R. · James R. · Cape Fear

Red River · Llano Estacado · Sabine River · Tombigbee R. · Stone Mountain · Clark Hill Lake · Savannah River · Oconee R. · Ocmulgee R. · Altamaha R.

Pecos River · Edwards Plateau · Brazos River · Colorado River · Sam Rayburn Reservoir · Toledo Bend Reservoir · Chattahoochee R. · Alabama R. · Okefenokee Swamp · St. Johns River

Rio Grande · Galveston Bay · Lake Maurepas · Lake Pontchartrain · Mobile Bay · Mississippi Delta · Cape Canaveral

Lake Okeechobee · Tampa Bay · Everglades · Cape Sable · Florida Keys · Straits of Florida

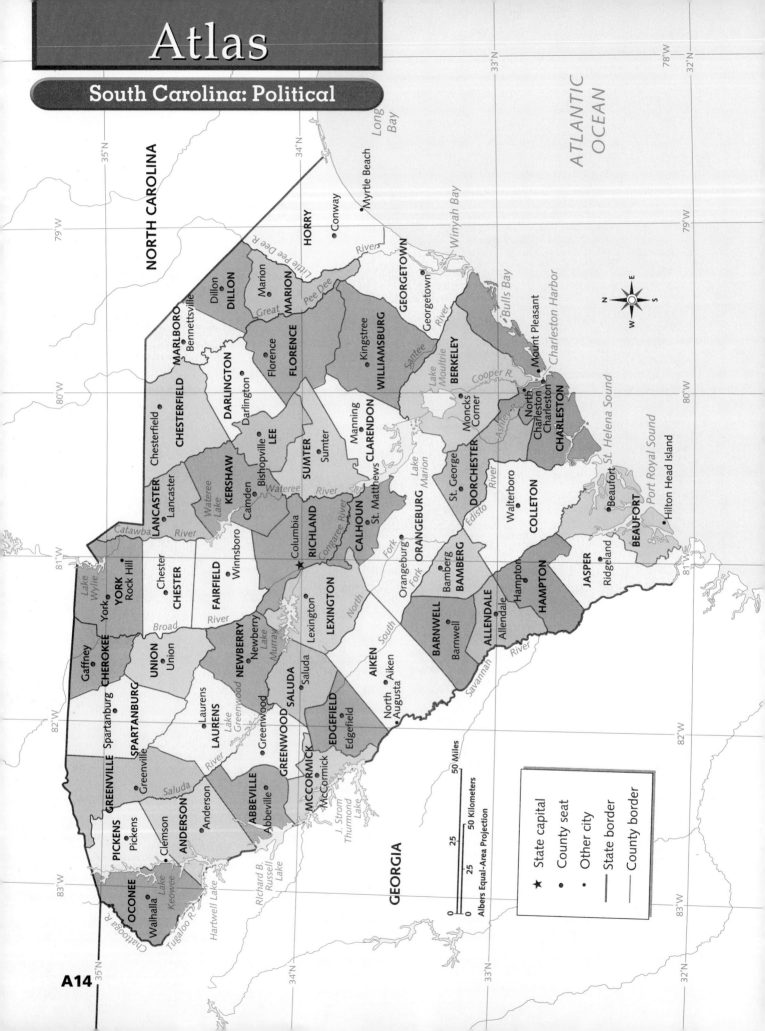

Atlas

South Carolina: Political

ATLANTIC OCEAN

NORTH CAROLINA

GEORGIA

Long Bay

Winyah Bay

Bulls Bay

Charleston Harbor

St. Helena Sound

Port Royal Sound

Cities and places:

Myrtle Beach
Conway — HORRY
Little Pee Dee R.
Pee Dee River
Great Pee Dee
Dillon — DILLON
Bennettsville — MARLBORO
MARION — Marion
FLORENCE — Florence
Kingstree — WILLIAMSBURG
GEORGETOWN — Georgetown
Santee River
Lake Moultrie
BERKELEY
Moncks Corner
Cooper R.
Mount Pleasant
North Charleston
CHARLESTON — Charleston
Ashley R.
CHESTERFIELD — Chesterfield
DARLINGTON — Darlington
LEE — Bishopville
KERSHAW — Camden
SUMTER — Sumter
Manning — CLARENDON
St. Matthews — CALHOUN
Lake Marion
DORCHESTER — St. George
Edisto River
COLLETON — Walterboro
Beaufort
Hilton Head Island
BEAUFORT
Wateree Lake
Wateree River
Congaree River
Columbia — RICHLAND
ORANGEBURG — Orangeburg
North Fork
South Fork
Bamberg — BAMBERG
Ridgeland — JASPER
HAMPTON — Hampton
Allendale — ALLENDALE
BARNWELL — Barnwell
LANCASTER — Lancaster
Lake Wylie
Catawba River
YORK — Rock Hill, York
CHESTER — Chester
FAIRFIELD — Winnsboro
Broad River
LEXINGTON — Lexington
AIKEN — Aiken
North Augusta
Savannah River
CHEROKEE — Gaffney
UNION — Union
NEWBERRY — Newberry
Lake Murray
Lake Greenwood
SALUDA — Saluda
EDGEFIELD — Edgefield
SPARTANBURG — Spartanburg
LAURENS — Laurens
GREENWOOD — Greenwood
McCORMICK — McCormick
J. Strom Thurmond Lake
GREENVILLE — Greenville
Saluda River
ABBEVILLE — Abbeville
PICKENS — Pickens
ANDERSON — Anderson, Clemson
OCONEE — Walhalla
Lake Keowee
Hartwell Lake
Richard B. Russell Lake
Tugaloo R.
Chattooga R.

Legend:

★ State capital
● County seat
• Other city
— State border
— County border

0   25   50 Miles
0   25   50 Kilometers
Albers Equal-Area Projection

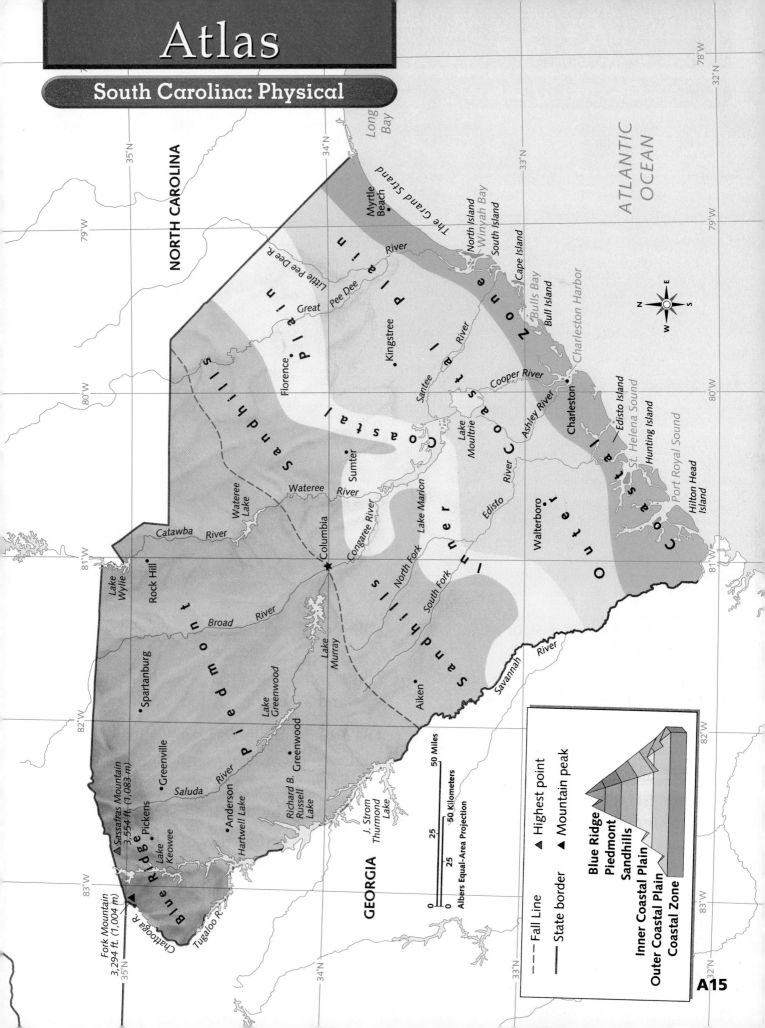

Atlas

South Carolina: Physical

NORTH CAROLINA

ATLANTIC OCEAN

Long Bay

Myrtle Beach

The Grand Strand

Coastal Plain

Little Pee Dee R.

Great Pee Dee River

Florence

Kingstree

Sandhills

River

North Island
Winyah Bay
South Island

Cape Island

Bulls Bay
Bull Island

Santee River

Inner Coastal

Sumter

Cooper River

Charleston Harbor

Wateree River

Lake Moultrie

Ashley River

Charleston

Edisto Island

St. Helena Sound

Hunting Island

Wateree Lake

Congaree River

Lake Marion

River

Columbia

North Fork

Edisto River

Walterboro

Port Royal Sound

Hilton Head Island

Catawba River

Lake Wylie

Rock Hill

Broad River

Lake Murray

South Fork

Sandhills

Outer Coastal

Coastal Zone

Spartanburg

Piedmont

Lake Greenwood

Aiken

Savannah River

Greenville

Saluda River

Anderson

Hartwell Lake

Lake Greenwood

Richard B. Russell Lake

Greenwood

J. Strom Thurmond Lake

GEORGIA

△ Sassafras Mountain 3,554 ft. (1,083 m)

Pickens

Lake Keowee

Blue Ridge

▲ Fork Mountain 3,294 ft. (1,004 m)

Chattooga R.

Tugaloo R.

50 Miles
25
0
50 Kilometers
25
0
Albers Equal-Area Projection

- - - Fall Line
—— State border

▲ Highest point
▲ Mountain peak

Blue Ridge
Piedmont
Sandhills
Inner Coastal Plain
Outer Coastal Plain
Coastal Zone

A15

Atlas

Geography Terms

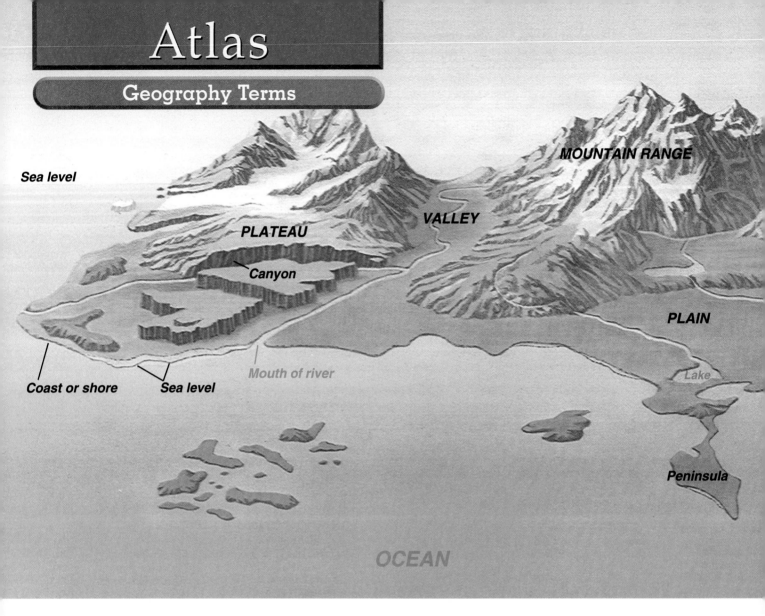

Sea level

MOUNTAIN RANGE

VALLEY

PLATEAU

Canyon

PLAIN

Coast or shore   Sea level

Mouth of river

Lake

Peninsula

OCEAN

bay part of a lake, sea, or ocean with land around some of it

bluff high, steep face of rock or earth

canyon deep, narrow valley with steep sides

cliff high, steep face of rock or earth

coast land along a sea or ocean

delta triangle-shaped area of land at the mouth of a river

desert dry land with few plants

foothills hilly area at the base of a mountain range

gulf body of water with land around some of it, but larger than a bay

harbor area of water where ships can dock safely near land

hill rolling land that rises above the land around it

island land that has water on all sides

lake body of water with land on all sides

mountain highest kind of land

mountain range row of mountains

mouth of river place where a river empties into another body of water

oasis area of water and fertile land with desert on all sides

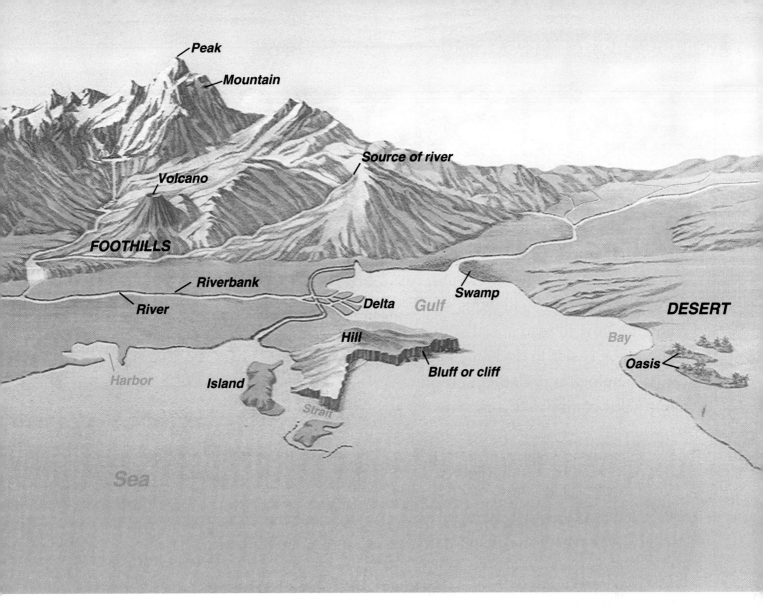

Peak

Mountain

Volcano

Source of river

FOOTHILLS

Riverbank

River

Delta

Gulf

Swamp

DESERT

Hill

Bay

Oasis

Bluff or cliff

Harbor

Island

Strait

Sea

ocean body of salt water larger than a sea

peak top of a mountain

peninsula land that has water around most of it

plain flat land

plateau large area of high, flat land with steep sides

river large stream of water that flows across the land

riverbank land along a river

sea body of salt water smaller than an ocean

sea level level that is even with the surface of an ocean or sea

shore land along the edge of a lake, sea, or ocean

source of river place where a river or stream begins

strait narrow body of water that joins two larger bodies of water

swamp area of low, wet land with trees

valley low land between hills or mountains

volcano mountain that has poured out hot rock

Read Social Studies

1. Why Learn This Skill?

Social studies is made up of stories about real people, places, and events. You may read these stories in library books or in textbooks like this one. Knowing how to read social studies can make it easier to do homework. It can also help you understand more about your community and state.

▲
In the Unit Preview each Key Concept word is highlighted in bright yellow. The meaning of each word is shown in a sentence and in photographs. You will see these words again as you study the unit.

2. Getting Started

Your book has six units. Each begins with several pages that help you preview, or look ahead at, the unit.

▲
Each Unit Introduction opens with a paragraph that tells what the unit is about and a list of Key Concepts, or important vocabulary words. You will also read about a project you can complete as you study the unit.

▲
After the Unit Preview comes a piece of literature, or a story, that is connected with what you will learn in the unit. The literature will help you begin to think about the important ideas of the unit.

3. The Parts of a Lesson

Each unit is divided into lessons. The first two pages and the last two pages of a lesson are shown below.

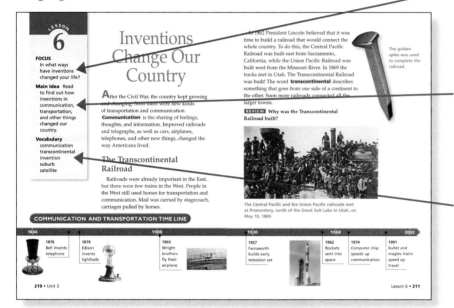

This question helps you see how the lesson connects with life today.

This statement gives you the lesson's main idea. It tells you what to look for as you read the lesson.

These are the new terms you will learn in the lesson.

The first time a vocabulary term appears in the lesson, it is highlighted in yellow.

Each lesson, like each unit, ends with a review. The questions and activities in the Lesson Review help you check your understanding and show what you know.

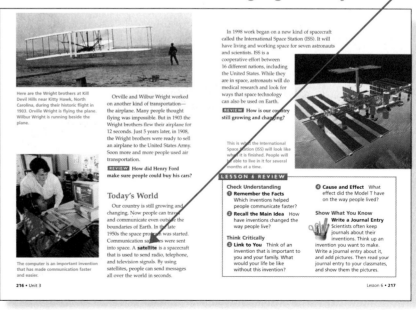

4. Understand the Process

You can follow these steps to read any lesson in this book.

1 Preview the whole lesson.

- Look at the title and the headings to find out what the lesson is about.
- Look at the pictures and maps and their captions, or words next to them. Captions explain what you are looking at. Pictures and maps show some of the important ideas in the lesson.
- Look at the questions to get an idea of what is most important in the lesson.
- Read the Focus question at the beginning of the lesson to see how the lesson connects with life today.
- Read the Main Idea statement to find out the main idea of the lesson.
- Look at the Vocabulary list to see what new terms you will learn.

2 Read the lesson to learn more about the main idea. As you read, you will come to questions with the label **REVIEW**. Be sure to answer these questions before you begin to read the rest of the lesson.

3 When you finish reading the lesson, say in your own words what you have learned.

4 Look back over the lesson. Then answer the Lesson Review questions—from memory if you can. These questions will help you check your understanding of the lesson. The activity at the end of the review will help you show what you know.

5. Special Features in a Unit

In each unit you will find special features. These give you interesting details about people, places, and events. Some of them are shown here.

The Geography feature gives the name of a place and shows its location on a map. Then it tells why that place is important.

The Biography feature gives the name of a person and the years when he or she lived. Then it tells what important thing that person did.

Young citizens listening to a storyteller in a library

Leaders Help Solve Problems

In *City Green* the people in Marcy's neighborhood worked together to solve a problem. Before a community can solve a problem, a leader may need to bring the people together. Marcy acted as a leader when she told her neighbors how they could solve a problem. She and Miss Rosa brought people together to make a garden from an empty lot.

In communities all over the United States, leaders help make things happen. Wilma Mankiller is a leader who helped solve problems in Cherokee communities. For many years she was the Chief of the Cherokee Nation. Her office was located in Tahlequah (TA•luh•kwaw), Oklahoma. One of the many communities she worked with was Bell, Oklahoma. Bell is a rural community where about 350 people live. Most of its citizens are Cherokees, like Wilma Mankiller.

City and town governments provide many services to their citizens. A **government service** is a service that is provided for all the citizens of a community. Fire and police protection are government services. Most city governments also provide libraries, street and traffic signs, sewers, and water for their citizens.

City governments can provide services like these because the community's **citizens** pay taxes. Taxes are paid to a government to run a city. People also pay taxes to run their county, state, and national governments. The government uses taxes to pay wages to the workers who provide services. The government also uses taxes to build new buildings and to buy equipment, such as police cars and fire engines.

REVIEW How do city governments pay for government services?

Firefighters provide an important government service.

342 • Unit 5

GEOGRAPHY

Tahlequah, Oklahoma

The community of Tahlequah is located in the northeastern part of Oklahoma. This area of Oklahoma, known as the Ozark Plateau, has many fast-moving streams and deep river valleys. Southeast of Tahlequah is the Cherokee Heritage Center, where people can learn about Cherokee history and culture. This center includes the Cherokee National Museum and the Tsa-La-Gi Ancient Cherokee Village.

Wilma Mankiller

Lesson 1 • 343

The Telegraph and Telephone

Samuel Morse was a painter who had many ideas for inventions. An **invention** is something that has been made for the first time. Morse's most important invention was the telegraph, a machine that used a code of dots and dashes to send messages over wires. When telegraph wires were strung across the country, people could get news quickly from people far away.

In 1876, Alexander Graham Bell invented the telephone. People could speak to and hear others who were far away. Since then, the telephone has changed many times. Today deaf people can use a special telephone to communicate. Bell's invention led the way to how we communicate today.

REVIEW What two inventions helped people communicate quickly with others far away?

Samuel Morse

▲ Early telegraph

TELEPHONES THEN AND NOW

1876
1919
1954
1968
1997
Today

LEARNING FROM PHOTOGRAPHS How have telephones changed over the years?

212 • Unit 3

BIOGRAPHY

Helen Keller
1880–1968

When Helen Keller was a child, she had an illness that left her both blind and deaf. Her parents asked Alexander Graham Bell (shown here) how they could help her. He sent a teacher named Anne Sullivan to work with her. Sullivan communicated with Helen by tapping letters into her student's hand. When Helen caught on, she quickly learned to tap letters back. At last she could communicate! Later she went to college. Helen Keller showed the world the great things one person can do.

The Lightbulb

When he was 15 years old, Thomas Edison went to work in a telegraph office. He began thinking of ways to make the telegraph machine better. Soon he became a full-time inventor. Thomas Edison thought up more than 1,000 inventions! The phonograph, the microphone, and the movie camera were some of his inventions. But the invention that he is most famous for is the lightbulb.

Edison with two of his lightbulbs

Lesson 6 • 213

The History feature gives the name of an important event. Then it tells a short story that explains why the event is remembered.

Crossing Points

When a land route meets a river, travelers need a way to cross the river. They may use a bridge, a ferry, or a ford. A bridge is a road built over a waterway. A **ferry** is a boat that carries people and goods across a waterway. A **ford** is a shallow place in a waterway that can be crossed by walking, riding, or driving.

Places on both sides of a bridge, a ferry, or a ford are good for building cities or towns. Many famous cities began as crossing points at rivers. Do you know this song?

> 66 London Bridge is falling down,
> Falling down, falling down,
> London Bridge is falling down,
> My fair lady! 99

The song is about the bridge that was in the city of London, England, for hundreds of years. London Bridge crossed the Thames (TEMZ) River at a place where the water is deep. Ships from the sea sailed up the river to the bridge. Wagons from farms and mills used the river to cross the river.

This black-and-white drawing shows London Bridge in the 1660s. You can see that homes and shops were built right on the bridge. This bridge has been rebuilt many times.

A ferry crossing Elliot Bay in Seattle, Washington

Bridges on the Thames River—London, England

Human-Environment Interactions
■ Why do you think there are now many bridges that cross the Thames River?

HISTORY

London Bridge

London Bridge helped the city of London grow. The last time it was rebuilt, business people in the United States bought the old bridge. They moved it to Lake Havasu City, Arizona! Many tourists go to see it there, thousands of miles from London.

Farmers long ago went to London Bridge with grains, wool, butter, and pigs to trade for cloth or leather goods carried there by ships. Sometimes the farmers needed to see a doctor, so doctors went to live near London Bridge. Soon many people settled close to the bridge, and a city grew up there. Today more than 9 million people live in and around London.

REVIEW Why is a crossing point a good place to build a city?

LESSON 3 REVIEW

Check Understanding

❶ **Remember the Facts** What are some ways travelers can cross rivers?

❷ **Recall the Main Idea** Why are cities and towns built at places where people meet?

Think Critically

❸ **Personally Speaking** What might be good and bad about living near a crossing point? Would you want to live there?

Show What You Know
Research and Writing Activity Choose one bridge in or near your community and find out more about it. You may need to use books or talk to people to get your information. Write a three-paragraph report about the bridge. In your paragraphs, tell when and why the bridge was built. Share your report with your classmates.

114 • Unit 2

Lesson 3 • 115

6. Other Features in the Book

Your textbook has many other features to help you learn. Some of them are shown here.

The Skills lessons help you build basic study skills. They also help you build citizenship skills as you work with others. ▼

The Counterpoints pages show you some of the different points of view people may have about certain questions. ▼

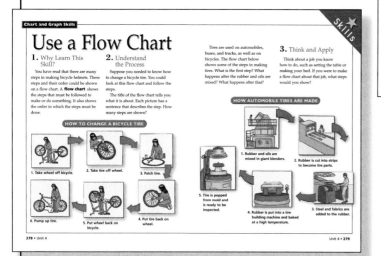

The feature called Making Social Studies Real shows how social studies is connected with your life and the lives of other people like you. ▼

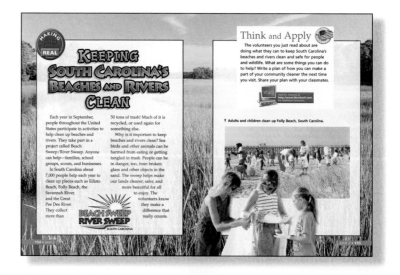

7. The Back of the Book

At the back of your book is a section called For Your Reference. It has reference tools you can use.

- Discovering the History of Your Community
- Biographical Dictionary
- Gazetteer
- Glossary
- Index

Some of these pages are shown here.

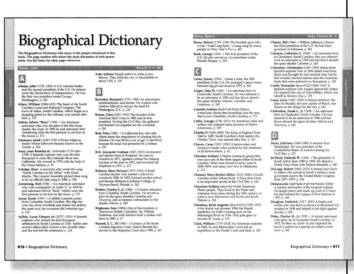

The Biographical Dictionary lists many of the people discussed in your book. It also includes page numbers that tell you where to find the persons in your book.

The Discovering the History of Your Community pages tell you how you can learn more about your community.

8. Think and Apply

Use the four steps on page 20 each time you read a lesson in your book.

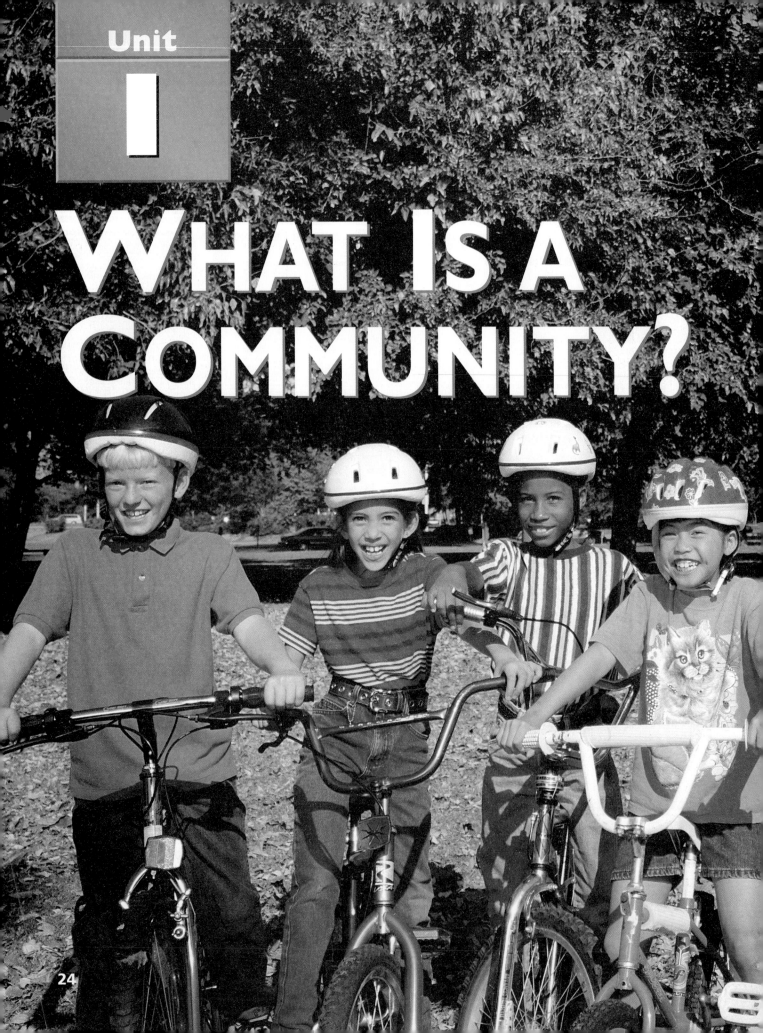

WHAT IS A COMMUNITY?

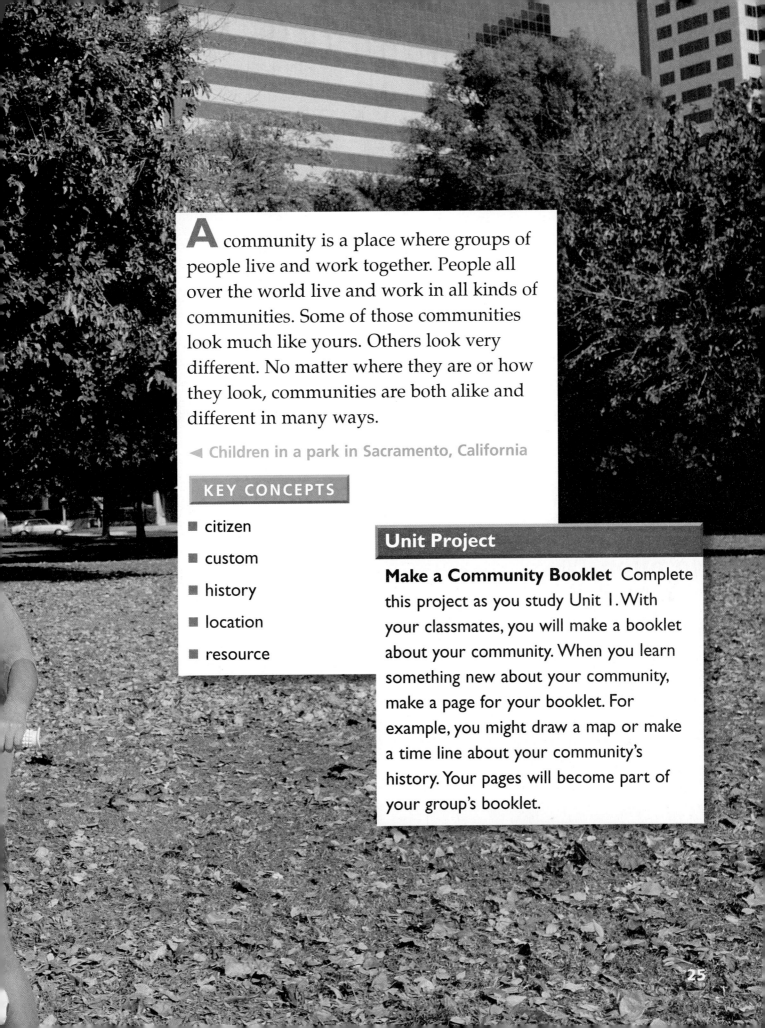

A community is a place where groups of people live and work together. People all over the world live and work in all kinds of communities. Some of those communities look much like yours. Others look very different. No matter where they are or how they look, communities are both alike and different in many ways.

◄ **Children in a park in Sacramento, California**

KEY CONCEPTS

- citizen
- custom
- history
- location
- resource

Unit Project

Make a Community Booklet Complete this project as you study Unit 1. With your classmates, you will make a booklet about your community. When you learn something new about your community, make a page for your booklet. For example, you might draw a map or make a time line about your community's history. Your pages will become part of your group's booklet.

citizen A person who lives in a community.

location Where something is found.

The United States

RUSSIA

ALASKA

CANADA

PACIFIC OCEAN

0   400 Miles

0   400 Kilometers

0   200   400 Miles

0   200 400 Kilometers

CANADA

WASHINGTON

OREGON

IDAHO

MONTANA

WYOMING

NORTH DAKOTA

SOUTH DAKOTA

MINNESOTA

WISCONSIN

Lake Superior

Lake Huron

Lake Michigan

MICHIGAN

Lake Ontario

Lake Erie

VERMONT

MAINE

NEW HAMPSHIRE

NEW YORK

MASSACHUSETTS

RHODE ISLAND

CONNECTICUT

PENNSYLVANIA

NEW JERSEY

NEVADA

UTAH

COLORADO

NEBRASKA

IOWA

ILLINOIS

INDIANA

OHIO

WEST VIRGINIA

DELAWARE

MARYLAND

CALIFORNIA

ARIZONA

NEW MEXICO

KANSAS

MISSOURI

KENTUCKY

VIRGINIA

OKLAHOMA

ARKANSAS

TENNESSEE

NORTH CAROLINA

SOUTH CAROLINA

ATLANTIC OCEAN

PACIFIC OCEAN

MISSISSIPPI

ALABAMA

GEORGIA

TEXAS

LOUISIANA

FLORIDA

PACIFIC OCEAN

HAWAII

0   100 Miles

0   100 Kilometers

MEXICO

Gulf of Mexico

N
W   E
S

history The story of what has happened in a place.

custom A people's way of doing something.

resource Something that people use to make what they need.

27

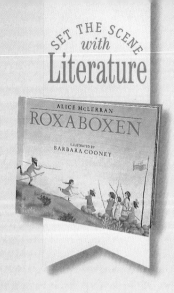

ROXABOXEN

by Alice McLerran   illustrated by Barbara Cooney

In this story some children build a make-believe community on a hillside in their neighborhood. Using old boxes and desert stones, they build a place where wonderful things can happen.

Marian called it Roxaboxen.
(She always knew the name of everything.)
There across the road, it looked like any rocky hill—
nothing but sand and rocks, some old wooden boxes,
cactus and greasewood and thorny ocotillo—
but it was a special place.

The street between Roxaboxen and the houses curved like a river,
so Marian named it the River Rhode.
After that you had to ford a river to reach Roxaboxen.

Of course all of Marian's sisters came:
Anna May and Frances and little Jean.
Charles from next door, even though he was twelve.
Oh, and Eleanor, naturally,
and Jamie with his brother Paul.
Later on there were others, but these were the first.

Well, not really the first.
Roxaboxen had always been there
and must have belonged to others, long before.

When Marian dug up a tin box filled with round black pebbles
everyone knew what it was:
it was buried treasure.
Those pebbles were the money of Roxaboxen.
You could still find others like them if you looked hard enough.
So some days became treasure-hunting days, with everybody trying to
    find that special kind.
And then on other days you might just find one without even looking.

A town of Roxaboxen began to grow, traced in lines of stone:
Main Street first, edged with the whitest ones,
and then the houses.
Charles made his of the biggest stones.
After all, he was the oldest.
At first the houses were very plain, but soon they all began to
    add more rooms.
The old wooden boxes could be shelves or tables or anything you wanted.
You could find pieces of pottery for dishes.
Round pieces were best.

Later on there was a town hall.
Marian was mayor, of course;
that was just the way she was.
Nobody minded.

After a while they added other streets.
Frances moved to one of them and built herself a new house outlined
    in desert glass,
bits of amber, amethyst, and sea-green:
a house of jewels.

And because everybody had plenty of money,
there were plenty of shops.
Jean helped Anna May in the bakery—
pies and cakes and bread baked warm in the sun.
There were two ice cream parlors.
Was Paul's ice cream the best, or Eleanor's?
Everybody kept trying them both.
(In Roxaboxen you can eat all the ice cream you want.)

Everybody had a car.
All you needed was something round for a
 steering wheel.
Of course, if you broke the speed limit you had to go to jail.
The jail had cactus on the floor to make it uncomfortable,
and Jamie was the policeman.
Anna May, quiet little Anna May, was always speeding—
you'd think she liked to go to jail.

But ah, if you had a horse, you could go as fast as the wind.
There were no speed limits for horses,
and you didn't have to stay on the roads.
All you needed for a horse was a stick and some kind of bridle,
and you could gallop anywhere.

Sometimes there were wars.
Once there was a great war, boys against girls.
Charles and Marian were the generals.
The girls had Fort Irene, and they were all girl scouts.
The boys made a fort at the other end of Roxaboxen, and they were
   all bandits.

Oh, the raids were fierce, loud with whooping and the stamping
   of horses!
The whirling swords of ocotillo had sharp thorns—
but when you reached your fort you were safe.

Roxaboxen had a cemetery, in case anyone died,
but the only grave in it was for a dead lizard.
Each year when the cactus bloomed, they decorated the grave
   with flowers.

Sometimes in the winter, when everybody was at school and the
    weather was bad,
no one went to Roxaboxen at all, not for weeks and weeks.
But it didn't matter;
Roxaboxen was always waiting.
Roxaboxen was always there.
And spring came, and the ocotillo blossomed,
and everybody sucked the honey from its flowers,
and everybody built new rooms, and everybody decided to have
    jeweled windows.
That summer there were three new houses on the east slope
and two new shops on Main Street.

And so it went.
The seasons changed, and the years went by.
Roxaboxen was always there.

The years went by, and the seasons changed,
until at last the friends had all grown tall,
and one by one, they moved away
to other houses, to other towns.
So you might think that was the end of Roxaboxen—
but oh, no.

Because none of them ever forgot Roxaboxen.
Not one of them ever forgot.
Years later, Marian's children listened to stories of that place
and fell asleep dreaming dreams of Roxaboxen.
Gray-haired Charles picked up a black pebble on the beach
    and stood holding it,
remembering Roxaboxen.

More than fifty years later, Frances went back
and Roxaboxen was still there.
She could see the white stones bordering Main Street,
and there where she had built her house
the desert glass still glowed—
amethyst, amber, and sea-green.

FOCUS
Why might you need to find out where places are?

Main Idea Learn the ways to describe where a community is found.

Vocabulary
location
map
continent
ocean
globe
hemisphere
equator

Where on Earth Is Roxaboxen?

You have just read a story about Roxaboxen, a make-believe community in the real city of Yuma, Arizona. Marian and her friends built streets, homes, stores, and other buildings. Then they pretended to live and work in the community they built. If someone asked you how to find Roxaboxen, what could you say?

Children looking at a map of Yuma

Where on a Map?

The children built Roxaboxen on a hill in their neighborhood. In the book, the author tells that the hill was at the corner of 2nd Avenue and 8th Street. This corner was Roxaboxen's location. A **location** is where something is found.

To show someone where to find Roxaboxen, you might draw a map. A **map** is a picture that shows the location of something. A map can show the whole Earth or just a small part of it, such as a neighborhood. This map shows where in Yuma Roxaboxen was located.

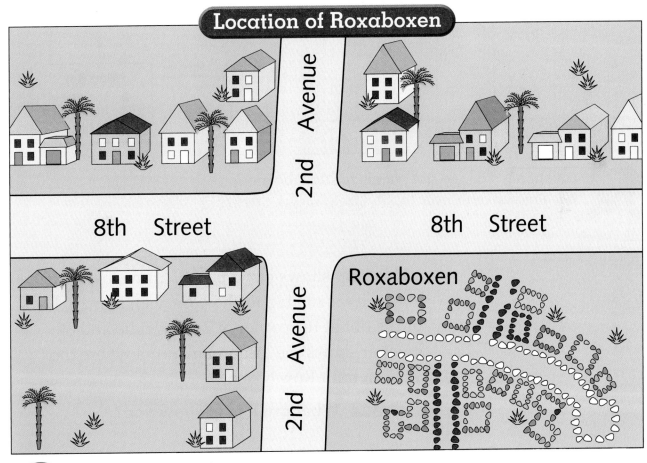

Location of Roxaboxen

2nd Avenue

8th Street   8th Street

Roxaboxen

2nd Avenue

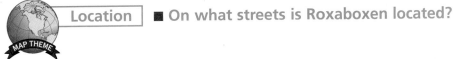

Location ■ On what streets is Roxaboxen located?

A Neighborhood in Yuma, Arizona

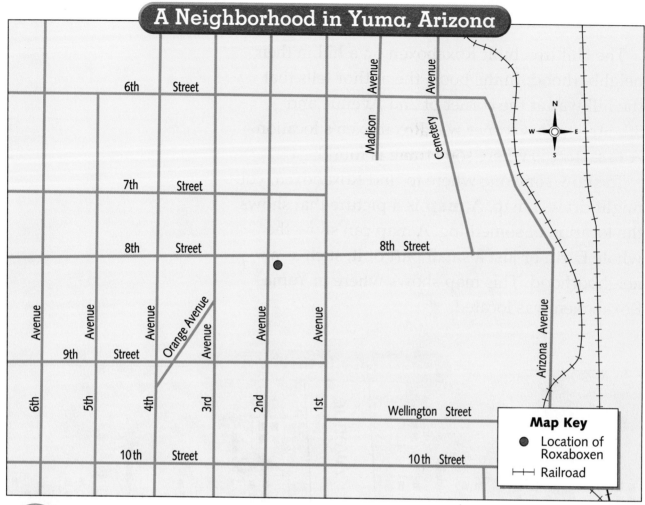

Location | The red dot stands for Roxaboxen.

■ Is Roxaboxen closer to 8th Street or 9th Street?

This map shows just a part of Yuma, because the whole city is too big to show on a small map. Look for the dot at the corner of 2nd Avenue and 8th Street. It shows the location in Yuma where the children built Roxaboxen.

REVIEW **What can a map show you?**

Where Is Yuma?

The city of Yuma is located in Arizona. Arizona is one of the 50 states that make up our country. Our country is the United States of America. Most people call it the United States for short.

This map shows all 50 states in the United States. It shows you the location of Arizona in the United States. The dot tells you the location of Yuma in the state of Arizona.

REVIEW How many states make up the United States of America?

The United States

Location ■ Which state is Yuma located close to?

Countries, Continents, and Oceans

The United States is one of the countries on the continent of North America. A **continent** is one of the seven main land areas on the Earth. The United States, Canada, and Mexico are the countries that make up the biggest part of North America. This map shows where Yuma, Arizona, is located in North America.

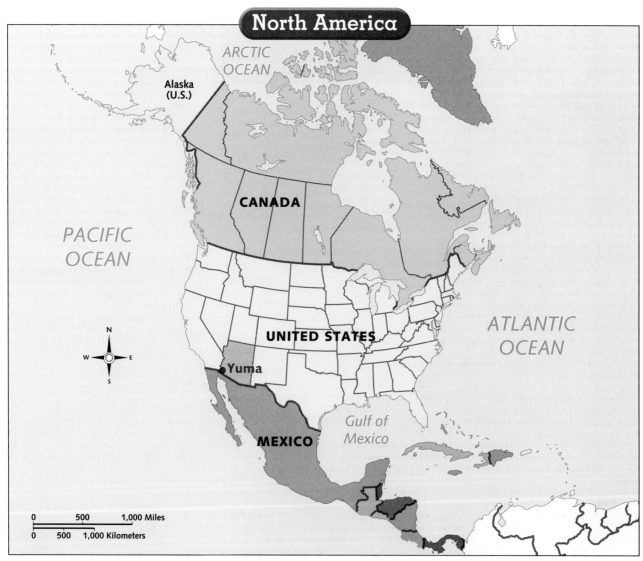

North America

ARCTIC OCEAN

Alaska (U.S.)

CANADA

PACIFIC OCEAN

UNITED STATES

ATLANTIC OCEAN

Yuma

Gulf of Mexico

MEXICO

N W E S

0   500   1,000 Miles
0   500   1,000 Kilometers

Location ■ Which country is Yuma located close to?

MAP THEME

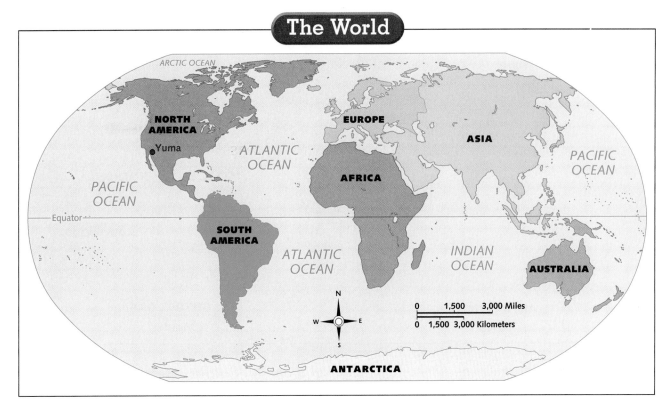

The World

Location ■ **Which ocean is Yuma located close to?**

This map of the world shows the seven continents. They are Africa, Antarctica, Asia, Australia, Europe, North America, and South America. Each continent, except for Australia and Antarctica, is made up of different countries.

This map also shows that much of the world is covered by oceans. An **ocean** is a large body of salt water. The largest oceans are the Pacific Ocean, Atlantic Ocean, Indian Ocean, and Arctic Ocean.

Where on Earth is Roxaboxen? You can now answer the question. Roxaboxen is on the corner of 2nd Avenue and 8th Street. It is in Yuma, Arizona, in the United States, in North America.

Where is North America? You can find out on the next page.

REVIEW **What are the seven continents?**

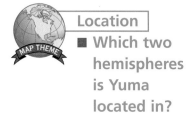

Western Hemisphere

North Pole

NORTH AMERICA
•Yuma
ATLANTIC OCEAN
Equator
SOUTH AMERICA
PACIFIC OCEAN
ANTARCTICA

South Pole

Eastern Hemisphere

North Pole

EUROPE
ASIA
PACIFIC OCEAN
AFRICA
Equator
ATLANTIC OCEAN
INDIAN OCEAN
AUSTRALIA
ANTARCTICA

South Pole

Location

■ Which two hemispheres is Yuma located in?

A globe is a model of the Earth.

Hemispheres

Maps of the whole Earth do not always show the true shape of the planet or the true sizes of all seven continents. That is because maps are flat, and the Earth is round. A **globe** is a better model of the Earth because it is round, too. However, a map is easier to carry with you.

Each of the maps above shows half of the Earth. Another way of saying "half of the Earth" is to use the word **hemisphere** (HEH•muh•sfir). *Hemi* means "half." *Sphere* means "ball" or "globe."

If you cut a globe in half from the North Pole to the South Pole, you would get two hemispheres. One half would be the Western Hemisphere. The other half would be the Eastern Hemisphere.

Another way to divide the Earth is along the equator. The **equator** is an imaginary line that is halfway between the North Pole and the South Pole. If you cut a globe in half at the equator, you still get two hemispheres—the Northern Hemisphere and the Southern Hemisphere.

You can see that North America, including Yuma, Arizona, is north of the equator. It is in the Northern Hemisphere. It is also in the Western Hemisphere. Every place on the Earth is in two hemispheres at the same time.

REVIEW In which two hemispheres can you find North America?

LESSON I REVIEW

Check Understanding

1 **Remember the Facts** What line divides the Northern from the Southern Hemisphere?

2 **Recall the Main Idea** How would you tell someone where to find Roxaboxen?

Think Critically

3 **Link to You** Imagine that you have a new pen pal. In your first letter, you will write about your community's location. How would you tell your pen pal your location on the Earth? Which vocabulary words from this lesson would you use?

Show What You Know

Map Activity Use the map on page 43 to draw the shape of your state. Show where your community is located. Then explain your map to a family member.

Read a Map

1. Why Learn This Skill?

Maps can tell you a lot about a place. They can show you places to visit, help you find their locations, and tell you how far away they are. Imagine that you are visiting the city of Yuma for the first time. You can use the map on page 49 to help you get where you need to go.

2. Understand the Process

Most maps have the same parts. If you know what each part does, you can read a map more easily.

1 **Title**—The title tells you what a map is about. The title is often at the top of a map. What is the title of the map shown on page 49?

2 **Map Key**—Most maps use **symbols** to stand for things that are real on the Earth. Some symbols do not look exactly like what they stand for. Look at the box that is at the bottom of the map. This box is the map key. A **map key** tells what the symbols on the map stand for. What symbol stands for a park?

3 **Scale**—The map of Yuma has a **distance scale**. You can use it to measure the distance, or how far it is, between two places on the map. To do this, you need a sheet of paper. Place the paper on the map, just below Carver Park and city hall. Make one mark on the paper where Carver Park is and another mark where city hall is. Then place the first mark under the zero on the distance scale. Check to see where the second mark is. The marks you made on the paper should show that the distance from Carver Park to city hall is one mile. How far is it from the library to the courthouse?

4 **Directions**—Find the drawing that shows the letters **N, S, E,** and **W.** This drawing is the compass rose. A **compass rose**

tells you directions, or which way you need to go to get someplace. **N** stands for *north*, **S** for *south*, **E** for *east*, and **W** for *west*. These four directions are called **cardinal directions**. Suppose you are at city hall. In which direction would you go to get to Fort Yuma? From city hall, in which direction would you go to get to the cemetery?

3. Think and Apply

Write five questions about finding location and distance. Ask a classmate to use this map to answer your questions. Then try answering his or her questions!

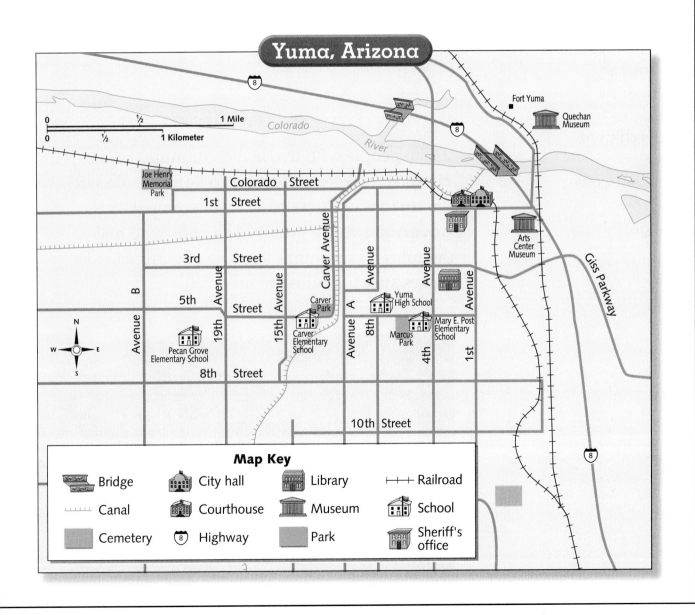

Yuma, Arizona

Map Key

Bridge	City hall	Library	├──┤ Railroad
⊥⊥⊥⊥ Canal	Courthouse	Museum	School
Cemetery	⑧ Highway	Park	Sheriff's office

FOCUS

Why do people in your community need to work together?

Main Idea Read to find out how people in communities work together to solve problems.

Vocabulary

cooperate
citizen
government
law
consequence
mayor
judge

Getting Along in a Community

Like the children in Roxaboxen, people in real communities such as Yuma, Arizona, do things together. Sometimes they get along. Sometimes they do not. People must **cooperate**, or work together, to keep their community a safe and peaceful place to live.

Governing a Community

The people who live in a community are its **citizens**. To keep order and to keep people safe, the citizens of Yuma have a government. A **government** is a group of citizens who make the rules for a community. The government also makes sure the rules are followed.

Citizens working together

A community government makes rules called laws. **Laws** are written to make the community a safe place to live. Traffic laws tell citizens how to travel safely through the streets of the community. Without traffic laws, many people might be hurt in accidents. They might ride their bikes without stopping at stop signs and be hit by cars.

If people break laws, they may face consequences. A **consequence** is something that happens because of something a person does. Being hurt in an accident is one kind of consequence. Having to pay a fine, or money, is another kind of consequence. If a person breaks a very important law, he or she may have to go to jail. In Roxaboxen the children went to jail if they drove too fast.

Jamie was the police officer in Roxaboxen. Police officers in Yuma and other communities work to keep people safe and to see that all citizens follow the laws.

REVIEW What are the rules a community makes called?

Police officer in Roxaboxen

Police officer in Yuma

The mayor of Roxaboxen

How Laws Are Made

Each community has a way to make laws and to see that they are followed. In Roxaboxen, Marian was the mayor. A **mayor** is the leader of a city or town government. The mayor's job is to see that things get done that will make the community a good place to live.

In Yuma, groups of citizens are chosen to make laws for all the people. The groups meet with the mayor to talk about problems in the community. Then they decide how to solve them.

MARILYN R. YOUNG
MAYOR

The mayor of Yuma

A judge in Yuma

Courts make up another part of the government in Yuma and in most other communities. **Judges** are citizens who are chosen to work as leaders in the courts. Judges decide if a person has broken the law. They also decide the consequences for people who have broken the law. Judges work in the courts to make sure that citizens are treated fairly.

REVIEW **What is the leader of the city government called?**

LESSON 2 REVIEW

Check Understanding

① **Remember the Facts** What is a government?

② **Recall the Main Idea** How do people in communities work together to solve problems?

Think Critically

③ **Personally Speaking** Think about some rules your school has. What consequences do you face if you do not follow the rules?

Show What You Know

Poster Activity Think about how laws can keep you safe in your community. Choose one law, and make a poster that shows why people should follow it. At the bottom of your poster, write a sentence that tells what could happen if the law is not followed. Hang up your poster in the classroom, and talk about it with classmates.

Act as a Responsible Citizen

1. Why Learn This Skill?

Each citizen in a community has responsibilities. **Responsibilities** are things citizens must do. One responsibility is to understand and obey the law. When citizens obey the law, they keep their community safe and peaceful.

Children in Philadelphia, Pennsylvania, show how responsible citizens can help clean up their communities.

2. Remember What You Have Read

Many community laws are like the traffic laws you read about in Lesson 2. If people break laws, they may face consequences. Responsible citizens know laws are important, so they follow them.

3. Understand the Process

Here are some ways you can be a responsible citizen.

➊ **At Home**—Pick up and put away your things so that people do not trip over them.

➋ **At School**—Follow the directions of the crossing guard. Look both ways before crossing. What are other ways to show you are a responsible citizen?

4. Think and Apply

Some laws are made to keep people safe. Is there a law in your community that says that children must wear helmets when riding a bicycle? Why should laws like this be followed? Explain your answer.

Getting What We Need

FOCUS
What kinds of things do you need to live?

Main Idea Read to find out how people in communities meet their needs.

Vocabulary
resource
volunteer

To have a safe and healthy life, people need food, clothing, and a place to live. People in communities can help one another meet these needs. They can work together as Marian, Charles, and others did in Roxaboxen.

Meeting Needs with Resources

Some of the needs people have can be met with resources. A **resource** is something that people use to make what they need. The children in Roxaboxen used white stones to mark their streets. They used old wooden boxes to make shelves and tables. The stones and boxes were resources the children used to meet their needs. People in Yuma use many resources, too. Soil, water, and plants are important resources.

A worker in Yuma uses resources to build a house.

The children used resources to build Roxaboxen.

55

A community has another important resource—its people. Their work and skills can be used to help the community.

The children of Roxaboxen used their skills in many ways. Jamie was the police officer. Marian was the mayor. Jean and Anna May worked in the bakery. In Yuma some people cook meals and some sell clothing. Others build roads, while still others paint buildings and keep them clean.

In any community there are many jobs that need to be done. People depend on one another in many ways.

REVIEW **What are some important resources in a community?**

Workers at a bakery in Roxaboxen

Workers at a bakery in Yuma

People Make a Difference

Some people work in a community without being paid. These people are **volunteers**. Volunteers spend their free time doing things to make their community a good place to live.

Volunteers can help solve many problems in the community. For example, community food banks collect food given by people. Then volunteers take it to places where people who have no food can get a free meal.

Volunteers help people when there has been an earthquake or a flood. They collect food, clothing, blankets, and medicine for people who need them.

In some cities, volunteers work on weekends with a project called "Habitat for Humanity." A habitat is a place to live. These volunteers help people who are not able to build or fix up their own homes.

REVIEW **How do volunteers help make their communities good places to live?**

Volunteers at a food bank

Volunteers in Yuma help with a community project.

LESSON 3 REVIEW

Check Understanding

1. **Remember the Facts** Why are people an important kind of resource?

2. **Recall the Main Idea** How do people in communities meet their needs?

Think Critically

3. **Link to You** What are some ways you can help in your community as a volunteer?

Show What You Know

Collage Activity Make a collage to show resources you and your family have used in the last week. Look through magazines for pictures of resources. You may also want to use some real resources, such as pieces of cotton or wood. Give your collage a title that explains what it is about. Then add your collage to a class bulletin board.

FOCUS
Why is learning about the past important?

Main Idea Read to find out how Yuma has changed over the years.

Vocabulary
history
ancestor
missionary
biography

Communities Have Histories

Every community has a history. **History** is the story of what has happened in a place. The story begins even before people begin to live and work there. Roxaboxen's history started long before Marian and her friends set up their streets and buildings. Many real communities have a long history. Yuma's history started hundreds of years ago with Native Americans, or American Indians. They were the first Americans.

Long, Long Ago

The first people to live in the place that is now called Yuma were the Quechan (KECH•uhn) Indians. They farmed land along the Colorado

River and also lived in parts of southern California. The Quechans were part of a larger group of Indians known as the Yumas. Many people who live near Yuma today have ancestors who were Yuma Indians. An **ancestor** is someone in a person's family, such as a great-great-grandparent, who lived a long time ago.

This photograph of Quechan Indians was taken in 1882.

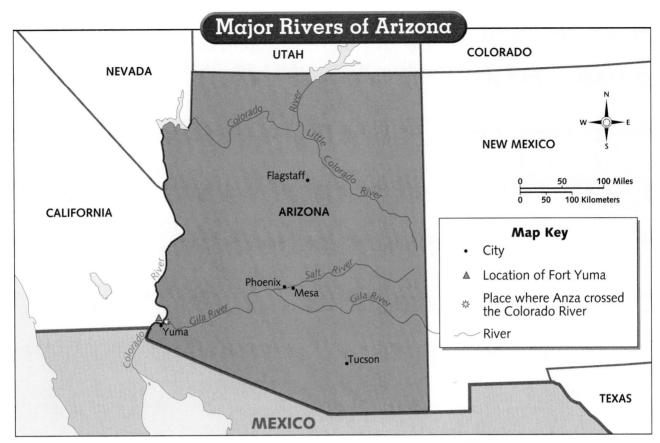

Major Rivers of Arizona

NEVADA

UTAH

COLORADO

Colorado River

Little Colorado River

Flagstaff.

ARIZONA

CALIFORNIA

NEW MEXICO

N
W — E
S

| 0 | 50 | 100 Miles |
| 0 | 50 | 100 Kilometers |

Map Key

- City

▲ Location of Fort Yuma

☀ Place where Anza crossed the Colorado River

〰 River

Colorado River

Phoenix
Mesa

Salt River

Gila River

Gila River

▲☀ Yuma

Colorado

.Tucson

TEXAS

MEXICO

Place ■ What rivers flow through Arizona?

MAP THEME

Beginning in the 1500s explorers from the country of Spain explored the land along the Colorado River. One was Juan Bautista de Anza (HWAN bow•TEES•tah day AHN• sah). In 1774 he and his group of men looked for a way to cross the Colorado River into what is now California. This was hard to do because the river was wide and rough. Anza learned that the best place to cross was near where Yuma is now.

With the help of the Quechans, the men safely crossed the river on February 9. To celebrate the safe crossing, Anza gave the Quechans an ox and set off fireworks. In his diary he later wrote,

66 The Yuma nation numbered thirty-five hundred. Their lands were very rich bottom lands and capable of high cultivation (good for growing crops). 99

The Quechans made clay jars like this one to sell or trade.

Lesson 4 • 59

San Xavier del Bac Mission in Tucson, Arizona

More Spanish people came to the Yuma area in 1780. A group of missionaries came to teach the Indians the Spanish way of life. A **missionary** is a person who is sent to tell others about his or her church. The Spanish missionaries built a mission, or church, and tried to make the Indians change what they believed. The Quechan Indians turned against the missionaries in 1781 and made them leave.

In 1821 Yuma became part of the country of Mexico. The ancestors of many people who live in Yuma today were Spanish or Mexican.

REVIEW Who were the first people to live along the Colorado River near Yuma?

Anglos and Chinese Move to Yuma

In 1850 United States soldiers built a fort across the river from Yuma. Soon many people began to travel through Yuma on their way to look for gold in California. In 1854 an agreement with Mexico made Yuma a part of the United States. Then many people gave up looking for gold. They stopped in Yuma and stayed. The Spanish people of Yuma called these new citizens Anglos. Anglos are white Americans whose ancestors were not Spanish.

This painting shows how Fort Yuma looked in 1850.

Another group of people who moved to Yuma were the Chinese. In 1877 thousands of Chinese workers came to help build the railroads. Chinese families still live in Yuma.

REVIEW **What brought the Anglos to Yuma?**

Changes over Time

Over the years there have been many changes in Yuma. The name of the town has changed, too—three times. First it was Colorado City. Then it was Arizona City. Finally the town was named Yuma after the larger group of Indians the Quechans belonged to.

Yuma grew from just a few buildings into the modern city it is today. The pictures on these pages show some of the ways Yuma has changed in almost 100 years.

The photograph on the left shows how Main Street in Yuma looked during a parade in 1909. The photograph above shows how the street looks today.

Many changes have taken place, but much has stayed the same. The weather in Yuma is still sunny and warm. People still live and work in this town next to the Colorado River. They raise their families and enjoy the location and weather.

Many groups have made Yuma their home—Yuma Indians and Spanish, Mexican, Chinese, and Anglo people. They all have interesting stories about how they came to live in Yuma. Knowing a community's history can help you understand the community today. In the same way, reading a biography (by•AH•gruh•fee) can help you understand a person. A **biography** is the story of a real person's life.

REVIEW What has stayed the same in Yuma over the years?

Cesar Chavez
1927–1993

Cesar Chavez was born on a farm near Yuma, Arizona. His parents lost their farm and business when he was a young boy. Chavez and his family had to go to work harvesting crops all over Arizona and California. Chavez saw that farm workers were not always treated fairly. When he grew up, Cesar Chavez spent his life working for fair treatment for all farm workers.

LESSON 4 REVIEW

Check Understanding

1 Remember the Facts What groups of people have lived in Yuma over the years?

2 Recall the Main Idea How has Yuma changed over time?

Think Critically

3 Think More About It Why do you think the Quechan Indians turned against the Spanish missionaries?

Show What You Know

Interview Activity Find a person who has been living in your community for a long time. Make a list of questions you would like to ask about how the community has changed. Then interview the person to find out what changes he or she has seen. Share with your classmates the changes you learn about.

Read a Time Line

1. Why Learn This Skill?

When you study Social Studies, you sometimes need to keep track of when events happened. To help you keep these dates in order, you can use a time line. A **time line** shows when important events took place.

2. Understand the Process

You read most time lines from left to right, just like a sentence. The things on the left happened first. The things on the right happened later. Look at the time line shown here. The first thing it shows is that Anza crossed the Colorado River in 1774. The last thing the time line shows is when Chinese workers started to build the railroads. In what year did they do that?

3. Think and Apply

Use the time line to help you answer these questions.

1 Which was built first, Fort Yuma or the railroads?

2 Did Yuma become part of the United States before or after the building of Fort Yuma?

3 In what year did the missionaries leave Yuma?

4 When did Yuma become part of the United States?

TIME LINE OF YUMA'S HISTORY

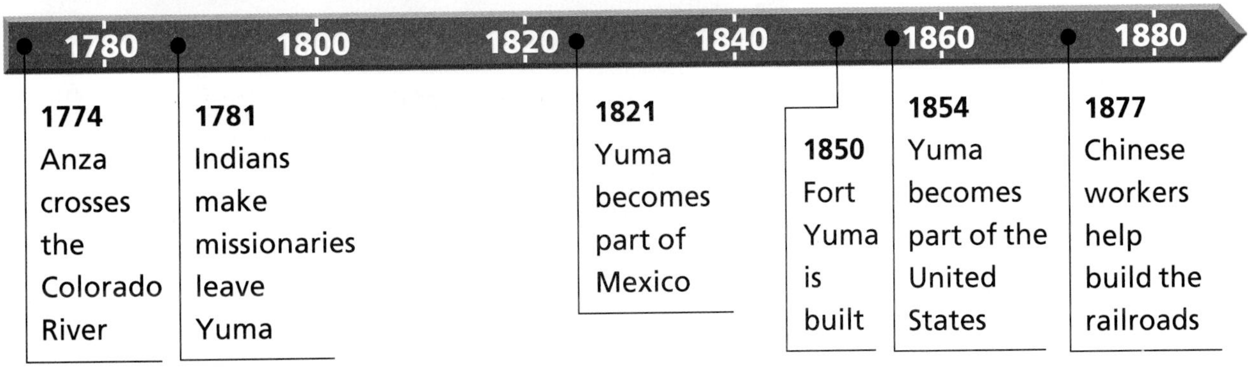

1780 — 1800 — 1820 — 1840 — 1860 — 1880

1774 Anza crosses the Colorado River

1781 Indians make missionaries leave Yuma

1821 Yuma becomes part of Mexico

1850 Fort Yuma is built

1854 Yuma becomes part of the United States

1877 Chinese workers help build the railroads

FOCUS

Why do you think most communities are made up of different groups of people?

Main Idea Read to find out how groups of people come to live together in communities.

Vocabulary

custom
culture
founder

Many People, Many Ways of Life

In most communities people with the same interests or background form groups. In Roxaboxen the girls formed one group and the boys formed another. Today the city of Yuma, like most other large communities, has many groups of people. Native Americans and people whose ancestors came from Asia, Mexico, Europe, Africa, and other places all live there.

What Makes Groups of People Special?

In any community the people in a group often share the same customs. A **custom** is a way of doing something. In the United States one custom is for people to greet each other by shaking hands.

People from many different groups live in Yuma.

In the United States it is a custom for people to shake hands when they meet.

In Japan one custom is for people to remove their shoes when they enter a house. Shoes are left in a room just inside the front door.

The customs that people have are part of their culture. The **culture** of a group is made up of things the people share. They usually speak the same language and often believe the same things. They may enjoy the same kinds of art, music, dance, and literature.

REVIEW What things make up the culture of a group of people?

People in Nikko, Japan, take off their shoes before entering this temple, a place where they worship.

This painting by John Innes shows Captain George Vancouver pointing to the land that would later become the city of Vancouver.

How Do Groups of People Start Communities?

A community begins when a group of people start to live together. The people who start the community are called its **founders**. Marian and the other children who started Roxaboxen were its founders.

Some communities are made up of just one group of people who share the same culture. Other communities are made up of many groups with different cultures, all living and working together.

Vancouver is a city in Canada, the country to the north of the United States. Like Yuma, Vancouver is a community made up of many groups of people from different parts of the world. The Musqueam (MUHS•kwee•uhm) Indians were the first people to live on the land where the city was built. The ancestors of some of the people who live in Vancouver today were Musqueam Indians.

Vancouver is named for British sea captain George Vancouver, who explored the area in 1792. He said that the land and the water would become part of his country, Great Britain. However, George Vancouver was not the founder of the city. The founders of Vancouver were the people who built a lumber mill there in 1865. The city of Vancouver grew up around that lumber mill.

REVIEW **Who are the founders of a community?**

The men in the photograph are William Hailstone, Sam Brighouse, and John Morton. These men founded Vancouver when they built Hastings Mill there in 1865.

Vancouver, British Columbia

CANADA

BRITISH COLUMBIA

PACIFIC OCEAN

Vancouver

UNITED STATES

0   150   300 Miles
0   150   300 Kilometers

Map Key
🌲 Forest

ARCTIC OCEAN

BRITISH COLUMBIA

CANADA

Vancouver

PACIFIC OCEAN

UNITED STATES

Yuma

ATLANTIC OCEAN

MEXICO   Gulf of Mexico

0   700 Miles
0   700 Kilometers

Human-Environment Interactions The founders of Vancouver built a lumber mill.
■ What resource was there for them to use?

Different People Make Up a Community

The groups of people who make up a community often have different cultures. However, they can still get along with one another.

People from many parts of the world have made Vancouver their home. Many who live there today have Native American ancestors. The children and grandchildren of people who came from Russia, England, Scotland, and Ireland live in Vancouver, too. People also came to Vancouver from other countries in Europe, such as Germany and Italy. In the 1850s miners came from the United States and Australia to search for gold. In the 1880s thousands of Chinese workers came to help build the railroads. Then, in 1904, a large group of Sikhs (SEEKS) moved to Vancouver from India to cut trees in Canada's forests.

Sikh tree cutters

LEARNING FROM PHOTOS

This photo shows a street in Vancouver around 1910.
- How is this place the same as your community? How is it different?

This classroom in Vancouver is filled with children of many different cultures. It is an interesting place to learn in.

Today four out of every ten students in Vancouver speak English at school and another language at home. Having different languages can make it hard for people to talk with one another. Different customs can make it hard for people to understand one another. But the differences between people make Vancouver an interesting city to live and work in.

REVIEW **What were three main reasons people moved to Vancouver from other countries?**

Communities Celebrate

The people of the different groups in a community like to celebrate their own holidays. In Vancouver the Chinese people celebrate the Chinese New Year. They hold a parade and set off fireworks. This day most often comes in February.

At other times all the people of a community celebrate a holiday together. For example, on July 1 everyone in Vancouver celebrates Canada Day, the country's birthday. This holiday is like the Fourth of July in the United States. Canadians gather to watch parades and fireworks. They listen to speeches and sing their country's special songs.

Chinese people in Vancouver celebrate the Chinese New Year.

This is one of the stamps that celebrates the Chinese New Year.

Fireworks in the night sky over Vancouver

Each group that lives in Vancouver has its own customs and culture. But all the people are Canadian citizens. They are proud of their flag and their country.

REVIEW How do citizens of Vancouver celebrate Canada Day?

LESSON 5 REVIEW

Check Understanding

1 Remember the Facts What kinds of things do people of the same culture share?

2 Recall the Main Idea How do different groups of people come to live together in a community?

Think Critically

3 Explore Viewpoints Why might people with the same interests or backgrounds want to form groups?

Show What You Know

Bulletin Board Activity Cut from old magazines pictures that show customs from around the world. You may also want to draw pictures to show customs you have seen yourself or read about in books. Write a paragraph that explains each custom. Then add your pictures and paragraph to a class bulletin board. Invite other classes to see your bulletin board, and explain the customs shown.

FOCUS
How would you describe the location of your community?

Main Idea Learn some ways to describe your community's location in the world, in the country, and in your state.

Vocabulary
region
tidewater
piedmont

Where on Earth Is Your Community?

In this unit you learned about two communities in two different locations. First you read about Yuma, Arizona. Then you read about Vancouver, British Columbia. Yuma is in the United States, and Vancouver is in Canada. Both communities share a location on the continent of North America. Both also are located in the Northern and Western hemispheres. If someone were to ask you to describe the location of your community in the same way that you can describe Yuma and Vancouver, what could you say?

You could use a globe like this one to show where your community in South Carolina is located.

Where on a Globe?

You can say that your community is in the Northern and Western hemispheres, just like both Yuma and Vancouver. Your community is on the continent of North America, too. Like Yuma, your community is in one of the 50 states of the United States. The state where you live is called South Carolina.

South Carolina is not a large state. Only ten of the fifty states in the United States are smaller in size than South Carolina. Driving across South Carolina in any direction takes just a few hours. Although it is small in size, South Carolina offers many different places for people to live, work, and have fun.

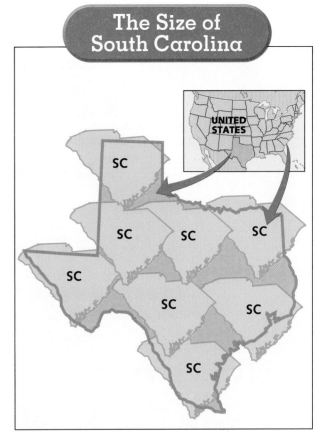

This map gives you an idea of South Carolina's size. Almost eight South Carolinas can fit into the state of Texas.

Where on Earth Is South Carolina?

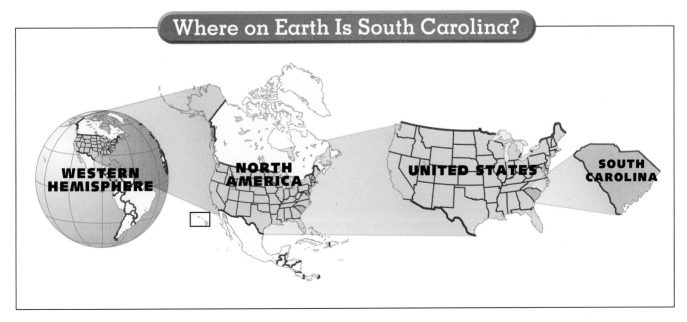

WESTERN HEMISPHERE

NORTH AMERICA

UNITED STATES

SOUTH CAROLINA

LEARNING FROM DIAGRAMS South Carolina is a state in the southern part of the United States.

■ Which continent is South Carolina located on?

This map shows you where South Carolina is located on North America and in the United States. South Carolina is in the southern part of the United States. The state is shaped like a rough triangle. The Atlantic Ocean and the states of North Carolina and Georgia form the three sides of the triangle.

REVIEW **Where is South Carolina located?**

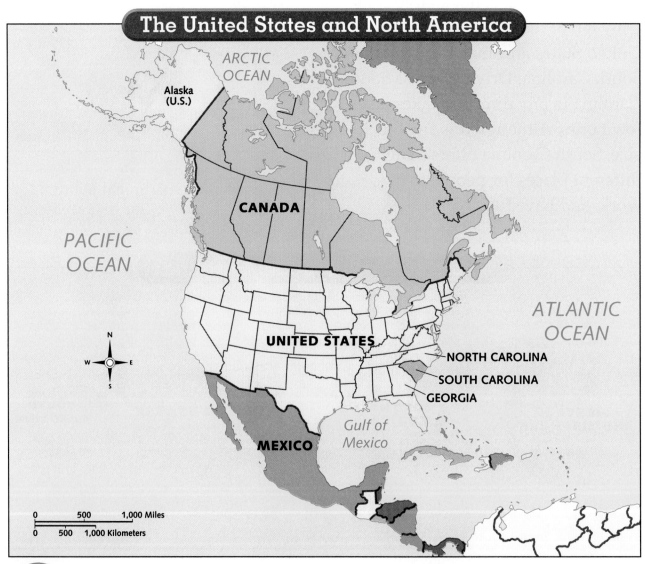

The United States and North America

ARCTIC OCEAN

Alaska (U.S.)

CANADA

PACIFIC OCEAN

UNITED STATES

ATLANTIC OCEAN

NORTH CAROLINA

SOUTH CAROLINA

GEORGIA

Gulf of Mexico

MEXICO

N
W E
S

0   500   1,000 Miles

0   500   1,000 Kilometers

Location ■ **Which ocean touches South Carolina?**

MAP THEME

Where in South Carolina?

People in South Carolina divide their state into different regions. A **region** is a place with at least one feature that makes it different from other places. A region can be a place with a certain kind of land or plant life. It could also be a place where people share a language or a way of life. South Carolina's six natural regions are the Blue Ridge, Piedmont, Sandhills, Inner Coastal Plain, Outer Coastal Plain, and Coastal Zone.

REVIEW What are the six natural regions of South Carolina?

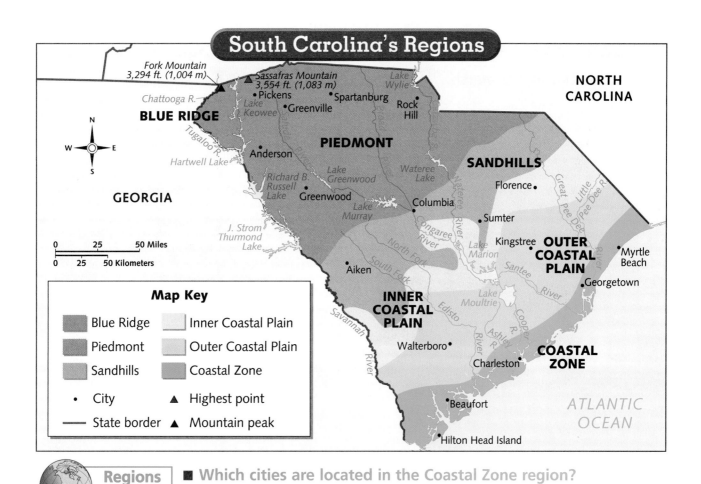

South Carolina's Regions

Fork Mountain
3,294 ft. (1,004 m)

Sassafras Mountain
3,554 ft. (1,083 m)

Lake Wylie

NORTH CAROLINA

Chattooga R.

Pickens

Spartanburg

Rock Hill

BLUE RIDGE

Lake Keowee

Greenville

Tugaloo R.

PIEDMONT

SANDHILLS

Hartwell Lake

Anderson

Lake Greenwood

Wateree Lake

Florence

GEORGIA

Richard B. Russell Lake

Greenwood

Lake Murray

Columbia

Sumter

Great Pee Dee R.

Little Pee Dee R.

0   25   50 Miles
0   25   50 Kilometers

J. Strom Thurmond Lake

Congaree River

Wateree River

Lake Marion

Kingstree

OUTER COASTAL PLAIN

Myrtle Beach

North Fork

Aiken

South Fork

Santee River

Georgetown

INNER COASTAL PLAIN

Lake Moultrie

Edisto

Cooper R.

COASTAL ZONE

Savannah River

Walterboro

Ashley R.

Charleston

Beaufort

ATLANTIC OCEAN

Hilton Head Island

Map Key

▨	Blue Ridge	▢	Inner Coastal Plain
▨	Piedmont	▢	Outer Coastal Plain
▨	Sandhills	▨	Coastal Zone
•	City	▲	Highest point
—	State border	▲	Mountain peak

Regions ■ Which cities are located in the Coastal Zone region?

MAP THEME

The Low Country

South Carolinians often call the Inner Coastal Plain, the Outer Coastal Plain, and the Coastal Zone regions the Low Country. It covers two-thirds of South Carolina. This area of lowland is part of a larger area of lowland that stretches from New York in the north to Florida in the south.

Marshes and waterways make up much of the Low Country near the ocean. This part of the Low Country is often called the **tidewater** area. Here the ocean waters rise and fall twice a day with the tide. Farther inland up the rivers are many swamps. One of the largest is the Congaree (KAHNG•guh•ree) Swamp.

▲ **Great Blue Heron in a marsh**

▼ **Charleston**

▼ **Historic schoolhouse in Allendale**

MISS ARNOLD'S
SCHOOL HOUSE
EST. 1875

Many of South Carolina's earliest communities were in the regions of the Low Country. Today some of the largest communities in the Low Country include Charleston, Myrtle Beach, Georgetown, and Port Royal along the ocean. Farther inland are Allendale, Florence, and Sumter.

REVIEW **What is the tidewater area?**

GEOGRAPHY

The Grand Strand

The Grand Strand is a long group of beaches that stretches 60 miles (97 km) from Little River to Georgetown. This map of South Carolina shows that the Grand Strand is a long, curved section of land along the Atlantic Ocean.

▼ **Myrtle Beach**

The Up Country and Midlands

South Carolinians often call the Blue Ridge and Piedmont regions the Up Country. It covers about one-third of the state in the western part of South Carolina. Some of the largest communities in the Up Country include Columbia, Spartanburg, Greenville, and Rock Hill.

The Blue Ridge Mountains are part of the larger Appalachian (a•puh•LAY•chee•uhn) Mountains. This chain of mountains runs through the eastern United States from Maine in the north to Alabama in the south. The Piedmont (PEED•mahnt) is a region of rolling hills. The name **piedmont** means "the foot of the mountain."

The Low Country and the Up Country are not divided by a straight and exact line. Long ago ocean waters covered much of the Low Country and formed a beach along its western edge. Today that ancient beach is a strip of land known as the Sandhills. Some people call the Sandhills region the Midlands because it is between the Low Country and the Up Country.

REVIEW How are the Up Country and the Midlands different from the Low Country?

▲ Table Rock State Park

▼ Spartanburg

▼ Peach orchard near Lexington

GEOGRAPHY

Sassafras Mountain

The highest point in the Up Country is Sassafras (SAS•uh•fras) Mountain. It is located in the Blue Ridge Mountains, at the edge of South Carolina. The mountain is named for its sassafras trees, which can be used to make tea and perfume. Sassafras Mountain reaches 3,554 feet (1,083 m), making it the highest point in all of South Carolina. From the top of Sassafras Mountain you can see four different states—Tennessee, North Carolina, South Carolina, and Georgia.

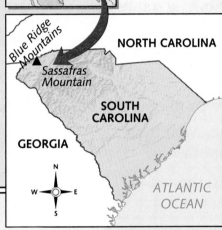

▲ **This photograph was taken at the top of Sassafras Mountain.**

LESSON 6 REVIEW

Check Understanding

1 Remember the Facts What are South Carolina's six natural regions?

2 Recall the Main Idea How would you tell someone where to find South Carolina?

Think Critically

3 Link to You Describe your location in South Carolina using the vocabulary from this unit.

Show What You Know

Map Activity Locate your community on a map of South Carolina. Use what you have learned in this unit to draw a map of your street. On the map, write the name of your street and show your house or apartment number. Add your map to a class bulletin board.

A Community
GUIDANCE CARD

The tiny community of Kotzebue (KAHT•sih•byoo) had a problem. Over the years some people had lost their feeling of responsibility to the community. There were problems with fighting and crime. Members of the community wanted to do something to help bring the community back together. So they created a community guidance card.

On the card is a list of ideas about the community that are important to the people of Kotzebue. "They give us all a sense of belonging, a sense of peace," says Rachel Craig, a community leader. Some of these ideas are

- Cooperation
- Family roles

- Hard work
- Humor
- Love for children
- Respect for nature
- Respect for others
- Responsibility to community
- Sharing

Many community members, young and old, carry these cards with them wherever they go. The cards help remind the people of the ideas that are most important to them. Today there are fewer problems in Kotzebue. A small card has made a big difference in this community.

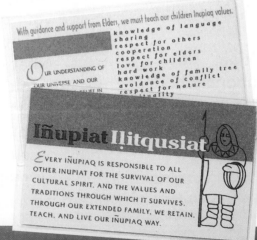

With guidance and support from Elders, we must teach our children Inupiaq values.

OUR UNDERSTANDING OF OUR UNIVERSE AND OUR PLACE IN

knowledge of language
sharing
respect for others
cooperation
respect for elders
love for children
hard work
knowledge of family tree
avoidance of conflict
respect for nature
spirituality

Iñupiat Ilitqusiat

EVERY IÑUPIAQ IS RESPONSIBLE TO ALL OTHER INUPIAT FOR THE SURVIVAL OF OUR CULTURAL SPIRIT, AND THE VALUES AND TRADITIONS THROUGH WHICH IT SURVIVES. THROUGH OUR EXTENDED FAMILY, WE RETAIN, TEACH, AND LIVE OUR IÑUPIAQ WAY.

Kotzebue, Alaska

UNITED STATES

ARCTIC OCEAN

RUSSIA • Kotzebue
Arctic Circle
• Nome
Fairbanks •
CANADA
A L A S K A
• Anchorage
Bering Sea
Gulf of Alaska
Juneau •

N W E S

0   200   400 Miles
0   200   400 Kilometers
PACIFIC OCEAN

Think and Apply

BUILDING CITIZENSHIP

Now it is your turn to make a guidance card. First, brainstorm a list of ideas that are important to you and your classmates. Then, pick five of the most important ideas. Next, cut out a blank card from cardboard or construction paper. Last, write the ideas on the card. Carry your card with you, and show it to a family member. Explain why the ideas on it are important to you and your classmates.

HARCOURT BRACE

Visit the Internet at
http://www.hbschool.com
for additional resources.

UNIT 1
REVIEW

VISUAL SUMMARY

Study the pictures and captions to help you review the events you read about in Unit 1.

Make a Picture Puzzle

Compare the community you live in with the one shown here. Then tell about your community by making a picture puzzle. Draw the outlines of puzzle pieces on a sheet of heavy paper. On each puzzle piece, draw a picture and write a sentence about it. The picture and sentence should be about something interesting in your community. Cut out the puzzle pieces, and ask a classmate to put them together again.

1 A community has a location on Earth.

3 People in a community use resources to meet their needs.

2 Citizens in a community form governments and work together to solve problems.

4 A community changes over time.

5 A community is made up of different groups of people who live and work together.

CONNECT MAIN IDEAS

Complete this graphic organizer by writing one detail about each community. The details should tell more about each lesson's main idea. A copy of the organizer is on Activity Book page 12.

Lesson 5
A community is made up of different groups of people who live and work together.
1. Roxaboxen
2. Yuma

Lesson 1
A community has a location on Earth.
1. Roxaboxen
2. Yuma

Lesson 2
Citizens in a community form governments and work together to solve problems.
1. Roxaboxen
2. Yuma

Lesson 4
A community changes over time.
1. Roxaboxen
2. Yuma

What Is a Community?

Lesson 3
People in a community use resources to meet their needs.
1. Roxaboxen
2. Yuma

WRITE MORE ABOUT IT

Write a Postcard   In this unit you visited the city of Vancouver. Think about a community you have really visited. Imagine that you are there now. Make a postcard that shows the community. On the back, write to a friend about the community and the people there.

Use Vocabulary

Roxaboxen was an imaginary community. Imagine a community of your own, and write sentences about it. Use each word below in your sentences.

1. citizen
2. custom
3. law
4. location
5. region

Check Understanding

6. What can you use to show where your community is located?
7. Why can people be called a resource?
8. Why is Vancouver made up of different groups of people?
9. What kind of land makes up South Carolina's Low Country?

Think Critically

10. **Link to You** What is one law in your community that is important to you and your family? Tell why it is important.
11. **Personally Speaking** How can people from different cultures make your life more interesting?

12. **Cause and Effect** What might happen if people stopped volunteering to help others?

Apply Skills

Read a Map Use the map to answer the questions.

13. What symbol stands for an airport?
14. Suppose you were at the zoo. In which direction would you travel to reach the hospital?
15. How far is it from the school to the police station?

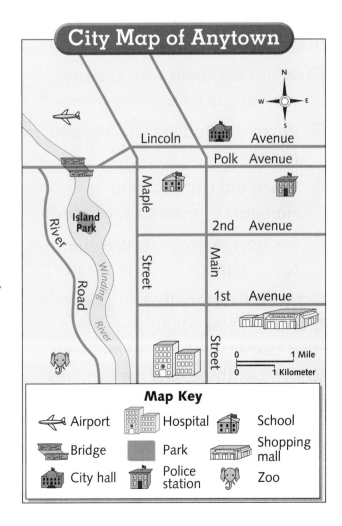

City Map of Anytown

N W E S

Lincoln   Avenue
Polk   Avenue
Maple
Island Park
River
2nd   Avenue
Street
Main
Road
1st   Avenue
Winding River
Street
0   1 Mile
0   1 Kilometer

Map Key

Airport   Hospital   School
Bridge   Park   Shopping mall
City hall Police station   Zoo

TIME LINE OF ANYTOWN'S HISTORY

1900		1930				1960	
1901 Founders start Anytown	**1920** Bob Stevens becomes mayor	**1935** Tornado destroys movie theater	**1940** Grace Diez builds new movie theater	**1952** 122 citizens from Hometown move to Anytown		**1961** City park is built	

Read a Time Line The time line shows when things happened in an imaginary town named Anytown. Use the time line to help you answer these questions.

16 Which was built first, the city park or the new movie theater?

17 When did Bob Stevens become mayor?

18 When did citizens from Hometown move to Anytown?

19 For how many years was the town without a movie theater?

Act as a Responsible Citizen Think about the rules students must follow at your school. List three, and explain why each is important. Then tell what the consequences are for not following these rules.

READ MORE ABOUT IT

All Around Town: The Photographs of Richard Samuel Roberts by Dinah Johnson. Henry Holt. Learn about the community of Columbia, South Carolina, in the 1920s and 1930s through the photographs of Richard Samuel Roberts.

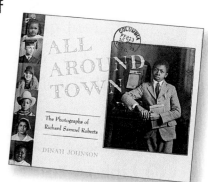

HARCOURT BRACE

Visit the Internet at
http://www.hbschool.com
for additional resources.

REMEMBER

- Share your ideas.
- Cooperate with others to plan your work.
- Take responsibility for your work.
- Help one another.
- Show your group's work to the class.
- Discuss what you learned by working together.

ACTIVITY

Make a Model

Roxaboxen was a community made by a group of children. They built Roxaboxen with stones and old boxes. Work with a group of classmates to plan an imaginary community of your own. Then build a model of your community. You can use empty boxes and rinsed milk cartons for buildings. You can cut paper to make roads and sidewalks. Work together to make your model community a safe and peaceful place to live.

Unit Project Wrap-Up

Make a Community Booklet With your classmates, work in small groups to complete your booklet. Together, look at all the pages you have made. Decide which ones will be in your booklet. Glue each page onto a sheet of construction paper. Then punch holes and tie the sheets together with yarn or string. Add your booklet to your classroom library.

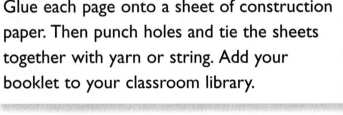

WHERE PEOPLE START COMMUNITIES

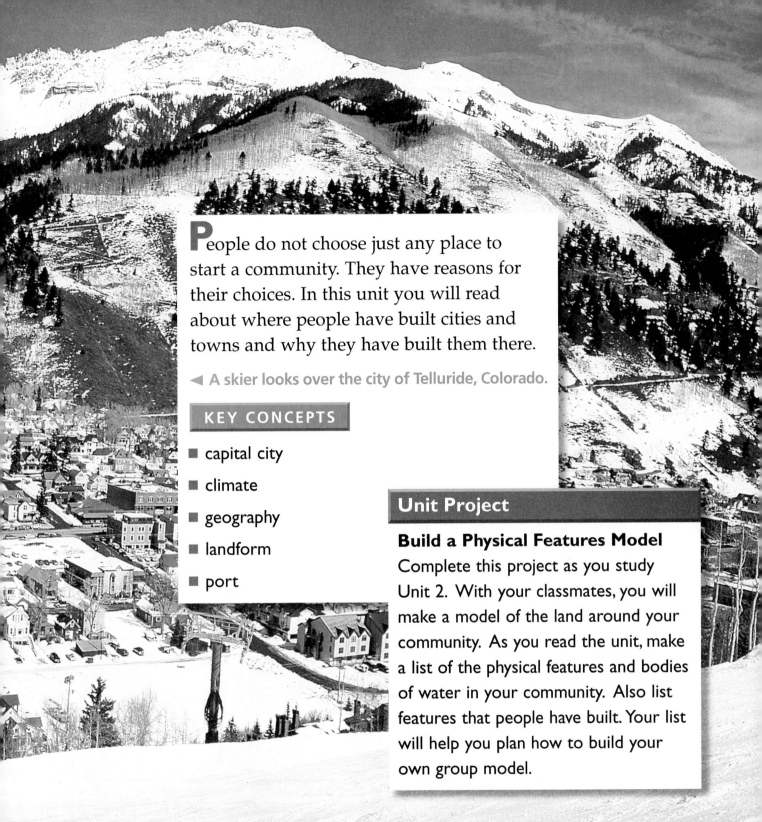

People do not choose just any place to start a community. They have reasons for their choices. In this unit you will read about where people have built cities and towns and why they have built them there.

◄ A skier looks over the city of Telluride, Colorado.

KEY CONCEPTS

- capital city
- climate
- geography
- landform
- port

Unit Project

Build a Physical Features Model
Complete this project as you study Unit 2. With your classmates, you will make a model of the land around your community. As you read the unit, make a list of the physical features and bodies of water in your community. Also list features that people have built. Your list will help you plan how to build your own group model.

geography The study of the Earth's features or shapes.

port A place where ships can dock.

capital city The place where the leaders of a country or state meet and work.

climate The kind of weather a place has each season year after year.

landform The natural shape of the land.

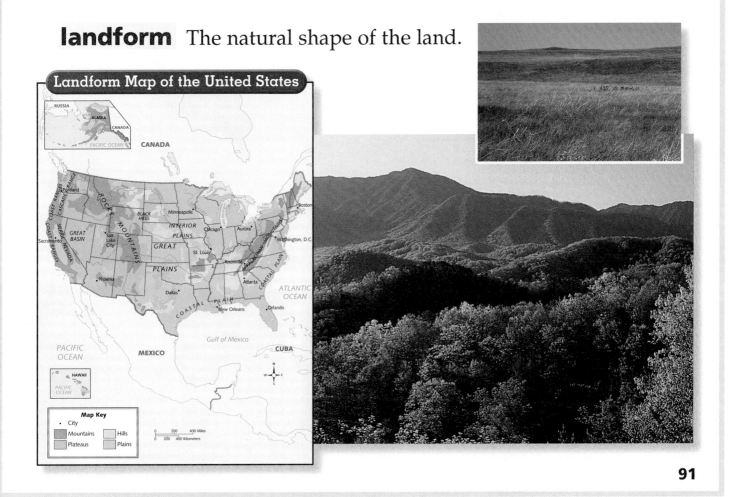

Landform Map of the United States

RUSSIA
ALASKA
CANADA
PACIFIC OCEAN

CANADA

COAST RANGES
CASCADE RANGE
Portland
SIERRA NEVADA
COAST RANGES
Sacramento
ROCKY MOUNTAINS
GREAT BASIN
Salt Lake City
BLACK HILLS
Minneapolis
INTERIOR PLAINS
Chicago
Aurora
Lake Michigan
Boston
APPALACHIAN MOUNTAINS
Washington, D.C.
GREAT PLAINS
St. Louis
Knoxville
Phoenix
Dallas
Atlanta
COASTAL PLAIN
New Orleans
Orlando
ATLANTIC OCEAN

PACIFIC OCEAN
MEXICO
Gulf of Mexico
CUBA

HAWAII
PACIFIC OCEAN

Map Key
• City
Mountains
Hills
Plateaus
Plains

0   200   400 Miles
0   200   400 Kilometers

91

AURORA
Means Dawn

by Scott Russell Sanders
illustrated by Jill Kastner

Read this story about the first family to live in the town of Aurora, Ohio. The family arrived in the year 1800, when Aurora had a name but no people.

This is the story of Mr. and Mrs. Sheldon and their seven children. They built Aurora's first house and cleared land for its first farm. As you read, think about the problems people might face in building a community.

AURORA
Means Dawn

by Scott Russell Sanders
illustrated by Jill Kastner

When Mr. and Mrs. Sheldon reached Ohio in 1800 with seven children, two oxen, and a bulging wagon, they were greeted by a bone-rattling thunderstorm. The younger children wailed. The older children spoke of returning to Connecticut.

The oxen pretended to be four-legged boulders and would budge neither forward nor backward, for all of Mr. Sheldon's thwacking. Lightning toppled so many oaks and elms across the wagon track that even a dozen agreeable oxen would have done them no good, in any case.

They camped. More precisely, they spent the night squatting in mud beneath the wagon, trying to keep dry.

thwacking
(THWAK•ing)
hitting with
something flat

squatting
(SKWAHT•ing)
bending low with
knees bent

deluge
(DEL•yooj) pouring
rain

perish
(PAIR•ish) to die

destination
(des•tuh•NAY•shuhn)
a place to which a
person is going

surveyor
(ser•VAY•er) a
person whose work
is measuring the
land

Every few minutes, Mrs. Sheldon
would count the children, touching each
head in turn, to make sure none of the
seven had vanished in the deluge.

Mrs. Sheldon remarked to her husband
that there had never been any storms
even remotely like this one back in
Connecticut. "Nor any cheap land," he
replied. "No land's cheap if you perish
before setting eyes on it," she said. A
boom of thunder ended talk.

They fell asleep to the roar of rain.

Next morning, it was hard to tell just
where the wagon track had been, there
were so many trees down.

Husband and wife tried cutting their
way forward.

After chopping up and dragging aside
only a few felled trees, and with half the
morning gone, they decided Mr. Sheldon
should go fetch help from Aurora, their
destination.

On the land-company map they had
carried from the East, Aurora was
advertised as a village, with mill and
store and clustered cabins. But the actual
place turned out to consist of a surveyor's
post topped by a red streamer.

So Mr. Sheldon walked to the next
village shown on the map—Hudson,
which fortunately did exist, and by
morning he'd found eight men who
agreed to help him clear the road.

Their axes flashed for hours in the sunlight. It took them until late afternoon to reach the wagon.

With the track cleared, the oxen still could not move the wagon through the mud until all nine men and one woman and every child except the toddler and the baby put their shoulders to the wheels.

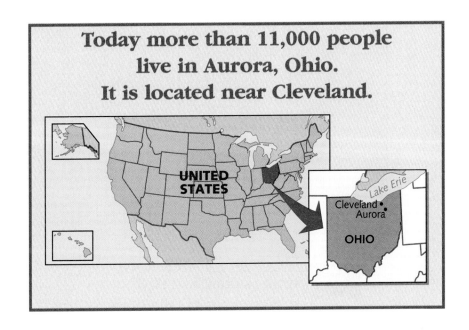

They reached Aurora at dusk, making out the surveyor's post in the lantern light. The men from Hudson insisted on returning that night to their own homes. Ax blades glinted on their shoulders as they disappeared from the circle of the campfire.

Huddled together like a basketful of kittens, the children slept in the hollow of a sycamore tree. Mr. and Mrs. Sheldon carried the lantern in circles around the sycamore, gazing at this forest that would become their farm. Aurora meant dawn; they knew that. And their family was the dawn of dawn, the first glimmering in this new place.

The next settlers did not come for three years.

Today more than 11,000 people live in Aurora, Ohio. It is located near Cleveland.

UNITED STATES

Lake Erie

Cleveland
Aurora

OHIO

FOCUS
What makes the
place where you
live different from
other places?

Main Idea Read to
find out some of
the things that
make places
different.

Vocabulary
geography
physical feature
landform
mountain range
valley
plateau
plain
peninsula
coast
climate
desert
human-made
    feature

Communities Are in Different Places

The Sheldon family knew little about Aurora. The land-company map showed a mill, a store, and some cabins. But when the family got there, they found only a post topped by a red streamer. The place called Aurora was nothing more than a clearing in a forest.

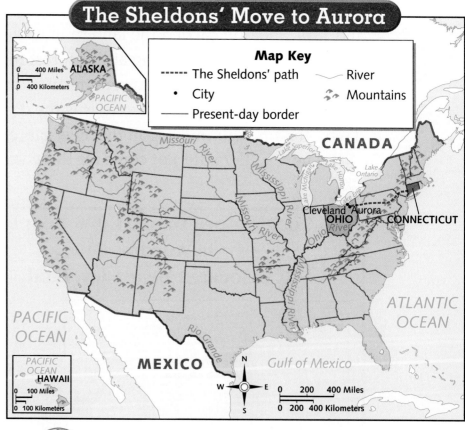

The Sheldons' Move to Aurora

Map Key
- - - - - The Sheldons' path
• City
——— Present-day border
River
Mountains

ALASKA
PACIFIC OCEAN

CANADA

Missouri River
Lake Superior
Lake Michigan
Lake Huron
Lake Ontario
Lake Erie
Mississippi River
Missouri River
Cleveland Aurora
OHIO
Ohio River
CONNECTICUT

PACIFIC OCEAN

Mississippi River

ATLANTIC OCEAN

PACIFIC OCEAN
HAWAII
0 100 Miles
0 100 Kilometers

MEXICO
Rio Grande
Gulf of Mexico

N
W   E
S

0   200   400 Miles
0 200 400 Kilometers

Movement Follow the Sheldons' path from Connecticut to Ohio.
■ What kind of land did they cross?

What Makes Places Different?

All places on the Earth have features, or things that are special about them. The study of the Earth's features is called **geography**. You can describe a place by talking about its geography.

The Sheldons first arrived in Ohio during a terrible thunderstorm. They had never seen storms like this back in Connecticut. The kind of weather a place has is one of its physical features. A **physical feature** is something found in nature, such as weather and plant life. Land and water are also physical features. People build communities in places with many different physical features.

REVIEW What are some physical features of a place?

This family is hiking through a meadow in Yosemite National Park. The park is in California.

Highlands and Lowlands

People build cities or towns on many kinds of land, or **landforms**. Some communities are in the highlands, which rise above the land around them. Some are in the lowlands, where the land is lower and often flatter.

Mountains are one kind of highland. There are many mountains in the United States. The two largest **mountain ranges**, or groups of mountains, are the Rocky Mountains and the Appalachian Mountains. **Valleys** are the lowlands between hills and mountain ranges.

The Rocky Mountains are in the western part of our country. The Appalachians are in the eastern part. These mountain ranges are different from each other. The Rocky Mountains are very high, and their tops are mostly pointed. The Appalachians are lower, and their tops are rounded. That is because the Appalachians are older. Over many, many years wind and rain have worn down their tops.

Mountain range

Valley

Pointed tops of the Rocky Mountains

Rounded tops of the Appalachians

Plateaus

Plains

Hills are highlands, too. However, hills are not as high as mountains. **Plateaus** (pla•TOHZ) are also highlands. They have steep sides like some mountains, but their tops are flat.

Plains are lowlands. They are flat or nearly flat. In the middle of our country, between the Rocky Mountains and the Appalachians, much of the land is lowland. Because this area is so large, the western part of it is called the Great Plains.

REVIEW What are some kinds of landforms?

Waterways and Bodies of Water

Many communities in the United States are built near flowing waterways or bodies of water. They may be built on peninsulas. A **peninsula** is a piece of land that has water almost all the way around it. Communities are also built on **coasts**—the land next to oceans—or on the shores of lakes, or along rivers.

Many cities and towns are built along rivers that start high in the Rocky or Appalachian mountains. These rivers flow down toward the middle of the country and into the Mississippi River. The Mississippi is the longest river in the United States. It flows into the Gulf of Mexico, a part of the Atlantic Ocean.

Other cities and towns are built along rivers that also start in the mountains but flow west or east toward the ocean coasts. These rivers flow into the Pacific Ocean on the west coast or the Atlantic Ocean on the east coast.

Peninsula

River

▲ The Yampa River winds through Dinosaur National Monument in Colorado.

Coast

◀ Waves crash against the rocky coastline of the Big Sur area in California.

Many communities in the United States are built on the ocean coasts. Others are built on the shores of the country's five largest lakes. These lakes are called the Great Lakes because of their size. They are Lakes Superior, Michigan, Huron, Erie, and Ontario. The Great Lakes lie between the United States and Canada.

REVIEW Along what kinds of waterways and bodies of water do people build communities?

Climate and Plant Life

The climate and plant life of a place are physical features, too. **Climate** is the kind of weather a place has in each season year after year. How hot or cold it gets and how much rain or snow falls are part of a place's climate.

Because of its size, the United States has many climates. They may be hot, warm, mild, cool, or cold, as well as wet or dry. People live in all these different climates.

These photographs show two places that have different climates. What is the climate like where you live?

Once you know the climate of a place, you can understand its plant life. Places with hot, dry climates, such as **deserts**, have plants that do not need much water. Some plants grow well in cool, dry climates, while others need warm, wet climates. Most trees need a lot of rain, so only places with wet climates have thick forests.

REVIEW **What is climate?**

Desert

LEARNING FROM DRAWINGS In this drawing you can compare how a peninsula and an island are the same and different.

■ Which of these landforms or bodies of water are near your community?

mountain

hill

plateau

lake

valley

river

plain

coast

island

peninsula

ocean

What People Add to a Place

When you describe a place, you might also talk about the features that people have added to it. These are its **human-made features**. The farm that the Sheldons built was one of Aurora's earliest human-made features. The post topped by a red streamer was the first!

Today Aurora is a city that has many human-made features. Its buildings, houses, bridges, and roads are features it did not have when the Sheldon family moved there. The roads now join Aurora to many other communities. Each of these communities has features that make it different from all other places.

REVIEW What is one kind of human-made feature?

Both children and adults like to visit the library in Aurora, Ohio.

LESSON 1 REVIEW

Check Understanding

1. **Remember the Facts** How is a human-made feature different from a physical feature?

2. **Recall the Main Idea** What are some things that make places different from one another?

Think Critically

3. **Think More About It** What kinds of physical features might make a place a good location for building a community?

Show What You Know

Map Activity Draw a map of the community where you live. Be sure to show at least one physical feature and one human-made feature. Label each feature, and explain the map to a family member.

Read a Land

1. Why Learn This Skill?

Have you ever visited a friend who lived in another part of the United States? Did you know anything about the geography of the place before you got there?

The Sheldon family knew very little about Aurora before they got there. The map that the land company gave them showed only a mill, a store, and some cabins.

Some maps show streets and roads to help you get where you need to go. Other maps show you other features. The landform map of the United States shows the shape of the land. It tells where the mountains, hills, plateaus, and plains are located.

2. Understand the Process

Follow the steps to read the map. It will help you understand the landforms of the United States.

1 Find the purple box in the map key. The key tells you that mountains are shown with the color purple on the map. Where are the Appalachian Mountains?

2 Look at the map key again. What things are shown with the colors brown, yellow, and green? The key tells you what each color stands for on the map. Brown stands for plateaus. Yellow stands for hills. Green stands for plains.

3 Which city is on higher ground, Salt Lake City or Sacramento?

4 Which cities are on the plains?

5 On what kind of land is Atlanta?

3. Think and Apply

Look at the landforms shown on a map from your state and another state. Then write two paragraphs. In your first paragraph, describe the landforms of your state. In your second paragraph, compare your state's landforms to the state you picked.

form Map

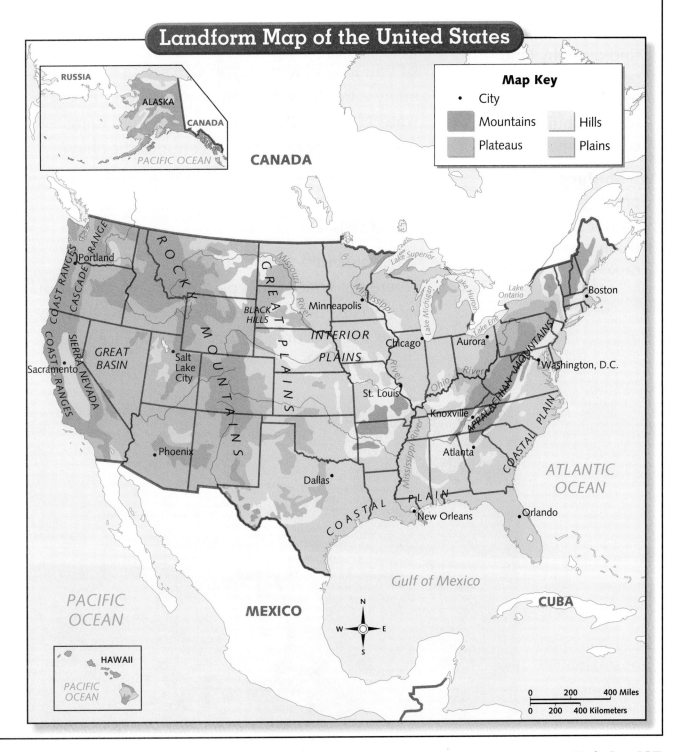

Landform Map of the United States

Map Key
- City
- Mountains
- Plateaus
- Hills
- Plains

RUSSIA
ALASKA
CANADA
PACIFIC OCEAN

CANADA

COAST RANGES
CASCADE RANGE
Portland
ROCKY MOUNTAINS
GREAT PLAINS
Missouri River
BLACK HILLS
Minneapolis
Mississippi
Lake Superior
Lake Michigan
Lake Huron
Lake Ontario
Lake Erie
Boston

SIERRA NEVADA
COAST RANGES
Sacramento
GREAT BASIN
Salt Lake City
INTERIOR PLAINS
Chicago
Aurora
APPALACHIAN MOUNTAINS
Washington, D.C.

Phoenix
Mississippi River
St. Louis
Ohio River
Knoxville
COASTAL PLAIN

Dallas
Atlanta
ATLANTIC OCEAN

COASTAL PLAIN
New Orleans
Orlando

PACIFIC OCEAN
MEXICO
Gulf of Mexico
CUBA

N
W E
S

HAWAII
PACIFIC OCEAN

0   200   400 Miles
0   200   400 Kilometers

FOCUS
Why are many cities and towns built near water?

Main Idea Read to find out why land next to water is often a good place to build a community.

Vocabulary
port
harbor
trade center
rapids

Communities Are Built Near Water

If you look at a map, you will see that many cities have been built where land meets water. People often start communities along waterways. Some of these communities have grown from small towns into large cities.

Bodies of Water

People build cities and towns along coasts where the water is deep, often where rivers run into oceans or lakes. A community next to deep water may become a great **port**, a place where ships can dock.

Many ships dock at the harbor of Petersburg, Alaska.

All port cities have harbors. A **harbor** is a place where ships can stay safe from high waves and strong winds. Nature makes some harbors. People make others.

Roads cross the land and come together at ports. Roads help people and goods get to the ships that can take them to places far away.

Long ago, goods were bought and sold at ports where ships docked. Wood that came into a port was made into furniture there, and then the furniture was shipped out. Iron that came in was made into steel, and then the steel was shipped out.

Many large cities grew from ocean ports. Port cities and harbors are all along the coasts of our country. They are on the west coast next to the Pacific Ocean. They are also on the east coast next to the Atlantic Ocean. Port cities are also located along the shores of the Great Lakes.

REVIEW Why is land next to a body of water a good place to build a community?

Waterways

People have built many cities and towns along waterways, too. Flowing water makes it easy to move heavy loads. It takes many railroad cars and a lot of fuel to move a huge load of coal over land.

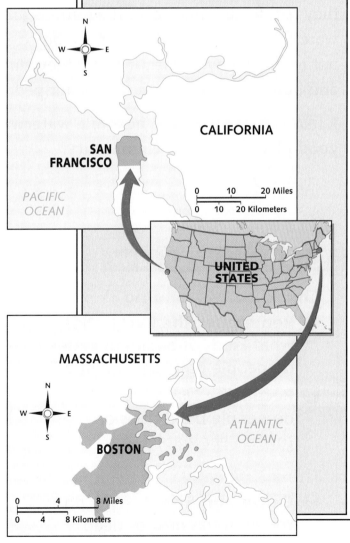

GEOGRAPHY

Boston and San Francisco

San Francisco and Boston are port cities on peninsulas. Boston's harbor on the Atlantic coast makes the city a busy seaport. In 1849 San Francisco became a supply center for gold miners. Today both Boston and San Francisco are large and important cities.

CALIFORNIA

SAN FRANCISCO

PACIFIC OCEAN

0   10   20 Miles
0   10   20 Kilometers

UNITED STATES

MASSACHUSETTS

BOSTON

ATLANTIC OCEAN

0   4   8 Miles
0   4   8 Kilometers

The same amount of coal can be moved over water on one ship using less fuel.

Many settlements that were built along deep waterways became trade centers. **Trade centers** are communities where buying and selling goods is the main work.

Places next to waterfalls and rapids are also good for building cities and towns. **Rapids** are the parts of rivers where the water runs very fast, often over rocks. Long ago, people used the tumbling water to turn waterwheels. The waterwheels turned millstones to make flour. They also ran machines in factories.

When people traveled by boat along rivers, they had to stop and carry their goods around waterfalls and rapids. Sometimes they decided not to travel any farther. Instead, they stayed and built towns where they had stopped.

REVIEW Why is land next to a waterway a good place to build a community?

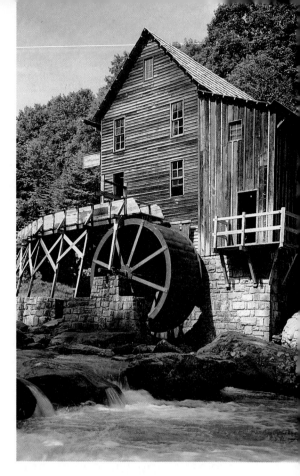
Waterwheel at Mabry Mill on the Blue Ridge Parkway, Virginia

LESSON 2 REVIEW

Check Understanding

1. **Remember the Facts** Near what kinds of bodies of water do people build communities?

2. **Recall the Main Idea** Why do people build cities or towns near water?

Think Critically

3. **Cause and Effect** Why do communities next to deep water often grow into large port cities or trade centers?

Show What You Know

Creative Writing Activity Write a four-line poem about a city or town in your state that is built near water. The lines do not have to rhyme. Read your poem to other class members.

Read a Table

1. Why Learn This Skill?

Lists of facts are often shown in a table. A **table** is a way to organize information. Knowing how to use a table will help you compare information and numbers more easily.

2. Understand the Process

You have read that San Francisco and Boston grew from ocean ports into large cities. Suppose you want to compare the populations of several port cities. **Population** is the number of people who live in a place. You could use a table like the one shown here.

This table has two columns and six rows. Columns go up and down, and rows go across. To find the population of a city, find its name in the first column. Then read the number that appears in the same row as the city's name. What is the population of Detroit?

3. Think and Apply

Use the table below to help you answer these questions.

1 Which city has the largest population?

2 Compare the populations of San Francisco and Seattle. How can you find out how many more people live in San Francisco than in Seattle?

3 What tables do you use when you are not in school? Work in a small group to list three kinds of tables you have used. Share your list with the other groups.

Populations of Cities

CITY	POPULATION
Anchorage, Alaska	248,296
Boston, Massachusetts	547,725
Detroit, Michigan	992,038
New Orleans, Louisiana	484,149
San Francisco, California	734,676
Seattle, Washington	520,947

FOCUS
Where do people meet in your town?

Main Idea Read to find out why cities and towns are built at the places where people meet.

Vocabulary
route
crossroads
ferry
ford

Communities Are Built Where People Meet

People start communities for different reasons. Sometimes communities grow at places where people meet each other or where roads cross.

Routes and Crossroads

A **route** is a path from one place to another. A route can be a river, a road, a railroad, or even a hiking trail.

These drawings show how a community can change and grow over the years.

TODAY

LEARNING FROM DRAWINGS Compare this drawing
with the others. Many changes have taken place at this
crossroads, but some things have stayed the same.

■ What are the things that have not changed in the
drawings?

Some cities and towns started at a **crossroads**, a
place where two routes cross. Perhaps a trader built
a store there to sell supplies to travelers. Then a
restaurant and hotel were built to feed the travelers
and give them a place to rest. Before long, people
settled at the crossroads instead of going on. Those
who stayed built houses, churches, and schools.
Soon they had a town. Some of these towns grew
into cities.

REVIEW What is the place called where two
routes meet?

Crossing Points

When a land route meets a river, travelers need a way to cross the river. They may use a bridge, a ferry, or a ford. A bridge is a road built over a waterway. A **ferry** is a boat that carries people and goods across a waterway. A **ford** is a shallow place in a waterway that can be crossed by walking, riding, or driving.

Places on both sides of a bridge, a ferry, or a ford are good for building cities or towns. Many famous cities began as crossing points at rivers.

Do you know this song?

A ferry crossing Elliot Bay in Seattle, Washington

> London Bridge is falling down,
> Falling down, falling down,
> London Bridge is falling down,
> My fair lady!

The song is about the bridge that was in the city of London, England, for hundreds of years. London Bridge crossed the Thames (TEMZ) River at a place where the water is deep. Ships from the sea sailed up the river to the bridge. Wagons from farms and mills used the bridge to cross the river.

HISTORY

London Bridge

London Bridge helped the city of London grow. The last time it was rebuilt, business people in the United States bought the old bridge. They moved it to Lake Havasu City, Arizona! Many tourists go to see it there, thousands of miles from London.

This black-and-white drawing shows London Bridge in the 1660s. You can see that homes and shops were built right on the bridge. This bridge has been rebuilt many times.

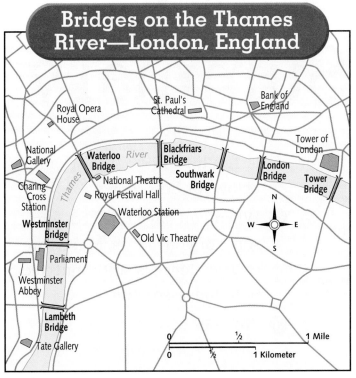

Bridges on the Thames River—London, England

Human-Environment Interactions
■ Why do you think there are now many bridges that cross the Thames River?

Farmers long ago went to London Bridge with grains, wool, butter, and pigs to trade for cloth or leather goods carried there by ships. Sometimes the farmers needed to see a doctor, so doctors went to live near London Bridge. Soon many people settled close to the bridge, and a city grew up there. Today more than 9 million people live in and around London.

REVIEW Why is a crossing point a good place to build a city?

LESSON 3 REVIEW

Check Understanding

1 Remember the Facts What are some ways travelers can cross rivers?

2 Recall the Main Idea Why are cities and towns built at places where people meet?

Think Critically

3 Personally Speaking What might be good and bad about living near a crossing point? Would you want to live there?

Show What You Know

Research and Writing Activity Choose one bridge in or near your community and find out more about it. You may need to use books or talk to people to get your information. Write a three-paragraph report about the bridge. In your paragraphs, tell when and why the bridge was built. Share your report with your classmates.

Write a Summary

1. Why Learn This Skill?

A summary gives the main ideas of a story in fewer words. When you write a summary, you give only the main ideas and leave out the details.

2. Understand the Process

1 Choose a lesson from this unit, and write down the lesson title. Then, for each paragraph of the lesson, write one sentence telling the main idea. Each main idea should be connected with the lesson title. Look at the example below for Lesson 3.

2 When you have finished, join some of your ideas. Make sure each sentence is still connected with the lesson title.

3 Put your ideas together and write a paragraph. Give your paragraph a title. You have just written a summary paragraph!

3. Think and Apply

Read a magazine article or a story. Then write a summary paragraph. Read your summary to a classmate.

Remember What You Have Read
COMMUNITIES ARE BUILT WHERE PEOPLE MEET
People start communities where roads cross.
A route is a path from one place to another.
People settle and start towns where routes meet.
When a route meets a river, people must find a way to cross the river.
Places on both sides of a river are good locations to build towns.
People built the London Bridge to cross the Thames River.
Many people settled near London Bridge and a city grew up there.

Why Did People Build Cahokia and St. Louis?

FOCUS
What features of a place might make people want to build a community there?

Main Idea Read to find out why two groups of people chose to build their communities near the same place.

Vocabulary
riverbank
branch
gateway
manufacture

Sometimes people living at different times have built communities near the same places. This happened along the Mississippi River with Cahokia and St. Louis, Missouri.

Cahokia Long Ago

Nearly 1,500 years ago Native Americans built a city that today we call Cahokia (kuh•HOH•kee•uh). They built Cahokia at the place where the Missouri River flows into the Mississippi River, in the middle of what is now the United States. This settlement was built before people came from Europe.

Long ago, as this painting shows, Native Americans lived and worked in their community of Cahokia.

Lesson 4 • 117

An artist in Cahokia made this bottle in the shape of a mother and her child.

Cahokia was built on the **riverbank**, the land beside the river. The rich soil along the riverbank was good for growing corn, beans, and squash.

The Mississippi River and its branches were very important to the people of Cahokia. A **branch** is a smaller river that flows into a larger one. The people traveled on these rivers in boats, moving themselves, their crops, and other goods. Along the way they met other Indian people and traded goods and ideas with them.

Cahokia soon became a trade center, where people bought and sold many goods. In its markets people could buy food, tools, and jewelry. With all this trade Cahokia grew and grew. Soon it became a city where about 40,000 people lived.

The Mississippi River and Its Branches

Location ■ What rivers are west of the Mississippi River?

Then something happened to Cahokia. No one is sure just what happened or when it happened. Whatever it was, the Cahokians left their city and did not return.

REVIEW Why were the branches of the Mississippi River important?

St. Louis Long Ago

Other people came to live along the river near where Cahokia once stood. Both the Iowa and Osage (oh•SAYJ) Indians built settlements. Their settlements were much smaller than Cahokia.

To get what they could not grow or make, the Iowa and Osage Indians traded with other people. They traveled the waterways just as the Cahokians had done, trading food and furs for other items. At first the Iowa and Osage people traded with other Indians. Later they also traded with people who had come from Europe.

In 1764 a European boy named René Auguste Chouteau (ruh•NAY ah•GUST shoo•TOH) arrived at this place. He was 14 years old. He and his stepfather built a small trading post on the riverbank, across the Mississippi River from where Cahokia had once stood.

René Auguste Chouteau lived most of his life near the trading post he and his stepfather built.

Floods

Some people think that a huge flood destroyed the city of Cahokia hundreds of years ago. Today floods are still a problem for people who live in the area.

BEFORE

AFTER

These photographs show the Mississippi River area before and after a flood.

Indians and Europeans from up and down the river came to Chouteau's trading post to trade goods with one another. They traded all kinds of items. There were pots, pans, metal tools, blankets, food, and other supplies.

With all this trading, more people came to live and work near Chouteau's trading post. They formed a community, and the settlement grew and grew. People named the settlement St. Louis to honor a past king of France. As Cahokia had done earlier, St. Louis grew to be a great city at the place where the Missouri River flows into the Mississippi.

REVIEW **Why was the location of Chouteau's trading post a good one?**

Why St. Louis Grew

Over the years, things changed in St. Louis. Hotels were built. Churches, stores, banks, and houses were also built for the people living and working there.

In the 1800s thousands of people came to St. Louis on their way to settle in Oregon or California. They stopped in St. Louis to buy wagons and supplies. The city became a **gateway**, or entrance, to the West.

Sallie Hester, a young girl traveling by wagon train to California, kept a journal. In it she wrote that her family's wagon carried "a cooking stove made of sheet iron, a portable table, tin plates and cups, cheap knives and forks." A covered wagon was a home on wheels to pioneers.

▲ A clock that would sit on a fireplace mantel.

▲ A cup, plates, and silverware that were used to eat meals.

A family of settlers stops on the trail to rest. Below are some of the things that a family might take on the long trip.

◀ A spider, or three-legged skillet, was used to cook meals over the fire.

Camp Needs		
1	tent	$15.00
1	10-gallon water tub	$ 1.25
2	water buckets	$ .50
1	small tin pail	$ 1.00
1	75-foot rope	$ 2.50
2	axes	$ 2.50
1	10 pounds nails	$ .75
1	misc. hand tools	$ 2.50
1	whetstone	$ .10
	TOTAL	$26.10

▲ A list of items needed for the trip.

▲ An oxhide-covered trunk held many of the family's belongings.

Soon people arrived to build factories and **manufacture**, or make, all kinds of goods. They manufactured shoes, cereal, and farm supplies. They shipped these goods on steamboats to other cities along the Mississippi River and its branches. St. Louis became a trade center and a manufacturing center, and it grew bigger.

As time passed, bridges were built across the Mississippi River. Trains and trucks from St. Louis could now reach new towns over land. More factories and bridges were built, and St. Louis grew even more. Later, airports were added. Airplanes could reach cities all over the world. And the city kept growing!

Better land and air routes let people live and work away from the river. Many of the buildings along the riverfront became empty and started to fall apart. The leaders of St. Louis decided to make some changes.

HISTORY

First Steel Arch Bridge to Cross the Mississippi River

The Eads Bridge at St. Louis, Missouri, was the bridge people said could not be built. They thought the river was too deep and too strong. Bridge builder James Buchanan Eads did not agree. In 1867 he and his workers started building the bridge. At last the bridge was opened on July 4, 1874. People from many countries came to see the bridge and to ask Eads to build bridges for them.

The Gateway Arch welcomes people to the city of St. Louis.

One person had the idea of making a park. Another person wanted to build a museum. Neither idea seemed just right. Then someone said that something should be built that would stand for St. Louis. A young artist from Michigan sent in a drawing of a tall, slim arch made of stainless steel. The idea seemed perfect!

Today the Gateway Arch is a symbol of St. Louis's past. The arch stands over the place where young Chouteau and his stepfather built their trading post long ago. The Gateway Arch is also a symbol for today. People still think of St. Louis as a gateway to the West for business and trade.

Eero Saarinen
1910–1961

Eero Saarinen (AIR•oh SAR•uh•nuhn), the designer of the Gateway Arch, came to the United States from Finland when he was 13 years old. He had already won a prize for designing a building. He won many more when he became an architect, or building designer. Visitors to St. Louis enjoy the great arch he designed as a symbol of the city. But Saarinen himself never saw it. He died before the Gateway Arch was built.

Flowing past the Gateway Arch is the Mississippi River. The mighty river is as important to St. Louis today as it ever was. Many people live along its banks, farm on land near it, and use it to move themselves and their goods, just as people did long, long ago.

REVIEW What does the Gateway Arch stand for?

LESSON 4 REVIEW

Check Understanding

1 Remember the Facts What waterways were important for people in both Cahokia and St. Louis?

2 Recall the Main Idea Why might people who lived at different times choose to build their communities near the same place?

Think Critically

3 Explore Viewpoints When cities grow, there will be new jobs for people. However, the land may become crowded or dirty. Choose two people who might have different feelings about the growth of your community. Tell what each might say.

Show What You Know

Art Activity Choose a symbol in your community or your state that stands for something from the past. Make a model of it, and display it for the class. Explain what it stands for.

Find Intermediate Directions on a Map

1. Why Learn This Skill?

You use directions when you want to tell someone where you have been or where you are going. North, south, east, and west are the cardinal directions. They are the most important. There are also four "in-between" directions. Northeast, southeast, southwest, and northwest are **intermediate directions**. Each one is between two of the cardinal directions.

2. Understand the Process

Find St. Louis on the map. It is the center point of a large compass rose. Put your finger on St. Louis, and trace the compass rose line toward North. Now slowly move your finger toward East. The part of the country between North and East on this map is the land northeast of St. Louis. Keep moving your finger toward South to find the land that is southeast of St. Louis. Move your finger toward West to find the land

southwest of St. Louis. Move it toward North again to find the land northwest of St. Louis.

3. Think and Apply

Use the map to help you answer these questions.

1 From St. Louis, in which direction is Orlando?

2 If you went from Los Angeles to New York, in which direction would you go?

3 If you traveled northwest from St. Louis, what city would you reach?

The United States and Intermediate Directions

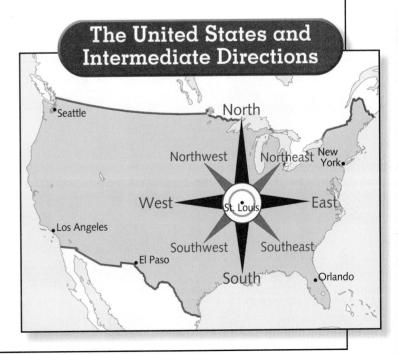

FOCUS
Why do you think cities and towns are built near resources?

Main Idea Read to find out why people build communities in places near fuels, mineral supplies, and water.

Vocabulary
crop
natural resource
growing season
mineral
fuel
ghost town

Communities Are Built Near Resources

The first settlers leaving St. Louis headed west across the Great Plains, where the tall grasses rippled like ocean waves. While most people kept moving across the vast plains, a few settled along the way.

On the Land

The people who settled on the Great Plains began to farm the land. Some farmers raised chickens, hogs, and cows. Others grew **crops**, or plants used by people for food or other needs.

Although these farms were different from one another, they all needed the same natural resources. A **natural resource** is something found in nature that people can use. Trees, water, animals, and soil are examples of natural resources.

A farmer holds peanuts that were grown in a field like this one near Atlanta, Georgia.

Much of the corn grown in Nebraska is used to feed cattle.

Farmers sell their goods in Omaha and shop in the city's stores.

Crops will not grow if the weather is too cold for them. That is why farmers in places with cold climates plant in the spring, when the cold winter weather is over.

The months in which crops can grow are called the **growing season**. Growing seasons depend on the climate of a place. In places with long, cold winters, the growing season is short. In places with short, warm winters, the growing season is long.

In places where there were plenty of resources nearby for farming, cities and towns grew up. Omaha, Nebraska, is a city on the plains. The rich soil is good for farming, and around Omaha, corn grows well.

REVIEW What are some natural resources important to farmers?

Inside the Earth

Oil wells near the busy port city of Long Beach, California

Some communities grew up in places where natural resources were found deep in the Earth. Towns started quickly in places where minerals and fuels were found. A **mineral**, such as silver, gold, or iron, is a resource found inside the Earth. Minerals can be used to make metal tools, glass, or jewelry. Some kinds of **fuels**, such as coal and oil, are also found inside the Earth. Fuels can be burned for heat and for power to make machines work.

People dug mines and drilled oil wells to get the resources from the Earth. They found that they could earn a lot of money from selling minerals and fuels. They built communities near these resources, even in places with physical features that made their lives hard. They also built in places with very cold or very hot climates if resources they wanted could be found there.

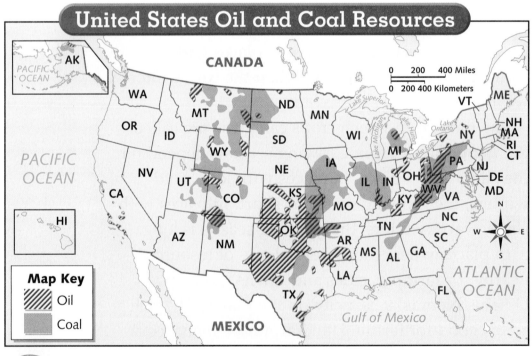

United States Oil and Coal Resources

Map Key
- Oil
- Coal

Human-Environment Interactions ■ What states on this map have only coal resources?

A lot of people must work to get minerals and fuels out of the ground. Then more people must work to get these materials ready to be sold and used. People are needed to sell clothes and food to the workers and to provide them with other things they may need. With all these people moving in, many towns near places with underground resources grew fast.

Some towns grew into cities. Others did not grow at all. When the minerals and fuels ran out in these places, the people left. These towns became **ghost towns**, with buildings but no people. Today some ghost towns have come back to life—at least a little. People like to visit the old buildings to find out what life was like for the people who lived there.

Today people visit Kennecott, Alaska, an old mining town, to look at the empty buildings and old mining tools.

REVIEW **Why do people build communities in locations that make life difficult?**

LESSON 5 REVIEW

Check Understanding

❶ **Remember the Facts** Why have some people chosen to live in places that have very hot or very cold climates?

❷ **Recall the Main Idea** Why do people build communities near natural resources?

Think Critically

❸ **Cause and Effect** Explain some of the things that can happen to a farm, a factory, or a town when resources run out.

Show What You Know

Travel Brochure Activity Make a travel brochure that would make people want to visit your community. Be sure to tell about resources and climate. Add pictures of features people would like about your community. Display your brochure.

Use a Product Map

1. Why Learn This Skill?

Sometimes it is easier to learn something if you can picture it. By learning to interpret, or explain, symbols on a map, you can understand information more easily.

2. Understand the Process

Many people in California make their living in agriculture. **Agriculture** is the raising of crops and farm animals. The map shows the location of the most important crops and farm animals raised in California. Each symbol stands for a different product raised on California farms. These symbols are explained in the map key.

3. Think and Apply

❶ Look on the map to find where cotton is grown. Does the northern or southern area of California raise more cotton?

❷ Find the symbol for nuts. Near what cities are nuts grown?

❸ What symbols stand for things that are not planted? Are these products found mostly near the northeastern or the southeastern border of California?

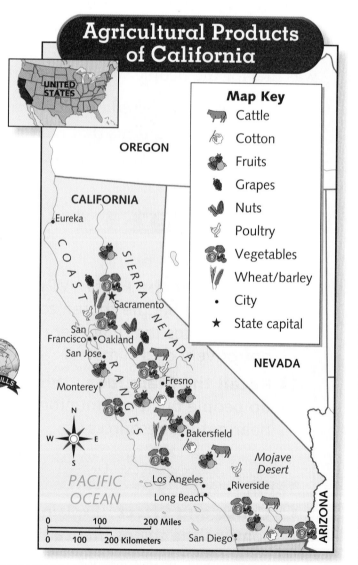

Agricultural Products of California

Map Key
- Cattle
- Cotton
- Fruits
- Grapes
- Nuts
- Poultry
- Vegetables
- Wheat/barley
- • City
- ★ State capital

Communities Are Built for Government

FOCUS
Why would location be important in choosing where to build a capital city?

Main Idea Read to find out why location was important in building Washington, D.C., and other places of government.

Vocabulary
capital city
capitol
state capital
county
county seat

The early leaders of the United States decided it was time to build a new city where the country's laws would be made. The people of Virginia and Maryland gave the country some land along the Potomac River on which to build the new city.

The Story of Washington, D.C.

George Washington rode out on his horse to look at the land along the Potomac River. The new nation was going to build a **capital city** where the leaders of the country could meet and work. President Washington wanted to find a good place to build this city.

Each day from the middle to the end of October 1791, he rode along the riverbank. It was hard to choose just the right place to build the nation's capital.

A painting of George Washington, the first President of the United States, by John Trumbull

The United States Capitol building as it looked in 1800

The Capitol building as it looks today

George Washington talked with Thomas Jefferson and other leaders about the problem. At last a good place was chosen.

George Washington chose an area of low wetlands and woods for the new capital. But he did not choose the place so much for its physical features as for its good location. It was halfway between the states of Vermont and Georgia. In 1791 this was right in the middle of the United States.

Building the capital city in the place that was chosen had its good points and bad points. A good point was that lawmakers from all over the country could easily get to the capital. A bad point was that the place was a swamp! The first lawmakers would not stay there in the summer because of the heat and the mosquitoes. The physical features of the place were not perfect for the capital, but the location was.

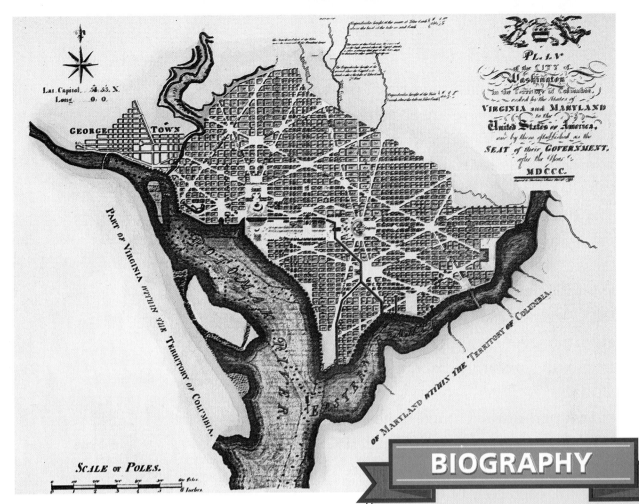

From this drawing by Pierre L'Enfant, the city of Washington, D.C., began to take shape.

Two former clock makers, Andrew Ellicott and Benjamin Banneker, measured the land. An engineer, Pierre L'Enfant (pee•AIR lahn•FAHN), used their measurements to plan the city's streets and buildings. The first thing built was the **capitol**, the building where lawmakers meet. Today, the capital city of every state has a capitol building.

REVIEW **Why was the capital city built in the middle of the country?**

BIOGRAPHY

Benjamin Banneker
1731–1806

This picture of Benjamin Banneker was drawn when he was a young man. Thomas Jefferson knew that Banneker had many skills. So Jefferson told George Washington that Banneker would be a good person to help mark where the streets of Washington, D.C. would go.

State Capitals and County Seats

The United States has one capital city for the whole country. But there are 50 state capitals, one for each of the 50 states in our country. A **state capital** is a city where lawmakers meet to make laws for a state.

A city does not have to be the biggest in the state to be the state capital. In fact, none of the five largest cities in the United States is a state capital. Los Angeles is not the capital of California, even though it is the largest city in California. Sacramento is the capital.

Just as a part of the United States is called a state, a part of a state is called a **county**. And just as each state has a state capital, each county has a county seat. A **county seat** is a city or town where county leaders meet.

Like every other state capital, Sacramento, California, has its own capitol building.

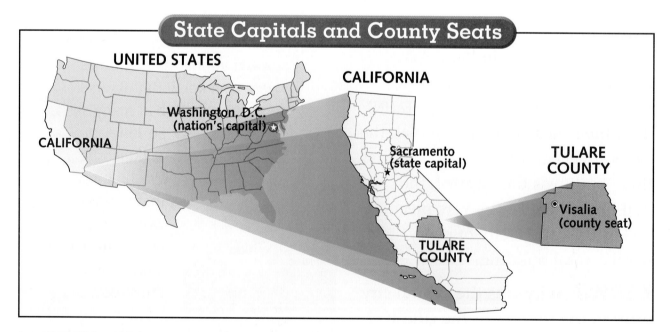

State Capitals and County Seats

UNITED STATES

CALIFORNIA

Washington, D.C. (nation's capital)

CALIFORNIA

Sacramento (state capital)

TULARE COUNTY

Visalia (county seat)

TULARE COUNTY

LEARNING FROM DIAGRAMS In what part of Tulare County is the county seat located?

Many cities were chosen to be state capitals or county seats for the same reason Washington, D.C., was built where it is. Being in the middle of a state or a county makes the city or town easier for lawmakers and others to get to.

REVIEW Why were many cities chosen to be capitals or county seats?

Capitol building in Juneau, Alaska

LESSON 6 REVIEW

Check Understanding

❶ **Remember the Facts** Where do people meet to make laws for a country or for a state?

❷ **Recall the Main Idea** Why is location important for places of government?

Think Critically

❸ **Personally Speaking** Do you think the nation's capital should be moved to what is today the middle of the United States? Why or why not?

Show What You Know

Collage Activity Use pictures from magazines and newspapers to make a collage about your state or county. Be sure to show something about the state capital or county seat. Display your collage on a class bulletin board.

Find State Capitals

1. Why Learn This Skill?

Look at the map of the United States on page 137. It shows the states and the state capitals.

You can use this map to find the location and shape of your state. You can also use it to find the location of your state's capital.

2. Understand the Process

The symbol of a star tells you that a city is a state capital. Find the state capital symbol in the map key. Then look for the capital of the state of California.

The symbol of a star in a circle shows the nation's capital. Find this symbol in the map key. Now find Washington, D.C., on the map.

This map also shows national and state borders. **Borders** are the lines on a map that show where one country or one state ends and another begins.

Borders are also called **boundaries**. The states that are just north of the Georgia border are Tennessee, North Carolina, and South Carolina. Which state is on the eastern border of Georgia?

3. Think and Apply

Use the map key to help you answer these questions.

1 What is your state capital?

2 What neighbors are to the north, south, east, and west of your state? What are the capitals of those states?

and Borders

States and Their Capitals

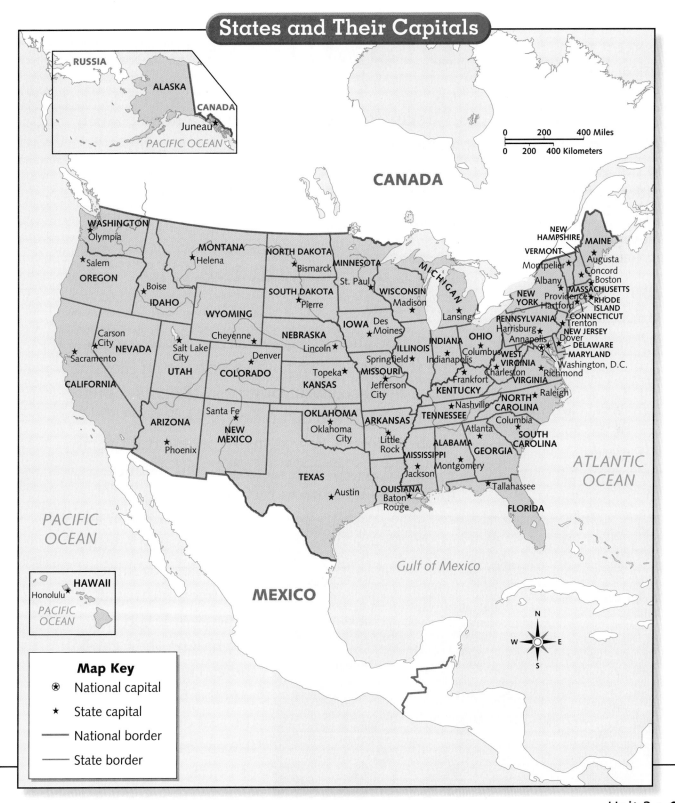

Communities Move— Brasília, Brazil

The city of Brasília sits high on a huge plateau in the middle of Brazil. Thick forest grows all around it. People said that a city could not be built in this location. It was built, but the job was not easy.

A Problem with the Old Capital

Brazil is the largest country in South America and the fifth-largest in the world. From the time Brazil had become a country in 1822, its capital city had been Rio de Janeiro (REE•oh DAY zhuh•NAIR•oh). Rio, as many people call the city, is known for its sandy beaches and its high mountains that run to the coast.

Rio was chosen as Brazil's capital because it was close to mineral resources. However, some people did not like having their capital there. They thought it was too far away from the rest of the country. It was "off in a corner of Brazil," they said.

Rio de Janeiro is located on a bay of the Atlantic Ocean. Sugarloaf Mountain, shown below, is a famous landmark.

138

Leaders in Brazil thought of the same things leaders in the United States did when they decided where to build Washington, D.C. The new capital of Brazil also needed to be close to the center of the country. But government leaders in Brazil had another reason for moving the capital. There were few people living inland, away from the coast. They wanted more people to move there.

REVIEW Why did Brazil's leaders want to move the capital city?

A City Called Brasília

Brazil covers almost half the continent of South America. A huge **rain forest**, or thick forest with a wet climate, covers much of the land. The Amazon River flows through this rain forest. The Amazon is Brazil's longest river and the second-longest in the world. Only the Nile River in Africa is longer.

Place Find Brasília and Washington, D.C., on the map.

■ What things are the same about these two capitals? What things are different?

The United States and Brazil

UNITED STATES

Washington, D.C.

NORTH AMERICA

PACIFIC OCEAN

Gulf of Mexico

ATLANTIC OCEAN

N
W   E
S

0   1,000   2,000 Miles
0   1,000   2,000 Kilometers

Map Key
⊛ National capital
— National border
⁀ River
🌴 Brazil's rain forest
🌲 United States' rain forest

Amazon River

SOUTH AMERICA

BRAZIL

Brasília

Rio de Janeiro

The place the government leaders chose to build the new capital was on a plateau rising from the rain forest. They chose this place for its location, not for its physical features. There were no roads. And because it was so hard to travel through the rain forest, everything that was needed to build the new city had to be taken there by airplane.

Like Washington, D.C., Brasília was carefully planned. A city planner named Lúcio Costa designed every detail of the city—every street and even every park bench. Costa laid out the city in the shape of an airplane. The "body" is 4 miles (about 6 km) long. The "wings" stretch 12 miles (about 19 km) across. Costa put houses and businesses along the wings and government buildings along the body. He put the most important buildings, where the government leaders meet, at the "nose" of the airplane.

Twenty-six people sent in ideas for Brasília's city plan. Lúcio Costa's plan was the one chosen.

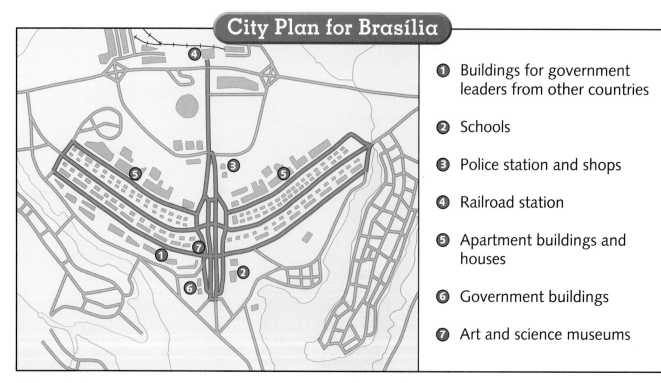

City Plan for Brasília

① Buildings for government leaders from other countries

② Schools

③ Police station and shops

④ Railroad station

⑤ Apartment buildings and houses

⑥ Government buildings

⑦ Art and science museums

LEARNING FROM DIAGRAMS What is located at the "tail" of this city plan?

Brasília has been called a city of the future. Some of its buildings look as if they could be from a future time.

It took less than 10 years to build Brazil's new capital city. In 1960 the government began meeting there instead of in Rio de Janeiro. Today more than two million people live in Brasília.

REVIEW Why did people think Brasília could not be built?

These photographs show the outside and the inside of the Metropolitan Cathedral in Brasília. This church is made of glass and concrete. It is one of many places in Brasília the famous builder Oscar Niemeyer built.

LESSON 7 REVIEW

Check Understanding

1. **Remember the Facts** Why did the people of Brazil want to move the capital city?

2. **Recall the Main Idea** Why was the location of Brasília more important than the place's physical features?

Think Critically

3. **Past to Present** How was building Brasília like building Washington, D.C.? How was it different?

Show What You Know

Poster Activity Make a poster that shows a plan for a city you would like to build. First, decide where you will build the city. What physical features or bodies of water will it be near? Why? Next, draw your city plan and label the important places on it. Share your poster with your classmates. Explain why you chose to build your city where you did.

FOCUS
Why would location be important for a state capital?

Main Idea Read to find out why location was important in deciding to build Columbia.

Vocabulary
junction

South Carolina's Capital Cities

Columbia is South Carolina's state capital and largest city. There was a time, however, when Columbia was not the largest city in the state. There was a time, too, when it was not the state's capital.

Charleston

Charleston, South Carolina's first capital city, is one of our country's oldest cities. Settlers built it in 1670 and named it Charles Town for King Charles II of England. The city's people later changed the name to Charleston.

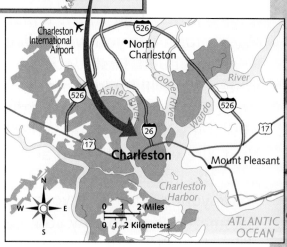

Charleston is located close to the midpoint of the South Carolina coast. It is on a peninsula formed by the Ashley and Cooper rivers. The English settlers found that living near the ocean made trade and travel easier. Charleston Harbor made it easy for ships to get to the Atlantic Ocean. Because of this, the settlers could send wood and crops such as rice to England. Charleston became an important port city.

From 1670 to the middle of the 1700s, Charleston was the center of life in South Carolina. It was South Carolina's capital and largest city. Back then most of the people in South Carolina lived in Charleston or in the Low Country around it.

This drawing shows South Carolina's first State House, or capitol building.

REVIEW **Where is Charleston located?**

This painting shows Charleston Harbor as it looked around 1740.

Columbia

At the time when Charleston was South Carolina's most important city, Congaree (KAHNG•guh•ree) Indians were living where Columbia is now. They lived there until the 1700s, when many English settlers began moving into the middle of South Carolina. These newcomers built farms in the Up Country on what had been the Congarees' lands. By the late 1700s, more people lived there than in the Low Country. State leaders decided it would be best to move the capital.

In 1786, they chose a place for the new capital on the Congaree River, near the junction of the Broad and Saluda rivers. A **junction** (JUNK•shun) is a place where rivers or roads meet. Having the capital at the junction of these two rivers made it easier for people from different parts of the state to travel there.

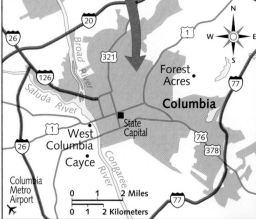

▼ This bridge crosses the junction of the Broad and Saluda rivers. The city skyline of Columbia is in the background.

The State House today

State leaders called the new capital *Columbia,* a name that some people also used for the United States. The state government first met in Columbia in 1790.

REVIEW Why was the capital of South Carolina moved from Charleston to Columbia?

HISTORY

Hail Columbia!

Columbia is a name people in the past sometimes called the United States. They thought that the country should have been named after the explorer Christopher Columbus. That is why, today, many towns and counties have that name.

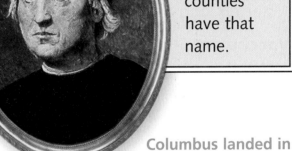

Columbus landed in the Americas in 1492.

LESSON 8 REVIEW

Check Understanding

1 Remember the Facts What two cities have been the capital of South Carolina?

2 Recall the Main Idea How was location important in deciding to build Columbia?

Think Critically

3 Think More About It Why do you think people in the Up Country wanted the state capital moved from Charleston to Columbia?

Show What You Know

Map Activity Imagine a state of your own, and draw a landform map of it. Show rivers and lakes on your map. Decide where you think the capital city should be, and put a star there. Explain why you chose this location.

FOCUS
Why was your community in South Carolina started where it is?

Main Idea Learn where and why some of South Carolina's communities were started long ago.

Vocabulary
sound
bay
frontier
fall line

More Communities in Our State

You have just read about South Carolina's capital cities. You learned when and why state leaders moved the capital from Charleston to Columbia. Every community in South Carolina has a story to tell about where and why it was started. Here are a few.

Starting on the Coast

South Carolina's earliest permanent, or long-lasting, towns were started along the coast of the Atlantic Ocean. Each was built on a natural harbor by English settlers.

Charleston was the first. As you already learned, it was built in 1670 on Charleston Harbor. By 1710, Charleston was home to hundreds of people. Its port was always busy. Today, the Port of Charleston is still a busy place. Each week tons of goods are loaded on and off ships there. Charleston is one of the busiest ports on the entire Atlantic Ocean.

In 1710 the English founded a second town on Port Royal Sound. A **sound** is a long passage of water separating a mainland and an island.

The busy Port of Charleston, South Carolina

The settlers named the town Beaufort (BYOO•furt) for the Duke of Beaufort, a leader of the Carolina colony. Beaufort's location on a natural harbor also made it an important trade city. Today, instead of trade ships, fishing ships and pleasure boats keep Beaufort's port busy.

South Carolina's third town, Georgetown, was started in 1730 on Winyah (WIN•yaw) Bay. A **bay** is a body of water that is part of a sea or ocean and is partly enclosed by land. Like Charleston, Georgetown's location on a natural harbor made it an important port town in its early days. Trade with other places helped Georgetown grow. Like Beaufort, however, Georgetown's port is now home to mostly fishing ships and pleasure boats.

REVIEW On what three bodies of water were South Carolina's first three permanent towns built?

Myrtle Beac

Surfside Beach

Georgetown

Winyah Bay

Francis Marion National Forest

Cape Romain National Wildlife Refuge

Intracoastal Waterway

Charleston

Mount Pleasant

Seabrook Island

Folly Beach

Kiawah Island

Edisto Island

ATLANTIC OCEAN

Beaufort

St. Helena Island

St. Helena Island

Parris Island

Port Royal Sound

Savannah National Wildlife Refuge

Hilton Head Island

Hilton Head Island

N
W   E
S

0   20   40 Miles
0   20   40 Kilometers

South Carolina's Population

YEAR	POPULATION
1720	18,000
1734	29,000
1749	64,000
1760	84,000
1763	105,000
1765	130,000
1773	175,000

LEARNING FROM TABLES
What happened between 1720 and 1734 that helped South Carolina's population grow?

Moving Inland

Before 1730 the only part of South Carolina settled by Europeans was a 20-mile-wide strip of land between Georgetown in the north and Beaufort in the south. Then in 1730 South Carolina's governor, Robert Johnson, had a plan. To settle South Carolina's inland regions, the state would give land away. Newcomers came from other places, such as Pennsylvania, Maryland, and Virginia, and from countries such as Germany, Switzerland, Ireland, and Wales. They moved as far inland as the area that is now Orangeburg and Florence.

The people who settled the **frontier**, or outlying areas, lived difficult lives. They cut trees to build their houses. For food, they hunted, fished, and grew corn.

By the 1760s Johnson's plan was a success. Many parts of the Midlands and Up Country had been settled. The town of Winnsboro near the center of South Carolina, for example, was settled about 1755. About ten years later, the first settlers arrived in the Anderson, Greenville, and Spartanburg areas.

This painting shows that people who settled the frontier had to work hard.

While newcomers from other locations began settling the Midlands and Up Country, many English settlers began moving inland from Charleston to find more farmland. In doing so, they started new communities, too.

Not long after Jacob Motte started his new farm across the harbor from Charleston, a community of farm workers and other business people was founded. Motte's farm soon became the town of Mount Pleasant.

English settlers also went up the Ashley and Cooper rivers and started more new communities there. Along the Ashley, they founded Summerville. Along the Cooper, people moved into North Charleston and made new homes in areas that are now Goose Creek and Hanahan.

By the time Columbia became South Carolina's capital city in 1790, more people lived in the Midlands and Up Country than in the Low Country. Over time, more people moved inland and started even more new communities.

REVIEW When did settlers in South Carolina start moving inland?

One of Mount Pleasant's beautiful city parks

Historical Museum in Summerville

▲ Winthrop College in Rock Hill

▲ One of Aiken's early railroad depots

Growth in South Carolina

Many inland South Carolina towns got their start when the railroads were built across the state in the 1850s. In 1852 workers building a railroad from Charlotte, North Carolina, to Augusta, Georgia, made a stop on a rocky hill in South Carolina. They called the place "Rock Hill." Today the town of Rock Hill is known as a railroad and business center.

Aiken is a community that started as a depot, or stopping point, for the South Carolina Canal and Railroad Company. It was named for the head of the company, William Aiken.

Florence also began as a railroad town in the 1850s. Florence's location halfway between New York City and Miami, Florida, made it an important shipping center for goods. Trains traveling between Florida and New York in the 1850s stopped in Florence to pick up ice. The ice was used to keep certain goods, like fresh fruit and vegetables, cold. Railroads at that time did not have refrigerated train cars.

Florence County Museum ▶

In addition to railroads, mills and factories helped new communities get started in the state's inland regions. Communities such as Anderson, Greenville, and Spartanburg grew up near the Fall Line. A **fall line** is the place where rivers drop from higher to lower land. People used the power of the rushing water to run machines in mills and other factories. Today these mills and factories are powered by electricity, but the goods they make are still important to their communities.

REVIEW Why were towns started near or along the Fall Line?

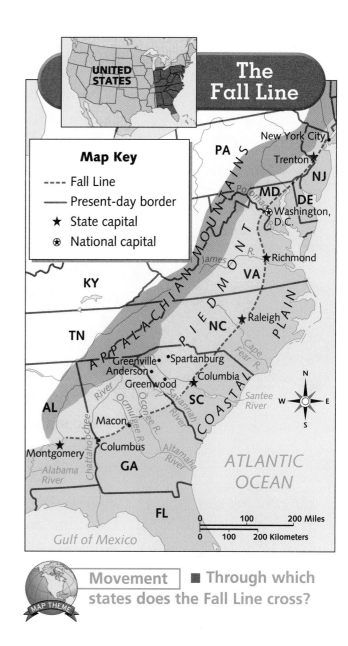

The Fall Line

UNITED STATES

Map Key

---- Fall Line
—— Present-day border
★ State capital
⊛ National capital

PA
New York City
Trenton
NJ
MD
DE
Washington, D.C.
Potomac
James R.
Richmond
VA
KY
PIEDMONT
NC
Raleigh
COASTAL PLAIN
TN
APPALACHIAN MOUNTAINS
Greenville • Spartanburg
Anderson •
Cape Fear R.
Greenwood •
Columbia
SC
Santee River
River
Oconee R.
Ocmulgee R.
Savannah River
AL
Macon •
Columbus
Montgomery
Chattahoochee River
Altamaha River
GA
ATLANTIC OCEAN
Alabama River
FL
Gulf of Mexico

0   100   200 Miles
0   100   200 Kilometers

N W E S

Movement ■ Through which states does the Fall Line cross?

MAP THEME

Greenville, South Carolina

AMERICAN FEDERAL

New Growth on the Coast

New communities in South Carolina continued to be founded in the 1900s. Some grew as a result of military bases that had been started in the state. One of South Carolina's earliest military bases is at Parris Island. Since 1915, Parris Island has been a Marine Corps Recruit Depot. Each year, thousands of young men and women from all over the United States go to South Carolina to live and get military training. As a result, communities grew up around Parris Island and other military bases in the state.

More communities also grew in recent times because many people started visiting the state. Two popular areas known for their natural beauty are along the Grand Strand and on Hilton Head Island. The Grand Strand is a strip of beaches on the northern part of the South Carolina coast. On one of these beaches, the community of Myrtle Beach grew to become one of the state's largest cities.

Harbor Town Lighthouse, on the southern tip of Hilton Head Island, was built in 1969.

On the southern part of the state's coastline is Hilton Head Island, an island once covered with trees. After the trees were cut down for lumber, a bridge was built connecting the island with the mainland. The bridge made it easier for people to reach the island. Soon a town grew. Today visitors from all over the world come to Hilton Head to spend their vacations.

REVIEW What has caused the growth of South Carolina communities in recent times?

◄ Marines training at Parris Island

▲ This photograph was taken from an airplane. It shows you a bird's-eye view of Myrtle Beach.

LESSON 9 REVIEW

Check Understanding

1 Remember the Facts What is South Carolina's most important port city?

2 Recall the Main Idea What did early settlers want their communities to be near?

Think Critically

3 Personally Speaking Suppose you wanted to start a new community. How would you decide on the location?

What natural features would you want to be near?

Show What You Know

Poster Activity Find out what resources are used in your community. Use your school library to find information. Draw and label some of these resources on a poster. Share your poster with the class. Explain why the resources you picked are important.

KEEPING SOUTH CAROLINA'S BEACHES AND RIVERS CLEAN

Each year in September, people throughout the United States participate in activities to help clean up beaches and rivers. They take part in a project called Beach Sweep/River Sweep. Anyone can help—families, school groups, scouts, and businesses.

In South Carolina about 7,000 people help each year to clean up places such as Edisto Beach, Folly Beach, the Savannah River, and the Great Pee Dee River. They collect more than 50 tons of trash! Much of it is recycled, or used again for something else.

Why is it important to keep beaches and rivers clean? Sea birds and other animals can be harmed from eating or getting tangled in trash. People can be in danger, too, from broken glass and other objects in the sand. The sweep helps make our lands cleaner, safer, and more beautiful for all to enjoy. The volunteers know they make a difference that really counts.

BEACH SWEEP RIVER SWEEP
SOUTH CAROLINA

Think and Apply

The volunteers you just read about are doing what they can to keep South Carolina's beaches and rivers clean and safe for people and wildlife. What are some things you can do to help? Write a plan of how you can make a part of your community cleaner the next time you visit. Share your plan with your classmates.

Visit the Internet at
http://www.hbschool.com
for additional resources.

▼ **Adults and children clean up Folly Beach, South Carolina.**

VISUAL SUMMARY

Study the pictures and captions to help you review the events you read about in Unit 2.

Write a Paragraph Choose one of the pictures from the visual summary, then write a paragraph that describes what the picture shows. In your paragraph, give details and examples that will help the reader understand more about the picture.

1 People often build communities near water.

4 Some people build towns so they will be near resources.

2 Communities sometimes start at places where people meet.

3 Over time, different groups of people may build communities near the same place.

5 The leaders of a country think about location before they build places of government.

UNIT 2 REVIEW

CONNECT MAIN IDEAS

Complete this graphic organizer by writing the main idea of each lesson. A copy of the organizer appears on Activity Book page 31.

Lesson 1
Communities are in different places.
_____
_____

Lesson 2
Communities are built near water.
_____
_____

Lesson 7
Communities move—Brasília, Brazil.
_____
_____

Lesson 6
Communities are built for government.
_____
_____

Where People Start Communities

Lesson 3
Communities are built where people meet.
_____
_____

Lesson 5
Communities are built near resources.
_____
_____

Lesson 4
Why did people build Cahokia and St. Louis?
_____
_____

WRITE MORE ABOUT IT

Write a Diary Entry Imagine that you are living in Charleston, South Carolina, at the time the new capital is being built. Your family may decide to move there. Tell how you feel about moving from Charleston to Columbia.

Write a Letter Work in a group to write a letter to a third-grade class in another part of your state. Tell that class about the physical features and human-made features of your class's community.

USE VOCABULARY

Sometimes the name of a place tells something about it. What vocabulary words from this unit are in the names of the cities listed below? Write a sentence to show the meaning of each vocabulary word.

1. Port Jefferson, New York
2. Safety Harbor, Florida
3. Bonners Ferry, Idaho
4. Rocky Ford, Georgia
5. Farmers Branch, Texas
6. Laurel Bay, South Carolina

CHECK UNDERSTANDING

7. How did St. Louis grow from a small trading post into a large city?
8. Why did towns grow near railroad junctions?
9. What are crossroads?

THINK CRITICALLY

10. **Link to You** Name two places in your community where people meet.
11. **Think More About It** At times, waterways are called river highways. What do you think that means?

12. **Personally Speaking** What would you tell people who plan to start a new community?

APPLY SKILLS

Find Intermediate Directions on a Map This map shows a classroom and some of the things in it. Find the orange-colored desk in the center of the map. Imagine that this is your desk. Then use the compass rose at the bottom of the map to answer these questions.

13. From your desk, in what direction is the clock?
14. If you wanted to walk from your desk to the teacher's desk, in which direction would you go?

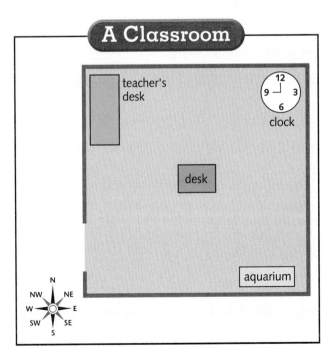

A Classroom

teacher's desk

12
9   3
6
clock

desk

aquarium

N
NW   NE
W   E
SW   SE
S

UNIT 2 REVIEW

Find State Capitals and Borders

The map below shows the state of Idaho. It shows the state capital and some of the county names. Use the map to answer these questions.

⑮ What is the name of the state capital?

⑯ In which county is the capital?

⑰ Which counties border the state capital's county?

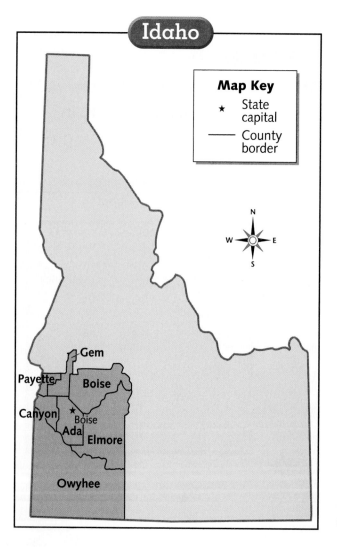

Idaho

Map Key
★ State capital
— County border

Gem
Payette
Boise
Canyon
★ Boise
Ada
Elmore
Owyhee

Read a Landform Map

Draw a map that shows the physical features and human-made features outside your school. Use colors to stand for different features, for example, green for trees and blue for water.

Write a Summary

Choose one of the lessons in this unit to read again. Use what you have learned to write a summary paragraph of the lesson.

Use a Product Map

Find out what crops or farm animals are raised in your county. Draw a map of your county. Add symbols to show where the crops and the animals are raised.

READ MORE ABOUT IT

New Hope by Henri Sorensen. Lothrop, Lee & Shepard. When Jimmy visits his grandfather in the town of New Hope, he learns that the town got its start when a wagon broke down!

HARCOURT BRACE
Visit the Internet at
http://www.hbschool.com
for additional resources.

REMEMBER

- Share your ideas.
- Cooperate with others to plan your work.
- Take responsibility for your work.
- Help one another.
- Show your group's work to the class.
- Discuss what you learned by working together.

ACTIVITY

Draw a Map

Work with a group of classmates to decide where the most important meeting places are in your school. Draw a map that shows these meeting places. Add a map key to explain the colors or symbols you used. Then write a title that tells what the map is about.

Unit Project Wrap-Up

Build a Physical Features Model   With your classmates, work in small groups to plan and build a model of the land around your community. Study your list to decide what things to include. Use clay to show the shape of the land. Then put the clay on a thick piece of cardboard. Next, paint the bodies of water on the cardboard. Now label the physical features and the roads, bridges, and important meeting points in your community. Share your model with other classes and explain it to them.

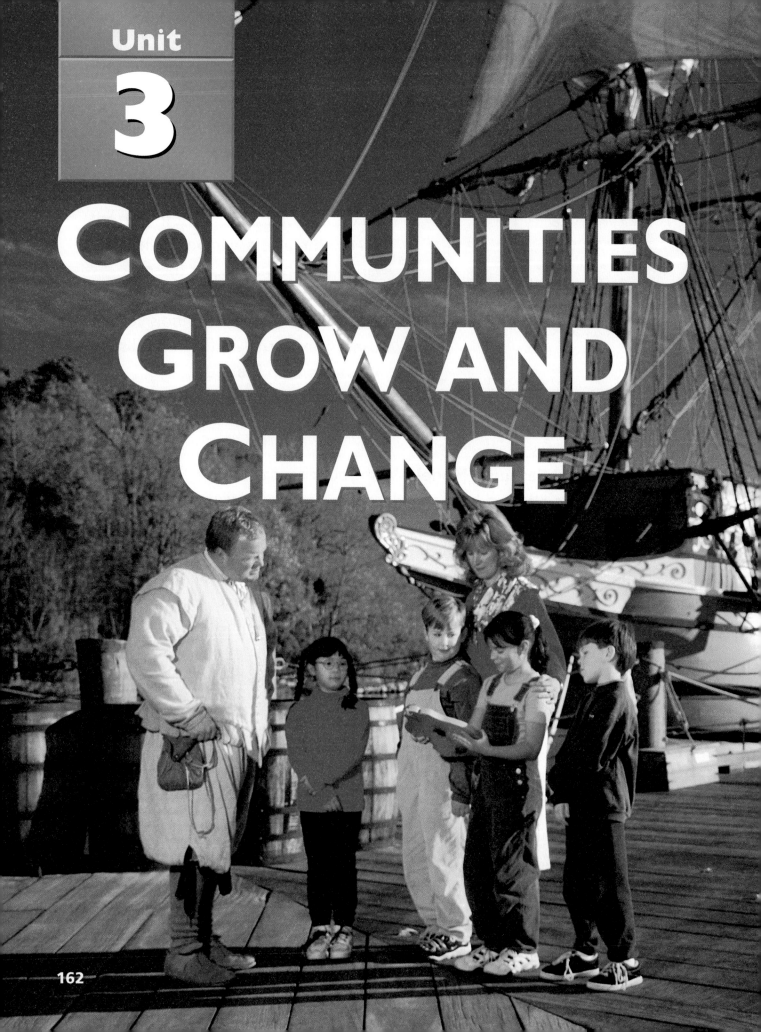

Unit 3

COMMUNITIES GROW AND CHANGE

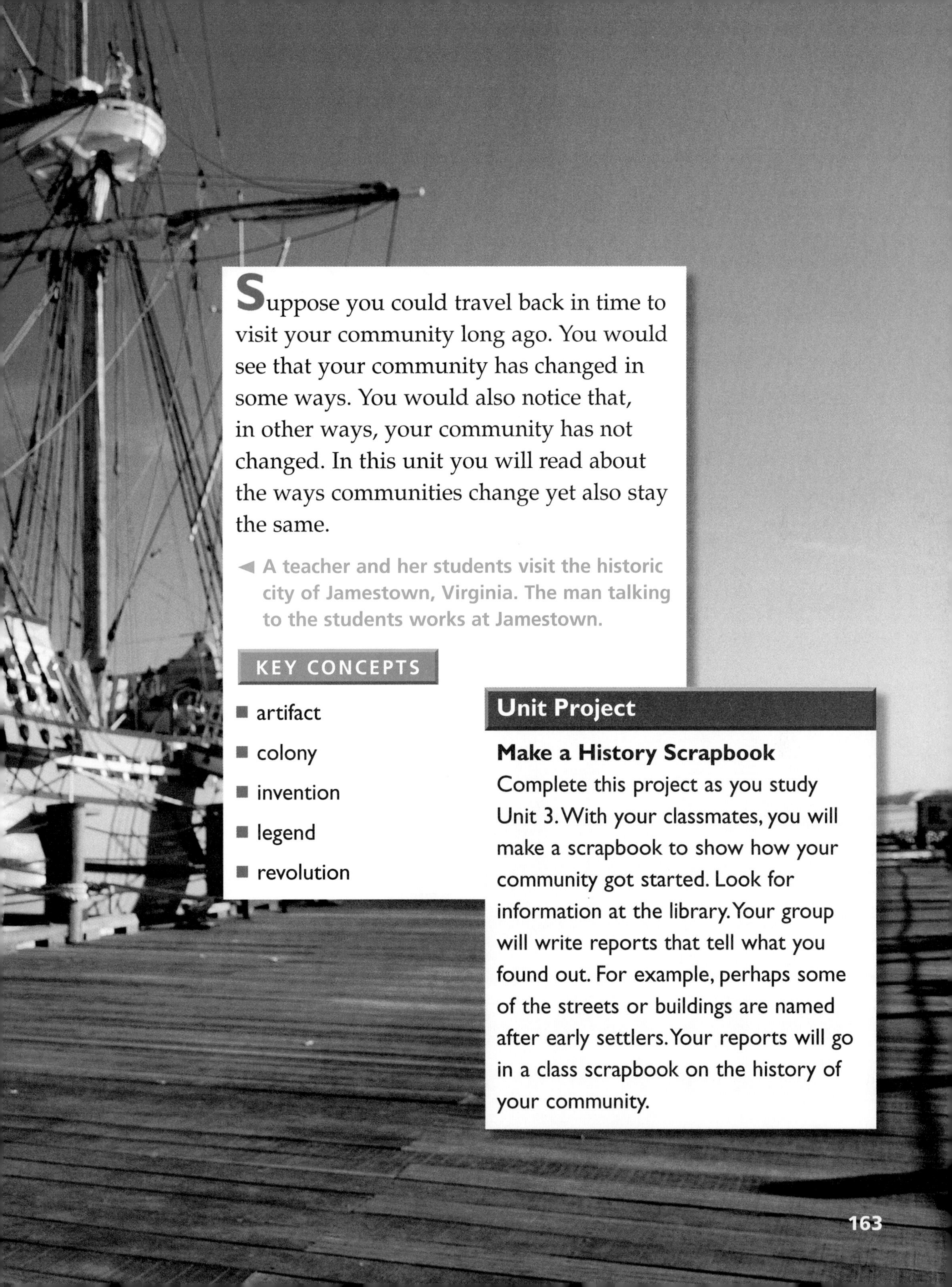

Suppose you could travel back in time to visit your community long ago. You would see that your community has changed in some ways. You would also notice that, in other ways, your community has not changed. In this unit you will read about the ways communities change yet also stay the same.

◀ A teacher and her students visit the historic city of Jamestown, Virginia. The man talking to the students works at Jamestown.

KEY CONCEPTS

- artifact
- colony
- invention
- legend
- revolution

Unit Project

Make a History Scrapbook
Complete this project as you study Unit 3. With your classmates, you will make a scrapbook to show how your community got started. Look for information at the library. Your group will write reports that tell what you found out. For example, perhaps some of the streets or buildings are named after early settlers. Your reports will go in a class scrapbook on the history of your community.

artifact An object that we find that was used by people in the past.

invention Something that has been made for the first time.

colony A settlement that is ruled by another country.

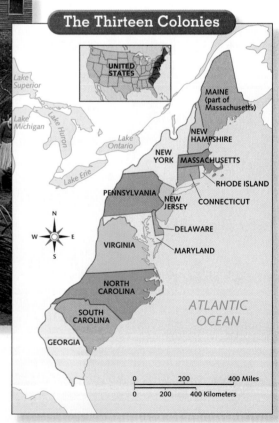

The Thirteen Colonies

UNITED STATES

Lake Superior
Lake Michigan
Lake Huron
Lake Ontario
Lake Erie

MAINE (part of Massachusetts)
NEW HAMPSHIRE
NEW YORK
MASSACHUSETTS
RHODE ISLAND
PENNSYLVANIA
NEW JERSEY
CONNECTICUT
DELAWARE
VIRGINIA
MARYLAND
NORTH CAROLINA
SOUTH CAROLINA
GEORGIA

ATLANTIC OCEAN

N W E S

0   200   400 Miles
0   200   400 Kilometers

legend A story that teaches a lesson or explains something.

WASHINGTON CROSSING THE DELAWARE

revolution A fight for change in government.

SHAKER LANE

ALICE AND MARTIN PROVENSEN

SHAKER LANE

written and illustrated
by Alice and Martin Provensen

All communities change over time. Some change
takes place slowly. Some change happens quickly.
In this story you will have an opportunity to see
how change affects the people who live in the tiny
community called Shaker Lane.

ot so long ago, if you went down School House Road and crossed Fiddler's Bridge, you would come to Shaker Lane. A Shaker Meeting House once stood at the crossroads. Nothing was left of it but a few stones.

Scrub brush covered the old farmland on both sides of the road. The farm belonged to the Herkimer sisters, Abigail and Priscilla. They were old ladies. They sat all day in their front yard facing the road. No one mowed their fields. No one fixed the fences.

In order to live, the Herkimer sisters sold off pieces of the farm, a half-acre here, an acre there. They sold it cheap. In a year or two there was a row of houses along Shaker Lane.

In the first house along the road lived Virgil Oates
with his wife, Sue Ann, their five kids, and Sue Ann's
brother, Wayne. Next to it was Sam Kulick's place.
Across the road lived Norbert La Rose. His wife's
name was Charlene. They had four kids. They also
had three dogs, five cats, and a duck named Lucy.

The people who lived on Shaker Lane took things easy. Their yards were full of stuff— old dressers waiting to go inside, cars that would never roll again, parts of old trucks, stovepipes, piles of rotten rope, rusty tin, bedsprings, bales of old wire and tin cans. Some people would have liked to see Shaker Lane disappear forever.

When the big yellow school bus came down Shaker Lane, the kids would yell, "Aker, baker, poorhouse shaker!"

Sometimes there were fights.

Here is Old Man Van Sloop's house. Dozens of
dogs lived here, as well as chickens and a goat
named Shem. The dogs came and went just as
they felt like. They fought and slept and chewed
on the bones that Old Man Van Sloop found for
them somewhere.

Sometimes an angry man showed up, looking
for a runaway. Old Man Van Sloop didn't care.
"Plenty more where that one came from!" he
would shout.

The man would frown and say, "Public
nuisance!" and take his dog away.

Next to Old Man Van Sloop lived the Whipple boys, Jesse and Ben. They were twins and did yard work. People never knew if it was Jesse or Ben who weeded their gardens.

Back of the Whipple house was the Peach place. Bobbie Lee Peach and his wife, Violet, lived here with their children—Emma, Zekiel, Sophie, Harvey, and Ralph. Violet's father, Chester Funk, lived with them too.

Here is Big Jake Van der Loon. Big Jake could do anything. He had four helpers: Little Jake, Herman, Matty, and Buddy. Big Jake dug wells, moved barns, put up fences.

He put up a telephone pole for the Herkimer sisters. He moved a chicken coop for Sam Kulick. When an enormous maple tree blew down in a storm, Big Jake cut up firewood for everyone.

The Van der Loon family lived in four houses on Shaker Lane. One for Big Jake, one for his brother-in-law, Harold Prideux; one for LeRoy and Milly Cobb; and one for Big Jake's mother, Big Ethel.

One day Ben Whipple came running up to Big Ethel. "We're going to be flooded out!" he shouted. "They're building a dam on Bosey's Pond!"

It was true. Ed Rikert, the County Land Agent, came to Shaker Lane. "A reservoir is to be built," he said. "Most of you folks will have to move. The county will pay you for your land."

Virgil Oates was the first to leave. "Can't swim," he said. Then the Whipple boys and the Peaches packed up and left. One by one, the other families followed.

The bulldozers came. Huge painted monsters, like
iron dinosaurs, chewed up Shaker Lane. Until, at last,
the excavation was complete.

The water rose slowly but surely. It crept over the
last chimney. Only the Herkimer house was still
there, high on the hill.

What was left of Shaker Lane changed its name to
Reservoir Road. You wouldn't know the place.

Old Man Van Sloop is
still here. He has a houseboat.
He has his chickens and Shem,
the goat.

Lots of dogs still come to
visit.

"I like the water," says Old
Man Van Sloop.

FOCUS
In the time you can remember, how has your community changed and how has it stayed the same?

Main Idea Read to find out some of the ways change takes place in communities.

Vocabulary
reservoir
decade
century
transportation
disaster

Communities Change Yet Stay the Same

Communities change every day. People move into a community, and others leave. An old building might be torn down to make way for a new building. A new shop might open for business in an old building. Some communities change quickly. Others change slowly.

Many Things Change

Many changes took place at Shaker Lane. The Herkimer sisters sold off pieces of their farm, and people built houses on them. Then the people were told they would have to move. A **reservoir**, or lake used for collecting and storing water, was to be built. After the reservoir was built, water covered much of Shaker Lane.

This was Dillon, Colorado, in the 1950s. The state government decided to build a reservoir there. Some buildings were torn down. Others were moved to a new location.

THEN

NOW

This is Dillon Reservoir. The community of Dillon is now in a new location, several miles away.

1900

TODAY

1950

LEARNING FROM PHOTOGRAPHS

■ Compare the three photographs to see how Atlanta, Georgia, has changed in a century.

A new community soon grew nearby. Many communities in the United States have changed in the same way.

Change can take a day, a decade, or even a century. A **decade** is 10 years. A **century** is 100 years. Some kinds of change take place so slowly that you hardly notice them. To see those changes, you can compare photographs that have been taken of the same place at different times.

REVIEW How many years are in a decade? a century?

THEN

NOW

This photograph was taken in 1997. City workers still do their jobs in the Custom House.

This photograph of the United States Custom House in New Orleans, Louisiana, was taken in 1900. The Custom House was built to give city workers a place to work.

Many Things Stay the Same

Many changes took place at Shaker Lane, but some things stayed the same. The reservoir was built, but Old Man Van Sloop stayed. He moved his animals and his belongings onto a houseboat and lived right on the reservoir.

In communities everywhere, many things seem to stay the same. Many old buildings are still used. They may have new things, such as telephones and computers. But the kinds of work people do inside the buildings are much the same as they were a century ago.

REVIEW What things stayed the same at Shaker Lane?

Slow, Steady Change

Charlotte, North Carolina, is a city that has changed in many ways over the years. Catawba (kuh•TAW•buh) Indians lived where Charlotte is now until European settlers came in the 1740s. The settlers built a town, which soon began to grow. Many people who lived in Charlotte at that time were farmers. Then in 1799 gold was found near Charlotte. Many miners moved to the community to look for gold. Other people built stores where the miners could buy things they needed.

In 1910 workers look for gold at the Parker Gold Mine in Stanley County, North Carolina.

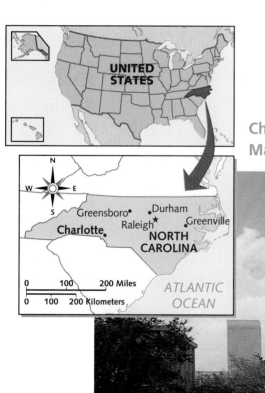

Charlotte is the largest city in North Carolina. Many businesses have grown up there.

The North Carolina Railroad
was finished in 1900.

At the Discovery
Place, a science
museum in
Charlotte,
students can
learn about
ocean life.

In the late 1800s people began to build
factories in Charlotte. Over the next century
many more factories and businesses were
built there. People moved to Charlotte for
jobs, and the city grew and changed.
Charlotte grew even larger after the North
Carolina Railroad was built. By the early
1900s six railroads connected Charlotte with
other cities in states on the Atlantic Coast.
Charlotte became an important center of
transportation. **Transportation** is the way
something moves from one place to another.
In 250 years Charlotte has grown to become
the largest city in North Carolina.

REVIEW How has Charlotte changed?

Fast Change

Some communities change very quickly. Sometimes something happens that causes them to disappear, as Shaker Lane did.

Terlingua, Texas, grew very quickly near the end of the 1890s. Thousands of people moved there to work in the mercury mines. Mercury is a kind of metal. But by the 1940s the mercury had all been mined. When the mines closed, all the people left. In just 50 years Terlingua grew from nothing into a busy community and then became a ghost town.

REVIEW **Why did Terlingua become a ghost town?**

Wagons were once used for transportation in Terlingua.

Terlingua, Texas, was once a busy community. Now it is a ghost town.

The Charleston Earthquake

On August 25, 1885, a strong hurricane destroyed most of Charleston. One year later, people were still rebuilding their homes when disaster struck again. On August 31, 1886, a powerful earthquake hit Charleston. Buildings were destroyed or damaged and many people died. Once again, the citizens of Charleston picked up the pieces of their homes and businesses and started to rebuild.

Unplanned Change

Sometimes a change happens that is not planned. A **disaster** is something that happens that causes great harm to a community. An earthquake can be a disaster. So can a flood, a fire, or a hurricane. Many disasters happen very quickly and without warning.

In 1906 a powerful earthquake hit San Francisco, California. Tall buildings and homes were flattened. Many businesses were destroyed. The changes caused by the disaster affected all the people living in the community.

LEARNING FROM PHOTOGRAPHS Taken from the Ferry Building, the photograph below shows the damage along Market and Sacramento streets after the 1906 San Francisco earthquake.
■ What do you think the people in the photograph are doing?

Earthquakes still happen today. Because so many earthquakes happen in California, children practice earthquake drills. Even though scientists know a lot about earthquakes, they cannot tell exactly when one will happen. That is why it is important to know what to do before an earthquake hits.

REVIEW How do earthquakes cause so much damage?

▲ People look at the damage caused by the 1989 earthquake in the San Francisco Bay area.

◄ Cleanup work begins soon after the earthquake.

LESSON 1 REVIEW

Check Understanding

1. **Remember the Facts** What are some kinds of disasters?

2. **Recall the Main Idea** In what ways does change take place in communities?

Think Critically

3. **Cause and Effect** What are some things that can cause communities to change quickly?

Show What You Know

Creative Writing Activity Think about what your community may be like a decade from now. What things may be the same? What things may have changed? Describe how you think a third grader will live in your community 10 years from today. Share your description with a classmate.

Compare Maps from

1. Why Learn This Skill?

Comparing maps that show different times in the same place can help you see how that place has changed. You can also see how mapmaking has changed.

2. How Mapmaking Has Changed

Many years ago mapmakers made maps by hand, using pen and ink. They made most maps by observing and measuring the area. When they needed to add new information, they often had to draw the whole map again.

Today mapmakers use computers to draw maps more quickly and easily. Mapmakers can also use photographs taken from space to help them make maps more correct.

3. Understand the Process

Compare the two maps of the northwestern part of Charlotte, North Carolina. Then answer the questions to find out how Charlotte has changed.

1 Find the park on each map. How has the area to the west of the park changed?

2 Compare the roads on each of the maps. What do the roads tell you about how Charlotte has grown?

3 Find Stewart Creek on each map. What has stayed the same? What has changed?

4. Think and Apply

Compare an old map of your state or community with a newer map. What do you learn by comparing the two maps?

With a computer, a mapmaker can add new information to a map very quickly.

Different Times

Charlotte, North Carolina (Northwest)—1935

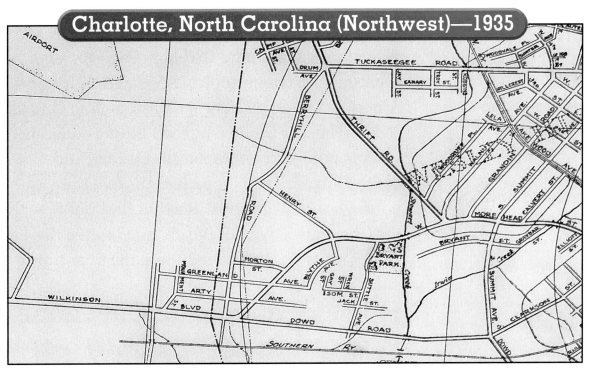

Charlotte, North Carolina (Northwest)—Today

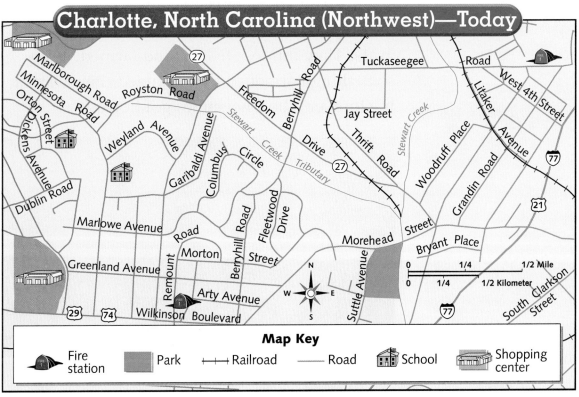

Map Key

Fire station | Park | Railroad | Road | School | Shopping center

FOCUS
What are some reasons your life has changed or has stayed the same?

Main Idea Read to find out how Native American ways of life changed and how they stayed the same long ago.

Vocabulary
lodge
tepee
legend

America's First Communities

Change is something that happened to even the first communities. Long ago, Native Americans lived all over what is now the United States. The Cheyenne (shy•AN) Indians lived in what is now Minnesota, North Dakota, and South Dakota. The Hoopa Indians lived in northwestern California. Read to find out how the Cheyennes' way of life changed while the Hoopas' way of life stayed the same over time.

Horses Change the Cheyenne Way of Life

For many years, the Cheyennes lived in **lodges**, homes made of logs, earth, and grass. They hunted, fished, and farmed. Then something happened that changed their way of life forever. The Cheyennes got horses.

In this painting on a buffalo hide, a Cheyenne artist shows how wild horses were caught.

The painting *Buffalo Chase* by Seth Eastman shows how the Cheyennes hunted buffalo.

Native American Groups

CHINOOK

YAKIMA

NEZ PERCE

CROW MANDAN

CHIPPEWA

CANADA

Great Lakes

WAMPANOAG

IROQUOIS

HOOPA

PAIUTE SHOSHONE

SIOUX

SIOUX

CHEYENNE

ERIE

POMO

SHOSHONE UTE

PAWNEE

IOWA

DELAWARE

ARAPAHO

MIAMI

ILLINOIS

POWHATAN

ATLANTIC OCEAN

PAIUTE

MISSOURI

KAW

YOKUTS

SHAWNEE

CHUMASH

HOPI APACHE

OSAGE

YUMA NAVAJO KIOWA

(QUECHAN) PUEBLO

QUAPAW

CHEROKEE

TUSCARORA

CATAWBA

CHICKASAW

CREEK

APACHE COMANCHE CADDO

CHOCTAW

NATCHEZ

PACIFIC OCEAN

MEXICO

TIMUCUA

SEMINOLE

Gulf of Mexico

N

W E

S

Caribbean Sea

0   300   600 Miles
0   300   600 Kilometers

Map Key

- California
- Eastern Woodlands
- Great Basin
- Northwest Coast
- Plains
- Plateau
- Southwest

Regions Native American groups who lived in the same areas shared cultures that were much the same.

■ To which Native American group do the Cheyennes belong?

Spanish explorers had brought horses with them to the southwestern part of the United States. After many years, horses that had gotten free began to roam the lands where the Cheyennes lived. The Indians caught some of these horses and began riding them. In the late 1700s the Cheyennes stopped farming. With horses, they could follow the buffalo herds across the Great Plains.

The Cheyennes lived in large groups, each with its own chief. The people of each group traveled and worked together.

The Cheyennes now needed shelters they could take with them. They began to live in tepees instead of in lodges. **Tepees** are triangle-shaped shelters made of buffalo skins stretched over poles.

The Cheyennes used buffalo meat for food and buffalo skins to make clothes and tepees.

Lesson 2 • **187**

This tool was made from a buffalo bone. It was used to scrape the animals' hides clean.

The women made clothes from the skins of the buffalo the men killed. They also cooked the meals and gathered berries and roots to use as foods and medicines. All the tools they used for their work they made themselves.

Cheyenne children learned to ride horses and help with cooking at an early age. Like children everywhere, Cheyenne children liked to play. They "played camp," setting up small tepees and catching and cooking fish. Their games helped them learn the jobs they would have as adults.

The Cheyenne believed in many gods and spirits and had festivals to honor them. At the festivals, the people wore special costumes and danced and played music.

REVIEW How did the horse change the Cheyennes' way of life?

This painting of the Cheyenne chief Wolf on the Hill was painted by George Catlin in 1832.

Hoopa Indian Life Stays the Same

For thousands of years the Hoopa Indians lived in the valley of the Trinity River in northwestern California. Few people came into their valley. The Cascade Range of mountains to the east and the Pacific Ocean to the west blocked the way. When European explorers and settlers came, the Hoopas had little contact with them. So their way of life stayed the same. It did not change as the Cheyennes' did.

The Hoopas had many villages along both sides of the Trinity River. To the north of the Hoopas lived two other tribes, the Karoks and the Yuroks. Because the three tribes lived so close together, they traded with each other and shared resources.

Shell necklaces like this one were given as gifts to Hoopa tribe members for following Indian laws. The shells were also used as money.

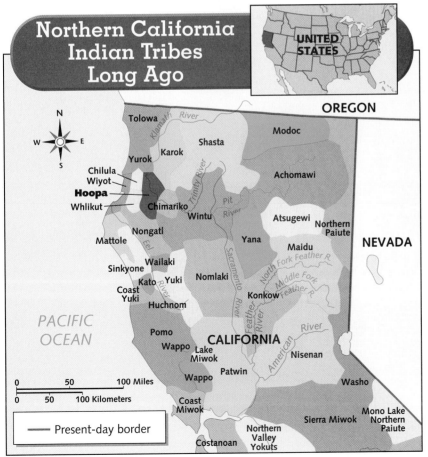

Northern California Indian Tribes Long Ago

UNITED STATES

OREGON

Tolowa — Klamath River
Modoc
Shasta
Yurok — Karok
Chilula
Wiyot
Hoopa
Whlikut
Chimariko
Wintu
Pit River
Achomawi
Atsugewi
Northern Paiute
Nongatl
Mattole
Yana
Maidu
NEVADA
Wailaki
Sinkyone
Kato — Yuki
Coast Yuki
Nomlaki
Konkow
North Fork Feather R.
Middle Fork Feather R.
Huchnom
PACIFIC OCEAN
Pomo
Wappo
Lake Miwok
CALIFORNIA
Nisenan
Patwin
Wappo
American River
Washo
Coast Miwok
Northern Valley Yokuts
Costanoan
Sierra Miwok
Mono Lake Northern Paiute

Feather River
Sacramento River
Eel River
Trinity River

0   50   100 Miles
0   50   100 Kilometers

— Present-day border

Location The Hoopa Indians lived in the northwestern part of California.

■ How did the Hoopas' location help keep their way of life the same?

Lesson 2 • **189**

Hoopa children spent much of their early childhood in basket cradles.

There were many resources near the Hoopas. They used the trees of the forest to make their homes and canoes. They fished for salmon in the streams and hunted for deer in the forest. They gathered acorns from the oak trees and ground them into flour to make bread and other foods. The Indians also used leaves, twigs, and roots to make baskets. Baskets were used to store, cook, and serve food. They were woven so tightly that liquids would not leak out. The baskets were also used as hats and cradles. The Hoopas made their baskets pretty as well as useful.

This Hoopa home was photographed in 1920. It is made of thick pieces of cedar and redwood. The round hole in the front of the home is the doorway.

This photograph, also taken in 1920, shows a Hoopa fisher. He is waiting to catch a trout or a salmon with his spear. The fence was built to trap the fish so they would be easier to catch.

Hoopa children learned some of the skills the adults used. They made baskets, fished, and hunted small animals. Hoopa children also liked to play. They played games in which they danced in a circle. Sometimes they went climbing in the nearby mountains or swam in streams.

At the center of all Indian culture is a deep respect for nature. It was important to the Hoopas to honor nature and the land. They held festivals to bring them success in hunting or to give thanks for plenty of salmon and acorns. At these festivals the people ate, sang, and danced.

REVIEW **What natural resources did the Hoopas use?**

This Hoopa drum is made of sealskin stretched over a wooden frame. Drums like this one were used at Hoopa festivals.

Native American Storytelling

Life today has changed for all Native Americans. However, they still keep the parts of their culture that are important to them. Storytelling is one important part of their culture. Stories are often **legends** that teach a lesson or help explain something. The stories do not have to be true. These stories are passed down from older members of the group to younger members. This legend is from the Gabrieleno Indians of southwestern California.

REVIEW What does this legend explain?

The TURTLE Story

Long ago, the trees, lakes, and rivers were all on the backs of giant turtles. This land was called California. But soon trouble came. The turtles wanted to leave, but they could not move.

"I want to swim to the East," said one. "I want to see the sunrise."

"The sunset is best. I want to swim to the West," said another.

The turtles argued for hours. One day three turtles swam east, and four turtles swam west. As they swam away from each other, the land began to shake. Then it cracked with a loud noise! The turtles stopped. Their backs hurt because the land each one carried was so heavy. The turtles knew they had to stay together to help each other, so they became friends again.

But sometimes the turtles that hold up California begin to argue again and want to move. Every time they do, the land shakes and cracks. The turtles soon decide to stay together, and the land returns to peace.

LESSON 2 REVIEW

Check Understanding

❶ **Remember the Facts** Why were natural resources important to the Cheyennes and Hoopas?

❷ **Recall the Main Idea** How has Native American life changed and stayed the same?

Think Critically

❸ **Think More About It** What might people who live near one another have in common?

Show What You Know

Poster Activity
Natural resources were important to Native Americans. On a poster, draw the natural resources that are important to your community. Then add labels and sentences that tell why these resources are important. Also show the ways people take care of these resources so they do not get dirty or run out. Display your poster so other classes can see it.

The Community of Tenochtitlán

Indian communities were not only in the United States. In what is now Mexico, the Aztec Indians built a great city and lived a life different from that of the Cheyennes and Hoopas.

A City on a Lake

The city of Tenochtitlán (tay•nawch•teet•LAHN) was started almost 700 years ago by the Aztec Indians. They believed that their gods wanted them to build a city in a special place. So when they saw an eagle sitting on a cactus with a snake in its mouth, they believed it was a sign that they had found the right place. The Aztecs saw this sign on an island in the middle of Lake Texcoco (tes•KOH•koh), in what is now Mexico.

FOCUS
In what ways did communities change many centuries ago?

Main Idea Find out how a community in Mexico changed many centuries ago.

Vocabulary
canal
causeway
empire

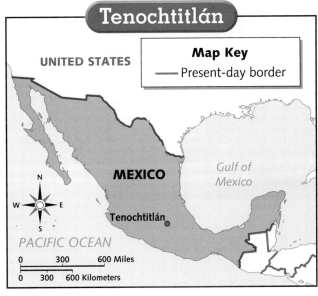

Tenochtitlán

UNITED STATES

Map Key
— Present-day border

MEXICO

Gulf of Mexico

Tenochtitlán

PACIFIC OCEAN

N W E S

0   300   600 Miles

0   300   600 Kilometers

◀ **A Spanish explorer's drawing of the city**

Lesson 3 • **193**

This painting, *The Great City of Tenochtitlán,* was made by the artist Diego Rivera in 1945.

This painting by José Muro Pico shows Aztecs building a floating garden.

The Aztecs built Tenochtitlán on that island. As many years passed, it became a great city. The Aztecs built huge temples and many homes. People traveled through the city on roads and canals. **Canals** are waterways built by people. Canoes were used to carry products to market. There were also causeways over the waters of Lake Texcoco. **Causeways** are roads built on soil piled up in shallow water. The causeways joined Tenochtitlán with other cities located around the lake.

The Aztecs used soil and reeds, or grasses that grow in water, to build floating gardens. These gardens floated like large rafts in the shallow waters around the city. The Aztecs planted them with crops, such as corn, beans, and tomatoes. These human-made "islands" produced a lot of food.

REVIEW How did canals and causeways help people in Tenochtitlán travel?

Changes in Government

Tenochtitlán was the capital city of the huge Aztec Empire. An **empire** is all the land and people under the control of a powerful nation. In the early 1500s there were millions of people in the Aztec Empire.

By 1521 the Aztec Empire was in ruins. Hernando Cortés (er•NAN•doh kawr•TEZ), a Spanish explorer, had led soldiers into Tenochtitlán. They fought a war with the Aztecs and destroyed the city. The Spanish built a new city in the same place and called it Mexico City. It became the capital of the Spanish Empire in Mexico. The Spanish began draining Lake Texcoco in the 1600s to make room for their growing city.

The Spanish ruled until the Mexican people formed their own government. Mexico became an independent country in 1821.

Hernando Cortés

A drawing of Mexico City in the 1600s. The city was built on top of the ruins of Tenochtitlán.

The Metro Cathedral was built by the Spanish in the 1600s.

The time line below shows some of the ways Tenochtitlán changed over time. However, some things did not change. This city, which was built in the middle of a lake, started as a capital city. After the city was destroyed, a new capital, Mexico City, was built.

REVIEW What new city did the Spanish build on the ruins of Tenochtitlán?

■ **LEARNING FROM TIME LINES** For how long did the Aztecs use Tenochtitlán as their capital city?

TIME LINE OF TENOCHTITLÁN'S HISTORY

1300	1400	1500	1600	1700	1800	1900

1325
Tenochtitlán started by the Aztecs

1521
Tenochtitlán destroyed by the Spanish who begin building Mexico City

1635
Spanish keep draining Lake Texcoco

1821
Mexico forms its own government with Mexico City as the capital

LESSON 3 REVIEW

Check Understanding

1 Remember the Facts How did the Aztecs decide where to build Tenochtitlán?

2 Recall the Main Idea How did Tenochtitlán grow and change many centuries ago?

Think Critically

3 Cause and Effect How did people change Lake Texcoco over the years?

Show What You Know

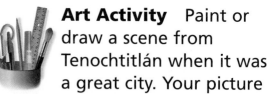

Art Activity Paint or draw a scene from Tenochtitlán when it was a great city. Your picture might be of a temple or a floating garden. Use the pictures in this lesson and pictures from encyclopedias for ideas. Give your painting or drawing a title. Then add your artwork to a bulletin board display.

Learn from Artifacts

1. Why Learn This Skill?

Objects that we find that were used by people in the past are called **artifacts**. A tool or a piece of jewelry is an example of an artifact.

Scientists who look for artifacts and try to explain how they were used are called **archaeologists**. By explaining the uses of the objects they find, they help us learn about the past. The ways artifacts were used can give us clues about how people lived long ago.

2. Understand the Process

Look at the pictures and read the caption about the artifacts. Then answer the questions.

Some Mexicans use tools like these to prepare food.

① Where were these tools found? What are they made of?

② What present-day tools do they look like?

③ How did people use these tools?

④ What do these tools tell you about how people lived long ago?

3. Think and Apply

Corn-grinding tools have changed over time. Some things about them, however, have stayed the same. Compare the two pictures. Make one list of the things that have changed and another list of the things that have stayed the same.

Archaeologists found these stone tools in the Aztec ruins of Tenochtitlán. Other Indian groups such as the Navajos and Hopis also used tools like these. People put kernels of corn on the large stone and used the small stone to grind the corn into flour.

FOCUS
What problems do cities face today?

Main Idea Find out what problem Mexico City faces today.

Vocabulary
pollution

Mexico City Today

Today Mexico City is in the place where Tenochtitlán once stood. The beautiful capital of the Aztec Empire had huge temples and floating gardens. Mexico City has many interesting buildings, parks, and museums.

The Largest City in the World

Mexico City is the largest city in the world. The population of the city and the area around it is more than 21 million.

People walking in Chapultepec Park in Mexico City

Human-Environment Interactions

■ How have people changed the area where Lake Texcoco once was?

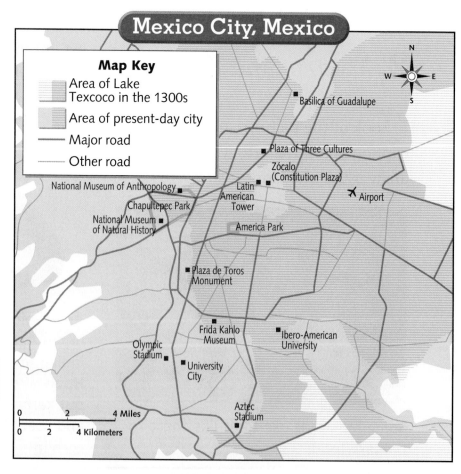

Mexico City, Mexico

Map Key

Area of Lake Texcoco in the 1300s

Area of present-day city

—— Major road

—— Other road

Basilica of Guadalupe

Plaza of Three Cultures

Zócalo (Constitution Plaza)

National Museum of Anthropology

Latin American Tower

✈ Airport

Chapultepec Park

National Museum of Natural History

America Park

Plaza de Toros Monument

Frida Kahlo Museum

Ibero-American University

Olympic Stadium

University City

Aztec Stadium

0   2   4 Miles
0   2   4 Kilometers

As in other big cities around the world, Mexico City's large population has created problems. For example, the people living in the city use many vehicles—buses, trucks, and cars. All of these vehicles produce exhaust, a kind of smoke. This exhaust, along with smoke from factories, causes pollution. **Pollution** is anything that makes the air, land, or water unclean.

The air in Mexico City is so thick with pollution at times that the citizens cannot see the mountains around their city. The air is not healthful to breathe.

REVIEW How many people live in and around Mexico City?

▲ A scene in Alameda Park in Mexico City. The Latin American Tower is in the background.

▼ What are some of the types of transportation these people might have used to get to downtown Mexico City?

199

Pieces of an Aztec temple can be seen in the Museum of the High Temple, which is located in a subway station.

Solving the Pollution Problem

The people in Mexico City are working to solve their pollution problem. Some factories that produced harmful smoke have been closed. Many vehicles now use special fuels and have engines that produce less pollution. There is also a law called "No driving today." This means that car owners may not drive their cars at least one day each week.

Better public transportation has also helped. In the 1960s, the people of Mexico City voted to build a subway. A subway is a set of tunnels with trains that run under the city. Many people now use the subway, and this has cut down on the number of vehicles on city streets.

Building the subway also gave Mexico City's people a new way to enjoy the history of their city. While working underground, subway builders found part of an Aztec temple. The pieces of the temple were carefully uncovered and left where they were found. An underground museum was built around them. Now people can visit the museum on their way to work or school.

SYMBOLS

The Mexican Flag

The Mexican flag reminds people of Mexico's history. The center of the flag shows an eagle sitting on a cactus with a snake in its mouth. This symbol reminds people of the Aztec city of Tenochtitlán, which stood where Mexico City stands today.

The people of Mexico City have many reasons to be proud of their city. It has had a long and interesting history.

REVIEW Why is the subway in Mexico City important?

The Plaza of Three Cultures has the ruins of an Aztec temple as well as a Spanish church and several modern buildings. It is a place where people can see some of the many ways Mexico City has changed.

LESSON 4 REVIEW

Check Understanding

1. **Remember the Facts** What did workers find when they were building the subway?

2. **Recall the Main Idea** How are people working to solve Mexico City's air pollution problem?

Think Critically

3. **Cause and Effect** Why does Mexico City have a problem with air pollution?

Show What You Know

Design a Postcard Think about some special buildings in your community. Pick the place you like the best and make a postcard about it. On one side draw a picture of the place and on the other write a few sentences describing the place. Then pick a partner to address it to. Share the postcard with your partner and describe what makes the place you chose special.

Solve a Problem

1. Why Learn This Skill?

You probably have to solve problems every day. You can use a set of steps to help you solve problems. Knowing the steps can help you be ready to solve most problems when they happen.

2. Remember What You Have Read

The citizens of Mexico City had a big problem. The air in their city was not healthful for people to breathe because of pollution.

3. Understand the Process

Here are some steps to use to solve a problem.

1 **Identify the problem.**
The Mexicans saw that the air in their city was not healthful.

2 **Think of solutions to the problem.**

A big problem like air pollution needs many **solutions**, or ways to solve it. The Mexicans thought of many things they could do. They could shut down the factories that caused pollution. They could have vehicles use fuels that cause less pollution. They could have people leave their cars at home one day each week. They could build a subway.

3 **Compare the solutions.**
What are the good points and bad points of each solution? A good point of closing down factories is that there is less air pollution. A bad point is that some people lose their jobs. Name the good and bad points of each solution that was named in Step 2.

4 **Carry out one or more of the solutions.**
The Mexican people are working together to make each solution work. One group of citizens

designed the subway. Another group made special fuels.

5 **Think about how well each solution worked.**

The problem of air pollution in Mexico City is not yet solved, but the solutions are helping. The air is much cleaner today than it was 10 years ago.

Air pollution over Mexico City

4. Think and Apply

The problems you face every day may not be as big as Mexico City's, but they are important to you. Imagine that you do not have enough money to pay for your lunch. Use the five steps to find one or more solutions.

FOCUS
How have you changed and how have you stayed the same since you were in first grade?

Main Idea Read to find out how our country long ago changed and how it stayed the same.

Vocabulary
slave
colony
tax
revolution
independence
constitution
civil war
amendment

Our Country's Early History

Change is something that has always happened. Our country has changed in many ways. Europeans built settlements where Native Americans had lived for hundreds of years. In 1565 Spain started St. Augustine, the first long-lasting settlement in what is now the United States. In 1607 the English started Jamestown in what is now Virginia. The Powhatan (pow•uh•TAN) Indians who already lived there taught the English the skills they needed. So the settlement lasted, and our country began to grow. It changed as it grew, but its promise of freedom stayed the same.

The Time of the Colonies

More settlements were started. Many settlers came from England, but some came from other countries. In 1619 the first Africans were brought to Jamestown to work as slaves. A **slave** is a person who is owned by another person and is forced to work without pay.

1600 •   1675 •

1607
Captain John Smith leads Jamestown settlers

1620
Settlers on the *Mayflower* start a colony at Plymouth, Massachusetts

1682
William Penn founds Pennsylvania

Most of the settlements along the eastern coast were colonies of England. A **colony** is a settlement that is ruled by another country. The colonies had their own laws, but England made laws for them, too. By the 1730s there were 13 colonies along the Atlantic Ocean from present-day Maine to Georgia. These colonies were the beginning of what is now the United States of America. On the western coast, California's first settlement, San Diego, was founded in 1769 by the Spanish.

Many of the people living in the colonies felt that England's laws were unfair. The colonists had no say in making the laws. They also did not like paying a **tax**, or extra money, for the things they needed or wanted. A war, called the American Revolution, began in 1775 and lasted eight years. A **revolution** is a fight for a change in government.

REVIEW Why did the colonists want a change in government?

The Thirteen Colonies

UNITED STATES

Lake Superior
Lake Michigan
Lake Huron
Lake Ontario
Lake Erie

MAINE (part of Massachusetts)
NEW HAMPSHIRE
NEW YORK
MASSACHUSETTS
RHODE ISLAND
PENNSYLVANIA
NEW JERSEY
CONNECTICUT
DELAWARE
VIRGINIA
MARYLAND
NORTH CAROLINA
ATLANTIC OCEAN
SOUTH CAROLINA
GEORGIA

N W E S

0   200   400 Miles
0   200   400 Kilometers

Location This map shows the locations of the 13 colonies.
■ Why do you think the colonies were all built along the coast?

1700

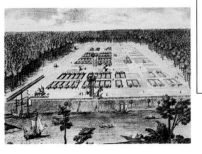

1733 Georgia becomes the 13th colony

1775

1775 American Revolution begins

The New Country

In 1776 John Adams, Benjamin Franklin, Thomas Jefferson, and other leaders wrote a statement telling why the colonies wanted independence. **Independence** is freedom from the rules of others and freedom to make your own rules. The statement they wrote was the Declaration of Independence. It said that all people are "created equal." On July 4, 1776, the leaders of the colonies voted to approve, or agree with, the Declaration of Independence. The colonists chose George Washington to lead their army. The colonists finally won their independence from England in 1783.

The leaders of the 13 new states then wrote the Constitution of the United States. A **constitution** is a plan of government. The Constitution was approved on June 21, 1788. George Washington was chosen to be the President of the new country. In the meantime, important events were also occurring in the West. California was ruled by the Spanish and then the Mexicans. It became a state in 1850.

REVIEW What important statement did the Declaration of Independence make?

This painting shows George Washington accepting the job of President of the United States of America on April 30, 1789, in New York City.

1776

1800

1776
Declaration of Independence signed

1783
American Revolution ends

1788
Constitution approved

1803
Meriwether Lewis and William Clark explore land west of the Mississippi

Lewis

The Civil War

Ways of life were changing. In the North, new factories in the cities needed workers. So people moved from farms and towns to get jobs. Life in the South did not change so quickly. Farming was the way most people made a living. The Southern states used slaves to do the work on the big farms. Disagreements over growth and slavery led the Southern states to split apart from the rest of the United States, or the Union. The Southern states formed the Confederate States of America, or the Confederacy. Jefferson Davis was their president.

President Abraham Lincoln hoped that the North and the South would find a way to agree. Instead, a civil war began. A **civil war** is a war in which two parts of one country fight each other. The Civil War started in 1861 and lasted four years.

Civil War States

Map Key

Union state

Confederate state

Border state

Territory

Human-Environment Interactions This map shows the border states that could not decide whether to join the North or the South.

■ A territory is land that belongs to a government but is not a state. Which territory borders a Union state, a Confederate state, and a border state?

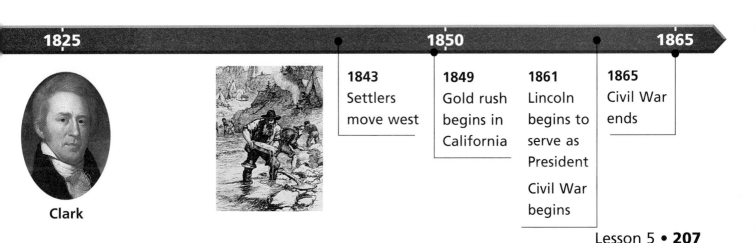

1825		1850		1865

1843 Settlers move west

1849 Gold rush begins in California

1861 Lincoln begins to serve as President

Civil War begins

1865 Civil War ends

Clark

LEARNING FROM PORTRAITS Here are the faces of five people who are important in our country's history.

■ Choose one of these people and tell why he or she is important.

George Washington

Benjamin Franklin

During the Civil War, former teacher Clara Barton delivered medical supplies to the battlefields. She also stayed with soldiers who had been hurt. Former slave Frederick Douglass made speeches to tell others why freedom was a right all people should have. Later Lincoln helped pass the Thirteenth Amendment to the Constitution. An **amendment** is a change to something that is already written. This amendment said that it was against the law to own slaves.

Lincoln hoped that the end of the war and the end of owning slaves would bring the country together. This did happen, but only very slowly.

LEARNING FROM DOCUMENTS
Lincoln signed a document like this one that said slaves in the Confederate states should be free. What does the eagle symbolize?

Abraham Lincoln

Clara Barton

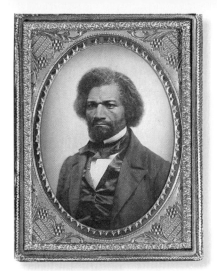
Frederick Douglass

Through all of the changes that have happened in our country, the promise of freedom has stayed the same. People have been willing to fight for this promise, and because they did fight, our country has survived.

REVIEW Why did many states leave the Union and start their own government?

LESSON 5 REVIEW

Check Understanding

1 Remember the Facts Why did settlers from England start colonies in America?

2 Recall the Main Idea How has our country changed, and how has it stayed the same?

Think Critically

3 Explore Viewpoints In what ways do you think the Civil War tore families apart? How did the end of the war help bring them back together?

Show What You Know

Make a History Minibook Make a minibook that shows how our country has changed over time. Your minibook should have six pages with pictures on them. The pictures should be in order from the earliest time to the latest time. Ask your classmates to look through the pages and talk about how our country has changed.

FOCUS

In what ways have inventions changed your life?

Main Idea Read to find out how inventions in communication, transportation, and other things changed our country.

Vocabulary

communication
transcontinental
invention
suburb
satellite

Inventions Change Our Country

After the Civil War, the country kept growing and changing. Soon there were new kinds of transportation and communication. **Communication** is the sharing of feelings, thoughts, and information. Improved railroads and telegraphs, as well as cars, airplanes, telephones, and other new things, changed the way Americans lived.

The Transcontinental Railroad

Railroads were already important in the East, but there were few trains in the West. People in the West still used horses for transportation and communication. Mail was carried by stagecoach, carriages pulled by horses.

COMMUNICATION AND TRANSPORTATION TIME LINE

1866

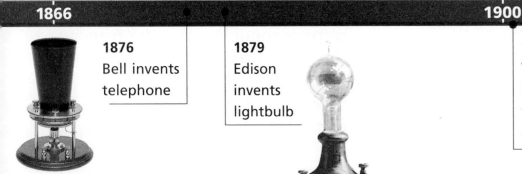

1876
Bell invents telephone

1879
Edison invents lightbulb

1900

1903
Wright brothers fly their airplane

In 1862 President Lincoln believed that it was time to build a railroad that would connect the whole country. To do this, the Central Pacific Railroad was built east from Sacramento, California, while the Union Pacific Railroad was built west from the Missouri River. In 1869 the tracks met in Utah. The Transcontinental Railroad was built! The word **transcontinental** describes something that goes from one side of a continent to the other. Soon more railroads connected all the larger towns.

The golden spike was used to complete the railroad.

REVIEW **Why was the Transcontinental Railroad built?**

The Central Pacific and the Union Pacific railroads met at Promontory, north of the Great Salt Lake in Utah, on May 10, 1869.

1930

1927
Farnsworth builds early television set

1968

1962
Rockets sent into space

1974
Computer chip speeds up communication

2002

1991
Bullet and maglev trains speed up travel

The Telegraph and Telephone

Samuel Morse was a painter who had many ideas for inventions. An **invention** is something that has been made for the first time. Morse's most important invention was the telegraph, a machine that used a code of dots and dashes to send messages over wires. When telegraph wires were strung across the country, people could get news quickly from people far away.

In 1876, Alexander Graham Bell invented the telephone. People could speak to and hear others who were far away. Since then, the telephone has changed many times. Today deaf people can use a special telephone to communicate. Bell's invention led the way to how we communicate today.

REVIEW **What two inventions helped people communicate quickly with others far away?**

Samuel Morse

▲ **Early telegraph**

TELEPHONES THEN AND NOW

1876

1919

1954

1968

1997

Today

LEARNING FROM PHOTOGRAPHS How have telephones changed over the years?

Helen Keller
1880–1968

When Helen Keller was a child, she had an illness that left her both blind and deaf. Her parents asked Alexander Graham Bell (shown here) how they could help her. He sent a teacher named Anne Sullivan to work with her. Sullivan communicated with Helen by tapping letters into her student's hand. When Helen caught on, she quickly learned to tap letters back. At last she could communicate! Later she went to college. Helen Keller showed the world the great things one person can do.

The Lightbulb

When he was 15 years old, Thomas Edison went to work in a telegraph office. He began thinking of ways to make the telegraph machine better. Soon he became a full-time inventor. Thomas Edison thought up more than 1,000 inventions! The phonograph, the microphone, and the movie camera were some of his inventions. But the invention that he is most famous for is the lightbulb.

Edison with two of his lightbulbs

Before there were lightbulbs, people used candles, oil lamps, or gas lamps for light. In 1879 Thomas Edison invited people to visit his workshop on New Year's Eve. When they arrived, the snowy road was brightly lit by lightbulbs in the trees. Soon news of this invention spread all over the world. Edison helped build the first power station in New York City in 1882. People could now have light any time they wished.

REVIEW What was Thomas Edison's most famous invention?

The Radio and the Television

Guglielmo Marconi (gool•YEL•moh mar•KOH•nee) studied the way the telegraph and telephone were made. These inventions could be used only where wires could carry the messages. Marconi thought of a way he could make a wireless telegraph. It could send messages from land out to ships at sea. Marconi's wireless telegraph later led to the invention of the radio.

▲Lewis Latimer worked with Thomas Edison. Latimer had many inventions of his own, such as the globe supporter shown in this drawing.

Fig: I.

Guglielmo Marconi

When Philo (FY•loh) Farnsworth was in high school, he learned how radios worked. He used what he learned about radios to build a television set in 1927. Today many people own both radios and television sets. These inventions bring us news from all over the world.

REVIEW **How did Marconi improve the telegraph?**

Philo Farnsworth with an early television set

The Automobile and the Airplane

Henry Ford changed the way people lived when he made the Model T automobile in 1908. Before that time, only rich people had cars. Henry Ford kept the price of his Model T low. As more and more people bought cars, the automobile became the main form of transportation. Many people moved to cities. The cities spread out, and people began to live in suburbs. **Suburbs** are communities near a city. Automobiles led to the building of highways all across the continent.

Henry Ford standing next to a 1921 Model T

Here are the Wright brothers at Kill Devil Hills near Kitty Hawk, North Carolina, during their historic flight in 1903. Orville Wright is flying the plane. Wilbur Wright is running beside the plane.

The computer is an important invention that has made communication faster and easier.

Orville and Wilbur Wright worked on another kind of transportation—the airplane. Many people thought flying was impossible. But in 1903 the Wright brothers flew their airplane for 12 seconds. Just 5 years later, in 1908, the Wright brothers were ready to sell an airplane to the United States Army. Soon more and more people used air transportation.

REVIEW How did Henry Ford make sure people could buy his cars?

Today's World

Our country is still growing and changing. Now people can travel and communicate even outside the boundaries of Earth. In the late 1950s the space program was started. Communication satellites were sent into space. A **satellite** is a spacecraft that is used to send radio, telephone, and television signals. By using satellites, people can send messages all over the world in seconds.

In 1998 work began on a new kind of spacecraft called the International Space Station (ISS). It will have living and working space for seven astronauts and scientists. ISS is a cooperative effort between 16 different nations, including the United States. While they are in space, astronauts will do medical research and look for ways that space technology can also be used on Earth.

REVIEW **How is our country still growing and changing?**

This is what the International Space Station (ISS) will look like when it is finished. People will be able to live in it for several months at a time.

LESSON 6 REVIEW

Check Understanding

❶ Remember the Facts Which inventions helped people communicate faster?

❷ Recall the Main Idea How have inventions changed the way people live?

Think Critically

❸ Link to You Think of an invention that is important to you and your family. What would your life be like without this invention?

❹ Cause and Effect What effect did the Model T have on the way people lived?

Show What You Know

Write a Journal Entry Scientists often keep journals about their inventions. Think up an invention you want to make. Write a journal entry about it, and add pictures. Then read your journal entry to your classmates, and show them the pictures.

FOCUS
What are some ways to find out about a community's history?

Main Idea Find out how you can learn about the history of your community.

Vocabulary
historical society

Every Community Has a History

History is the story of what happens to people and their communities over time. In this unit you have looked at how change affects communities. You have also seen that some things do not change. Now use what you have learned to find out more about the community where you live.

Learning About the History of Your Community

There are many ways you can learn about the history of your community. Every community has places where you can find information.

Older family members can tell you what life was like before you were born.

A neighbor talks about the history of a community.

A good place to start is with your family. Maybe you have older family members you can interview about your community. Ask them questions. Find out what life was like when they were your age. Look at old family photos or movies. Some family members might be able to show you artifacts that were used long ago.

Maybe your family has just moved to a new community or your family members do not live in your community. Then you might interview other members of your community—perhaps some of the workers at your school. Your neighbors may also share what they know about your community.

Family members may have artifacts like this butter churn that pioneers used long ago.

This photograph shows a fire truck from the 1920s. People who work in historical museums like this one often have a special interest in history. They may be glad to share information about your community.

Many communities have special places where you can find information. The library may have books, maps, and other displays that you can learn from. Your community may also have a museum or a historical society. A **historical society** is a group of people, usually volunteers, who have a special interest in the history of their community. They may have collections of photographs and artifacts.

REVIEW Who can you ask about the history of your community?

Using History Skills

You can use your social studies skills as you learn about the history of your community. You could make a time line that shows when important events happened in your community. You could also compare maps or photographs from different times to see how things have changed. You might make a chart or graph to show how the population of your community has changed over the years.

Soccer Team Wins Championship

By Toby Taylor
Daily News Sports Correspondent

It was a very close game, but the Doraville Eagles defeated the Fairburn Bluejays 5-4 to win the district soccer championship. The Eagles were behind 4-1 at the half, with the only goal scored by Brittany Williams. In the beginning of the second half, an outstanding pass by Marquis Wilson to Sal Mendoza helped pull the Eagles within one point. Then, in a scoring frenzy, the Eagles netted 3 more to win in the last two minutes of the game. Goalie Scott Tow had an outstanding day with 4 saves. Williams, Mendoza, Wilson, Andrea Garza, and Andrew Weekes each scored one goal.

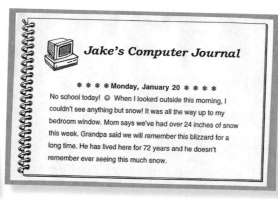

Jake's Computer Journal

✳ ✳ ✳ **Monday, January 20** ✳ ✳ ✳

No school today! ☺ When I looked outside this morning, I couldn't see anything but snow! It was all the way up to my bedroom window. Mom says we've had over 24 inches of snow this week. Grandpa said we will remember this blizzard for a long time. He has lived here for 72 years and he doesn't remember ever seeing this much snow.

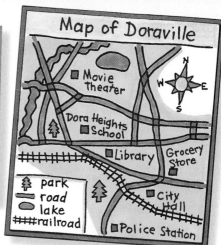

As you study your community's history, remember that history is happening every day. And *you* are a part of that history. You may wish to keep a journal or scrapbook of events that are important to you. Someday, when you have become an older member of your community, a group of third graders may ask you what life was like years ago. Just think how much fun it will be to tell them about it!

REVIEW What social studies skills can you use to tell others about the history of your community?

Students Help Plan New City Park

By Peggy Hamilton
Daily News Staff Writer

Third grade students at Dora Heights Elementary School met with city planners yesterday to provide input for the new park. The park will be located in the vacant lot on the west side of City Hall and will include a playground. The students were asked to describe the kinds of features they'd like to see in the playground, and the kids had plenty to say.

"We hope there will be lots of slides," said Zachary Herbst. "And many places for climbing."

Tamika Watson described how her sister, a wheel-chair user, has enjoyed the playground at the park in nearby Westville. That playground has specially designed ramps and areas that are built for wheel chair access.

"We want our new playground to have places where *all* children can play and have fun," said Tamika.

City officials will be looking for volunteers to help build the park, beginning sometime in May.

LESSON 7 REVIEW

Check Understanding

1 Remember the Facts What interest do members of a historical society share?

2 Recall the Main Idea What are three ways you can learn about the history of your community?

Think Critically

3 Explore Viewpoints Would two older members of your community tell the same story about your community's past? Explain your answer.

Show What You Know

Make a Time Capsule A time capsule is a container that holds papers and other objects. These items tell what life was like during a certain time. The time capsule is put in a safe place for people to open years later. What would you put in a time capsule to be opened a century from now? Make a list of five things, and explain to a partner why you chose each one. Then start collecting the items.

FOCUS

How has South Carolina changed, and how has it stayed the same?

Main Idea   Read to find out how Native Americans, Europeans, and Africans changed South Carolina long ago.

Vocabulary
plantation
Gullah
township

South Carolina's Early History

Like every community and country, every state has a history. South Carolina's history begins before it was a state or even a colony.

The Early People of South Carolina

Long before Europeans came to South Carolina, Native Americans lived on the land. They made good use of the natural resources around them. For food, they gathered plants, hunted, and fished. Those who also raised crops lived in villages, in shelters made of logs.

Some of the early Carolina Indians lived in small villages like the one shown here.

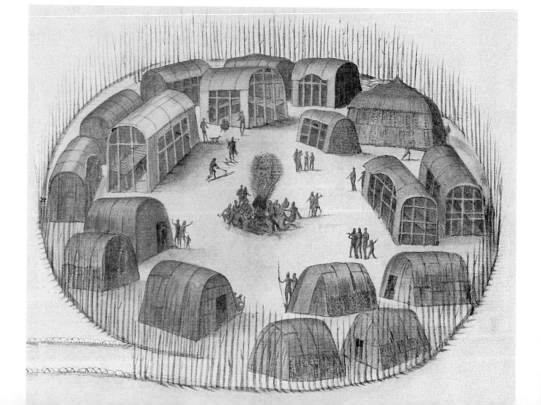

More than 25 Native American groups have lived in what is now South Carolina. The two largest groups were the Catawbas (kuh•TAH•buhz) and the Cherokees (CHAIR•uh•keez).

After European settlers arrived, the number of Native Americans living in South Carolina went down. Many died from diseases or moved to new land. A few stayed. Today there is a Catawba Indian community near Rock Hill.

Many of South Carolina's rivers and towns are named for Indian groups. Some of the state's highways follow their old trails. Interstate 26, for example, follows much of the old Cherokee Path. This trail led from Charles Town, along the Saluda and Congaree rivers, to the northwestern corner of the state.

REVIEW **Which two Native American groups in South Carolina were the largest?**

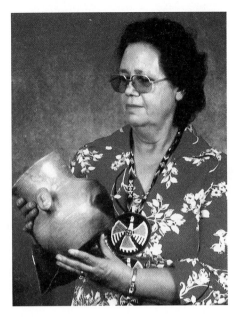

Sara Ayers, a Catawba from Columbia, looks at one of the pots she has made.

Major Native American Groups in South Carolina, 1670

NORTH CAROLINA

CHEROKEE

CATAWBA

CHERAW

WAXHAW

CHEROKEE

SOUTH CAROLINA   PEEDEE

SALUDA   WATEREE

YUCHI   CONGAREE

WACCAMAW

SANTEE

SAVANNAH   WINYAH

GEORGIA   KASIHATA   SEWEE

COOSAH   WAADO
ETIWAN

CUSABO   KIAWAH

WESTO   STONO
EDISTO

YAMASSEE   ESCAMACU   ATLANTIC
COMBAHEE   OCEAN
WIMBEE

N W E S

0   50   100 Miles
0   50   100 Kilometers

Regions This map shows where Native American groups lived in South Carolina long ago.

■ Did more groups live in the Piedmont or in the Coastal Zone region?

The Spanish and the French Arrive in Carolina

In the 1500s, Spanish explorers wore helmets like this one.

Christopher Columbus's voyage in 1492 opened the door for Europeans to set up colonies in North America and South America. In the early 1500s Spanish explorers led by Lucas Vásquez (VAHS•kays) de (DAY) Ayllón (eye•YOHN) looked for land for a colony along the eastern coast of what is now the United States. In 1526 they may have settled near where the city of Georgetown, South Carolina, is now.

The place had everything the Spanish settlers needed. They found water to drink, plants and animals for food, trees for shelters, and good soil for crops. However, because of illness, fighting with the Native Americans, and weather they were not used to, the Spanish settlers returned home.

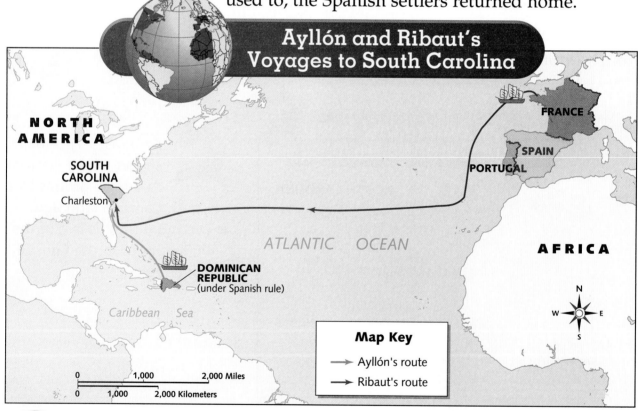

Ayllón and Ribaut's Voyages to South Carolina

NORTH AMERICA

SOUTH CAROLINA

Charleston

ATLANTIC OCEAN

DOMINICAN REPUBLIC (under Spanish rule)

Caribbean Sea

FRANCE

SPAIN

PORTUGAL

AFRICA

N
W   E
S

Map Key

→ Ayllón's route

→ Ribaut's route

0   1,000   2,000 Miles
0   1,000   2,000 Kilometers

Movement Explorers from Spain and France sailed to South Carolina.
■ Who traveled the greater distance to South Carolina, Ayllón or Ribaut?

The French were the next to set up a settlement in South Carolina. In 1562 they chose a location on Parris Island. During their first winter, the settlers ran out of food and had to give up the colony. They built a ship, using their shirts for sails, and left for home.

In 1566 the Spanish again tried to settle South Carolina. This time they chose a place near the old French settlement and named their town Santa Elena. The settlement lasted more than 20 years. However, there were many mosquitoes and the people did not like the weather. The Spanish government ordered the settlers to move in 1587.

REVIEW **Which countries tried to start colonies in South Carolina?**

Jean Ribaut
1520?–1565

In 1562 Jean (ZHAN) Ribaut (ree•BOH) led 150 men from France to North America. In late spring they reached Parris Island, along the Port Royal Sound in South Carolina. There they built a military post, or fort, called Charlesfort. Ribaut described Port Royal as "one of the greatest and fayrest (fairest) havens (harbors) of the world."[1]

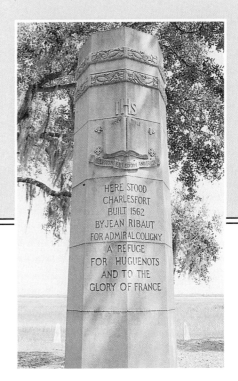

This monument on Parris Island honors Jean Ribaut, the leader of the early French settlers.

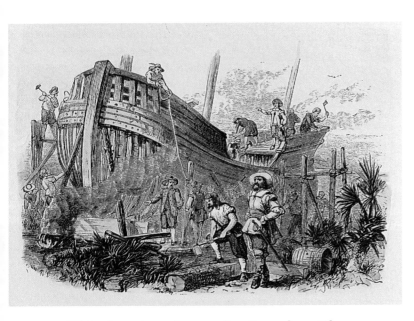

This drawing shows the French settlers building a ship to sail back to France after Ribaut left the settlement with his ship.

The English Come to Carolina

Like Spain and France, England also claimed land in what is now the United States. The English called their land between Virginia and Florida "Carolina." Carolina was made up of the land that is today North Carolina and South Carolina.

The first English settlers arrived on the Carolina coast in 1670 and built a settlement at Albemarle (AL•buh•marl) Point. They named this settlement Charles Town, which was later changed to Charleston. In 1680, the English moved Charles Town to a new location at Oyster Point. Charles Town was the first long-lasting European settlement in South Carolina.

This engraving shows the growing city of Charles Town in 1780.

Among the first English settlers in what is now South Carolina was Dr. Henry Woodward. Woodward did much to help the new settlement. He started a fur trade with the Native Americans, and he may have helped plant the first rice crop. Rice was grown on large farms called **plantations**. Fur trading and rice growing helped the Carolina colony grow.

Over time, more settlers arrived. By 1750 the number of people who lived in Carolina had grown to more than 80,000.

REVIEW Which group started the first long-lasting European settlement in South Carolina?

▲ During colonial times, slaves used these wooden tools to take off the outer shells of rice grains.

There are no pictures of Eliza Pinckney, so no one knows exactly what she looked like. However, the South Carolina Historical Society made this doll of her by looking at pictures of her children. The dress she is wearing is the color of the blue dye made from indigo. ▼

BIOGRAPHY

Eliza Lucas Pinckney
1722?–1793

Two of the main crops grown on plantations in South Carolina were rice and indigo (IN•dih•goh). Indigo is a plant from which a blue dye for coloring cloth is made. This crop was hard to grow, but Elizabeth "Eliza" changed that. She was 17 years old when she planted a different kind of indigo on her family's plantation near Charles Town. When it did well, she showed other people how to grow it. Soon indigo became an important crop.

This engraving from the 1700s shows how the workers passed fresh water through tubs or barrels to get the dye from the indigo plant.

Africans in Carolina

Most of the newcomers to Carolina were Africans. Europeans brought them from West Africa and the West Indies to North America as slaves. Many of the slaves lived and worked on the plantations in the Low Country near Charles Town. They cleared the land and planted and harvested cotton, rice, and other crops.

Some Africans were skilled workers—brickmasons, carpenters, cabinetmakers, woodcarvers, and blacksmiths. Many of the houses in Charles Town were built by African workers. The finer houses had beautiful woodwork carved by Africans.

Some Africans spoke their own special language called Gullah (GUH•luh). **Gullah** is made up of English and more than 4,000 African words. This language is still spoken today in the Low Country and on the Sea Islands of South Carolina.

REVIEW **Where did many slaves brought to Carolina live and work?**

Others Come to Carolina

In 1712 Carolina was divided into North Carolina and South Carolina. Governor Robert Johnson of South Carolina thought of a plan to bring in even more settlers. He promised settlers land, tools, and food if they would settle in planned communities called **townships**. Settlers from France, Scotland, Ireland, England, Holland, Switzerland, and Germany began to arrive. People from other English colonies in the north came as well.

Many of the townships were settled by people from one country. For example, people from France settled in the townships of New Bordeaux and Hillsborough. German and Swiss farmers settled in Purrysburg, Orangeburg, and Amelia. Scotch-Irish settlers lived in the townships of Londonsburg, and Williamsburg. Soon people were living all along the coast and into the Up Country.

REVIEW **When was Carolina divided?**

Governor Robert Johnson

LESSON 8 REVIEW

Check Understanding

1. **Remember the Facts** Who lived in South Carolina before the Europeans started colonies?

2. **Recall the Main Idea** How did Native Americans, Europeans, and Africans change South Carolina?

Think Critically

3. **Think More About It** Why do you think some people in South Carolina still speak Gullah today?

Show What You Know

Write a Journal Entry Settlers in new lands often keep journals about their experiences. Imagine that you are an early settler in South Carolina. Write a journal entry about how you feel in a land that is new to you. Share your journal entry with your classmates.

LESSON 9

FOCUS
What part has South Carolina played in our country's history?

Main Idea Read to learn how South Carolina changed our country's history during the American Revolution, the Civil War, and the years that followed.

Vocabulary
secede
Reconstruction

South Carolina's Role in War

In 1788 the colony of South Carolina became the eighth state of the United States. Many South Carolinians fought in the American Revolution. They wanted their colony and the others to be free from England. South Carolinians also helped create the Constitution of the United States, the plan for our country's government.

South Carolina in the American Revolution

Many important battles were fought in South Carolina during the American Revolution. One of the first battles was fought near Charles Town.

MAJOR HISTORICAL EVENTS

1775 — 1800

1776
Declaration of Independence is signed

1783
American Revolution ends

1788
South Carolina becomes the eighth state

Constitution approved

1801
South Carolina College, later called the University of South Carolina, is founded

230 • Unit 3

On June 28, 1776, the English army attacked the fort on Sullivan's Island. South Carolina soldiers led by Colonel William Moultrie (MOHL•tree) and Colonel William Thompson were ready for them. The English were surprised when their cannonballs thudded into the fort's walls and then landed in the sand. The fort's walls were built of palmetto (pahl•MEH•toh) logs, which are rather soft.

During the battle, a shot broke the fort's flagpole, and the flag fell to the ground outside the fort. Sergeant William Jasper climbed over the wall, picked up the flag, fixed the flagpole and put the flag back. His brave action gave the soldiers the courage to keep fighting. By the end of the day the English had been beaten.

REVIEW What was the fort on Sullivan's Island built of?

BIOGRAPHY

General Francis Marion 1732–1795

This painting shows General Francis Marion of South Carolina. He was an important leader in the American Revolution. He was called the Swamp Fox because he and his soldiers often hid in the swamps and made surprise attacks on the English soldiers.

1825   1850   1875

1821
South Carolina leads the nation in the production of cotton

1860
Lincoln elected President

South Carolina secedes from the United States

1865
Civil War ends

Reconstruction begins

South Carolina After the American Revolution

After the war ended in 1783, Americans no longer had to follow the rules of the English. They were free to make up their own rules. However, it took leaders many years to agree on the right set of rules for the new country.

Charles Pinckney (PINK•nee), a leader from Charleston, went to a meeting of the new country's leaders in Philadelphia, Pennsylvania, to share his ideas. Many of the ideas in the Pinckney Plan were used in the Constitution. More than 200 years later, the Constitution is still the plan that guides our country.

REVIEW Why did Charles Pinckney go to Philadelphia?

▲ This painting by James Earl shows Charles Cotesworth Pinckney, an important leader in South Carolina. Both he and his cousin, Charles Pinckney, signed the Constitution.

▼ Signing of the Constitution by Thomas P. Rossiter

South Carolina in the Civil War

During the 1800s cotton was the most important crop in the South, especially in South Carolina. Growing cotton was the way people in South Carolina made most of their money. Almost all of the planting and picking of the cotton was done by African slaves. Meanwhile, life in the North was changing as people moved from farms and towns to work in factories in the cities. People in the North and the South began to disagree about growth and slavery.

After Abraham Lincoln was elected President in 1860, the leaders of some of the Southern states thought they should **secede** (sih•SEED) from the United States. This means that they wanted to stop following the rules of the United States government and form their own country. South Carolina was the first state to secede from the Union. Ten other states seceded, too. Many different disagreements between the North and the South led to the Civil War.

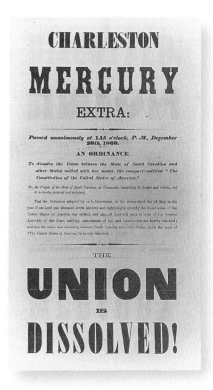

The states that seceded from the United States called their new country the Confederate States of America.

The Civil War started in April 1861 after shots were fired at Fort Sumter, in Charleston Harbor.

Mary Boykin Miller Chesnut 1823–1886

Mary Boykin Miller Chesnut lived in South Carolina during most of the Civil War. She wrote about her life and the lives of her friends. Her writings are among the most important of the Civil War period. People study her writings today to find out what life was like then.

The Civil War lasted for four years. Almost all the battles were fought in the South. Many people on both sides were killed or badly hurt. One of the events that finally ended the war was Sherman's March to the Sea.

General William T. Sherman of the Union believed he could get the Confederate army to give up. He and 60,000 of his troops marched across Georgia and through South Carolina. His large Union army burned public buildings and homes in several towns in South Carolina and Georgia. They also destroyed railroad tracks and bridges.

This photograph of Main Street in Columbia after the Civil War shows that many of South Carolina's soldiers came home to find their land, houses, and businesses destroyed.

In February 1865 Sherman and his troops took over the city of Columbia. While they were in Columbia, the city caught fire and the State House was burned. No one is sure how the fire started. The new, fireproof State House, which was being built when Sherman arrived in Columbia, survived the fire. However, it was damaged by Union guns.

The Civil War finally ended when Confederate General Robert E. Lee surrendered to Union General Ulysses S. Grant in Virginia. The Confederate states rejoined the Union. More than 18,000 South Carolinians had died in the war. After the Civil War the Thirteenth Amendment was passed. It made it against the law to own slaves.

REVIEW **Why did South Carolina secede from the Union?**

Robert E. Lee surrendered his troops to Ulysses S. Grant at the tiny Virginia town of Appomattox Court House.

South Carolina After the Civil War

Since much of South Carolina had been destroyed during the war, it had to be built again. The time after the Civil War is often called Reconstruction (ree•kuhn•STRUHK•shuhn). **Reconstruction** means "rebuilding." Reconstruction was a difficult time of change for the people of the South.

For several years after the war, much of the South was run by people from the North. Many Southerners, especially those who had been in power before the war, did not like being told what to do. Not all government leaders were from the North, though. Some were white Southerners who believed that slavery was wrong.

For the first time in the South's history, African Americans could take part in government. For most former slaves, however, life was almost as hard as it had been before the war. Many had no land of their own and little or no money.

These African Americans were the first to serve in the United States Congress. From left to right they are Hiram Revels, Benjamin Turner, Robert DeLarge, Josiah T. Walker, Jefferson Long, Joseph M. Rainy, and R. Brown Elliott. DeLarge, Rainy, and Elliott were from South Carolina. From 1868 to 1877 African Americans were the majority in South Carolina's government.

Many freed slaves and poor whites became tenant farmers, farmers who grew crops on land owned by someone else. Instead of paying rent, tenant farmers gave the landowners part of their crops. They had barely enough left to feed their families. Since they had nothing to sell, tenant farmers stayed poor.

Life after the Civil War was not easy for most South Carolinians. The fight for freedom meant different things to different people. However, it was the promise of freedom that kept our nation and South Carolina together. They would go through more change during the next century.

REVIEW What is the time after the Civil War called?

BIOGRAPHY

Robert Smalls
1839–1915

Robert Smalls of Beaufort, South Carolina, was one of the first African American heroes of the Civil War. A slave and a riverboat pilot, he took control of the *Planter*, a Confederate ship, and delivered it to the Union navy. The Union navy made him captain of the ship in 1863. After the war, he became a leader in the government.

LESSON 9 REVIEW

Check Understanding

1 **Remember the Facts** Why did South Carolinians fight in the American Revolution?

2 **Recall the Main Idea** What part has South Carolina played in our country's history?

Think Critically

3 **Past to Present** How do the events of South Carolina's past affect you today?

Show What You Know

Make a Venn Diagram Think about what happened during the American Revolution. Then find examples of people today who are fighting for freedom or independence. Use a Venn diagram to compare and contrast the present-day events with those of the American Revolution. Display your diagram on a bulletin board.

FOCUS
How has South Carolina changed in the last century?

Main Idea Read about South Carolina's roles in America's history in the twentieth century.

Vocabulary
textile
equal rights

South Carolina in the Twentieth Century

Many of the problems and bad feelings of Reconstruction stayed with the state well into the twentieth century, or the 1900s. South Carolina would go through many more changes to become the state it is today.

Textile Mills

For many years South Carolina had made most of its money through farming, mainly the growing of cotton. However, most of the mills that used cotton to make **textiles**, or woven cloth, were in the North. This changed in the years following the Civil War.

The photograph below shows workers in Mount Pleasant in 1875 carrying the day's cotton harvest. The photograph on the right shows the great spinning room of a textile mill in Columbia in 1903.

In the 1880s several textile mills were built in the Up Country counties of Anderson, Greenville, and Spartanburg. By the 1890s the state was in a textile boom, or time of quick growth. Farming was still important, but many people worked in textile mills, too.

South Carolina's textile industry continued to grow during the early 1900s. By 1915 South Carolina led the southern United States in textiles. Today South Carolina's textile business is still important to the state.

Textiles are made at Delta Woodside's Beattie Plant in Fountain Inn.

REVIEW In what counties did South Carolina's textile boom begin?

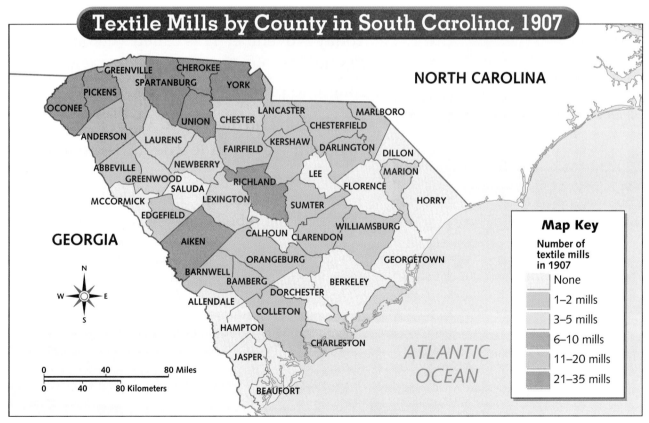

Textile Mills by County in South Carolina, 1907

NORTH CAROLINA

GEORGIA

GREENVILLE CHEROKEE
SPARTANBURG YORK
PICKENS
OCONEE
LANCASTER MARLBORO
UNION CHESTER CHESTERFIELD
ANDERSON LAURENS KERSHAW DARLINGTON DILLON
FAIRFIELD MARION
ABBEVILLE NEWBERRY LEE
GREENWOOD RICHLAND FLORENCE
SALUDA
MCCORMICK LEXINGTON SUMTER HORRY
EDGEFIELD
WILLIAMSBURG
AIKEN CALHOUN CLARENDON
ORANGEBURG GEORGETOWN
BARNWELL
BAMBERG BERKELEY
ALLENDALE DORCHESTER
COLLETON
HAMPTON
CHARLESTON
JASPER ATLANTIC OCEAN
BEAUFORT

Map Key

Number of textile mills in 1907

None
1–2 mills
3–5 mills
6–10 mills
11–20 mills
21–35 mills

0   40   80 Miles
0   40   80 Kilometers

Location ■ In 1907 how many counties had between 6–10 textile mills?

This World War I poster was drawn by James Montgomery Flagg in 1917.

World War I

In 1914 a war started in Europe. Many countries took part in the fighting. The United States joined this war, later called World War I, in 1917.

During the war South Carolina's textile mills became important to the rest of the country and the world. They made cloth for uniforms, blankets, tents, and many other important supplies.

Soldiers from all over the country came to South Carolina to train. People in the army trained in Columbia, in Greenville, and in Spartanburg. Marines trained at Parris Island and at the Charleston Navy Yard.

The war ended on November 11, 1918. Today November 11 is called Veterans Day. On this day we honor the people who fought to protect our country.

REVIEW During World War I, what was the cloth woven in textile mills used for?

▼ At Camp Jackson in Columbia, soldiers lived in these buildings, called barracks.

▲ In 1918 these men were photographed at Camp Jackson.

Camp Jackson · Columbia, S.C.
Taken from 100 foot tower

The Great Depression

After the war, South Carolina's textile industry slowed down. In the 1920s insects called boll (BOHL) weevils destroyed much of the cotton crop. Many cotton growers went out of business.

In 1929 a time known as the Great Depression began. Thousands of people in South Carolina and the rest of the United States did not have jobs or homes. Since people did not have money to spend, many businesses had to close. Hundreds of banks closed, too, because people who had borrowed money could not pay them back. The Great Depression lasted almost ten years.

In 1933 President Franklin D. Roosevelt (ROH•zuh•velt) started programs to end the Great Depression. One of these programs was the Civilian Conservation Corps, or CCC. The CCC hired thousands of people to do all kinds of jobs. In South Carolina CCC workers planted trees and built state parks. When people had work, they had money to spend, and the country began to recover.

During the Great Depression, life was very hard for many people.

REVIEW What was the Great Depression?

CCC workers at Table Rock State Park, South Carolina

The Tuskegee Airmen

The Tuskegee (tuh•SKEE•gee) Airmen were the first African American airplane pilots to serve in the United States military. They were some of the best pilots in World War II. Many of the Tuskegee Airmen were trained in Walterboro, South Carolina. A monument there honors their courage.

World War II

In 1939 countries around the world began fighting again. The United States did not enter the war at first. Then on December 7, 1941, Japanese planes attacked the navy base at Pearl Harbor, Hawaii. The next day, the United States joined World War II.

About 170,000 South Carolinians were sent all over the world to fight. South Carolina's training camps were busy again. South Carolina's textile mills were busy again, too.

With so many men away fighting, there were not enough workers at home. Before this time, most women had not worked outside their homes. Now women took jobs in the military, the government, and in factories to keep the country going. By August 1945 Germany and Japan had surrendered. Many people had died to keep our country free.

REVIEW **What did women do in wartime?**

◄ **Tuskegee flight instructors**

► **South Carolina Women's Air Force Service Pilots**

Freedom for All South Carolinians

More than one million African Americans fought in World War II. They fought for the freedom of all Americans. However, they were still not free in their own country.

In the South, African Americans were still separated from whites. They had to go to different schools and churches. The government said that having separate places for African Americans and whites was allowed, as long as those places were equal. Most of the time, however, they were not equal.

Many people worked hard for change and the promise of freedom. Dr. Martin Luther King, Jr., was one African American who worked for **equal rights**, the same rights for all people. Dr. King led peaceful marches and held planning meetings at Penn Community Center on St. Helena Island.

Over many years, some things changed in South Carolina. African American children could go to the same schools as other children. In 1963 Harvey Gantt became the first African American to go to Clemson University. He later became the first African American mayor of Charlotte, North Carolina. Today people continue to work for equal rights.

REVIEW Where did Dr. King hold meetings?

Mary McLeod Bethune 1875–1955

Mary McLeod Bethune was born in Mayesville, South Carolina. As a child, she worked in the nearby cotton fields. Bethune wanted an education. She studied hard and became a teacher. After moving to Florida, she started a school for young African American women. It later became Bethune-Cookman College.

Dr. Martin Luther King, Jr., and Reverend Jesse Jackson in Frogmore, South Carolina in 1965

South Carolina Today

Farming continues to be an important way for South Carolinians to earn money. It is also an important way of life for many people in the state. Today South Carolina's most important crops are tobacco and soybeans. South Carolina is also second in the nation in peach growing.

Tourism has become more and more important to South Carolina. For example, people come to South Carolina to play golf or to watch auto racing in Darlington. People also come from all over the world to visit the beaches, mountains, and historic places and to go hiking and camping in South Carolina's state parks.

This researcher works at the Medical University of South Carolina in Charleston.

HISTORY

Hurricane Hugo

In 1989 Hurricane Hugo struck South Carolina. It destroyed many homes, but people worked together to rebuild.

The small photo shows people from McClellanville sharing a meal after the hurricane. The large photo shows damage in Charleston from the hurricane.

Today many people at the Medical University of South Carolina work on inventions to help doctors save lives. Several South Carolinians have been astronauts. Their work has made South Carolina a leader in science and space exploration.

Whatever the future brings to South Carolina, its people will work together to make their state a good place to live.

REVIEW Why do people visit South Carolina?

South Carolina's astronauts

1. Charles F. Bolden, Jr.   3. John H. Casper   5. Charles M. Duke, Jr.
2. Frank L. Culbertson   4. Catherine G. Coleman   6. Ronald E. McNair

---

LESSON 10 REVIEW

Check Understanding

❶ Remember the Facts What destroyed the cotton crops in the 1920s?

❷ Recall the Main Idea What roles did South Carolina play in the twentieth century?

Think Critically

❸ Personally Speaking What are some of the challenges that face your community today as it changes and grows?

❹ Link to You What can you do to make South Carolina a better place in which to live?

Show What You Know

Make a Storycloth
A storycloth is a way to show important events with pictures. Draw pictures or cut out pictures from newspapers and magazines to make a storycloth about South Carolina today. Label each picture, and give your storycloth a title. Share it with a classmate, and talk about its meaning.

HONORING THEIR ANCESTORS

Rena Duncan is always excited when she discovers an artifact buried in the soil. She is even more excited when her father takes her into the mountains to see the ancient rock drawings on the walls of caves. Rena and her family live near the Uinta (yoo•IN•tah) Mountains in Utah.

One day Rena's dad took her to the Utah State Capitol Building in Salt Lake City. He showed her two white marble sculptures of Native Americans. He explained that one of the men was her great-great grandfather, John Duncan. The other man was her great-great-great grandfather, Unca Som. Rena noticed something. Neither one of the sculptures had a label that told who the person was.

Later, Rena traveled to Salt Lake City with her family and gave a speech to the Utah State Legislature. She talked about the nameless sculptures and the Native American ancestors they showed.

Everyone heard Rena's message. "Respect our ancestors. Respect the heritage they have given to us. Do not leave these sculptures nameless."

Soon after that day, the Utah State Legislature passed a resolution to identify the sculptures. Who do you suppose was invited to help place the nameplates on the sculptures? Rena Duncan!

▲ John Duncan

▲ Unca Som

▲ These drawings were made by Rena's ancestors.

Think and Apply

BUILDING CITIZENSHIP

Rena Duncan helped everyone know the history of her family and her Indian community. You can help people know the history of your community by finding out about sculptures or other interesting landmarks. When you learn something you think everyone should know, make a speech to your class about it.

HARCOURT BRACE

Visit the Internet at
http://www.hbschool.com
for additional resources.

VISUAL SUMMARY

Study the pictures and captions to help you review the events you read about in Unit 3.

Write a Poem Choose one of the events on this visual summary, and write a poem about how the community changed. Tell how those changes affected the people in the community. Read your poem to the class.

1 Some things in a community change, and some things stay the same. Communities can change quickly and slowly.

3 Mexico City is near the place where Tenochtitlán once stood.

5 New inventions in communication and transportation changed our country.

2 The Cheyennes' way of life changed while the Hoopas' way of life stayed the same.

4 Our country changed and stayed the same long ago.

UNIT 3
REVIEW

Complete this graphic organizer by writing the main idea for each lesson. A copy of the organizer appears on Activity Book page 48.

Communities Grow and Change

Lesson 1
Communities change yet stay the same.

Lesson 2
Some Native American communities changed while others did not.

Lesson 3
Aztec communities grew and changed long ago.

Lesson 4
Change in a community can create problems.

Lesson 5
People moved from England and settled in what is now the United States.

Lesson 6
Inventions change communication and transportation.

Lesson 7
Every community has a history.

WRITE MORE ABOUT IT

Write a Letter How would you feel if you saw an old building being torn down? Imagine you have learned that your community government plans to tear down an old building. Write a letter to tell others why the government should or should not go ahead with its plans.

USE VOCABULARY

Words that describe time, culture, and freedom are important when you write about history. Write a paragraph about your community, using each of the following words in a sentence.

1. artifacts
2. century
3. decade
4. legend
5. independence

CHECK UNDERSTANDING

6. What can cause a community to change quickly?

7. Why did the Cheyennes use tepees as their homes?

8. Who did the colonists fight in the American Revolution?

THINK CRITICALLY

9. **Past to Present**   How can studying artifacts help you learn about people who lived long ago?

10. **Think More About It**   History is the story of what happens to people and their communities over time. How can you help make sure that the changes in your community will make it better?

11. **Personally Speaking**   Which of the following jobs would you choose to do? Tell how your job would help your community.

    Historian—A person who studies the past and writes about it.

    City Planner—A person who helps citizens decide where their city's new buildings, roads, and parks should be built.

APPLY SKILLS

Learn from Artifacts   This artifact is a tool called an adz. Answer the questions about this early tool.

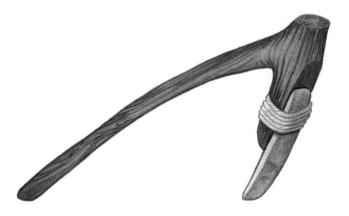

12. What do you think this tool is made of?

13. How do you think people long ago used this tool?

14. What present-day tool does it look like?

Compare Maps from Different Times

Compare this map to the map on pages A2–A3. Then answer the questions.

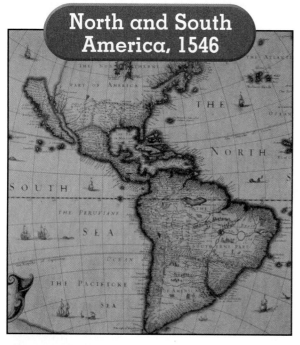

North and South America, 1546

15 Which map makes it easier to tell where countries are located?

16 How do you think each map was made? Why do you think that?

Solve a Problem

Read these paragraphs. Then answer the questions that follow.

An oil spill in the ocean near Valdez (val•DEEZ), Alaska, caused many problems for the otters that lived in the water. When an otter is covered with oil, its body cannot stay warm. If the otter becomes too cold, it will die.

To solve this problem, volunteers worked to wash the oil from the otters' fur. They brought the otters to special cleaning areas and washed them gently with soap. When their fur was dry, they washed them again until all the oil was gone. In the first summer after the spill, 348 otters were cleaned. Of those otters, 226 survived.

17 What steps did volunteers take to help solve the problem?

18 Do you think the rescue workers solved the problem? Why or why not?

READ MORE ABOUT IT

The Blue and the Gray by Eve Bunting. Illustrated by Ned Bittinger. Scholastic. Two boys discover how the Civil War changed the land that surrounds their homes.

Visit the Internet at **http://www.hbschool.com** for additional resources.

REMEMBER

- Share your ideas.
- Cooperate with others to plan your work.
- Take responsibility for your work.
- Help one another.
- Show your group's work to the class.
- Discuss what you learned by working together.

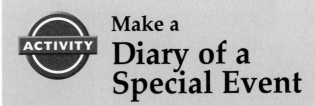

ACTIVITY

Make a Diary of a Special Event

Choose a special event that has happened to a community. Collect newspaper and magazine articles about it. Then imagine that you lived through it, and make a diary about it. In your diary, explain what caused the event to happen and how it affected the community. Tell how people in the community worked together to help each other.

Unit Project Wrap-Up

Make a History Scrapbook Work with a group of classmates to finish the History Scrapbook activity that was described on page 163. Together, look at the information you have gathered. Decide which information you will use and who will write a one-page report for each subject. Give the reports titles, and add maps, photographs, or drawings to them. Then put your reports in a class scrapbook. Share your History Scrapbook with community leaders.

PEOPLE WORKING TOGETHER

People in communities live together. They have fun together. They also help one another and work together to get things done.

◀ Young people work together washing cars to raise money.

KEY CONCEPTS

- consumer
- marketing
- product
- service
- technology

Unit Project

Make a Bulletin Board Display As you study Unit 4, complete this project to show the steps in a manufacturing process. Decide which process you will illustrate. Get information about the subject from newspapers, books, and businesses. Organize the information, and put it on the bulletin board. Invite other classes to see the display.

marketing Planning how to sell a product to a community.

product Something that people make or grow, often to sell.

service Something that one person does for another.

consumer The person who buys a product or service.

technology The use of machines, tools, and materials to make products faster and more easily.

REUBEN and the FIRE

by Merle Good   illustrated by P. Buckley Moss

This is a story about a boy who lives in an Amish (AH•mish) community. The Amish are a group of people who follow their own religious ideas. They live and work together in their own communities. The Amish depend on each other for meeting most of their needs. For some things, however, they get help from people outside of their community. The story begins when Reuben and his friends see that a neighbor's barn is on fire.

Reuben had never run so hard. It looked like the smoke was coming from his homeplace.

"I hope it's not our barn," he gasped to the twins as he ran, trying to see over the tops of the crops.

They saw the billowing smoke as they came over the ridge. The roof of a barn was burning.

"It's Abner Fisher's place," Sam said. The three of them stopped, staring at the frightening scene.

"We better go home and tell our parents," Sam said.

"Glad it's not our place," Reuben replied.

The twins nodded. "Yeah, but I feel sorry for Abner's family," Sam said.

Annie was hurrying out of the barn as Reuben came running around the corner. She looked upset.

"Can I go along over to the fire?" he asked.

"Better get a fork and a shovel if you're going," she said. "But be quick."

Annie Reuben's oldest sister

It was hot and scary close to the fire.
Neighbors were letting out the cows and horses.

"Can I help?" Reuben asked Abner.

"There are five little puppies in the milk house,"
Abner's oldest son answered. "See if someone can
help you move them to the house. But be careful."

The fire was still at the other end of the big barn.
Sam and Ben drove up with their father just in time
to help Reuben carry the pups to the back porch of
the house.

They could feel the heat of the fire as they ran,
big eyes and droopy ears in their arms.

Ben Sam's twin

Reuben had never seen so many fire trucks. They came from everywhere, lights flashing red.

At first, everyone was afraid the house would burn too, but the firemen quickly sprayed water on it.

It was past midnight when Reuben crawled into bed. Dawdi had waited for them and wanted to hear all about the fire.

Dawdi (DAW•dee)
Grandfather

At first Reuben couldn't sleep, his mind full of flashing lights and smoke. Then Mamm looked in on him and rubbed his forehead and his arm to help him relax. She was good that way.

Reuben dreamed that the puppies ran away on the fire truck.

Next morning Reuben could hardly stay awake during the milking. "Don't walk with your eyes closed," his sister Barbie complained.

At breakfast Datt announced the bad news. Reuben would have to stay home and bale the hay with Annie and Nancy.

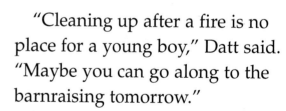

"Cleaning up after a fire is no place for a young boy," Datt said. "Maybe you can go along to the barnraising tomorrow."

Mamm baked all day, with Barbie and Mary helping. A lot of food was needed for the barnraising. Reuben drove the horses and Annie and Nancy stacked the bales.

A barnraising is like a holiday. It seemed to Reuben that everyone was there. His cousins from the southern end even came.

Ben and Sam brought their hammers, but they never got to use them. All the boys could do was watch and run errands if they were asked.

Big Henry Stoltzfus was the boss. Reuben liked him. By lunch the rafters were all in place. And the roof was going on before milking time.

"I'd like to be a carpenter like Big Henry," Sam said.

Ben laughed. "You better start growing."

Abner walked up to Datt and Reuben as they were leaving. He had one of the little pups in his arm. "Thanks for your help," he smiled. He looked tired.

"Gladly," Datt said. "We'll be back tomorrow if you can use us."

Abner smiled again. "Reuben, this puppy needs a home." Reuben couldn't believe it. He looked at Datt, afraid he'd say no. But his father nodded with a smile.

FOCUS
How do you work with others in your community, school, and home?

Main Idea Read to find out how people in the Amish community work together to meet their needs.

Vocabulary
basic needs
rural
service
product

People in an Amish Community Work Together

Reuben's Amish community has a way of life that is different from most communities. But the Amish have the same basic needs as people in every community. Those **basic needs** are food, clothing, and shelter.

The Amish Way of Life

The Amish way of life began in Europe. The name *Amish* comes from Jacob Ammann, an early leader. The first Amish people to move to the United States came from Switzerland in the early 1700s. They came to find a place where they could follow their religion and a simple way of life. For this reason, they did not settle in big cities. Instead, they started their own communities in rural areas. A **rural** area is in the countryside, away from cities and towns.

The Amish live much as their ancestors did more than 200 years ago. The women and girls wear long dresses, aprons, and caps. The men and boys wear plain shirts, pants with suspenders, and straw or black cloth hats.

Amish children enjoy playing games.

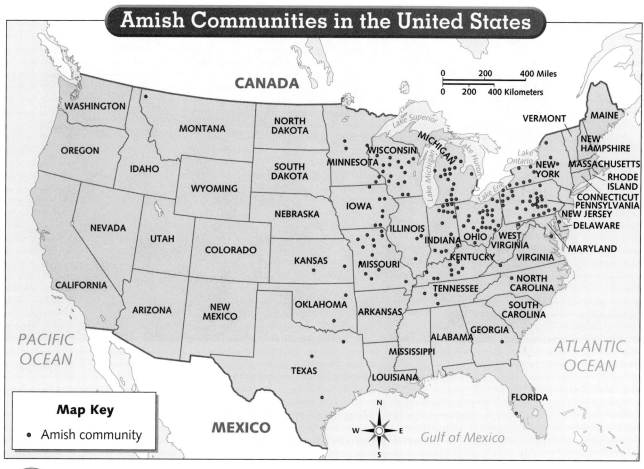

Amish Communities in the United States

CANADA

Map Key
• Amish community

Location ■ In which states are many Amish communities located?

Most Amish people are farmers. They grow most of the food used by their community. Amish farmers use horses instead of tractors to pull their plows.

Amish homes have no electricity. The Amish use lanterns to provide light for reading or sewing at night. They do not own or use computers, televisions, or radios. They live this way to keep their lives simple and free from other peoples' beliefs.

REVIEW Why did the Amish move to the United States from Switzerland?

The Amish do not own or drive cars. Instead, they drive buggies— small wagons pulled by horses.

A Barn Is Built

In "Reuben and the Fire," Reuben and his family
and friends help a neighbor build a new barn after
the old one burns down. Helping each other is an
important part of Amish community life. If one
Amish family has a problem, the rest of the Amish
community helps the family solve it. They say, "It
is better for a group to work together than for a
person to labor alone."

When a family in an Amish community needs
a new barn, the people get together for a barn
raising. As you learned in the story, men, women,
and children from the community gather early in
the morning with materials and tools. They work
all day long. By the time it is dark, they have built a
new barn. While the men and boys are building,
the women and girls are cooking and serving
meals. No one is ever paid money for working at a
barn raising. People do it to help each other. After
the barn is finished, families in the community may
even fill the new barn with their own hay.

The Amish build their own homes and barns. They also make their own clothing. They make by hand many of the things they need. By working together, they can meet most of the basic needs of their families and community.

REVIEW **What is a barn raising?**

Amish People Depend on the Outside World

Sometimes the Amish must get help from other people. In "Reuben and the Fire," firefighters from other communities helped put out the barn fire. Those firefighters provided a service. A **service** is something one person does for another. Police officers and teachers provide services. So do carpenters and plumbers. The Amish have no doctors in their communities. When a doctor's help is needed, the Amish must get this service from outside their community.

People outside the Amish community use Amish services, too. Some Amish men work as carpenters or blacksmiths. Blacksmiths work with iron to make horseshoes and tools.

Car-repair people provide a service by fixing cars.

◄ This doctor provides a service by helping people keep healthy.

This Amish blacksmith provides a service by making things from iron. ►

A quilt is made by sewing together small pieces of cloth. Amish women and girls make and sell quilts to earn money. They will save the money and use it to pay for the items and services they need.

Besides providing services, the Amish make products to sell to people outside the community. A **product** is something that people make or grow, often to sell.

Quilts are one kind of product Amish people make. Quilts are used as covers on beds or as wall hangings. Often they have interesting and beautiful designs. Amish women and girls work in groups to sew the quilts. Then they sell them to people from other communities. Other products the Amish sell are cheese, vegetables, jellies and jams, and tools made from wood.

The Amish buy products from outside their community that they cannot make themselves. They buy fuel for their lanterns and materials for building new barns and homes. They buy cloth for making clothes and quilts. They also buy shoes.

Amish children wear clothes that have been made by hand. But they buy athletic shoes because they last longer than handmade shoes.

The Amish have a different way of life. But in some ways their communities are just like others. People need to buy products they cannot make and services they cannot provide. To get the money to do this, they sell their products and services to others.

REVIEW What are some products and services the Amish buy from other communities?

The Amish sell their products to people from other communities.

Stores in any community offer products for people to buy.

LESSON 1 REVIEW

Check Understanding

❶ **Remember the Facts** Why are products and services important to people?

❷ **Recall the Main Idea** In what ways do Amish people help each other in their own communities?

Think Critically

❸ **Think More About It** What products and services are important to you and your family or community? Why?

Show What You Know

Quilting Activity Fold a sheet of paper into three parts, first the long way and then the short way. Now unfold it. You will have nine boxes like the squares of a quilt. In each box, draw a picture that shows something about the Amish way of life. Use your textbook or another book for ideas. Add your "Amish quilt" to a classroom display, and talk about your drawings.

Read Graphs

1. Why Learn This Skill?

Sometimes you need to compare sets of numbers. A graph can make it easier. There are several kinds of graphs. Two of them are shown on this page. A **pictograph** is a graph that uses symbols to show amounts of things. A **bar graph** uses bars to show amounts of things.

2. Understand the Process

Compare the two graphs. Each has a title that tells you what it is about. The pictograph has a key to explain what the pictures stand for.

The bar graph has labels that explain what the bars show. Use the graphs to answer these questions.

1 Were more quilts sold on Wednesday or on Saturday?

2 On which day were the most quilts sold? How many were sold that day?

3 How many quilts were sold in all?

3. Think and Apply

Think of something you would like to show on a graph. Then gather the information and make a pictograph and a bar graph. Share your graphs with your classmates.

Quilt Sales for One Week	
DAY OF THE WEEK	NUMBER OF QUILTS SOLD
Monday	◆ ◆ ◆
Tuesday	◆
Wednesday	◆ ◆ ◆ ◆
Thursday	◆ ◆
Friday	◆ ◆
Saturday	◆ ◆ ◆ ◆ ◆

◆ = 5 quilts

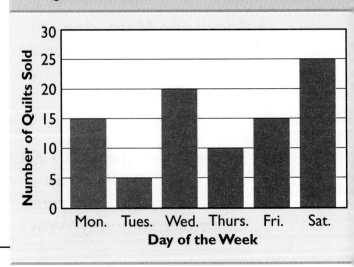

Quilt Sales for One Week

People Work Together to Make a Product

LESSON
2

FOCUS
How are most products made?

Main Idea   Read to find out how people work together to make products.

Vocabulary
technology
producer
raw materials
marketing
human resources
wage
industry

The Amish people work together to make their products by hand. But most of the products you use every day are manufactured, or made by machines.

Working Together in a Factory

Many of the products you use are made by machines, not by hand. Workers in factories use machines to make great numbers of products very quickly. The use of machines, tools, and materials to make products faster and more easily is called **technology**.

In one community in Illinois, a factory makes a certain product—bicycle helmets. The people who make a product are called **producers**. In that factory, work is done in steps to produce the helmets.

Products like crayons and bicycle helmets are made in factories.

273

1. Designing the Product

A group works together in the factory to design the helmets. Some people work with computers, and some work on paper. They use drawings and models to decide what the helmets should be like. Designers talk to scientists to find out whether there are new materials they might use in producing the helmets. They make a few sample helmets and test their safety. In some factories designers do these tests on computers without making samples first.

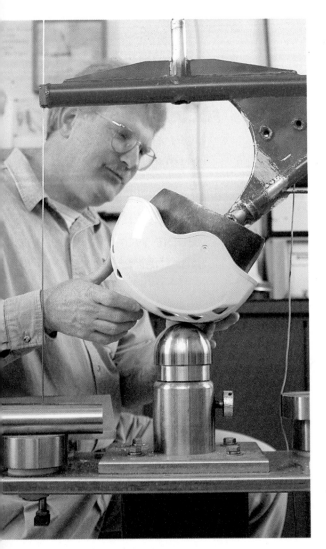

The helmet is tested for safety.

2. Getting the Materials

When all the safety tests have been passed, the raw materials, such as plastics, for making the helmets must be bought. **Raw materials** are the resources needed to make a product. These materials are shipped to the factory from places around the world.

Black foam pellets will be used as a cushion for the helmet.

Machines are used to make the outer shell of the helmet.

A plastic coating is added to the shell of the helmet.

3. Making the Product

Workers use machines to make each part of the helmets. One kind of machine makes the shell, or outside, of the helmets. Another kind of machine produces the straps. Some workers make the same part all the time. Other workers assemble, or put together, all the different parts.

4. Marketing the Product

Marketing means planning how to sell a product. The people who work in marketing plan how to get people to buy the helmets. They also decide the best places to sell them.

REVIEW How are most products made today?

Straps are attached to the helmet.

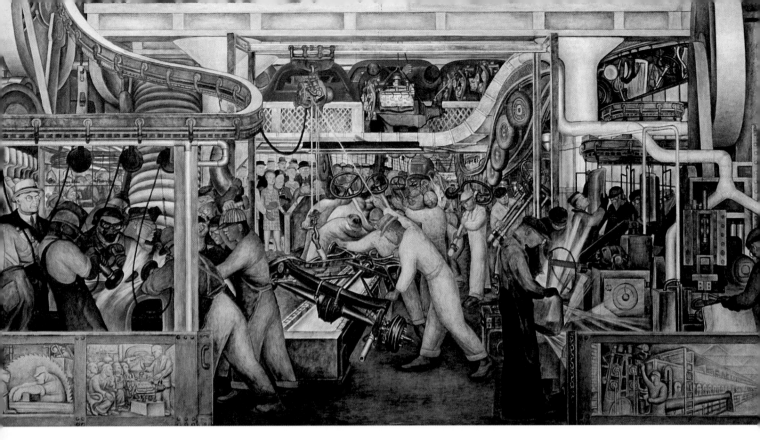

Money is one of the resources necessary for making products.

Using Resources

It takes more than raw materials to make helmets. It takes other kinds of resources, too. A company's most important resource is its people. **Human resources** are the people who work for a company. It takes many people working together to make a product.

Another important resource that is needed to make the helmets is money. Money is needed to build and keep up the factory. It is also needed to buy the machines and raw materials to make the helmets.

Money is needed to pay the workers, too. The workers are paid **wages** for the work they do. The people who own the factory must have enough money for all the resources they need. They must have this money before the first helmet can be made.

REVIEW What are human resources?

Industries

You have just read about how one factory produces bicycle helmets. There are more than 50 companies around the world that manufacture these helmets. The many companies that make bicycle helmets are part of an industry. An **industry** is made up of all the companies that make the same product or provide the same service.

The bicycle helmet industry is just one industry that is needed by people who ride bicycles. They also need the bicycle and bicycle tire industries. The shipping industry is important, too. Shipping companies move products from where they are made to where they are sold. Communities all over the world depend on both service and product industries to meet their needs.

REVIEW **What is an industry?**

The clothing industry produces the clothes you wear every day.

LESSON 2 REVIEW

Check Understanding

❶ **Remember the Facts** What kinds of resources are needed to manufacture a product?

❷ **Recall the Main Idea** How do people work together to make products in a factory?

Think Critically

❸ **Cause and Effect** How do you think the making of products in factories has changed the way people live and work?

Show What You Know

Writing Activity Think about a product you would like to make. What kinds of resources would you need to make your product? Where would you get these resources? Now write a how-to paragraph. In your paragraph, tell each of the steps you would follow in manufacturing the product. Share your paragraph with a small group of classmates. Then turn your idea into a real product.

Use a Flow Chart

1. Why Learn This Skill?

You have read that there are many steps in making bicycle helmets. These steps and their order could be shown on a flow chart. A **flow chart** shows the steps that must be followed to make or do something. It also shows the order in which the steps must be done.

2. Understand the Process

Suppose you needed to know how to change a bicycle tire. You could look at this flow chart and follow the steps.

The title of the flow chart tells you what it is about. Each picture has a sentence that describes the step. How many steps are shown?

HOW TO CHANGE A BICYCLE TIRE

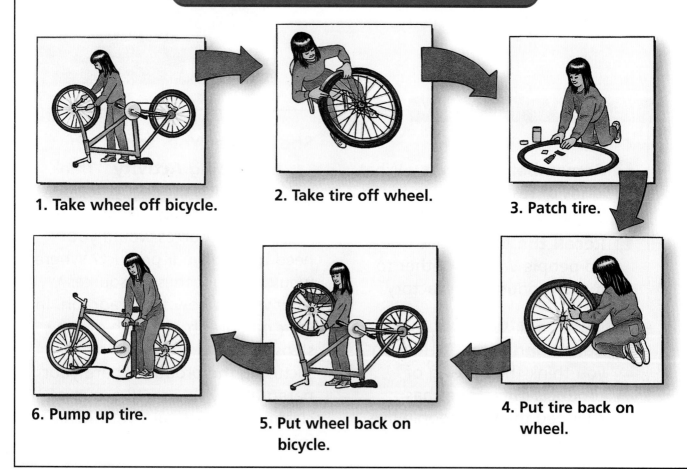

1. Take wheel off bicycle.

2. Take tire off wheel.

3. Patch tire.

4. Put tire back on wheel.

5. Put wheel back on bicycle.

6. Pump up tire.

Tires are used on automobiles, buses, and trucks, as well as on bicycles. The flow chart below shows some of the steps in making tires. What is the first step? What happens after the rubber and oils are mixed? What happens after that?

3. Think and Apply

Think about a job you know how to do, such as setting the table or making your bed. If you were to make a flow chart about that job, what steps would you show?

HOW AUTOMOBILE TIRES ARE MADE

1. Rubber and oils are mixed in giant blenders.

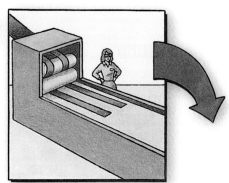

2. Rubber is cut into strips to become tire parts.

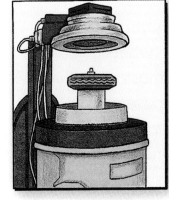

5. Tire is popped from mold and is ready to be inspected.

4. Rubber is put into a tire building machine and baked at a high temperature.

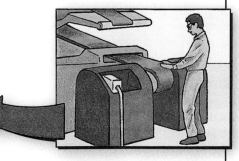

3. Steel and fabrics are added to the rubber.

FOCUS

What makes a person decide to buy one product or service rather than another?

Main Idea Read to find out how people decide to buy a product or service.

Vocabulary

consumer
price
competition
supply
demand
advertisement

People Buy Products and Services

People work together to make products and provide services. In communities everywhere, people buy those products and services every day.

Deciding What to Buy

The person who buys a product or a service is called a **consumer**. A consumer has to think about many things before buying. Suppose you were a consumer looking for new bicycle equipment. How would you decide what to buy?

Most people cannot have everything they want. Consumers have to decide what products they need or want the most and what things they can do without. Suppose you wanted to buy both a jacket and a bicycle helmet but had only enough money for one. You might decide that safety was more important than a new jacket. Then you would choose to buy the helmet and wear your old jacket.

These consumers have saved enough money to buy a bicycle helmet. Now they must decide which helmet they will buy.

Another thing consumers keep in mind is price. The **price** is the amount of money needed to buy a product or service. Factories decide the price they will charge the stores for the helmets they ship to them. Then the stores decide the price they will charge the consumers.

The price of a product can depend on competition. Companies that produce and sell the same product are in **competition** with one another. Each one tries to sell more of the product. There are several companies in the United States that make and sell bicycle helmets. Each company wants consumers to buy its helmets rather than those made by the others. So each company tries to make the best product and keep its price as low as possible.

Stores often put different companies' products side by side so that consumers can decide which one to buy. Many consumers choose the product with the lowest price.

When many companies are in competition, prices may be lower.

When stores are in competition, each tries to sell the same products at the lowest prices.

281

When the supply of a product is too high, stores often lower the price to raise demand for the product.

Competition takes place between stores, too. Two stores may sell the same product, but their prices may be different. A consumer who compares prices may choose to buy the product from the store that has the lower price.

The price of a product can also depend on supply and demand. **Supply** is the amount of a product or service there is to be sold. If there are many helmets waiting to be bought, the supply is high. If there are few helmets, the supply is low. **Demand** is the need or desire that people have for a product or a service. If there are many people who will buy bicycle helmets, the demand is high. If there are few people who will buy helmets, the demand is low.

REVIEW What can competition do to price?

Advertisements Affect Choices

You might want to buy a certain bicycle helmet because of its low price. However, there are other things to keep in mind. For example, you want to make sure that a helmet will protect your head in an accident. You might also want to know how much it weighs or what colors it comes in.

Where could you find this kind of information? You might look at advertisements on television or in magazines and newspapers. An **advertisement** is information that a producer provides about its products or services. Advertisements try to get consumers to buy a product or service.

Some advertisements are written for consumers your age. They use words, colors, and music that young people like. However, bright colors and popular music in an advertisement should not be the reason you choose a product. Consumers need to be careful. Sometimes they should get information from places other than an advertisement.

REVIEW What is an advertisement?

You'll be the coolest kid on the bike path when you wear the *Heads Up Helmet!*

AVAILABLE IN 5 NEON COLORS

MEETS THE HIGHEST STANDARDS FOR SAFETY

LEARNING FROM ADVERTISEMENTS
What information does this helmet advertisement give you? Would it make you want to buy the helmet?

Comparing Bicycle Helmets

BRAND	PRICE	WEIGHT (in ounces)	CRASH-TEST RESULTS	APPEARANCE
A	$30.00	8	very good	good
B	$25.00	8	good	very good
C	$40.00	10	very good	excellent
D	$30.00	12	excellent	good

LEARNING FROM TABLES Information about several bicycle helmets is shown in this table.

■ How can using a table make it easier for you to decide which helmet to buy?

This computer can be easily snapped on and off a bicycle.

Raising Demand

What fits in your hand and tells you the time, the temperature, and how far you have traveled? A bicycle computer can do all these things. When bicycle riders learned about this invention, demand for it grew very fast. Many bicycle riders wanted to own a bicycle computer. The demand was so great that factories could not make enough of this product for all the people who wanted to buy it.

The demand for products is always changing. New inventions and advertisements can cause greater demand. Two other things that can raise demand are new laws and better products.

Many people in communities have strong feelings about bicycle safety. They work with community leaders to pass laws that say bicycle riders must wear helmets. These laws have caused a demand for helmets. As more communities pass these laws, more people will buy helmets. Producers will have to make more helmets to keep up with the demand from consumers.

Demand also grows when a new material or new technology makes a product better. Early bicycle helmets were made of thick foam and plastic. They were heavy and did not fit well. Then scientists invented new materials to make helmets lighter and safer. These changes even made helmets cost less and look better! More bicycle riders are now wearing helmets, and many riders who wore the old kind have bought new ones.

REVIEW How does technology create demand?

BIOGRAPHY

Peter Beal
1985–

Two days after his eleventh birthday, Peter Beal was hit by a car while riding his bicycle. Peter is alive today only because he was wearing a bicycle helmet. In his California school, Peter tells other students about bicycle helmet safety. If he sees a student riding without a helmet, he tells that boy or girl how wearing a bicycle helmet saved his life.

LESSON 3 REVIEW

Check Understanding

1 Remember the Facts What is a consumer?

2 Recall the Main Idea How do people decide which product or service to buy?

Think Critically

3 Personally Speaking Do you think advertisements can help consumers make good choices? Why or why not?

Show What You Know

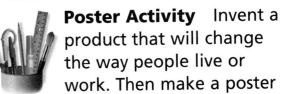

Poster Activity Invent a product that will change the way people live or work. Then make a poster that advertises your invention. Use bright colors and interesting words to persuade people to buy your product. You can make drawings or cut pictures from magazines for your poster. Now share your poster with the class.

Make an Economic

1. Why Learn This Skill ?

When you buy something at a store, you are making a choice about how to spend your money. Sometimes the choice is hard to make. In order to buy or do one thing, you have to give up buying or doing something else. This is called a **trade-off**. What you give up is the **opportunity cost** of what you get. Knowing about trade-offs and opportunity costs can help you make good choices.

2. Remember What You Have Read

All people today have to make choices about what to buy. They, too, face trade-offs and opportunity costs. Choices can be made both easier and more difficult by new inventions, technology, and advertisements. Consumers must be careful with their buying decisions.

3. Understand the Process

Imagine that you need to buy a bicycle helmet. You will have to make a choice. Should you buy the newest style of helmet from a bicycle store? Or should you buy a cheaper helmet from a discount department store?

1 Think about the trade-offs—the good and bad sides of your choice. The helmet at the bicycle store may be the newest style. It may have brighter colors and newer technology. However, it costs more. The helmet from the discount store may not have the style and bright colors, but it is still a safe helmet. It also costs less.

2 Next think about the opportunity costs. If you buy the helmet from the bicycle store, you will spend all your money. If you buy the helmet from the

Choice

discount store, you will have money left over that you can save or spend on something else.

Most of the time you cannot have everything you want, so there will always be opportunity costs as you trade off one product for another. The product you give up may be a good one, but another product may be a better choice for you. What choice will you make?

4. Think and Apply

Imagine that a family member has given you $20 for your birthday. How will you spend it? You do not have to spend all your money on one thing. You can choose some of one thing and some of another. Decide what you would buy with $20. Then explain to a partner the trade-offs and opportunity costs of your choice.

This boy is trying to decide which book to buy. He is making an economic choice.

Saturday Sancocho

written and illustrated
by Leyla Torres

Instead of using money to buy a product or service, people might sometimes *barter*, or trade, with one another. In this story you will meet Maria Lili and her grandparents. They live in a small town in South America. They want to make their special chicken sancocho (sahn•KOH•choh), a kind of stew. But they have no money for shopping. Read to find out how Maria Lili and her grandmother get what they need for their meal.

Every Saturday, Maria Lili looked forward to making chicken sancocho with her grandparents Mama Ana and Papa Angelino. Just the thought of stew simmering on the stove and filling the house with the aroma of cilantro made her mouth water. But one Saturday morning Papa Angelino announced, "There is no money for sancocho. Not even a penny to buy the vegetables, let alone a chicken. All we have is a dozen eggs."

"Then we will use the eggs to make sancocho," replied Mama Ana.

"Egg sancocho! Everyone knows sancocho is not prepared with eggs," said Maria Lili.

Smiling, Mama Ana removed her apron and asked Maria Lili to take two baskets and place the eggs in one of them.

"Come, my dear, we are going to the market."
And off they went.

cilantro
(sih•LAHN•troh)
a flavoring made
from the leaves of
a certain plant

At the market square they walked from stall to stall. First they found Don Eugenio and his son, Sebastian. Mama Ana persuaded Don Eugenio to accept six eggs for a bunch of green plantains. It did not take much bargaining; Sebastian was one of Maria Lili's classmates.

The next stop was the stall of Doña Carmen. She was not interested in the eggs, but Mama Ana managed to trade nine plantains for four pounds of thick cassava.

At first Don Mateo was not in the mood for bartering. It took some time for Mama Ana to convince him to take two pounds of cassava for six ears of corn. She gave him a couple of eggs as well. "So he doesn't pout," Mama Ana whispered, making sure the corn was fresh.

plantains
(PLAN•tuhnz) the bananalike fruits of a plant grown in warm countries for food

cassava
(kuh•SAH•vuh) the root of a plant grown in warm countries for food

Doña Dolores wanted all the corn for just eight carrots.

"All my corn? No, dear lady, your carrots are not that big," Mama Ana said. Doña Dolores settled for three ears of corn, and agreed that it was a fair exchange.

Under the noonday sun, Mama Ana and Maria Lili traded their remaining eggs for onions and tomatoes; tomatoes for cilantro; cilantro for garlic and garlic for cumin, always keeping some for themselves. But they still needed one more ingredient.

"The chicken. What about the chicken?" asked Maria Lili. "How are we going to get it?"

"I have an idea," said Mama Ana, wiping her brow. "Let's divide the vegetables equally between the two baskets."

Mama Ana offered one of the baskets to Doña Petrona in exchange for a large, red-feathered chicken.

"Impossible," Doña Petrona said, sniffing. "I'll give you this one instead." She showed Mama Ana a smaller one.

"No, it's much too skinny," said Mama Ana, frowning.

They haggled until Mama Ana added two more carrots and some cumin to the basket. Doña Petrona accepted the offer, handing Maria Lili a nice, potbellied chicken. It was not the largest one, but it was good enough for a wholesome stew.

haggled
(HA•guhld) argued over price

cumin
(KYOO•mihn) a spice made from seeds of the cumin plant

As Mama Ana and Maria Lili were leaving the marketplace, they passed Don Fernando's stall. He had always admired Mama Ana's hand-knit bags and suggested they trade the one Maria Lili was carrying for one of his wooden ladles. With a wink, he also handed her a colorful spinning top.

Papa Angelino plucked the chicken while Mama Ana boiled the water and peeled the vegetables. Maria Lili chopped the onions and the cilantro. This was a teary job.

That afternoon, no later than usual, they sat down to enjoy their chicken sancocho. Maria Lili ate slowly, blowing gently on each spoonful. The stew was delicious.

LITERATURE REVIEW

1. How did Maria Lili and Mama Ana get the things they needed to make the sancocho?

2. In bartering, why should the traded items be worth about the same amount? What would happen if you tried to trade a dozen eggs for a computer?

3. Think of a time when you traded one thing for another. What happened during your trade? Write a paragraph that explains what you traded and how you traded it. In your paragraph, also explain what made you decide to make a trade. Share your paragraph with your classmates.

Use a Map Grid

1. Why Learn This Skill?

One way to find a location is to use a map that has a grid. A **grid** is a set of lines the same distance apart that cross one another to form boxes. Learning to use a map grid will make it easier for you to quickly find locations on a map.

2. Understand the Process

Look at the grid below. You can see that a grid divides a space into boxes. Find the row labels—the letters along the sides of this grid. Now look for the column labels—the numbers at the top and at the bottom of this grid.

Find the box that is green, and put your finger on it. Now slide your finger to the left side of the grid. You will see that the green box is located in row C.

Put your finger on the green box again. Slide your finger to the top of the grid. You will see that the green

box is in column 4. To describe the location of the green box, you would say that it is at C–4. What is the location of the purple box?

Next look at the map of Quito, Ecuador on page 297. It has a grid. Use the map and its grid to answer these questions. Give a letter and a number when you are asked for a location.

1 Government buildings called embassies are located in different parts of the grid. Which countries' embassies can you find at A–4?

2 Where can you find the Supreme Court?

3 What buildings do you see in the box at D–5?

4 Where is the United States embassy?

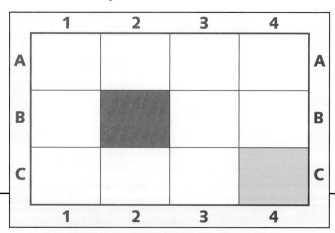

3. Think and Apply

Draw a map of a place you know. You might draw your neighborhood, your school, or your classroom. Add a grid so people can find places on your map.

Now share your map with a classmate or a family member. Ask that person to use the grid to give the location of something on the map.

Downtown Quito, Ecuador

ECUADOR
SOUTH AMERICA

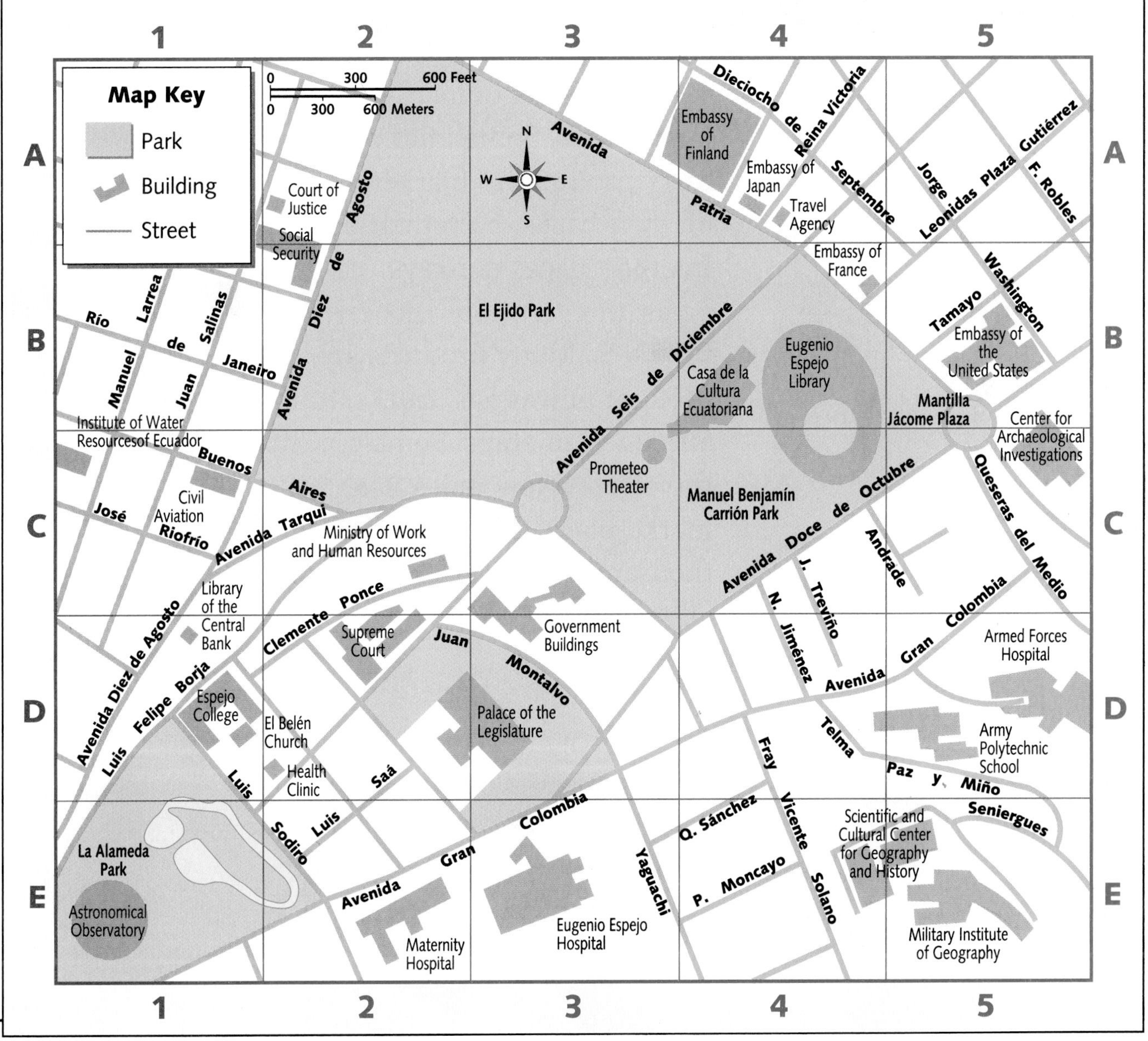
1
2
3
4
5
A
B
C
D
E
Map Key
Park
Building
Street
0
300
600 Feet
0
300
600 Meters
N
S
E
W
Court of Justice
Social Security
Avenida Diez de Agosto
Avenida
Patria
El Ejido Park
Embassy of Finland
Dieciocho de Septiembre
Reina Victoria
Embassy of Japan
Travel Agency
Embassy of France
Jorge
Leonidas Plaza Gutiérrez
F. Robles
Washington
Tamayo
Embassy of the United States
Mantilla Jácome Plaza
Center for Archaeological Investigations
Río de Janeiro
Larrea
Manuel
Juan
Salinas
Avenida Seis de Diciembre
Casa de la Cultura Ecuatoriana
Eugenio Espejo Library
Institute of Water Resourcesof Ecuador
Buenos Aires
Prometeo Theater
Manuel Benjamín Carrión Park
Avenida Doce de Octubre
Queseras del Medio
José
Riofrío
Civil Aviation
Avenida Tarqui
Ministry of Work and Human Resources
Andrade
J. Treviño
N. Jiménez
Library of the Central Bank
Clemente Ponce
Supreme Court
Juan Montalvo
Government Buildings
Avenida Gran Colombia
Armed Forces Hospital
Avenida Diez de Agosto
Luis Felipe Borja
Espejo College
El Belén Church
Health Clinic
Palace of the Legislature
Telma
Fray Vicente Solano
Paz y Miño
Army Polytechnic School
Luis Sodiro
Luis Saá
Seniergues
La Alameda Park
Astronomical Observatory
Avenida Gran Colombia
Yaguachi
Q. Sánchez
P. Moncayo
Scientific and Cultural Center for Geography and History
Maternity Hospital
Eugenio Espejo Hospital
Military Institute of Geography

FOCUS
How do people in your community buy products from other countries?

Main Idea
Read to find out how products all over the world get to marketplaces.

Vocabulary
international trade
communication links
import
export

The World Is a Marketplace

In "Saturday Sancocho" you read about a grandmother and granddaughter who took eggs to a marketplace. There they were able to barter the eggs for other products. In places all over the world, people take products to marketplaces.

International Trade

Products get to marketplaces in many ways. Sometimes people carry products to marketplaces on their backs or on their heads. In other places donkeys, goats, or even elephants carry products. Many products are brought in wagons, trucks, trains, airplanes, or ships. Some products travel just a few miles to a marketplace. Others may travel thousands of miles to marketplaces all over the world.

People take products to marketplaces in many different ways.

This painting shows European, African, and Asian traders in the early 1600s.

Today products from many countries can be bought in supermarkets.

Ships, trains, airplanes, and other types of transportation make it possible for people all over the world to trade with one another. Trade between people in different countries is called **international trade**.

People in different parts of the world have traded with one another for a very long time. Hundreds of years ago traders left their countries and traveled to new lands. They discovered things that they could not produce in their own countries. They returned home with new ideas as well as new products. The traders also discovered new trade routes that would make their trips easier and shorter. Their journeys, whether by ship, horse, or camel, often took months or even years.

REVIEW How is international trade today different from trade long ago?

The products being loaded onto this airplane will arrive at a marketplace in just one day.

Trading Becomes Easier and Faster

Today faster transportation and new technologies make trade between people in different nations almost as easy as trade between people who live in the same community. People living in different parts of the world can trade by using communication links. **Communication links** are machines that let people who are far apart communicate with one another. People use computers, telephones, and fax machines to buy and sell thousands of products and services. Today a person can use a telephone to order a product from someone on the other side of the world. With modern transportation, the product can arrive in a few days or weeks instead of in months or years.

An order for a product can be sent almost anywhere in the world by using a fax machine.

REVIEW How do communication links help trade?

Countries Depend on One Another

Many products, and many resources for making products, come from other countries. They are brought into the United States. To **import** is to bring a product or resource into one country from another country.

The United States also exports many products and resources to other countries. To **export** is to send a product or resource from one country to be sold in another country.

Most bicycle helmets are made in the United States, Australia, Canada, China, Great Britain, Italy, South Korea, and Taiwan. These countries export bicycle helmets to the rest of the world.

Some products are sent from one country to another by airplane. However, most large products, such as bicycles, are carried on container ships. These huge ships can carry thousands of tons of products from one port to another.

Movement
This map shows some of the products exported by different countries.
■ Which countries export products that people can eat or drink?

Some Major Worldwide Exports

Map Key

✈ Airplanes	👕 Clothing	💻 Computers	💎 Gems	🛢 Oil	🌾 Wheat
🚗 Cars	☕ Coffee	🌿 Cotton	🐂 Meat products	🌱 Soybeans	🧥 Wool products

The United States exports many kinds of products. At the same time, products made in other countries are imported into the United States. Think of all the things you use every day that were made in other parts of the world. Look at the labels in your clothing. You may read *Made in Hong Kong.* The shoes you wear may have been made in Spain, Italy, or Korea. Your toys may have come from Mexico, China, or Japan.

LEARNING FROM TABLES Which countries import natural resources? Which countries export manufactured products?

Major Imports and Exports

COUNTRY	MAJOR IMPORTS	MAJOR EXPORTS
Brazil	oil, chemicals, coal	coffee, iron ore, soybeans, sugar, shoes
France	oil, iron and steel products, chemicals	clothing, machinery, chemicals, cars, airplanes
India	oil, chemicals, fertilizer, machinery	gems, jewelry, clothing, cotton fabric
Saudi Arabia	manufactured products, food, cars	oil
South Africa	car parts, machinery, chemicals	gold, diamonds, minerals, metals
United States	oil, machinery, cars	machinery, chemicals, airplanes, grains, cars

Countries depend on one another for the products their citizens must have. The world is a huge marketplace that can supply things that people want and need.

REVIEW How is an export different from an import?

LESSON 5 REVIEW

Check Understanding

1 **Remember the Facts** What is trade between countries called?

2 **Recall the Main Idea** What are some of the ways products from all over the world get to marketplaces?

Think Critically

3 **Explore Viewpoints** In what ways do you think trade brings people around the world together? How could trade cause them to disagree?

Show What You Know

Map Activity First, make a list of products from other countries that you and your family use. Second, draw a simple map of the world, and label the continents. Next, draw a symbol for each product on the continent where it was made. Then, draw an arrow from that continent to where you live. Next, give your map a title, and make a map key that explains your symbols. Finally, share your map with a classmate.

Read a Cutaway

1. Why Learn This Skill?

Sometimes it is interesting to know how things work. To do that, it helps to see what something looks like inside. However, it is not always possible to take an object apart to see inside it. Do you wonder what computers or space shuttles look like inside and how they work?

2. Cutaway Diagrams

There is a kind of drawing that can help you answer this question. It is called a cutaway diagram. A **cutaway diagram** shows the outside and inside of an object at the same time. On a drawing of this type, part of the object has been "cut away" to make a kind of window. The window lets you see inside the object. A cutaway diagram can let you see inside a computer or a space shuttle. The photograph here shows a container ship. Inside each metal container are hundreds of products, such as bicycles or bicycle helmets.

3. Understand the Process

Now look at the cutaway diagram on page 305. It lets you see inside a container ship. Use the diagram to answer the questions below.

1 Find the cutaway "window" that shows the inside of the living area. What does this show you?

2 You can see that the container ship is divided into different parts. Why do you think the ship has more than one part?

3 Is the barge located closer to the bow or stern of the ship?

Container ship

Diagram

4. Think and Apply

Use library books to find out how something works, for example, a tape recorder or a toy. Draw a cutaway diagram of that object, and add a title and labels. Then use your diagram to explain to classmates how the object works.

A CONTAINER SHIP

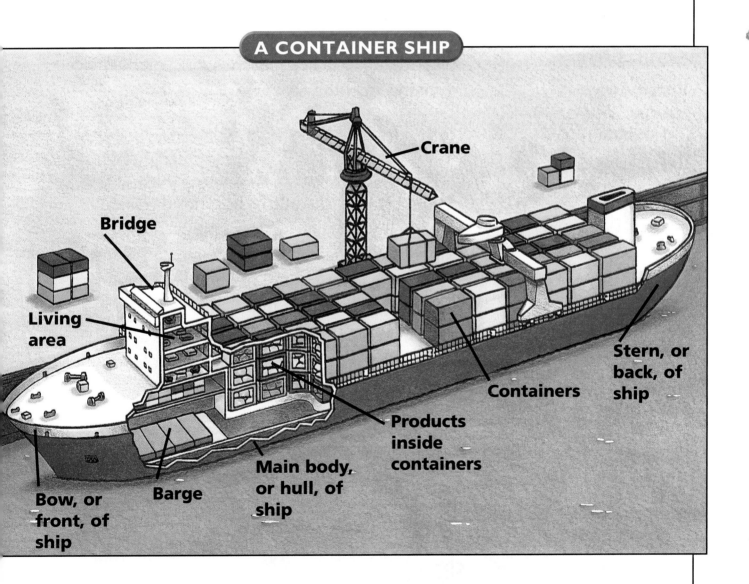

Crane

Bridge

Living area

Bow, or front, of ship

Barge

Main body, or hull, of ship

Products inside containers

Containers

Stern, or back, of ship

FOCUS
Why do many countries use South Carolina's ports?

Main Idea Read to find out why South Carolina's ports have an important job in the world marketplace.

Vocabulary
cargo
distribute

South Carolina and the World Marketplace

In the last lesson you learned that different types of transportation make international trade possible. You also found out that newer and better technology makes trade between nations faster and easier. South Carolina has an important job in keeping the world marketplace running smoothly.

The Port of Charleston

Charleston is one of the busiest ports in the United States. The port is busy for the same reason it was when settlers first lived in Charleston long ago. Its location on a peninsula makes it a great natural harbor. Its location next to the Atlantic Ocean makes it easy for ships from all over the world to dock, or stop, there.

Container ship at the Port of Charleston

The container ships that dock at the Port of Charleston carry all kinds of cargo. **Cargo** is the load of products a vehicle carries. The cargo may include anything from tennis shoes and gloves to candy and jams. Some of these products will be loaded onto trucks and trains and sent to locations in South Carolina or other parts of the United States. However, much of the cargo is loaded onto ships that will be sailing to other countries.

REVIEW What makes Charleston a busy port?

Workers at the port load trucks with cargo.

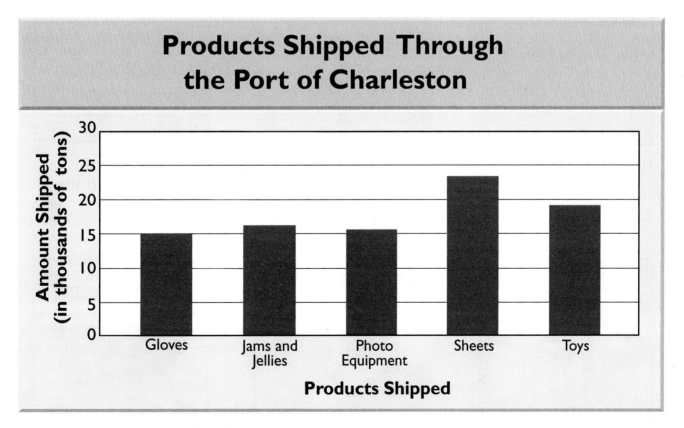

Products Shipped Through the Port of Charleston

LEARNING FROM GRAPHS Compare the amounts of sheets and gloves shipped through the Port of Charleston.

■ How many more tons of sheets than gloves are shipped?

Information Technology

Thousands of cargo containers come and go every day at the Port of Charleston. At the port, dock workers load and unload cargo. However, before cargo can be moved, information about the shipment must be shared.

Every container has a number. Each time the container is moved, the bar code is scanned electronically. The scan tells workers what time the container came in, what is in it, and where it needs to go.

LEARNING FROM DIAGRAMS
Which step shows a crane lifting containers off of the ship?

HOW CARGO IS BROUGHT INTO THE PORT OF CHARLESTON

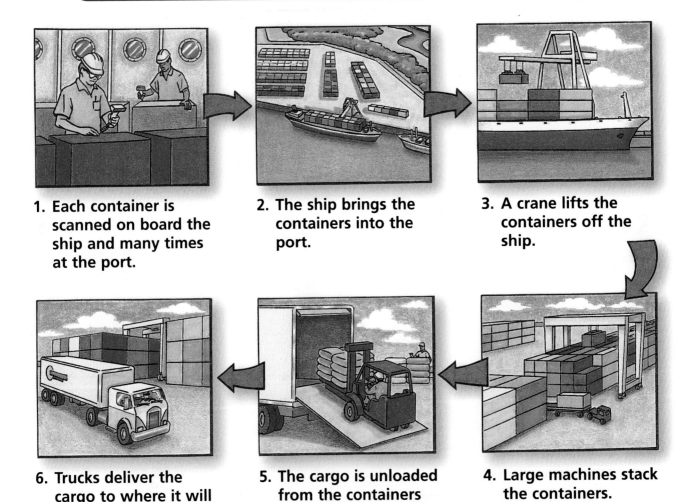

1. Each container is scanned on board the ship and many times at the port.

2. The ship brings the containers into the port.

3. A crane lifts the containers off the ship.

6. Trucks deliver the cargo to where it will be sold and used.

5. The cargo is unloaded from the containers and put on trucks.

4. Large machines stack the containers.

This technology helps businesses **distribute**, or send out, their products all over the world.

There are two smaller ports in South Carolina—Georgetown and Port Royal. All three ports bring jobs and business to the state. South Carolina's ports are an important resource.

REVIEW Why does each container have a number?

Workers at the Port of Georgetown stack cargo.

LESSON 6 REVIEW

Check Understanding

❶ **Remember the Facts** What are the names of South Carolina's most important ports?

❷ **Recall the Main Idea** What makes South Carolina an important part of the world marketplace?

Think Critically

❸ **Cause and Effect** If workers at the ports stopped using technology to help them do their jobs, what might happen?

Show What You Know

Research Activity
Choose a product that is imported to South Carolina through one of its ports. Find out where the product is made and why it is important to South Carolina. Use your school library or a computer to gather the information you need. Then share what you find with your classmates. Use a wall map to show where the product comes from and at which port it arrives.

Use Latitude

1. Why Learn This Skill?

If someone asked you where the Port of Charleston is, you could describe the exact location using latitude and longitude.

2. Understand the Process

Latitude and longitude are lines that mapmakers draw on maps and globes. **Lines of latitude** run east and west. Lines of latitude are measured in degrees (°) north and south from the equator. They go from 0° at the equator to 90° at each of the poles. Lines north of the equator are marked *N* for *north* and lines south of the equator are marked *S* for *south*.

Lines of longitude (LAHN•juh•tood), or meridians, run north and south from pole to pole. They go from 0° at the prime meridian near London, England, to 180° halfway around the globe.

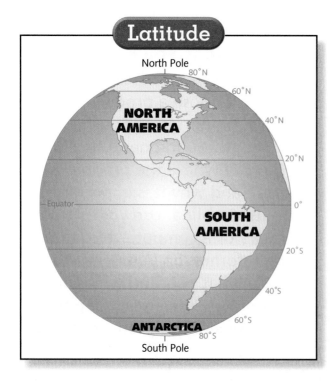

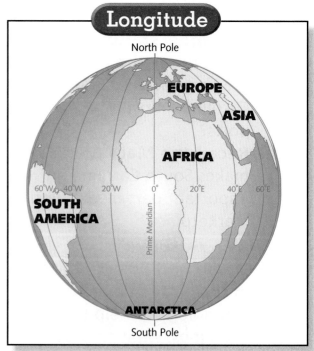

and Longitude

Lines west of the prime meridian are marked *W* for *west* and lines east are marked *E* for *east*.

Lines of latitude and longitude form a grid. You can give the exact location of any place on Earth by naming the line of latitude and line of longitude closest to it. Answer these questions from the map.

1 On which line of latitude is Allendale? On which line of longitude is Rock Hill?

2 Near which lines of latitude and longitude is Charleston? Name the latitude first and then the longitude. Charleston is located near 33°N, 80°W.

3. Think and Apply

Choose a city on the map and write its location using latitude and longitude. Tell a classmate how you found the location.

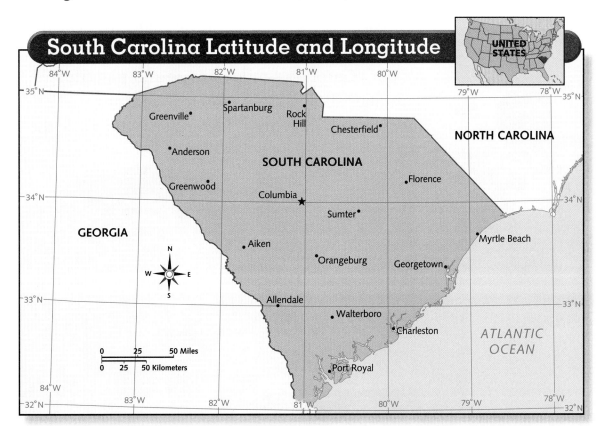

South Carolina Latitude and Longitude

UNITED STATES

84°W 83°W 82°W 81°W 80°W 79°W 78°W

35°N

Greenville
Spartanburg
Rock Hill
Chesterfield

NORTH CAROLINA

Anderson

SOUTH CAROLINA

Greenwood

Florence

34°N

Columbia

Sumter

GEORGIA

Aiken

Myrtle Beach

Orangeburg

Georgetown

33°N

Allendale

Walterboro

Charleston

ATLANTIC OCEAN

0 25 50 Miles
0 25 50 Kilometers

Port Royal

84°W 83°W 82°W 81°W 80°W 79°W 78°W

32°N

FOCUS
What kinds of jobs do people in your community have?

Main Idea Read to find out about the kinds of work people do in South Carolina.

Vocabulary
profit
renewable resource
nonrenewable resource
tourism

South Carolinians and Their Work

Like people everywhere, South Carolinians make their living in different ways. Some raise animals and grow food. Others make products such as clothes, lumber, and machine parts. Still others provide services. Together, they produce many of the things that people need and want.

Agriculture

Today many South Carolina farmers raise beef cattle, dairy cows, hogs, chickens, and turkeys. Tobacco is the state's leading cash crop. Farmers also grow cotton for the state's textile factories. South Carolina's mild climate and plentiful rainfall allow farmers to grow peaches, soybeans, and corn. The farmers who grow the

▲ A boy holds a hog.

A farmer harvests corn, one of the crops grown in South Carolina. ▶

products all try to make a profit. A **profit** is the amount of money left after all the costs of running a business or making a product have been paid.

All farming depends upon an important renewable resource—soil. A **renewable resource** is a resource that can be used again or made again by people or nature. Soil forms slowly and is destroyed easily. For that reason, farmers take care of their soil by adding minerals to it. They also plant and plow their fields in ways that will not destroy the soil.

REVIEW What animals do farmers in South Carolina raise?

Leading Cash Crops

CROP	ANNUAL SALES IN DOLLARS
Tobacco	213,298,000
Greenhouse and Nursery Plants	182,230,000
Cotton (fiber)	139,375,000
Soybeans	93,733,000
Corn	69,177,000
Wheat	50,313,000
Tomatoes	23,199,000
Peaches	21,771,000

LEARNING FROM TABLES What is the annual sales of corn?

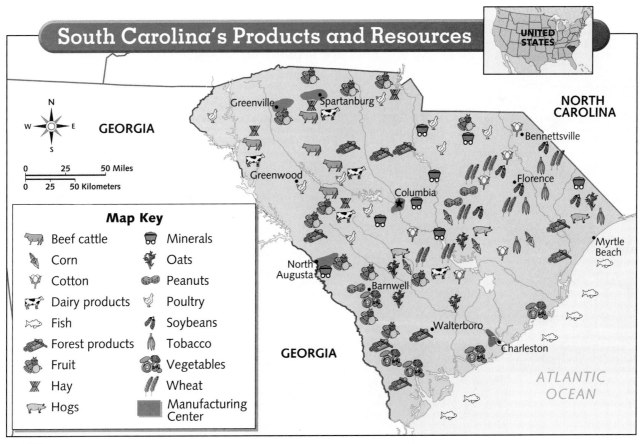

South Carolina's Products and Resources

UNITED STATES

Map Key

- Beef cattle
- Corn
- Cotton
- Dairy products
- Fish
- Forest products
- Fruit
- Hay
- Hogs
- Minerals
- Oats
- Peanuts
- Poultry
- Soybeans
- Tobacco
- Vegetables
- Wheat
- Manufacturing Center

Human-Environment Interactions ■ Are beef cattle raised in the eastern or western part of the state?

Manufacturing, Forestry, and Mining

The sheets on your bed or the clothes you wear may have been made in one of South Carolina's textile factories. Other factories in South Carolina make the machinery and dyes used in manufacturing textiles. Still others make medicines, power tools, and automobile tires.

Factories also use wood from the state's forests to make paper and wood products. Some of the companies that cut down trees have their own tree farms. Replanting trees is an important way to renew the supply of trees.

In Spartanburg, South Carolina, automobiles are manufactured.

◄ These workers are replanting trees.

▼ A worker in Sumter county uses a knuckle-boom loader to gather trees that have been cut down.

Mining makes up a small part of South Carolina's industry. The most important mineral resources are granite and limestone. These are **nonrenewable resources**, resources that cannot be replaced. Granite is mined from the Piedmont region. Limestone is mined from the Outer Coastal Plain region.

REVIEW What are some of the items made in South Carolina's factories?

▲ This train and truck are being loaded with minerals from a mine in Columbia.

Government

Someone living right on your street or in your neighborhood probably works for the government. The government employs, or gives jobs to, many South Carolinians.

Some of these people work for public schools and hospitals. Some build roads or care for parks. Others work at one of South Carolina's state colleges, universities, or technical schools. Some people work on military bases located in the state.

REVIEW What are some of the jobs government workers have?

▼ A college class at Clemson University

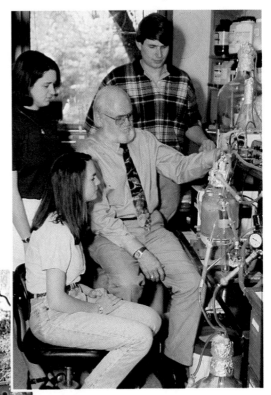

◀ The College of Charleston

BIOGRAPHY

Darla Moore
1954–

One of South Carolina's entrepreneurs (ahn•truh•pruh•NERZ) is Darla Moore. An entrepreneur is someone who starts and runs a business. Moore grew up in Lake City, South Carolina. After she finished business school, she became a banker and was soon known for her smart decisions. She has been so successful that she was able to give $25 million to the University of South Carolina.

Services and Tourism

Many South Carolinians own or work in businesses that provide services. The people who work in restaurants, banks, and stores all help provide services.

Many service workers are needed to take care of the tourists, or visitors, who come to South Carolina each year. **Tourism**, the selling of products and services to tourists, is an important industry in South Carolina. Tourists come to South Carolina to visit beaches, parks, and historic places. They spend a lot of money in the state, and this helps create more jobs. Tour guides, taxi drivers, and hotel clerks are just a few of the workers in the tourism industry.

Many people visit the Mann-Simons Cottage in Columbia to learn about early African Americans in the state.

Tourists also like to go to places where they can enjoy South Carolina's natural treasures. For that reason, tourists travel to every region of the state. Each region has its own physical features, plants, and animals. South Carolina has something for everyone.

REVIEW What kinds of places might tourists want to visit in South Carolina?

Tourists in Charleston view Church Street from a horse-drawn carriage.

Tourists enjoy rafting on the Chattooga (chuh•TOO•guh) River.

LESSON 7 REVIEW

Check Understanding

1 Remember the Facts What are some of South Carolina's crops?

2 Recall the Main Idea What kinds of work do people in South Carolina do?

Think Critically

3 Cause and Effect If paper-making companies did not plant new trees, what might be the effect on those companies and the environment?

Show What You Know

Art Activity Design a poster or a button that tells something about farming or manufacturing in South Carolina. Use your poster or button to explain how the product or activity helps people in your state earn a living.

Working Together Is Good Business

Each year, Mellichamp Elementary School students in Orangeburg, South Carolina, take field trips to a local supermarket. Store workers explain how they work together to help the supermarket run smoothly.

Back at the school, third and fourth graders talk about careers, or jobs, in the food business. They also talk about what workers do to make a store a success. Then these students set up stores of their own in their classrooms.

The classes are divided into different groups. One group writes Help Wanted advertisements and then interviews and hires classmates for the store jobs. Another group orders items for the store. They also keep track of how many of each item the store has. A third group prices the items and makes posters to help sell them. Working together, the students learn what it takes to run a business. They have fun doing it, too!

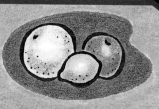

Think and Apply

Is there something your school needs? Maybe you and your classmates could earn the money to buy it. Think of something you could sell. Then make a plan, and decide what everyone in the group will do. Present your plan to your classmates.

Visit the Internet at **http://www.hbschool.com** for additional resources.

▼ **Students listen to supermarket workers explain about the produce–or fruit and vegetable–department.**

▼ **Back at school the students make Help Wanted advertisements for their classroom store.**

▼ **Students look at the newspaper to get ideas about the kinds of products they would like to sell in their store.**

VISUAL SUMMARY

Study the pictures and captions to help you review the events you read about in Unit 4.

Write a Paragraph   Choose one of the five summary statements on this visual summary. Then find the picture that goes with it. Write a paragraph to tell what the picture shows about the summary statement.

1 People work together to make products and provide services.

4 People trade with one another.

3 People choose the products and services they will buy.

2 Human resources and raw materials are important in the manufacturing process.

5 Products and services get to market in different ways.

CONNECT MAIN IDEAS ···

Complete this graphic organizer by writing details for the main idea of each lesson. A copy of the organizer appears on Activity Book page 66.

Lesson 1
People in a community work together.

1. _____
2. _____

Lesson 5
Products and services get to marketplaces in different ways.

1. _____
2. _____

People Working Together

Lesson 2
People work together to make products and provide services.

1. _____
2. _____

Lesson 4
People trade, or barter, with each other.

1. _____
2. _____

Lesson 3
People choose the products and services they will buy.

1. _____
2. _____

WRITE MORE ABOUT IT ···

Write a Speech   Imagine that your class has been given a box of bicycle helmets. Most of your classmates want to wear a helmet. A few do not. You know that helmets save lives. Write a speech that will make everyone want to wear a helmet. Then read it to your classmates.

USE VOCABULARY

Think of a time when you bought something special. Write a paragraph about that time. In your paragraph, use the vocabulary words below.

1. advertisement
2. basic needs
3. consumer
4. import
5. price
6. technology

CHECK UNDERSTANDING

7. Why are resources important to producers and consumers?

8. How do supply and demand affect the price of products?

9. How can advertising affect a consumer's choice?

THINK CRITICALLY

10. **Past to Present** How does population size affect demand for raw materials and products?

11. **Think More About It** Why is it important for people to use non-renewable resources carefully?

12. **Personally Speaking** Tell three ways new technologies have made your life easier or better.

APPLY SKILLS

Read Graphs This graph shows the five busiest container ports in the United States. Use the graph to answer the questions.

13. Which port moved the most containers?

14. Did the Port of Charleston move more containers than New York, NY? than Hampton Roads, VA?

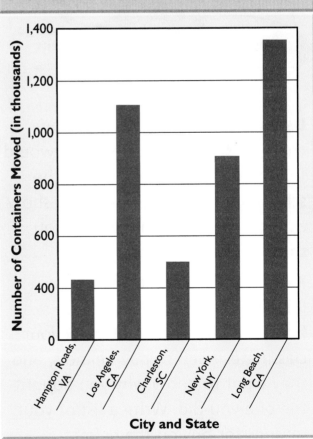

Five Busiest Container Ports in the United States

Number of Containers Moved (in thousands) — Hampton Roads, VA; Los Angeles, CA; Charleston, SC; New York, NY; Long Beach, CA

City and State

Read a Cutaway Diagram Look at this cutaway diagram of a cargo airplane. Use the cutaway diagram to answer the following questions.

15 Where is the flight deck located?

16 In what part of the plane is most of the cargo stored?

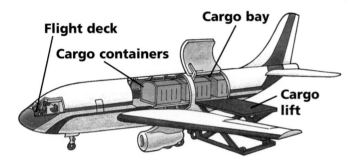

CARGO AIRPLANE

Flight deck

Cargo containers

Cargo bay

Cargo lift

Use a Flow Chart Make a flow chart that shows the steps you would follow to check a book out of the school library. What would you show as the first step? What would you show as the last step?

Make an Economic Choice Imagine that you have just bought a bicycle helmet. Now your classmates need to buy helmets, and they want to know why you bought the one you did. Write a list of your reasons for buying the helmet. Also explain the trade-offs and opportunity costs of your choice.

Use a Map Grid Draw a map of your classroom. On the map, draw a map grid. Along one side, label the rows by using letters. At the top, label the columns by using numbers. Hide an object someplace in the room. On your map, mark the location of the object. Then give your map to a classmate, and see if he or she can find the object.

READ MORE ABOUT IT

Carolina Shout! by Alan Schroeder. Dial. All day long Delia hears the songs of workers on the streets of Charleston, South Carolina.

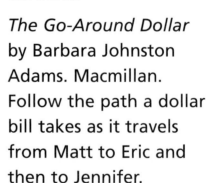

The Go-Around Dollar by Barbara Johnston Adams. Macmillan. Follow the path a dollar bill takes as it travels from Matt to Eric and then to Jennifer.

Visit the Internet at **http://www.hbschool.com** for additional resources.

REMEMBER

- Share your ideas.
- Cooperate with others to plan your work.
- Take responsibility for your work.
- Help one another.
- Show your group's work to the class.
- Discuss what you learned by working together.

Conduct a Survey

Write a list of questions you want to ask people about their favorite restaurants. You might ask what they like to eat and drink at the restaurants. Or you might ask about the prices of the food. Make copies of your list, and give them to classmates, friends, and family members. Have them answer each question and return the list to you. After you have the answers, show them in a chart. Display your chart for classmates to see.

Unit Project Wrap-Up

Make a Bulletin Board Display With your classmates, work in small groups to decide which manufacturing process you will display on the bulletin board. Look at the information you have gathered. Draw pictures or cut them out of magazines to illustrate your subject. After you have organized the information, put it on the bulletin board. Add numbers, labels, and arrows to help tell the steps in the process. Then invite other classes to see the display.

LIVING TOGETHER IN A COMMUNITY, STATE, AND NATION

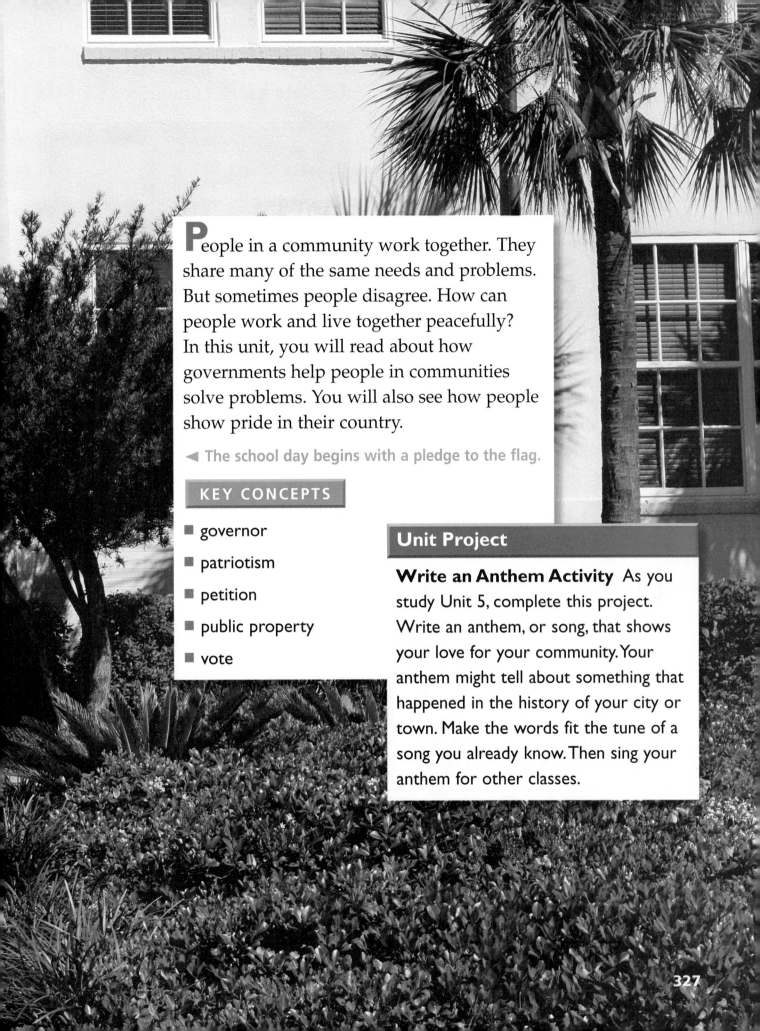

People in a community work together. They share many of the same needs and problems. But sometimes people disagree. How can people work and live together peacefully? In this unit, you will read about how governments help people in communities solve problems. You will also see how people show pride in their country.

◄ The school day begins with a pledge to the flag.

KEY CONCEPTS

- governor
- patriotism
- petition
- public property
- vote

Unit Project

Write an Anthem Activity As you study Unit 5, complete this project. Write an anthem, or song, that shows your love for your community. Your anthem might tell about something that happened in the history of your city or town. Make the words fit the tune of a song you already know. Then sing your anthem for other classes.

petition A written request that people sign to ask for government action.

governor The elected leader of a state's government.

patriotism The love that people have for their country.

public property Something that belongs to all citizens.

vote The way people show what they think a group should do.

City Green

written and illustrated
by DyAnne DiSalvo-Ryan

In this story, a wrecking ball is used to tear down an old apartment building in Marcy's neighborhood. All that is left is an empty lot covered with trash and broken glass. Find out how Marcy, her neighbors, and the city government work together to turn an ugly empty lot into a place that everyone can enjoy.

Miss Rosa and I go to see Mr. Bennett. He used to work for the city. "I seem to remember a program," he says, "that lets people rent empty lots."

That's how Miss Rosa and I form a group of people from our block. We pass around a petition that says: WE WANT TO LEASE THIS LOT. In less than a week we have plenty of names.

"Sign with us?" I ask Old Man Hammer.

"I'm not signin' nothin'," he says. "And nothin' is what's gonna happen."

But something did.

The next week, a bunch of us take a bus to city hall. We walk up the steps to the proper office and hand the woman our list. She checks her files and types some notes and makes some copies. "That will be one dollar, please."

We rent the lot from the city that day. It was just as simple as that.

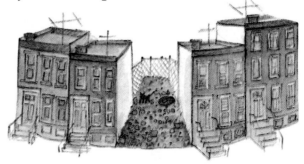

Saturday morning I'm up with the sun and looking at this lot. My mama looks out too. "Marcy," she says, and hugs me close. "Today I'm helping you and Rosa."

After shopping, Mama empties her grocery bags and folds them flat to carry under her arm. "Come on, Mrs. B.," Mama tells her friend. "We're going to clear this lot."

Then what do you know but my brother comes along. My brother is tall and strong. At first, he scratches his neck and shakes his head just like Old Man Hammer. But Mama smiles and says, "None of that here!" So all day long he piles junk in those bags and carries them to the curb.

Now, this time of day is early. Neighbors pass by and see what we're doing. Most say, "We want to help too." They have a little time to spare. Then this one calls that one and that one calls another.

"Come on and help," I call to Old Man Hammer.

"I'm not helpin' nobody," he hollers. "You're all wastin' your time."

Sour grapes my mama'd say, and sour grapes is right.

Just before supper, when we are good and hungry, my mama looks around this lot. "Marcy," she says, "you're making something happen here."

Next day the city drops off tools like rakes and brooms, and a Dumpster for trash. Now there's even more neighbors to help. Miss Rosa, my brother, and I say "Good morning" to Old Man Hammer, but Old Man Hammer just waves like he's swatting a fly.

"Why is Old Man Hammer so mean and cranky these days?" my brother asks.

"Maybe he's really sad," I tell him. "Maybe he misses his building."

"That rotten old building?" My brother shrugs. "He should be happy the city tore down that mess."

"Give him time," Miss Rosa says. "Good things take time."

Mr. Bennett brings wood—old slats he's saved—and nails in a cup. "I knew all along I saved them for something," he says. "This wood's good wood."

Then Mr. Rocco from two houses down comes, carrying two cans of paint. "I'll never use these," he says. "The color's too bright. But here, this lot could use some brightening up."

Well, anyone can tell with all the excitement that something is going on. And everyone has an idea about what to plant—strawberries, carrots, lettuce, and more. Tulips and daisies, petunias, and more! Sonny turns the dirt over with a snow shovel. Even Leslie's baby tries to dig with a spoon.

For lunch, Miss Rosa brings milk and jelly and bread and spreads a beach towel where the junk is cleared. By the end of the day a fence is built and painted as bright as the sun.

Later, Mama kisses my cheek and closes my bedroom door. By the streetlights I see Old Man Hammer come down his steps to open the gate and walk to the back of this lot. He bends down quick, sprinkling something from his pocket and covering it over with dirt.

In the morning I tell my brother. "Oh, Marcy," he says. "You're dreaming. You're wishing too hard."

But I know what I saw, and I tell my mama, "Old Man Hammer's planted some seeds."

Right after breakfast, I walk to the back of this lot. And there it is—a tiny raised bed of soil. It is neat and tidy, just like the rows we've planted. Now I know for sure that Old Man Hammer planted something. So I pat the soil for good luck and make a little fence to keep the seeds safe.

Every day I go for a look inside our garden lot. Other neighbors stop in too. One day Mrs. Wells comes by. "This is right where my grandmother's bedroom used to be," she says. "That's why I planted my flowers there."

I feel sad when I hear that. With all the digging and planting and weeding and watering, I'd forgotten about the building that had been on this lot. Old Man Hammer had lived there too. I go to the back, where he planted his seeds. I wonder if this was the place where his room used to be.

I look down. Beside my feet, some tiny stems are sprouting. Old Man Hammer's seeds have grown! I run to his stoop. "Come with me!" I beg, tugging at his hand. "You'll want to see."

I walk him past the hollyhocks, the daisies, the peppers, the rows of lettuce. I show him the strawberries that I planted. When Old Man Hammer sees his little garden bed, his sour grapes turn sweet. "Marcy, child." He shakes his head. "This lot was good for nothin'. Now it's nothin' but good," he says.

Soon summertime comes, and this lot really grows. It fills with vegetables, herbs, and flowers. And way in the back, taller than anything else, is a beautiful patch of yellow sunflowers. Old Man Hammer comes every day. He sits in the sun, eats his lunch, and sometimes comes back with supper.

Nobody knows how the sunflowers came—not Leslie, my brother, or Miss Rosa. Not Mr. Bennett, or Sonny, or anyone else. But Old Man Hammer just sits there smiling at me. We know whose flowers they are.

FOCUS
What can you do to help solve a problem in your community?

Main Idea Read to find out how people in a community can work together to solve problems.

Vocabulary
petition
council
government
service

People Make Communities Good Places to Live

In *City Green* you read about Marcy and her neighbors. They saw a problem in their community. There was an ugly empty lot near their apartments. Like people in communities everywhere, Marcy and her neighbors found that their problem could be solved. They could cooperate, or work together, to turn the lot into a garden.

City Government Helps People

To solve their problem, Marcy and her neighbors first found out how to cooperate with their city government. They learned that they could rent the lot from the city. So Marcy and Miss Rosa wrote a petition asking to rent the lot. A **petition** is a letter people sign that asks the government to do something. By signing the petition, people show that they support what it asks for.

Marcy and many of her neighbors signed the petition and took it to city hall. City hall is the building where people in city government work.

These students are asking people to sign a petition. The petition asks for a law that says all bicycle riders must wear helmets.

Help Make Bike Helmets a Law

After paying a dollar for rent, Marcy and her neighbors agreed to be responsible for the empty lot. They would begin by cleaning it up.

In communities everywhere, people work with their local government to solve problems. In some small communities, all the citizens are invited to attend town meetings. At a town meeting, citizens discuss problems in their community and ways to solve them. However, many towns and cities are much too large for all their citizens to fit into one room. These larger towns and cities are run by a council. A city or town **council** is a group of people who have been chosen by citizens to meet and solve problems. In many communities a council and a mayor make laws for everyone to follow.

This mayor and city council are holding a meeting in Austin, Texas. More than 500,000 people live in this city.

These citizens are taking part in a town meeting in Francestown, New Hampshire. About 1,200 people live in this community.

Young citizens listening to a storyteller in a library

Firefighters provide an important government service.

City and town governments provide many services to their citizens. A **government service** is a service that is provided for all the citizens of a community. Fire and police protection are government services. Most city governments also provide libraries, street and traffic signs, sewers, and water for their citizens.

City governments can provide services like these because the community's citizens pay taxes. Taxes are paid to a government to run a city. People also pay taxes to run their county, state, and national governments. The government uses taxes to pay wages to the workers who provide services. The government also uses taxes to build new buildings and to buy equipment, such as police cars and fire engines.

REVIEW How do city governments pay for government services?

Leaders Help Solve Problems

In *City Green* the people in Marcy's neighborhood worked together to solve a problem. Before a community can solve a problem, a leader may need to bring the people together. Marcy acted as a leader when she told her neighbors how they could solve a problem. She and Miss Rosa brought people together to make a garden from an empty lot.

In communities all over the United States, leaders help make things happen. Wilma Mankiller is a leader who helped solve problems in Cherokee communities. For many years she was the Chief of the Cherokee Nation. Her office was located in Tahlequah (TA•luh•kwaw), Oklahoma. One of the many communities she worked with was Bell, Oklahoma. Bell is a rural community where about 350 people live. Most of its citizens are Cherokees, like Wilma Mankiller.

Wilma Mankiller

One of the biggest problems in Bell was that there was no running water. In order to have water for their homes, most people had to get barrels of water from other communities. The community needed a pipe that would bring in running water.

Wilma Mankiller brought the people of Bell together to find a way to solve their problems. She held meetings where people could share ideas. She helped the citizens find other leaders in the community who could be in charge of building the pipeline. She asked the United States government for money to pay for the pipe. When the United States government and the citizens of Bell did not agree, Wilma Mankiller helped everyone find a way to make things work.

REVIEW **What problem did Wilma Mankiller help the people solve in Bell, Oklahoma?**

Wilma Mankiller goes to meetings where people can share their ideas for solving problems.

Success Means Working Together

Wilma Mankiller knew that the Cherokees had a tradition of working together. She helped the people in the community make plans, but she did not do the work herself. The United States government did not do the work, either. Volunteers from Bell built the pipeline.

In *City Green* Marcy, too, knew that the people in her neighborhood could solve their problem. Leaders like Marcy and Wilma Mankiller help people in a community make plans. Then the people can do the work themselves.

REVIEW Who built the new pipeline in Bell, Oklahoma?

BIOGRAPHY

Sarah Winnemucca
1844–1891

As a child, Sarah Winnemucca (wih•nuh•MUH•kuh) learned the cultures and languages of both the Indians and the white people. When settlers began to move onto Paiute (PY•oot) tribal lands, she wrote a book about it. It was one of the first books written in English by an Indian woman. She hoped that her words would help Indians and white people live together peacefully.

LESSON 1 REVIEW

Check Understanding

1 Remember the Facts How can a leader help a community get what its citizens need?

2 Recall the Main Idea How can people in communities work together to solve problems?

Think Critically

3 Cause and Effect What would happen if community leaders did not bring people together? Explain your answer.

Show What You Know

Speech-Writing Activity Imagine that you are going to take part in a city council meeting. Think about a subject that you feel is important to your commmunity. For example, perhaps your community needs a new park or a larger library. Work in a small group to write a speech about your subject and what action needs to be taken. Read your speech to the other groups.

Resolve Conflicts

1. Why Learn This Skill?

People take sides in conflicts in every country, every community, and every home. A **conflict** is a disagreement. In a conflict, people or groups disagree because they have different needs, wants, or ways of thinking. Learning how to settle conflicts will help you get along with others. You can use this skill all your life.

2. Remember What You Have Read

People in a conflict may or may not know one another well, but they can still follow the steps of conflict resolution. **Conflict resolution** is a way to solve, or resolve, disagreements among people or groups. Conflict resolution can lead to changes that help people understand one another better.

All of these students want to use the same computer. How can they resolve this conflict?

3. Understand the Process

You can follow these steps when there is a conflict. Remember that the same steps may not work every time. You may need to try more than one way to end your conflict.

1. **Walk away.** Just walk away without saying anything, and let some time pass. Later, people may not have such strong feelings about the conflict. They may be able to think better about what to say or do.

2. **Smile about it.** Make things seem less serious. People who can smile about something together may be able to work together to solve the problem.

3 **Make a compromise.** If you cannot walk away from a conflict or smile about it, you may be able to work out a compromise. In a **compromise** (KAHM•pruh•myz), each person gives up some of the things he or she wants. Each also gets some of the things he or she wants.

4 **Ask someone to help.** If you cannot compromise, you can ask someone to be a mediator.

A **mediator** is a person who helps both sides settle their disagreement. Sometimes the mediator has a helpful new way of looking at the problem.

4. Think and Apply

Describe the steps people at your school follow when there is a conflict. Talk with classmates. How were conflicts handled before these steps were used?

With the help of a mediator, the students decide to take turns using the computer.

Main Idea Read to find out how rules and laws helped people in communities resolve conflicts long ago.

Vocabulary
vote
election

Rules and Laws in a Community

Rules and laws help people in a community cooperate. In *City Green* you read how Marcy and her neighbors learned how to rent the empty lot from the city. By following those rules, they were able to solve their problem peacefully. As they do today, rules and laws also helped people cooperate long ago.

Native Americans Made Laws

Before the first Europeans settled in North America, native peoples lived here. In the 1500s there were five Iroquois (IR•uh•kwoy) tribes. They had many conflicts with one another. They disagreed over which tribes should be allowed to use the best land for hunting and farming. They often fought wars with one another because of their disagreements. One wise Iroquois leader named Dekanawida (deh•kahn•uh•WIH•duh) believed that the tribes must find a way to resolve their conflicts. If they did not, they would destroy their communities.

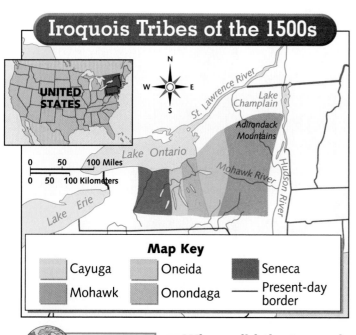

Iroquois Tribes of the 1500s

UNITED STATES

St. Lawrence River
Lake Champlain
Adirondack Mountains
Lake Ontario
Mohawk River
Hudson River
Lake Erie

0   50   100 Miles
0   50   100 Kilometers

Map Key
Cayuga
Mohawk
Oneida
Onondaga
Seneca
Present-day border

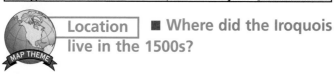

Location ■ Where did the Iroquois live in the 1500s?

Dekanawida thought of a way to bring peace to the five tribes. He made up a set of 13 laws he thought all the Iroquois could follow. The laws would help the tribes resolve their disagreements without fighting wars with one another. He asked all the tribes to follow these laws.

An Iroquois leader named Hiawatha (hy•uh•WAH•thuh) wanted to help Dekanawida tell others about the new laws. To do this, Hiawatha made a wampum belt. Wampum (WAHM•puhm) were beads made from polished shells. By using different-colored beads and designs, a person could weave a message into a belt. Hiawatha's wampum belt told about the laws. By showing this belt to other tribal leaders, Hiawatha and Dekanawida could better explain the new laws.

The tribes agreed to follow the new laws. Each tribe would have its own government. But conflicts among the tribes would be resolved by a Great Council. Members of each tribe would serve on the Great Council. Each council member would have one vote. People use a **vote** to show what they think the group should do. If all the members did not vote the same way, they would compromise until they reached an agreement.

Today the Iroquois continue to follow these laws that were created hundreds of years ago. The Great Council still meets to make decisions for the Iroquois. The laws from long ago still work today.

REVIEW How did Hiawatha and Dekanawida carry the message about the new laws to other Iroquois tribes?

This wampum belt was made by Iroquois people in the 1800s. It is like the belt made by Hiawatha.

Settlers in America Wrote New Laws

In 1620 a group of English settlers known as Pilgrims arrived in America. They had sailed on a small ship called the *Mayflower*. The Pilgrims had planned to settle in Virginia, where a government was already set up. But their ship was blown north so that they landed in what is now Massachusetts. Because they were the first settlers, there was no government there yet. So there were no settlers' laws for the Pilgrims to follow.

The Pilgrims wrote a set of laws they called the Mayflower Compact. A compact is a written statement that people agree to follow by signing their names. The Mayflower Compact said that the Pilgrims would form their own government. They would choose leaders, who would write new laws as they were needed. The people agreed to obey the laws for the good of everyone. The new laws helped the Pilgrims live and work together in their new homeland.

This painting shows the Pilgrims signing the Mayflower Compact.

REVIEW **What was the Mayflower Compact?**

Laws for a New Country

More than 150 years after the Mayflower Compact was signed, the 13 colonies in North America joined to form the United States of America. The new country's leaders wrote a set of laws called the United States Constitution. The Constitution is more than 200 years old, but it is still the most important set of laws in the United States. It describes how the United States government works. The ideas and laws of the Pilgrims helped our country's first leaders write the Constitution.

Students looking at the Constitution in Washington, D.C.

The Constitution also describes the rights, or freedoms, that all citizens have. Americans are free to enjoy their own cultures and to practice their religions. American citizens can work at any job for which they have the skills and can live and travel where they wish. The Constitution also says that Americans have the right to talk in public about their ideas and have the right to vote in elections. In an **election**, people vote to choose leaders. They may also vote for or against new laws.

This painting shows leaders such as George Washington and Benjamin Franklin meeting to sign the Constitution.

These children are obeying a law that keeps them safe.

Citizens have rights, but they also need to be responsible. A citizen is responsible for obeying the laws. Citizens who do not obey the laws must face the consequences of their actions. The consequences may be paying a fine or going to jail.

REVIEW **What does the Constitution describe?**

LESSON 2 REVIEW

Check Understanding

1 Remember the Facts What were the Iroquois laws and the Mayflower Compact?

2 Recall the Main Idea How did rules and laws help people in communities long ago resolve their conflicts?

Think Critically

3 Think More About It How is the Great Council of the Iroquois like a city council?

Show What You Know

Letter-Writing Activity Imagine that you are one of the Pilgrims. Write a letter that tells why you think people need laws. Think about what laws people need to live together peacefully. Make a list of laws for the Pilgrims to follow, and add it to your letter. Read your letter to your classmates, and together talk about your ideas.

Make a Choice by Voting

1. Why Learn This Skill?

You make choices every day. You choose what to eat and what to wear. You have different reasons for the choices you make. You can make a choice because you like one thing better than another or because one choice has better consequences than another. Understanding the reasons for your choices will help you make good ones.

2. Remember What You Have Read

People in communities also make choices. Voting is the way members of a community make important choices about their government. Perhaps you have voted at your school to choose a school slogan or a mascot.

Before voting, people need to learn as much as they can about the consequences of each choice. The more they know about a subject or

person, the better they will be able to make good choices. People should also talk to one another about the good and the bad points of each choice.

3. Understand the Process

Voting may be our most important right. It allows every citizen to make a choice. Here is how it works.

When people in communities need to make choices about their government, they hold an election. In an election people vote for or against a new law or a candidate. A **candidate** is someone who hopes to be elected for a job.

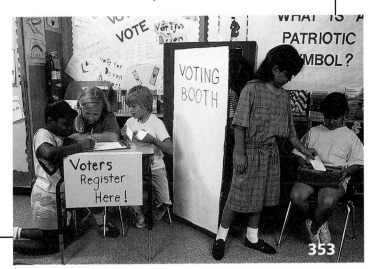

In some elections people mark paper ballots. A **ballot** lists all the possible choices. A person votes by making a mark next to his or her choice. The ballot is placed in a ballot box. It is kept there with all the other ballots until everyone has voted. Then the votes are counted and the winner is named.

In an election everyone's vote is kept a secret. Each person goes into a voting booth and makes a choice without anyone else watching. Also, the voters do not put their names on the ballots. This way, people can vote without worrying what other people may think about their choices.

Who wins an election? The voter usually has two or more candidates to choose from.

Sometimes voters are also asked whether they want to have a new law or to have the government spend money on a certain project. The candidate or the choice that gets the most votes wins. This is called **majority rule** because a majority, or more than half, of the people voting chose one candidate or decision. The people who did not vote for the winner are the minority. But in our country, those who do not vote for the winner still keep their rights. We call this idea **minority rights**.

The work of getting the voters to choose one candidate instead of another is called a **campaign**. Candidates look for every chance to tell the public about their ideas. Sometimes candidates make speeches

to hundreds of people at dinners or other special events. Two candidates running against one another might agree to discuss their different ideas at a public meeting. Today some candidates spend millions of dollars for television and radio advertisements to tell people about their ideas.

Often people want to help a candidate get elected. These volunteers hand out posters and buttons with the candidate's name and picture on them. Sometimes volunteers telephone voters to tell them why they should vote for one of the candidates. They may also telephone voters to tell them why they should or should not vote for a new law.

4. Think and Apply

Hold an election in your class using what you have learned. You and your classmates should choose two candidates for a special job. Then the class members should form three groups. One group should help each candidate decide what to say to the voters about his or her ideas. A second group should make posters and buttons. The third group should make ballots so each student in the school can vote in secret. This group will also make a ballot box to collect the ballots. Ask for volunteers to count them. The winner should make a speech accepting the special job.

FOCUS
How is a state government like other kinds of government?

Main Idea Read to find out how state governments affect the lives of citizens.

Vocabulary
governor
public property
private property
jury

State Governments

You have read how people and community governments work together to solve problems. Leaders bring people together to plan. Laws help people know what to do and what not to do. Another government that affects you and your community is your state government. Nearly all citizens of the United States live in one of the 50 states. Each state has its own government that affects the lives of its citizens.

State Governments Are Not All Alike

The 50 states are different from one another in many ways. Each state has its own climate, landforms, history, and resources. Its problems may be different from the problems of other states, too. Citizens in Florida, Texas, and Louisiana must plan ways to deal with hurricanes. Citizens in California and Alaska must plan ways to deal with earthquakes. Each state needs its own government to deal with its own problems.

REVIEW **Why does each state need its own government?**

National Guard troops help citizens get supplies after a hurricane.

The Governor Leads the State

Each state government has a leader called a **governor**. The governor is elected by the voters in the state. The governor's job is like the job of a city or town mayor in many ways. The governor suggests laws that he or she thinks will be good for the state. A governor also meets with governors from other states to share ideas and talk about ways to solve problems.

The governor of a state is also the leader of the state's branch of the National Guard. The National Guard can help citizens in an emergency such as a tornado or an earthquake. When tornadoes hit Florida in 1998, people whose homes and businesses were damaged could not go back to them right away. The National Guard protected their property until they could return. Property is land, buildings, and other things that belong to people.

One kind of property is public property. **Public property** belongs to all citizens. Parks and some museums are public property. Another kind of property is private property. **Private property** belongs to one person or a small group of people. Homes and businesses are private property.

REVIEW How is the governor's job like the job of the mayor of a city or a town?

The girl's bicycle is her private property.

Public property is for all citizens to use and enjoy.

Members of the National Governors' Association meet with President Clinton.

Lesson 3 • **357**

Lawmakers and Judges

Each state government also has lawmakers. The lawmakers are elected by voters in the state. Most states have two groups of lawmakers—senators and representatives—who write state laws. Nebraska, however, has only one group of lawmakers. Each state's lawmakers meet in the state capital.

State governments also have state judges. Many judges are not elected. Instead, they are chosen by the governor. Judges decide whether state laws are fair. State judges also help protect private property. If a person is accused of stealing or harming private property, that person must go to court.

In court a judge and a jury listen to both sides tell what happened. A **jury** is a group of 6 to 12 citizens. The jury decides whether the person accused of the crime is guilty or not guilty. If it decides the person is guilty, the judge tells what the consequences will be.

REVIEW What do state lawmakers and judges do?

A jury listening in a courtroom

Governments Have Different Responsibilities

There are some things that are done by both state governments and community governments. Both make laws and collect taxes from citizens. Both use tax money to provide services and to buy property that the public will own.

There are some things that are only done by state governments. State governments provide citizens with driver's licenses. They also build state highways and care for state parks.

There are some things that only community governments do. Community governments provide services such as fire protection and garbage collection.

REVIEW What are some of the things state governments do?

LEARNING FROM DIAGRAMS

This diagram shows how the state and community governments affect people in Bishopville, South Carolina.

■ What services do your state and community governments provide?

Two Levels of Government

UNITED STATES

SOUTH CAROLINA

Bishopville
Columbia★

CITY HALL

State Government of South Carolina
- solves problems in the state
- collects taxes
- provides a court system
- provides money for schools
- builds state highways
- provides state parks
- provides driver licenses

Community Government of Bishopville, South Carolina
- solves problems in the community
- collects taxes
- provides community services
- helps protect private property
- provides community parks

LESSON 3 REVIEW

Check Understanding

1 Remember the Facts Who is the leader of a state government?

2 Recall the Main Idea In what ways does a state government affect the lives of citizens?

Think Critically

3 Explore Viewpoints Why might different governors use different ways to solve the same problem?

Show What You Know

Map Activity Draw a map of your community. On your map, show where you live. Then use symbols to show some different kinds of private property. Also show places that are public property in and near your community. Give your map a title and a map key. Share your map with a classmate. Explain to your classmate the difference between private property and public property.

Measure Distance on a Map

1. Why Learn This Skill?

To find out how far apart two places on a map really are, you need a distance scale. A distance scale shows that a certain length on a map stands for some longer, real distance on the Earth.

2. Understand the Process

Look at the distance scale on the map of the state of Oregon. You can see that the top part of the scale has the word *Miles*. The bottom part of the scale has the word *Kilometers*. Kilometers are used in the metric system, which is another way of measuring. You can find distance with either part of the scale.

Use a ruler to measure the distance scale on the map. The scale is 1 inch long. Now read the number of miles on the distance scale. On this map, 1 inch stands for 150 miles on the Earth.

If two cities are 1 inch apart on this map, they are really 150 miles, or about 240 kilometers, apart. Now use the distance scale to find the distance in miles from Eugene to Ontario.

3. Think and Apply

Use the distance scale and the map of Oregon to answer these questions.

1. In miles, how far is it from Medford to Burns?

2. In kilometers, how far is it from the state capital to John Day?

3. Why is it important to know how to use a distance scale on a map?

The National Government

LESSON
4

FOCUS
How does our national government help you and your community?

Main Idea Read to find out how our national government works.

Vocabulary
Congress
Supreme Court

The governments of a community and of a state help keep people's lives safe and peaceful. The government of the United States, our national government, also affects people's lives.

Three Branches of Government

Most of the offices of the United States government are located in Washington, D.C., our nation's capital. The government is made up of three parts, each with a different job to do. The different parts of the government are sometimes called branches. The branches, like those on a tree, are separate but connected. The United States Constitution describes the job of each branch.

REVIEW How many parts make up the government of the United States?

THE BRANCHES OF THE UNITED STATES GOVERNMENT

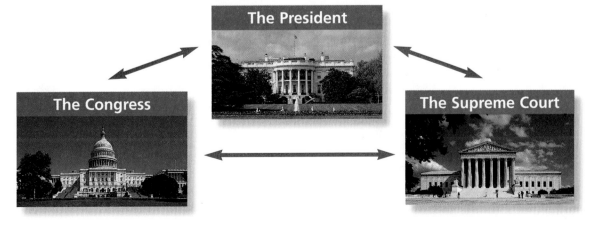

The President

The Congress

The Supreme Court

The President Leads the Government

One branch of our national government includes the President of the United States. The President leads the government and helps keep the country safe and peaceful. These pictures show some of the jobs of the President. They also show some past Presidents doing those jobs.

The President lives and works in the White House.

President Johnson

1. The President signs a new law.

President Nixon

2. The President visits other countries to build friendships with them.

PRESIDENTS OF THE UNITED STATES SINCE 1961

1960

1961–1963
John F. Kennedy

1963–1969
Lyndon B. Johnson

1970

1969–1974
Richard Nixon

1974–1977
Gerald Ford

President Carter

President Reagan

President Bush

3. The President signs treaties, or agreements with other countries.

4. The President communicates with citizens.

5. The President leads the Army, Navy, Air Force, and Marines.

President Clinton

6. The President tells lawmakers what the government is doing and what new laws are needed.

REVIEW What are some of the jobs of the President?

LEARNING FROM TIME LINES
Presidents are elected to four-year terms and may serve only two terms.
■ How many terms did President Jimmy Carter serve?

1980   1990

1977–1981   **1981–1989**   **1989–1993**   **1993–**

Jimmy Carter

Ronald Reagan

George Bush

Bill Clinton

Congress Makes New Laws

Congress meets in the Capitol building.

Another branch of the national government is **Congress**, which makes new laws. Congress has two parts. One is the House of Representatives, and the other is the Senate.

The House of Representatives has 435 members. Each state has a certain number of representatives based upon population. The more people who live in a state, the more representatives the state can send to Congress. California has the most representatives, 52, because more people live in California than in any other state. Alaska, Delaware, Montana, North Dakota, South Dakota, Vermont, and Wyoming each has only one representative because they have fewer people.

The Senate has 100 members. Each state, no matter how many people it has, sends two senators to serve in the Senate. Representatives and senators are like the members of a city or town council. They are elected by the people of the United States to work to solve national problems.

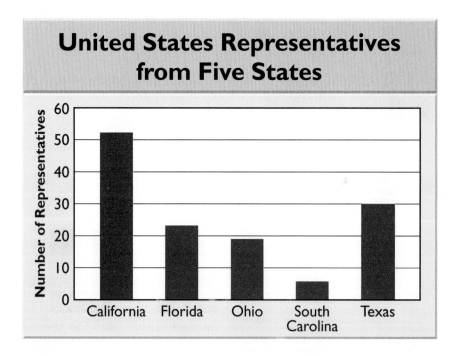

United States Representatives from Five States

Number of Representatives

60 · 50 · 40 · 30 · 20 · 10 · 0

California Florida Ohio South Carolina Texas

LEARNING FROM BAR GRAPHS Which two of the states shown here have the most representatives? Explain why.

Members of the House of Representatives

The Capitol building in Washington, D.C., has two large rooms called chambers. The House of Representatives meets in one chamber, and the Senate meets in the other. The members come together to discuss problems and to vote on how to solve them. They write new laws and decide how much money United States citizens should pay in taxes. The House and the Senate must agree on a new law before it can be passed. Then the President can sign it.

South Carolina ▶
Senator
Strom Thurmond

South Carolina
Senator
◀ Fritz Hollings

REVIEW **What are the two parts of Congress called?**

The Supreme Court Interprets Laws

The Supreme Court meets in the Supreme Court building.

The third branch of our national government is the courts. The **Supreme Court** is the highest, or most important, court in the United States. Nine judges, called justices, serve on the Supreme Court. Their leader is called the chief justice.

The Supreme Court is in charge of studying laws and deciding if they are fair or unfair. If a law is unfair, the justices can ask Congress to change it.

Chief Justice John Marshall once said that our nation's Constitution is "the outline of a government." This outline often does not tell lawmakers exactly what they need to know. The Supreme Court answers their questions when the Constitution is not clear about a subject.

BIOGRAPHY

Sandra Day O'Connor
1930–

Sandra Day O'Connor became the first woman to serve on the Supreme Court. She grew up on the Lazy B Ranch on the border between Arizona and New Mexico. After she received her law degree, she became a senator and an Arizona state judge. President Reagan met her and discovered that as a judge she was tough but fair. He wanted her to serve as a judge on the Supreme Court, and the Senate approved his choice. Sandra Day O'Connor's job has taken her far from the Lazy B Ranch, but she visits whenever she can.

Justices are not elected to the Supreme Court. Instead, they are chosen by the President. The President's choices must be approved by the Senate. A justice serves for life or until he or she decides to quit. When a justice is chosen to serve on the Supreme Court, he or she promises to "do equal right to the poor and to the rich."

REVIEW How are the justices of the Supreme Court chosen?

Nine justices serve on the Supreme Court.

LESSON 4 REVIEW

Check Understanding

1 Remember the Facts What are the branches of the United States government?

2 Recall the Main Idea What does each branch of the United States government do?

Think Critically

3 Think More About It The United States Constitution gives us "the outline of a government" and leaves the details to be filled in. Why do you think the writers of the Constitution did this?

Show What You Know

Problem-Solving Activity Read or listen to news reports to identify a real problem in our nation. The class should form small groups to talk about how the problem might be solved. Share your group's ideas with the whole class.

FOCUS

In what ways can you show that you are proud to be a citizen of your community and country?

Main Idea Read to find out how our flag brings people together all over the United States.

Vocabulary

patriotism
anthem
pledge
allegiance

Symbols of Pride

You have probably seen our country's flag in many places—for example, in front of your school, in your classroom, or at the post office. A flag may seem like just a piece of cloth with a simple design. However, most people honor their flag because it is a symbol of their country. The feeling of love people have for their country is called **patriotism**. A flag stands for the ideas the people of a country believe in.

A Flag for a New Country

There are many kinds of flags. Some rulers, such as the king or the queen of England, have personal flags that are used when the rulers are present. Other flags stand for cities, states, businesses, or sports teams. Of all the kinds of flags, a national flag is the most important. It stands for a country and all the people who live in it.

People show pride in their country when they display the flag.

The design of the flag of the United States of America has changed over time. On early United States flags, the number of both stars and stripes showed the number of states in the country. But as the country grew, there were too many states to show with stripes. Congress decided that only a star should be added to the flag when a new state joined the United States. The number of stripes would stay at 13, for the first 13 states.

Congress did not say how the stars should be grouped, so there were different designs. In 1912 it was decided that the stars should always be grouped in straight rows. The last change to the flag was in 1960. In that year the fiftieth star was added to stand for the state of Hawaii.

REVIEW **Why has the design of our country's flag changed many times?**

1777

1795

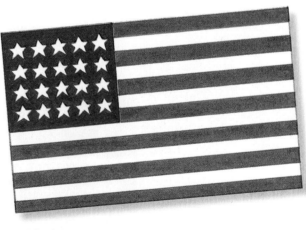

1818

Today

The National Anthem

Francis Scott Key

Many people, when they look at the flag, think of the freedom for which it stands. They also think about the people who fought and died in wars to protect the country's freedom. "The Star-Spangled Banner," our country's national anthem, was written because of the flag. An **anthem** is a song of patriotism.

Francis Scott Key, a lawyer from Washington, D.C., watched from a distance as Fort McHenry, in Baltimore, Maryland, was attacked by the British during the War of 1812. The battle, which had started during the day, went on into the night. Even after the fighting had stopped, Key could not see through the darkness to tell who had won. As the sun rose, he could see the American flag flying above the fort. Key knew then that the United States had won. His feeling of patriotism was so strong that he wrote a poem. That poem became the words to "The Star-Spangled Banner."

Most flags are flown only during the day. However, the flag flies day and night over Fort McHenry and over the grave of Francis Scott Key.

REVIEW **Who wrote "The Star-Spangled Banner"?**

★ THE STAR-SPANGLED BANNER ★

O say can you see by the dawn's early light
What so proudly we hailed at the twilight's last gleaming.
Whose broad stripes and bright stars through the perilous fight,
O'er the ramparts we watched, were so gallantly streaming?
And the rocket's red glare, the bomb bursting in air,
Gave proof through the night that our flag was still there,
O say does that star-spangled banner yet wave
O'er the land of the free and the home of the brave?

The Pledge of Allegiance

Saying the Pledge of Allegiance is a tradition for many citizens in the United States. A **pledge** is a promise, and **allegiance** means being true to something. Citizens respect the flag and the things it stands for. When you say that you "pledge allegiance to the flag," you are saying that you promise to be true to the flag and our country. People show their respect by standing when they say the pledge. They also place their right hands over their hearts in a salute and look at the flag as they say these words.

A third-grade class saluting the flag in 1900

> 66 I pledge allegiance to the Flag of the United States of America, and to the Republic for which it stands, one Nation under God, indivisible, with liberty and justice for all. 99

The Pledge of Allegiance was said for the very first time in 1892 by children in public schools. Many students all across the United States now join in this salute to the flag every school day.

REVIEW What is the Pledge of Allegiance?

A third-grade class saluting the flag today

371

The flag is used to honor soldiers and others who have died serving their country. This flag honored President John F. Kennedy at his funeral.

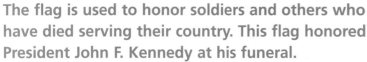
The flag is flown at voting places on election days.

Displaying the Flag

The flag gives people of all ages, who live in communities across our country, a shared symbol for their homeland. It brings them together and helps them remember the ideas that have made this country great. These photos show some of the places and events at which our national flag is displayed.

REVIEW What are some places or events at which our national flag is displayed?

The nation's flag is used to mark great discoveries. Astronaut Edwin Aldrin stands next to the flag he and Neil Armstrong placed on the moon.

United States winners at the Olympic Games proudly hold or wave the flag.

LESSON 5 REVIEW

Check Understanding

1 **Remember the Facts** What are some times when the flag is displayed?

2 **Recall the Main Idea** How does the flag help bring people from different communities together?

Think Critically

3 **Personally Speaking** In what ways can you show your patriotism?

Show What You Know

Design Activity Work with a group to design a flag for your class. Decide what colors and symbols you will use. Each color and symbol should stand for something that you think is important. Then use paper or cloth to make your flag. Explain to other groups what the colors and the symbols stand for. Then display your flag on a bulletin board.

Lesson 5 • **373**

Compare Patriotic

1. Why Learn This Skill?

Symbols are all around you. A flag is a symbol you can see and touch. An anthem is a symbol you can listen to or sing. Symbols are important because they stand for things people believe in. Knowing what symbols mean can help you learn more about your community, state, country, and world.

2. Understand the Process

All countries have their own symbols. Here are a few well-known symbols of the United States.

THE GREAT SEAL OF THE UNITED STATES This became an important symbol in 1782. Both sides of this seal can be seen on a dollar bill. The eagle holds an olive branch, which is a symbol of peace. The arrows the eagle holds are a symbol of strength. This seal is used on important government papers and can be seen on the walls of government buildings in the nation's capital.

UNCLE SAM Uncle Sam is a national symbol that stands for the United States. The most well-known image of Uncle Sam is shown in this poster drawn by James Montgomery Flagg in 1916–1917.

THE FLAG Displaying the flag is one way to show patriotism.

Symbols

THE BALD EAGLE

The powerful bald eagle is the national bird of the United States. It was chosen as a national symbol because it is found only in North America. This bird has been seen in every state except Hawaii.

THE NATIONAL ANTHEM

People sing "The Star-Spangled Banner," our national anthem, at many sports events.

NATIONAL SONGS

People also sing these patriotic songs about our country.

"America"

by Samuel Francis Smith

My country, 'tis of thee,
Sweet land of liberty,
Of thee I sing:
Land where my fathers died,
Land of the Pilgrims' pride,
From every mountainside
Let freedom ring.

▲ The Liberty Bell is a symbol for freedom. It hangs near Independence Hall in Philadelphia, Pennsylvania.

"America the Beautiful"

by Katharine Lee Bates

O beautiful for spacious skies,
For amber waves of grain,
For purple mountain majesties
Above the fruited plain!
America! America!
God shed his grace on thee
And crown thy good with brotherhood
From sea to shining sea!

Each state also has its symbols. Here are some state flags and birds for different states. How are these symbols different from those of the United States? How are they the same?

STATE FLAGS

▼ The Bear Flag is the state flag of California. It was first raised during a revolt on June 14, 1846.

▼ The Florida flag shows the state seal, which has many symbols for the state—sunshine, a palm tree, and rivers and lakes. This became the official state flag in 1899.

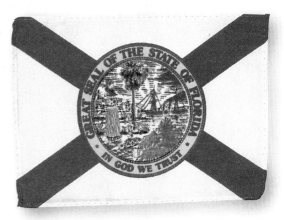

▼ There have been three different flags for Georgia. The flag in use now became the official state flag in 1956.

▼ In the center of the New York flag, ships are sailing on the Hudson River. This became the official state flag in 1901.

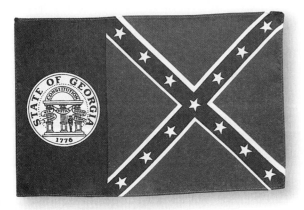

STATE BIRDS

▼ The California quail is the state bird of California.

▼ The eastern goldfinch is the state bird of New Jersey.

▼ The brown thrasher is the state bird of Georgia.

▼ The robin is the state bird of Michigan.

South Carolina has its own symbols that have become part of the state's identity. **Identity** is the sense of sameness people feel about something. For example, when most people see their state's flag, they feel proud. There are many state symbols that give South Carolina its identity.

STATE FLAG

▼ The state flag was adopted, or chosen, on January 28, 1861. The flag's blue background matches the blue uniform worn by the American soldiers at Fort Moultrie on Sullivan's Island.

STATE SEAL

▼ The official seal was used for the first time on May 22, 1777. The palmetto tree on the left side of the seal is a symbol of the battle on Sullivan's Island.

STATE PLEDGE

▼ The salute to the flag of South Carolina was adopted by the General Assembly in 1966. These are the words.

❝ I salute the Flag of South Carolina and pledge to the Palmetto State love, loyalty, and faith. ❞

THE STATE MOTTOES

▼ Both of the state mottoes are on the great seal of South Carolina. A **motto** is a saying that holds meaning for many people. These are the official mottoes.

❝ Ready in soul and resource. ❞

❝ While I breathe I hope. ❞

STATE ANIMAL

▶ The white-tailed deer became the official state animal in 1972.

STATE BIRD

▼ The Carolina wren became South Carolina's official state bird in 1948.

STATE FLOWER

▼ The Carolina jessamine (JEH•suh•muhn) became the state flower in 1924.

STATE TREE

▼ The Palmetto became the state tree in 1939. The palmetto is on the state flag and the state seal.

3. Think and Apply

Many states have more symbols than the ones shown on these pages. Do research to find out what other types of symbols South Carolina has. Share your research with a small group of classmates. Then, as a group, think of something that could be a symbol for your class. Make a poster that shows your idea.

FOCUS
How are governments in other countries like our government?

Main Idea Read to find out how the government of South Africa is solving problems.

Vocabulary
province

Solving Problems in South Africa

There are hundreds of countries in the world. Each country and each community has a government that works to solve its problems. Now look at one community in the country of South Africa to see how its government is working to solve problems.

An Unfair Government

South Africa is in the Southern Hemisphere. It is at the southern tip of the continent of Africa. South Africa touches both the Atlantic Ocean and the Indian Ocean. Near the big city of Johannesburg is the community of Soweto (suh•WAY•toh).

Farmers and hunters settled much of southern Africa almost 2,000 years ago. They were the ancestors of the black people who live in South Africa today.

In the 1600s and 1700s, many white people from Europe came to live in southern Africa. They took much of the land that the black people had lived on for hundreds of years. The Europeans set up communities, and in 1910 they formed the country of South Africa.

Frederik de Klerk was president of South Africa from 1989 to 1994.

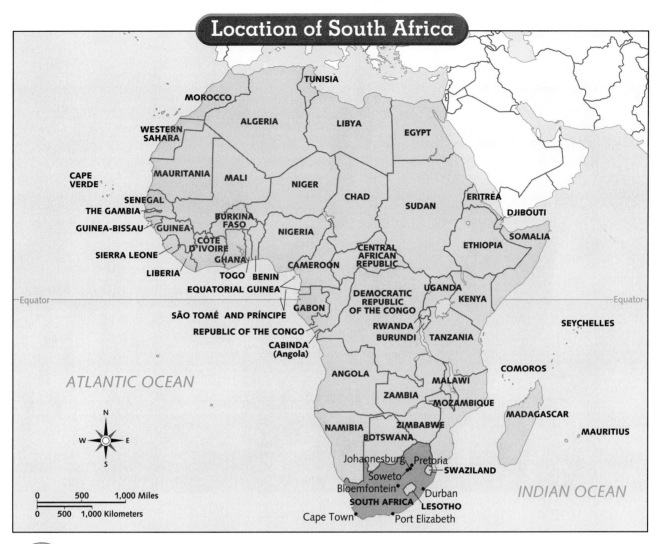

Location of South Africa

TUNISIA
MOROCCO
WESTERN SAHARA
ALGERIA
LIBYA
EGYPT
CAPE VERDE
MAURITANIA
MALI
NIGER
CHAD
SUDAN
ERITREA
DJIBOUTI
SENEGAL
THE GAMBIA
GUINEA-BISSAU
GUINEA
BURKINA FASO
NIGERIA
SOMALIA
CÔTE D'IVOIRE
SIERRA LEONE
GHANA
CENTRAL AFRICAN REPUBLIC
ETHIOPIA
LIBERIA
TOGO BENIN
CAMEROON
EQUATORIAL GUINEA
DEMOCRATIC REPUBLIC OF THE CONGO
UGANDA
KENYA
Equator
SÃO TOMÉ AND PRÍNCIPE
GABON
REPUBLIC OF THE CONGO
CABINDA (Angola)
RWANDA
BURUNDI
TANZANIA
SEYCHELLES
ATLANTIC OCEAN
ANGOLA
ZAMBIA
MALAWI
MOZAMBIQUE
COMOROS
MADAGASCAR
NAMIBIA
ZIMBABWE
BOTSWANA
MAURITIUS
Johannesburg Pretoria
Soweto SWAZILAND
Bloemfontein
SOUTH AFRICA Durban
Cape Town LESOTHO
Port Elizabeth
INDIAN OCEAN

N W E S

0   500   1,000 Miles
0   500   1,000 Kilometers

Place ■ What are the two small countries inside the borders of South Africa?

Not all the people who lived in South Africa could take part in running the country. Until 1994 only white people were allowed to vote. No black leaders were allowed in the national government. Yet many more black people than white people lived in South Africa. Because of this unfairness, there were many conflicts. Communities such as Soweto were not safe or peaceful places to live. Leaders of South Africa knew the problem had to be solved.

REVIEW **What was the problem in South Africa?**

Desmond Tutu is a leader who wanted to change the national government in South Africa.

On May 8, 1996, leaders in Cape Town, South Africa, gathered to accept a new constitution.

A New Constitution

In 1993 the leaders of South Africa began to write a new constitution to change the unfair laws in their country. Three years later, the new constitution was approved. Like the United States Constitution, the Constitution of South Africa explains how the government will work. It also names the basic rights of all South African citizens. Former president F. W. de Klerk spoke for many people when he said that South Africans were ready to "turn our back on the bitterness of the past, to build and develop, and to bring a better life to all our people."

In 1994 South Africa had its first election in which all adult citizens, black and white, were allowed to vote. Voters elected many black representatives to help run the national government. Leaders were also elected for South Africa's provinces. Some countries are made up of **provinces**, the way our country is made up of states. Each province has its own government. Leaders were elected for South Africa's many cities and towns, too.

South African citizens voting

REVIEW What did the new constitution give the citizens of Soweto and other South African communities?

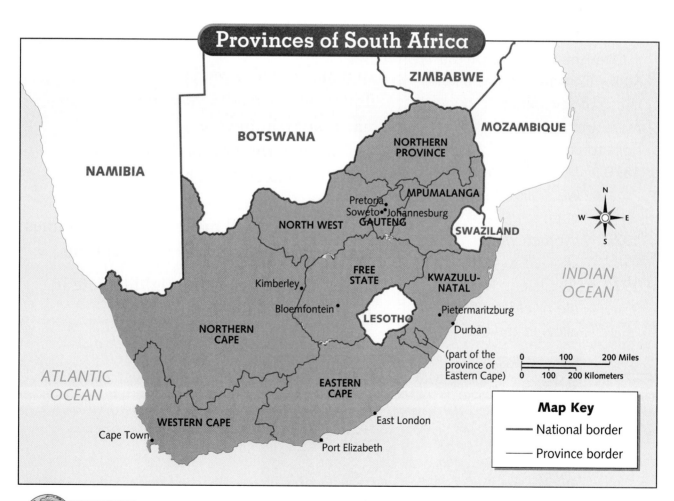

Provinces of South Africa

Place From 1910 to 1994, South Africa had four provinces. In 1994 the country was divided in a new way.
■ How many provinces does South Africa have now?

Governments Change to Solve Problems

The government of South Africa had to change to solve the nation's problems. The biggest change came in 1994. Before then, only white people could vote. Today in every South African community, all citizens who are 18 years old or older can vote to elect leaders and to make other decisions.

Years ago the United States had unfair voting laws, too. At one time only white men who owned land could vote. African Americans, Native Americans, and women could not vote. Lawmakers have made changes to the United States Constitution to make voting laws fair for everyone. Today all citizens 18 years old or older have the right to vote.

The governments of South Africa and the United States have made many changes. People in both countries hope these changes will make their communities safe and peaceful places for all citizens.

REVIEW Who has the right to vote in the United States?

HISTORY

Voting Rights

Over the years the United States Constitution has been changed several times to give more and more citizens the right to vote.

1870 Men of all races were allowed to vote.

1920 Women were allowed to vote.

1971 All citizens 18 years old or older were allowed to vote.

The President of South Africa

Like Marcy in *City Green* and Wilma Mankiller with the Cherokees, Nelson Mandela of South Africa made things happen. Because he spoke against the unfairness of keeping black people out of government, he was sent to prison for 28 years. After he was set free, the people of South Africa elected him as their president. Nelson Mandela became the first black South African to lead the national government.

Mandela brought change to South Africa by resolving many conflicts. He worked for a compromise between majority rule and minority rights. Since the majority of people in South Africa are black, now most of the country's leaders are black. Mandela wanted them to protect the rights of all people. This included protecting the rights of white people, who are in the minority.

Nelson Mandela, president of South Africa

REVIEW **How did Nelson Mandela bring change to South Africa?**

LESSON 6 REVIEW

Check Understanding

1 Remember the Facts Who was elected South Africa's first black president?

2 Recall the Main Idea How is the South African government solving problems?

Think Critically

3 Cause and Effect How do you think changes in the government of South Africa have affected the lives of its citizens?

Show What You Know

Creative Writing Activity Write a paragraph that will persuade all citizens to vote. In your paragraph, explain why responsible citizens should vote. Then trade paragraphs with a classmate, and compare your ideas.

FOCUS
How is South Carolina's government like the government of the United States?

Main Idea Read to find out how South Carolina's government affects the lives of all its citizens.

Vocabulary
education

▲ Inez Tenenbaum, South Carolina's State Superintendent of Education

► The University of South Carolina has had a separate library building since 1840.

South Carolina's Government

South Carolina's state government is like the government of the United States. Both have three branches—lawmakers, leaders, and judges. Each branch has a responsibility to help make your life safe and to make sure you have many different opportunities.

State Government

The voters of South Carolina elect people to make laws. These people form South Carolina's General Assembly. Like Congress, the General Assembly is divided into two parts—the Senate and the House of Representatives.

The lawmakers of the General Assembly have passed laws that say its citizens must pay sales tax and state income tax. These taxes help pay for state and community services, such as museums and libraries. They have also passed a law that says children from age 5 to 16 must

receive an education. **Education** is the knowledge you are given by your teachers. Education can help you get a good job when you are an adult.

South Carolina's leaders help make sure the people obey the laws. The chief leader of the state is the governor. Jim Hodges is South Carolina's governor.

South Carolina's Supreme Court is the highest court in the state. The General Assembly elects five Supreme Court justices to make sure that the laws in the state are fair.

REVIEW What two parts is South Carolina's General Assembly divided into?

Governor Jim Hodges of South Carolina

South Carolina's Supreme Court includes Chief Justice Ernest Finney, Jr., and Justices Jean Toal, John Waller, E.C. Burnett III, and James Moore.

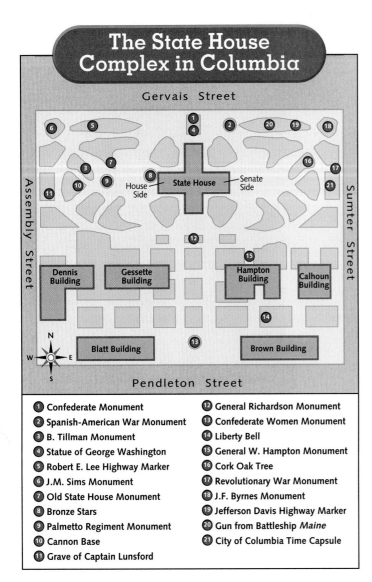

The State House Complex in Columbia

Gervais Street

Assembly Street

Sumter Street

House Side — State House — Senate Side

Dennis Building
Gessette Building
Hampton Building
Calhoun Building

N W E S

Blatt Building
Brown Building

Pendleton Street

1. Confederate Monument
2. Spanish-American War Monument
3. B. Tillman Monument
4. Statue of George Washington
5. Robert E. Lee Highway Marker
6. J.M. Sims Monument
7. Old State House Monument
8. Bronze Stars
9. Palmetto Regiment Monument
10. Cannon Base
11. Grave of Captain Lunsford
12. General Richardson Monument
13. Confederate Women Monument
14. Liberty Bell
15. General W. Hampton Monument
16. Cork Oak Tree
17. Revolutionary War Monument
18. J.F. Byrnes Monument
19. Jefferson Davis Highway Marker
20. Gun from Battleship *Maine*
21. City of Columbia Time Capsule

LEARNING FROM DIAGRAMS What monuments are located directly south of the State House?

From the steps of the State House, Governor Jim Hodges speaks to South Carolina's citizens.

The State House

It is an exciting day at the State House in Columbia when the new governor begins his job. Lawmakers shake hands and greet one another. Then everyone listens as the governor shares his ideas and plans for all of South Carolina's citizens.

The General Assembly meets in the State House and is made up of 46 senators and 124 representatives. There is one senator for each county. The number of representatives is based upon South Carolina's population. The governor and many other government workers also have offices in the State House.

REVIEW Where do South Carolina state senators and representatives meet?

Local Government

The state of South Carolina is divided into 46 counties. Each of these counties has its own government. There are several towns in each county. The town where the county government is located is the county seat.

Voters in each county elect a group of people to run the county government and to make laws for the county. This group is called the County Council.

The Saluda county courthouse

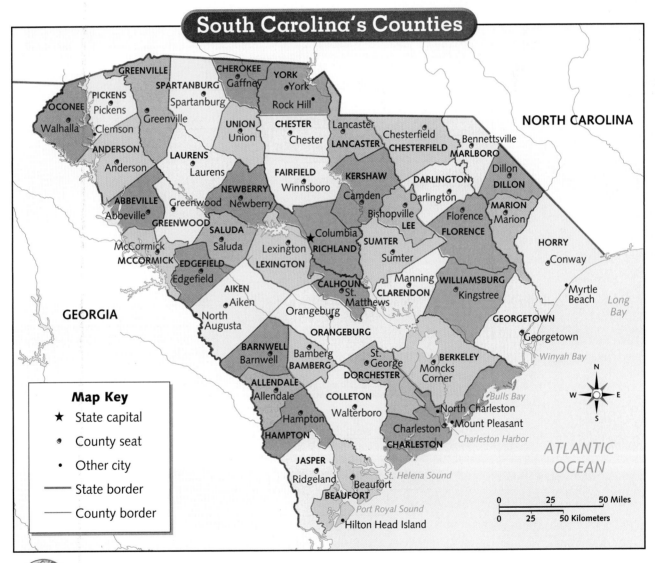

South Carolina's Counties

NORTH CAROLINA

GEORGIA

ATLANTIC OCEAN

Long Bay

Winyah Bay

Bulls Bay

Charleston Harbor

St. Helena Sound

Port Royal Sound

Map Key
- ★ State capital
- ◦ County seat
- • Other city
- State border
- County border

0   25   50 Miles
0   25   50 Kilometers

N / S / E / W

GREENVILLE, CHEROKEE, YORK, SPARTANBURG, Gaffney, PICKENS, Pickens, Spartanburg, York, OCONEE, Greenville, Rock Hill, Walhalla, Clemson, UNION, CHESTER, Lancaster, Chesterfield, Bennettsville, Union, Chester, LANCASTER, CHESTERFIELD, MARLBORO, ANDERSON, LAURENS, Anderson, Laurens, FAIRFIELD, KERSHAW, Dillon, DILLON, NEWBERRY, Winnsboro, Camden, DARLINGTON, ABBEVILLE, Greenwood, Newberry, Bishopville, Darlington, MARION, Abbeville, GREENWOOD, SALUDA, Columbia, LEE, Florence, Marion, McCormick, Saluda, Lexington, RICHLAND, SUMTER, FLORENCE, HORRY, MCCORMICK, EDGEFIELD, LEXINGTON, Sumter, Conway, Edgefield, AIKEN, CALHOUN, Manning, WILLIAMSBURG, Aiken, St. Matthews, CLARENDON, Kingstree, Myrtle Beach, Orangeburg, North Augusta, ORANGEBURG, GEORGETOWN, BARNWELL, Bamberg, St. George, BERKELEY, Georgetown, Barnwell, BAMBERG, DORCHESTER, Moncks Corner, ALLENDALE, Allendale, COLLETON, North Charleston, Hampton, Walterboro, Mount Pleasant, HAMPTON, Charleston, CHARLESTON, JASPER, Ridgeland, Beaufort, BEAUFORT, Hilton Head Island

Regions South Carolina has 46 counties.
■ Which of South Carolina's counties border the county you live in?

Lesson 7 • **389**

Cities and towns also have their own governments. There are three types of city government in South Carolina. One is the mayor-council type of government. Voters in a city elect the mayor and the council members. The mayor and the council together help run the city.

A second type of city government is the council government. The council members are elected by the voters to run the city. In this type of government, the mayor is the leader of the council.

LEARNING FROM DIAGRAMS

Which type of local government has a city manager?

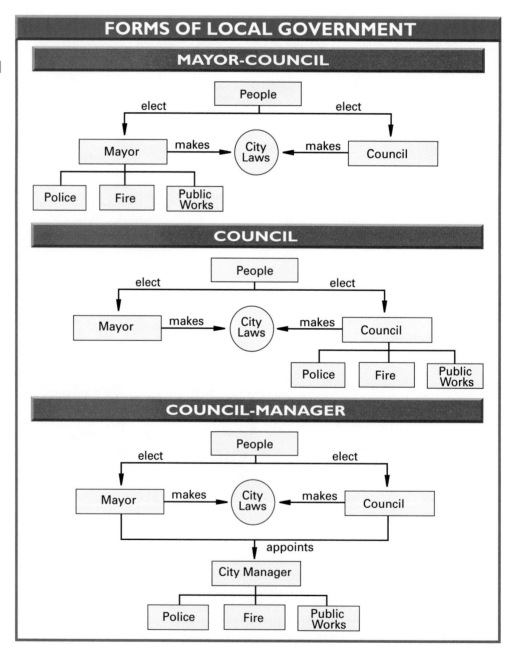

FORMS OF LOCAL GOVERNMENT

MAYOR-COUNCIL

COUNCIL

COUNCIL-MANAGER

A third type of city government is the council-manager government. In this type of government the mayor and council hire a city manager to help run the daily activities of the city.

REVIEW What are the responsibilities of the County Council?

Reuben Greenberg 1943–

In 1982 Reuben Greenberg was appointed, or chosen, by the mayor of Charleston to serve as the Chief of Police. Since then, he and the rest of the police department have made Charleston a safer place for people to live. Greenberg has received many awards for finding ways to reduce crime and resolve conflicts. Chief Reuben Greenberg is someone who has made a difference.

LESSON 7 REVIEW

Check Understanding

1 Remember the Facts What are the three branches of South Carolina's state government?

2 Recall the Main Idea How does the state government of South Carolina affect your life every day?

Think Critically

3 Think More About It Compare the government of South Carolina with the national government. How are they alike? different?

Show What You Know

Interview Activity Find a person to interview in your community. Make a list of questions you would like to ask the person, including what his or her responsibilities are. Remember to take notes and send a thank-you note after the interview. Share what you learned with the class.

LESSON

8

LEARN
ABOUT SOUTH
CAROLINA'S
PATRIOTIC
SONGS
through
Literature

Carolina

by Henry Timrod

South Carolina has two state songs that people sing to show their pride in the state. The first state song, "Carolina," was written by the South Carolina poet Henry Timrod. In 1911 the General Assembly adopted "Carolina" as the official state song of South Carolina.

Peach, the
state fruit

White-tailed deer,
the state animal

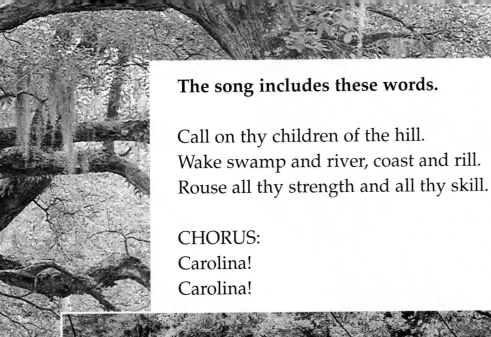

The song includes these words.

Call on thy children of the hill.
Wake swamp and river, coast and rill.
Rouse all thy strength and all thy skill.

CHORUS:
Carolina!
Carolina!

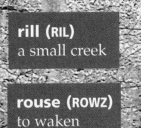

rill (RIL)
a small creek

rouse (ROWZ)
to waken

Carolina wren,
the state bird

Up Country
waterfall

SOUTH CAROLINA ON MY MIND

BY HANK MARTIN AND BUZZ ARLEDGE

The second state song, "South Carolina on My Mind," was written by Hank Martin and Buzz Arledge. These musicians were both born in South Carolina. Their song became so popular that in 1984 the General Assembly adopted "South Carolina on My Mind" as the second state song of South Carolina.

Cherokee foothills ▶

▼ Loggerhead turtle, the state reptile

The song includes these words.

At the foothills of the Appalachian chain,
down through the rivers, to the coastal plain,
there's a place that I call home and I'll never be alone,
singin' this Carolina love song.

CHORUS:
I've got South Carolina on my mind,
remembering all those sunshine summertimes,
and the autumns in the Smokies when the
    leaves turn to gold
touches my heart and thrills my soul
to have South Carolina on my mind,
with those clean snow-covered mountain wintertimes
and the white sand of the beaches and those
    Carolina peaches,
I've got South Carolina on my mind.

thrills (THRILZ)
causes
excitement

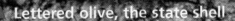

Lettered olive, the state shell

LITERATURE REVIEW

1. What is South Carolina's state animal?
2. What do these state songs tell you about South Carolina's identity?
3. Write a poem or song of your own about an idea or event important to South Carolina.

The Turkey OR

For many years lawmakers tried to decide on a design for the Great Seal of the United States. But they could not agree. Finally, on June 20, 1782, Congress chose a design that showed an eagle. On that day, the bald eagle became a national symbol for the United States.

Benjamin Franklin, a member of the committee that chose the design, had wanted the rattlesnake for a national symbol. Later he had agreed that a bird would be a better choice.

The Turkey

However, in a letter to his daughter, Sarah, Franklin wrote,

> 66 I wish the Bald Eagle had not been chosen as the Representative of our Country. . . . The Turkey is a much more respectable Bird. 99

Franklin thought the eagle was a coward because it could be chased away by smaller birds. Also, he had heard that the eagle took food away from other birds. He felt that the turkey would be a better symbol of America because it was a bird with courage. It was also an important food source for settlers.

The Great Seal of the United States

The turkey—a national symbol?

The Eagle?

The Eagle

Over the years many people have disagreed with Franklin. In the 1930s the animal scientist Francis Hobart Herrick wrote,

66 The bald eagle is an expert fisherman . . . he is never driven from the neighborhood by any other living being excepting a man armed with a gun. 99

The National Symbol Today

People did not let Franklin's ideas change their minds. The eagle had long been a symbol of freedom and power. The choice of the bald eagle as the American symbol was so well liked that pictures of the bird began to be used on quilts, furniture, and dishes. Today the eagle can be seen on coins, paper money, stamps, and government papers.

These are some of the kinds of objects on which an eagle is shown.

Compare Viewpoints

1. Why did Benjamin Franklin think the eagle was not a good choice for a national symbol?

2. Why did Francis Hobart Herrick think the eagle was a good choice?

Think and Apply

Do you agree or disagree with the decision to make the bald eagle a national symbol? Write a letter to Benjamin Franklin to let him know your point of view. Share your letter with your classmates.

HONORING OUR Veterans

▲ The *Yorktown*

November 11 is Veterans Day. On Veterans Day we honor the men and women who have fought for our country.

Veterans Day is an exciting day for hundreds of students from schools near Charleston, South Carolina. They travel to Patriot's Point and walk onto a ship named the *Yorktown*. On the *Yorktown*, they attend a program for World War II veterans.

Speakers talk about the freedom we enjoy in the United States. They tell how veterans have fought to keep our country and other countries free. Then students share their ideas about why we honor our veterans. The group sings the national anthem and other patriotic songs. When the program is over, everyone feels proud to be an American.

Think and Apply

Our veterans gave up certain things to serve in our country's armed forces. What do you think some of those things were? Discuss your ideas with your family. Then write a few paragraphs that tell why we owe veterans our thanks. Share your writing with a veteran.

HARCOURT BRACE

Visit the Internet at **http://www.hbschool.com** for additional resources.

▼A World War II veteran shares a story with a student.

▲ A color guard marches as part of the Veterans Day celebration.

UNIT 5
REVIEW

Study the pictures and captions to help you review the events you read about in Unit 5.

Draw a Map Look for the patriotic symbols shown on the visual summary. Now draw a map of your community to show where flags or other patriotic symbols are displayed. Add a title, a compass rose, and a map key. Then share your map with a family member.

1 People in communities work together to solve their problems.

3 The parts of our government work together to keep the country strong.

2 Rules and laws are made to help everyone in a community.

4 Citizens show pride in their country in many ways.

5 Governments in other countries also work to solve problems.

UNIT 5 REVIEW

Complete this graphic organizer by writing details for the main idea of each lesson. A copy of the organizer appears on Activity Book page 79.

Lesson 6
Solving problems in other countries
1. _____
2. _____

Lesson 1
Solving community problems
1. _____
2. _____

Lesson 5
Patriotic symbols
1. _____
2. _____

Living Together in a Community, State, and Nation

Lesson 2
Rules and laws
1. _____
2. _____

Lesson 4
Branches of national government
1. _____
2. _____

Lesson 3
State governments
1. _____
2. _____

WRITE MORE ABOUT IT

Write a Letter Think of something that you would like to see changed in your community. Then write a letter to a community leader. In your letter, explain what you think needs to be done. Also explain what the first step might be in making this change. Read your letter to a family member, and talk about the change you have written about.

USE VOCABULARY

Look at the words below. Write a sentence for each word. Then write one more sentence that tells how these words are connected.

1 allegiance

2 anthem

3 patriotism

4 pledge

CHECK UNDERSTANDING

5 What group of people helps a city's mayor make laws?

6 What is the set of laws for our country's government called?

7 What are the jobs of the branches of the national government?

THINK CRITICALLY

8 **Past to Present** How have lawmakers of the past affected your life today?

9 **Think More About It** Why is it important for citizens to get an education?

10 **Personally Speaking** If you could have a job in government, which job would you choose? Explain.

APPLY SKILLS

Resolve Conflicts Imagine that two children have a conflict. Each child wants an apple, but there is only one apple. Write a story that tells how the children might resolve the conflict.

Compare Patriotic Symbols The design of the United States flag has changed many times. Look at the pictures, and then answer the questions below.

11 How are these two flags different?

12 Why do you think the flags are different in this way?

Measure Distance on a Map

Use the distance scale and the map of South Carolina to answer the questions in miles and kilometers.

South Carolina

NORTH CAROLINA

Spartanburg
Greenville
Rock Hill
Anderson
SOUTH CAROLINA
Abbeville
Columbia
Florence
Sumter
GEORGIA
Aiken
Kingstree
Orangeburg
Myrtle Beach
Walterboro
Charleston
ATLANTIC OCEAN
Hilton Head Island

0   50   100 Miles
0   50   100 Kilometers

13 What is the distance from Abbeville to Florence?

14 What is the distance from Rock Hill to Orangeburg?

Make a Choice by Voting

One way citizens can take part in their government is by voting in elections. Use the words at the top of the next column to fill in the blanks in the paragraph. It tells about an election.

**ballot   campaign   candidate
election   vote**

Rebecca Lawson is a _____ for the United States Senate. She will begin her _____ for election in January. She hopes that many people will _____ for her. The voters can choose her name from those on the _____. If the majority of the people choose her name, she will win the _____.

READ MORE ABOUT IT

Stars & Stripes: Our National Flag by Leonard Everett Fisher. Holiday House. This book will take you on a journey through the history of our nation's flag.

The Buck Stops Here: The Presidents of the United States by Alice Provensen. Harcourt Brace. Illustrations give details about each one of the presidents.

Visit the Internet at
http://www.hbschool.com
for additional resources.

REMEMBER

- Share your ideas.
- Cooperate with others to plan your work.
- Take responsibility for your work.
- Help one another.
- Show your group's work to the class.
- Discuss what you learned by working together.

Write a Constitution

A constitution includes a written set of laws for people to follow. Working in a group, brainstorm a list of rules for your classroom. Then meet with other groups and talk about your rules. Vote on which rules to list in a "Classroom Constitution." Write the rules, and display your Classroom Constitution.

Unit Project Wrap-Up

Write an Anthem Activity Work with a group of classmates to finish the Anthem Activity that was described on page 327. Look at the words each of you has written. Decide which sentences you would like to put into an anthem. Then fit the words to the tune of a song you already know, and practice your song. Sing your song for other classes. Before you sing, tell your audience what makes the song an anthem for your community.

THE MANY PEOPLE OF A COMMUNITY

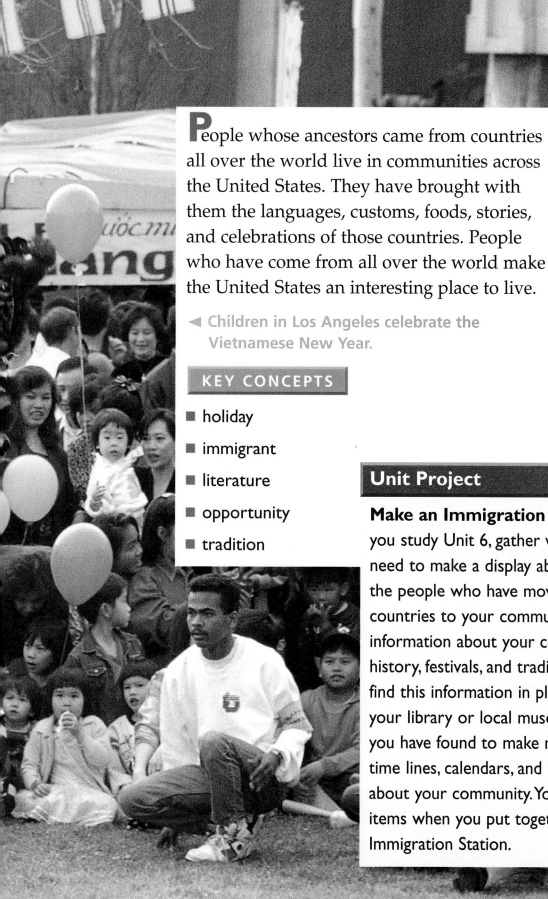

People whose ancestors came from countries all over the world live in communities across the United States. They have brought with them the languages, customs, foods, stories, and celebrations of those countries. People who have come from all over the world make the United States an interesting place to live.

◀ Children in Los Angeles celebrate the Vietnamese New Year.

KEY CONCEPTS

- holiday
- immigrant
- literature
- opportunity
- tradition

Unit Project

Make an Immigration Station As you study Unit 6, gather what you will need to make a display about immigrants, the people who have moved from other countries to your community. Collect information about your community's history, festivals, and traditions. You can find this information in places such as your library or local museum. Use what you have found to make maps, posters, time lines, calendars, and brochures about your community. You will use these items when you put together your Immigration Station.

tradition A way of doing something that has been passed on from parents to children.

literature The books, poetry, stories, and plays written by people to share ideas.

immigrant A person who moves from one country to live in another.

opportunity The chance to find a job, get an education, or have a better way of life.

holiday A special day for remembering a person or an event that is important to a community.

Grandfather's Journey

written and illustrated by
Allen Say

This is the story of a man who leaves Japan, his home country, and moves to the United States. After many years he returns to Japan and marries his girlfriend. They then decide to live in the United States.

Whether the man is in Japan or in the United States, he is homesick for the other place. As you read, think about what it would be like to move to a country where the culture is different from your own.

My grandfather was a young man when he left his home in Japan and went to see the world.

He wore European clothes for the first time and began his journey on a steamship. The Pacific Ocean astonished him.

For three weeks he did not see land. When land finally appeared it was the New World.

He explored North America by train and riverboat, and often walked for days on end.

Deserts with rocks like enormous sculptures amazed him.

The endless farm fields reminded him of the ocean he had crossed.

Huge cities of factories and tall buildings bewildered and yet excited him.

He marveled at the towering mountains and rivers as clear as the sky.

He met many people along the way. He shook hands with black men and white men, with yellow men and red men.

The more he traveled, the more he longed to see new places, and never thought of returning home.

Of all the places he visited, he liked California best. He loved the strong sunlight there, the Sierra Mountains, the lonely seacoast.

After a time, he returned to his village in Japan to marry his childhood sweetheart. Then he brought his bride to the new country.

They made their home by the San Francisco Bay and had a baby girl.

As his daughter grew, my grandfather began to think about his own childhood. He thought about his old friends.

He remembered the mountains and rivers of his home. He surrounded himself with songbirds, but he could not forget.

Finally, when his daughter was nearly grown, he could wait no more. He took his family and returned to his homeland.

Once again he saw the mountains and rivers of his childhood. They were just as he had remembered them.

Once again he exchanged stories and laughed with his old friends.

But the village was not a place for a daughter from San Francisco. So my grandfather bought a house in a large city nearby.

There, the young woman fell in love, married, and sometime later I was born.

When I was a small boy, my favorite weekend was a visit to my grandfather's house. He told me many stories about California.

He raised warblers and silvereyes, but he could not forget the mountains and rivers of California. So he planned a trip.

But a war began. Bombs fell from the sky and scattered our lives like leaves in a storm.

When the war ended, there was nothing left of the city and of the house where my grandparents had lived.

So they returned to the village where they had been children. But my grandfather never kept another songbird.

The last time I saw him, my grandfather said that he longed to see California one more time. He never did.

And when I was nearly grown, I left home and went to see California for myself.

After a time, I came to love the land my grandfather had loved, and I stayed on and on until I had a daughter of my own.

But I also miss the mountains and rivers of my childhood. I miss my old friends. So I return now and then, when I can not still the longing in my heart.

The funny thing is, the moment I am in one country, I am homesick for the other.

I think I know my grandfather now. I miss him very much.

FOCUS

What parts of the world have people in your community come from?

Main Idea Find out why people from many places come to live in a community.

Vocabulary

opportunity
religion
immigrant

During the late 1800s and early 1900s, millions of Europeans arrived at Ellis Island, in New York Harbor.

People from Many Places

People move from one place in the world to another for many reasons. Sometimes, as in *Grandfather's Journey*, a person moves to a new country for adventure. Allen Say's grandfather traveled all over the United States. He found the country beautiful and exciting. But adventure is not the only reason people move to new places.

People Move for Many Reasons

Many people who move from one part of the world to another are hoping to find opportunities in their new country. An **opportunity** is a chance—to find a job, to get an education, to have a better way of life.

Sometimes people move because they are not allowed to follow their religion in their home country. A **religion** is a set of ideas a person believes about God or a set of gods. People may move to a country where they will be free to believe as they wish.

Some people move because a war is making life hard for them. They need safety. Others move because of hunger in their country. They want to live in a country where there is enough to eat.

REVIEW **Why do people move from one country to another?**

Many People Move to the United States

People have moved to the United States from countries all over the world. People who move from one country to live in another country are called **immigrants**.

From 1881 until 1920 almost 24 million immigrants came to the United States. The immigrants came from all over the world. The greatest number of them were from Europe. When their ships arrived at Ellis Island, in New York Harbor, or Angel Island, in San Francisco Bay, many decided to make New York City or San Francisco their new home. Some looked for opportunities in other cities along the west and east coasts. Other immigrants traveled to the middle of the United States and worked as farmers.

These immigrants traveled by boat to Ellis Island.

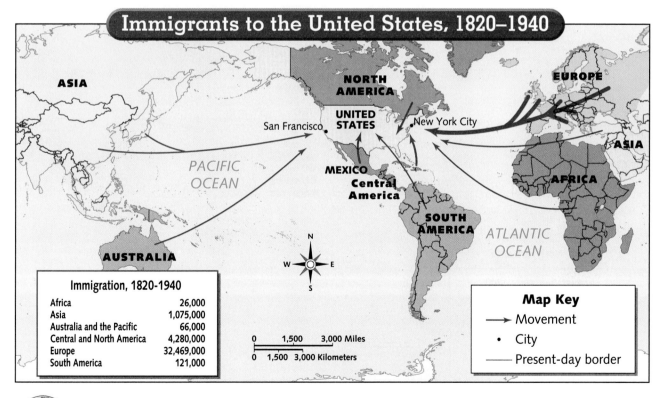

Immigrants to the United States, 1820–1940

ASIA

NORTH AMERICA

EUROPE

UNITED STATES

San Francisco

New York City

ASIA

PACIFIC OCEAN

MEXICO

Central America

AFRICA

SOUTH AMERICA

ATLANTIC OCEAN

AUSTRALIA

Immigration, 1820-1940

Africa	26,000
Asia	1,075,000
Australia and the Pacific	66,000
Central and North America	4,280,000
Europe	32,469,000
South America	121,000

0   1,500   3,000 Miles
0   1,500 3,000 Kilometers

N   W   E   S

Map Key
→ Movement
• City
— Present-day border

Movement ■ **What part of the United States did most of the immigrants from Europe reach first?**

The Statue of Liberty

As their ships entered New York Harbor, many immigrants from Europe saw the Statue of Liberty. It has come to stand for freedom to many people.

Today, immigrants still come from Europe. Others come from Africa. However, greater numbers are now coming to the United States from Mexico and Central and South America. Others come from countries on islands in the Caribbean Sea, between Florida and South America. Large groups of immigrants also come from China, the Philippines, Vietnam, India, and other countries in Asia.

REVIEW **What is an immigrant?**

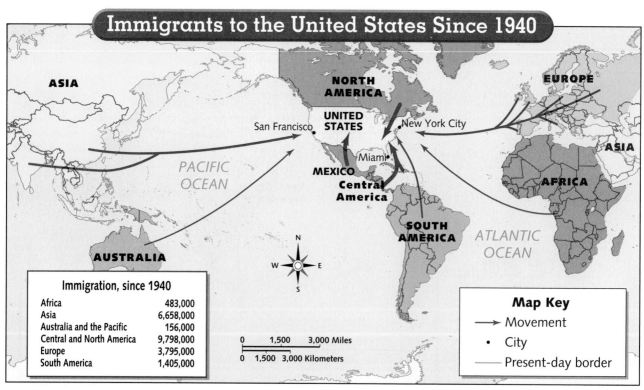

Immigrants to the United States Since 1940

ASIA

NORTH AMERICA

EUROPE

UNITED STATES

San Francisco

New York City

ASIA

PACIFIC OCEAN

Miami

MEXICO

Central America

AFRICA

AUSTRALIA

SOUTH AMERICA

ATLANTIC OCEAN

N W E S

Immigration, since 1940	
Africa	483,000
Asia	6,658,000
Australia and the Pacific	156,000
Central and North America	9,798,000
Europe	3,795,000
South America	1,405,000

0 1,500 3,000 Miles
0 1,500 3,000 Kilometers

Map Key	
→	Movement
•	City
—	Present-day border

Movement ■ **Which places in the United States do many of these immigrants today reach first?**

MAP THEME

A City of Many Cultures

Like the author of *Grandfather's Journey*, many immigrants feel homesick. They feel sad because they miss their home and family and the language and customs of their culture.

Often people move to neighborhoods where others from their home country have lived for a long time. The people in these neighborhoods help new immigrants learn about their new country. They also help new immigrants not to miss their home country so much. In these communities the immigrants can speak the language and follow the customs of their culture. The city of Los Angeles, California, has several neighborhoods in which many of the people have immigrated from the same country.

Chinatown in Los Angeles

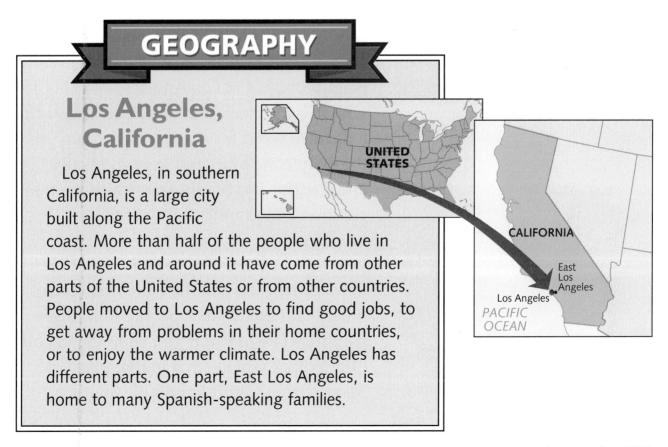

GEOGRAPHY

Los Angeles, California

Los Angeles, in southern California, is a large city built along the Pacific coast. More than half of the people who live in Los Angeles and around it have come from other parts of the United States or from other countries. People moved to Los Angeles to find good jobs, to get away from problems in their home countries, or to enjoy the warmer climate. Los Angeles has different parts. One part, East Los Angeles, is home to many Spanish-speaking families.

▲ Many people shop at this fish market in East Los Angeles.

▲ A shopper choosing papaya at an outdoor market

▲ A woman at an outdoor market making tortillas

East Los Angeles is one of the largest neighborhoods in Los Angeles. The people who live there call it the *barrio* (BAR•ee•oh), a Spanish word for *neighborhood*. Many of the people are immigrants from Mexico and Central and South America or are the children and grandchildren of these immigrants.

In East Los Angeles, grocery stores and outdoor markets sell the fruits, vegetables, meats, and breads that people from these countries like to eat. If you shop there, you might think you are in a marketplace in Mexico or in Central or South America.

There are many other neighborhoods in Los Angeles where groups of people share a culture. The picture below shows one of these groups.

REVIEW What is the Spanish word for *neighborhood*?

▲ People of many cultures enjoy a meal at this restaurant in Los Angeles.

◀ A Korean festival in Los Angeles, California

LESSON 1 REVIEW

Check Understanding

1 **Remember the Facts** Why do immigrants often move to certain neighborhoods in their new countries?

2 **Recall the Main Idea** Why do some communities have many different cultural groups living there?

Think Critically

3 **Explore Viewpoints** What do you think would be the hardest thing to learn if you moved to another country? What do you think would be the easiest? What things do you think are hard for new immigrants to the United States to learn? Why?

Show What You Know

"Packing for a Journey" Activity
Work in a group of four. On a sheet of paper, one person should draw a large suitcase shape. Take turns writing or drawing in it things you would take if you were moving to another country. Talk about why these things are important to you. Then share with the class what the members of your group "packed."

FOCUS
What kinds of stories, poems, art, and music are part of your community?

Main Idea Find out about the culture of a New York City neighborhood called Harlem.

Vocabulary
literature
heritage

Culture in Harlem

New York City is another community that is made up of many neighborhoods. In several neighborhoods in New York City, people who share a culture live together. One of those neighborhoods is Harlem. Many of the people of Harlem did not move there from other countries. They came from other parts of the United States.

The South Moves North

During the early 1900s many African Americans who lived in the South decided to move to the North to find jobs. They left small farms in the South to find opportunities in large cities like New York City, Detroit, and Chicago. Many of them found work in factories.

This African American family moved from the rural South to Chicago.

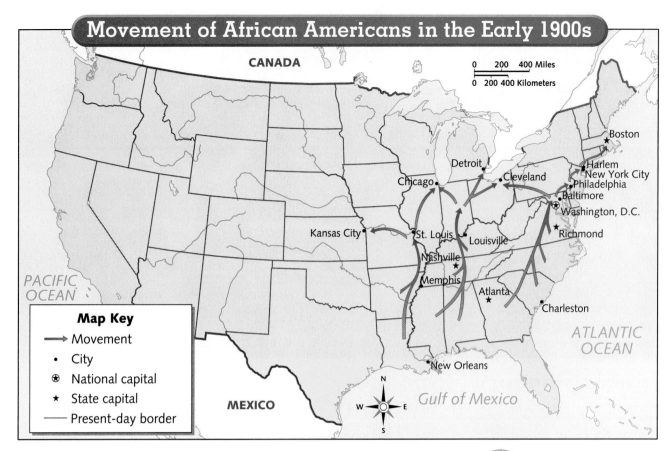

Movement of African Americans in the Early 1900s

CANADA

0   200   400 Miles
0   200 400 Kilometers

Boston

Detroit
Chicago
Cleveland
Harlem
New York City
Philadelphia
Baltimore
Washington, D.C.

Kansas City
St. Louis
Louisville
Richmond

Nashville

Memphis
Atlanta
Charleston

New Orleans

PACIFIC
OCEAN

ATLANTIC
OCEAN

Gulf of Mexico

MEXICO

Map Key
→ Movement
• City
⊛ National capital
★ State capital
— Present-day border

The New York City neighborhood known as
Harlem soon became one of the largest African
American neighborhoods in the country. A writer,
Loften Mitchell, described Harlem in the 1900s.

66 The small town of black Harlem . . . was
crowded with togetherness, love, human
warmth, and neighborliness. 99

In Harlem, African Americans created an exciting
place to live. They were proud of themselves and
their culture. This pride began to show in the
stories and poems people wrote. It also began to
show in the art they made and in the music they
played.

REVIEW **Why did many African Americans
leave the South and move to cities in the North?**

Movement
■ What do the
arrows show
you about where African
Americans moved in the
early 1900s?

In the 1930s a family
takes a Sunday afternoon
walk in Harlem.

Children in an art class in Harlem in the 1930s

Zora Neale Hurston

Literature and Art in Harlem

In the 1920s and 1930s, Harlem became well known for its literature and art. **Literature** is the books, poetry, stories, and plays people write to share their ideas. Like language and customs, literature and art are part of a culture.

Langston Hughes and Zora Neale Hurston were two writers who lived and worked in Harlem during the 1920s and 1930s. They wrote about the lives of African Americans in a new way. They used the language that people use every day to make their poems and stories sound real. Their writing showed that they were proud of their African heritage. **Heritage** is the culture handed down to people by their ancestors.

Many other artists in Harlem wanted to share their African heritage. They created paintings and other works of art that showed what it was like to be African American.

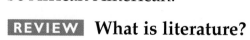 **REVIEW** What is literature?

A photo from the 1920s shows King Oliver's Creole (KREE•ohl) Jazz Band.

Jazz Comes to Harlem

Another important part of Harlem's culture in the 1920s and 1930s was its music. People from all over New York City went to Harlem to hear a new kind of music called jazz. It had been started by African Americans in other parts of the United States. But this new kind of music quickly became an important part of Harlem's culture.

Jazz bands played in restaurants and jazz clubs in Harlem. The music was fun to listen to because jazz musicians would often make up the music while they were playing or singing.

Judith Jamison
1944–

Judith Jamison has been a ballet dancer since she was a child. In the 1970s she became a member of the famous Alvin Ailey American Dance Theater in New York City. Many dances were created just for her. Ms. Jamison is now the artistic director of a dance company. She also teaches dance and creates dances for others to perform. She is the dancer in the center of this photograph.

Jazz is a style of music that began in the United States. Jazz is enjoyed by people all over the world.

Today, people of many cultures live in Harlem. But it is still a neighborhood where African Americans celebrate and enjoy their culture through art, literature, and music.

REVIEW **What form of music became popular in Harlem?**

LESSON 2 REVIEW

Check Understanding

1 **Remember the Facts** Name two important writers from Harlem.

2 **Recall the Main Idea** What was the culture of Harlem like in the 1920s and 1930s?

Think Critically

3 **Personally Speaking** Think about how important music is in your own life. How can music tell about a culture?

Show What You Know

Poster Activity Choose a musician, and make a poster to advertise the next performance of that person. Use words and details that will interest others. Show the kind of instrument the musician plays. Try to find a recording by the musician to share with your classmates. Many libraries have records, tapes, and CDs that you can borrow.

TALL TALES FROM AMERICA

People express their heritage and culture in many ways. Storytelling is one way. Zora Neale Hurston, a writer who lived in Harlem, collected stories. One that she collected was "John Henry." The story of John Henry is a **tall tale**, a story that tells about someone who does something impossible. Tall tales often start with a real person. Then as the story is told over and over again, things are added that did not really happen. Pioneers and immigrants told tall tales about super-strong characters like John Henry and Paul Bunyan to help themselves feel strong in a place where life was hard. Since that time, many writers have retold those tall tales in books.

retold and
illustrated by
Ezra Jack Keats

JOHN HENRY

Starting in the 1870s railroad workers sang songs and told stories about John Henry. In this part of the story, he is working on a tunnel for the railroad. Workers bring in a steam drill, a machine they say will help dig the tunnel faster. Find out what happens when John Henry works against the steam drill.

Down the tunnel came a group of men with a strange machine.

"This is a steam drill. It can drill more holes faster than any six men combined," a new man bragged.

"Who can beat that?"

John Henry stepped forward. "Try me!"

He and L'il Bill took their work places. John Henry gripped his hammer. L'il Bill clutched his steel drill.

A hoarse voice counted, "One, two—THREE!"

The machine shrieked as it started. John Henry swung his hammer—and a crash of steel on steel split the air!

Clang! Bang! Clang!

Hiss! Whistle! Rattle!

Men frantically heaved coal into the hungry, roaring engine and poured water into the steaming boiler.

Whoop! Clang! Whoop! Bang!

John Henry's hammer whistled as he swung it.

Chug, chug! Clatter! rattled the machine. Hour after hour raced by. The machine was ahead!

clutched
held tightly

steel
a metal made of iron

shrieked
cried out

boiler
a large tank in which water is heated to make steam used for running engines

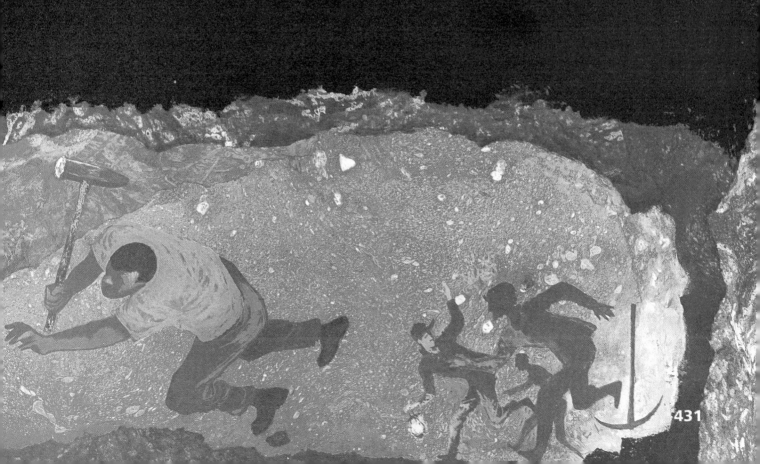

Great chunks of rock fell as John Henry ripped hole after hole into the tunnel wall. The machine rattled and whistled and drilled even faster. Then John Henry took a deep breath, picked up two sledge hammers, and swung both mighty hammers—faster and faster. He moved so fast the men could see only a blur and sparks from his striking hammers. His strokes rang out like great heart-beats.

At the other side of the tunnel the machine shrieked, groaned and rattled, and drilled. Then all at once it shook and shuddered—wheezed—and stopped. Frantically men worked to get it going again. But they couldn't. It had collapsed! John Henry's hammering still rang and echoed through the tunnel with a strong and steady beat.

Suddenly there was a great crash. Light streamed into the dark tunnel. John Henry had broken through! Wild cries of joy burst from the men. Still holding one of his hammers, John Henry stepped out into the glowing light of a dying day. It was the last step he ever took. Even the great heart of John Henry could not bear the strain of his last task. John Henry died with his hammer in his hand.

If you listen to the locomotives roaring through the tunnels and across the land, you'll hear them singing—singing of that great steel-driving man—John Henry.

Listen!

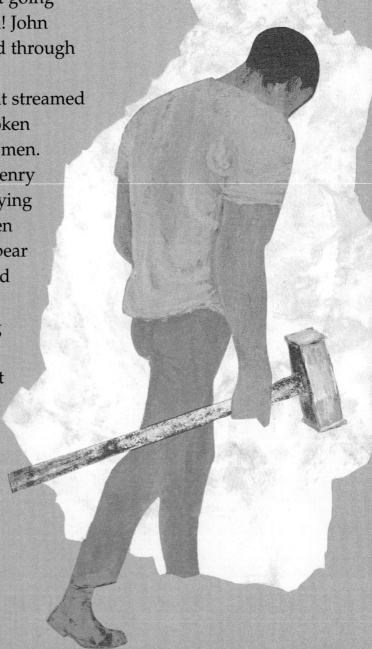

strain great force or weight	**locomotives** (loh•kuh•MOH•tivz) engines used to pull the cars of railroad trains

PAUL BUNYAN

retold by Mary Pope Osborne
illustrated by David McCall Johnston

Like John Henry, the story of Paul Bunyan is about a super-strong character who helped America grow. This tall tale probably grew out of the stories lumberjacks told. Lumberjacks are workers who cut down trees to make lumber. Carl Sandburg, a famous American writer said, "The people, the bookless people, they made up Paul and had him alive long before he got into the books for those who read." In Paul Bunyan stories, Paul gets help from his friend, Babe the Blue Ox. Read now to find out how Paul and Babe changed the shape of the land.

In those times, huge sections of America were filled with dark green forests. And the forests were filled with trees—oceans of trees—trees as far as the eye could see—trees so tall you had to look straight up to see if it was morning, and maybe if you were lucky, you'd catch a glimpse of blue sky.

glimpse
a quick look

Lesson 3 • 433

It would be nice if those trees could have stayed tall and thick forever. But the pioneers needed them to build houses, churches, ships, wagons, bridges, and barns. So one day Paul Bunyan took a good look at all those trees and said, "Babe, stand back. I'm about to invent logging."

"*Tim-ber!*" he yelled, and he swung his bright steel ax in a wide circle. There was a terrible crash, and when Paul looked around, he saw he'd felled ten white pines with a single swing.

Paul bundled up the trees and loaded them onto the ox's back. "All right, Babe," he said. "Let's haul 'em to the Big Onion and send 'em down to a sawmill."

Since both Babe and Paul could cover a whole mile in a single step, it took them only about a week to travel from Maine to the Big Onion River in Minnesota.

felled
cut down

sawmill
(SAW•mil) a building in which machines saw logs into lumber

After that Paul and Babe traveled plenty fast through the untamed North Woods. They cut pine, spruce, and red willow in Minnesota, Michigan, and Wisconsin. They cleared cottonwoods out of Kansas so farmers could plant wheat. They cleared oaks out of Iowa so farmers could plant corn. It seems that the summer after the corn was planted in Iowa, there was a heat wave. It got so hot the corn started to pop. It popped until the whole state was covered with ten feet of popcorn.

When next heard of, Paul and Babe were headed to Arizona. Paul dragged his pickax behind him on that trip, not realizing he was leaving a big ditch in his tracks. Today that ditch is called the Grand Canyon.

untamed
not settled, wild

pickax
(PIK•aks) a tool used for breaking rocks and loosening dirt

LITERATURE REVIEW

❶ What is a tall tale?

❷ When people made up the story of John Henry, what do you think they were saying about railroad work?

❸ Use the library to find out what stories are told about your community or state. Write a story down, and add drawings to it. Share your story with another classmate.

Understand Point

1. Why Learn This Skill?

In *Grandfather's Journey*, author and artist Allen Say uses words and pictures to tell the story of his grandfather's life. Say's pictures also tell you about his point of view. A person's **point of view** is the way he or she feels about something. If you know what to look for in a photograph or a piece of art, you can understand what the artist is saying to you.

2. Understand the Process

In the 1950s and 1960s, Martin Luther King, Jr., worked for the rights of African Americans. He wanted them to have the same opportunities as others. In 1963 he gave his most famous speech in Washington, D.C. In his speech he said that his hope was for all people to live and work together peacefully.

There are many ways a photographer can show his or her point of view. Look at the photograph of Martin Luther King, Jr., on page 437, and ask yourself these questions.

- Who is the person in the photograph? What is he doing? What feeling does his face show?

- What kinds of items are shown in the background of the photograph? What do these items tell you about the person?

3. Think and Apply

Look again at the photograph and answer the questions.

1 The photographer could have shown Martin Luther King, Jr., in many ways. Why do you think he chose to show King looking off into the distance?

2 In the photograph King is standing near a painting of Mahatma (muh•HAHT•ma) Gandhi (GAHN•dee).

# of View

Gandhi was a leader who helped India gain independence from Britain through a nonviolent revolution. Why do you think the photographer had King pose near this painting?

Martin Luther King, Jr., in his Atlanta office

FOCUS
How do you celebrate your favorite holiday?

Main Idea Find out how a holiday can be celebrated in many different ways.

Vocabulary
holiday
tradition

Holiday Customs and Traditions

People all over the world celebrate holidays. A **holiday** is a special day for remembering a person or an event that has importance for the people in a community. The Fourth of July and Thanksgiving are holidays that celebrate the beginning of this country. They are important holidays to people in the United States, but not to people who live in other countries.

The United States is home to people from many cultures. Each group celebrates its own holidays with special customs. Here are some ways that people celebrate the New Year's holiday in the United States.

Suc

Mikesha and her mother

Aya

Chet

438

A Japanese Tradition

Aya was born in the United States, but her parents came from Japan. They still follow many Japanese traditions. **Traditions** are customs, or ways of doing things, that are passed on from parents to children. In Japan the New Year's holiday is called *Oshogatsu* (oh•shoh•GAHT•soo). It is one of the most important holidays of the year there.

There are many traditions for the Japanese celebration of the New Year. One of the most important is to begin the New Year with everything in order. First, Aya and her family clean the house. Next, they try to pay back any money they have borrowed. Then, they take the time to solve any personal problems they might have. Last, the family puts on new clothes and visits friends, and together they eat a special soup called *ozoni* (oh•ZOH•nee). Japanese people say this soup will bring them a long, good life.

All of the foods eaten on *Oshogatsu* have a special meaning. Snapper, a kind of fish, is eaten for happiness. *Soba* (SOH•bah) noodles are for long life. *Mochi* (MOH•chee), which is made of sweet rice balls, is for wealth. *Kuro mame* (KOO•roh MAH•meh), black beans, are for good luck.

REVIEW What traditions are important to Japanese people for the New Year's holiday?

Foods eaten on the Japanese New Year have a special meaning.

Aya holds a tray of foods she and her family eat to celebrate *Oshogatsu*.

A Vietnamese Custom

One tradition of the Vietnamese New Year is the giving of a red envelope.

In another part of the United States lives Suc (SOOK), whose parents moved to this country from Vietnam. Suc and his family call their New Year's celebration *Tet*. Like Aya's family, the members of Suc's family clean their house, pay back money they have borrowed, and wear new clothes. But the foods they make are very different. Suc and his family eat special rice cakes called *banh day* (BYN ZAY) and *banh chung* (BYN CHUHNG). Each child receives a small red envelope with money inside. Suc likes that part the best!

REVIEW **What do Vietnamese people call the New Year's holiday?**

Suc opens the red envelope he was given during *Tet*. The red color stands for good luck.

An African American Celebration

Mikesha (my•KEE•shuh) and her family celebrate Kwanzaa (KWAHN•zuh), a festival that honors their African American heritage. It lasts for one week and ends on New Year's Day. On each day of the celebration, Mikesha lights a candle in the *kinara* (KIN•uh•ruh), a candle holder with places for seven candles, and thinks about that day's special meaning. She looks forward to the *karamu* (KAR•uh•muh), the big feast that takes place on New Year's Day. During Kwanzaa, Mikesha hears many words in Swahili, a language of her African ancestors.

Making special foods and giving gifts are traditions during Kwanzaa.

REVIEW What is Kwanzaa?

During Kwanzaa, Mikesha lights the candles in the *kinara*.

Celebrating at Times Square

Each culture celebrates the New Year in different ways.

Chet and his family live in New York City. They celebrate the New Year with hundreds of thousands of other people. They ride the subway to Times Square, where New Yorkers gather each year to celebrate the holiday. There they wait in a huge crowd for the big clock on the top of a building to show it is midnight. When it does, the New Year has begun. The crowd cheers and sings "Auld Lang Syne," which means "good old times." This song was written more than 200 years ago in Scotland by a poet named Robert Burns.

> " Should auld acquaintance be forgot,
>   And never brought to mind?
>   Should auld acquaintance be forgot
>   And days of auld lang syne? "

Chet wears a party hat and blows noisemakers to celebrate the New Year at Times Square in New York City.

New Year's is a time to remember old times and old friends and to get ready for the new ones. People plan to make changes in their lives in the year that is starting. People everywhere celebrate the New Year, but they do it in their own special ways.

REVIEW Why do many people celebrate the New Year's holiday at Times Square?

These people in Times Square are waiting for the clock to strike midnight so they can welcome the New Year.

LESSON 4 REVIEW

Check Understanding

1 Remember the Facts What do the Japanese call the celebration of their New Year?

2 Recall the Main Idea What are some of the many ways people in the United States celebrate the New Year?

Think Critically

3 Think More About It Why do you think many people in the United States sing a song to celebrate the New Year?

Show What You Know

Write a Report Choose one holiday that your family likes to celebrate. List some traditions you follow during it. Then choose one tradition to write a report about. You might choose a special food, a piece of clothing, a song, or an activity that goes with the holiday. If you wish, you can make drawings or find pictures to go with your report. Share your report with your classmates.

Follow a Sequence

1. Why Learn This Skill?

When Allen Say decided to write about his grandfather, he wanted to make it easy for everyone to understand. So he decided to tell about his grandfather's life by using sequence. **Sequence** (SEE•kwuhns) is the order in which things happen. Say begins the story when his grandfather is a young man. He ends the story when his grandfather dies. Understanding the sequence of events can help you remember what happened.

2. Remember What You Have Read

In Lesson 4 you learned about Aya and her family and how they celebrate *Oshogatsu*. What sequence do they follow as they celebrate it?

3. Understand the Process

To follow a sequence, you can look for certain clues. Some authors use word clues like *first, next, then,* and *last*. These words help put events in sequence. Another way to understand a sequence of events is to look for dates. Dates often give clues to the sequence you are reading in a social studies book.

Look at the second paragraph on page 439. Find the words that tell what Aya and her family do to celebrate *Oshogatsu*. What do they do last? How can you tell?

4. Think and Apply

Choose four activities that you do every day. Write a paragraph about them with the sentences in sequence. Use the words *first, next, then,* and *last*. Read your paragraph to a partner. Ask him or her to draw a time line for your day.

Aya helps clean her family's house.

Different Countries, Different Cultures

FOCUS
Compare the way you live with the way a person your age in another country lives.

Main Idea Find out how life in India is like life in the United States and how it is different.

Vocabulary
folktale

In *Grandfather's Journey* the author's grandfather traveled back and forth between two countries—Japan and the United States. He enjoyed the beautiful physical features of the United States. Landforms such as the mountains and coasts amazed him. He also discovered that interesting people lived in the United States. He met many people from different cultures.

Traveling is one of the ways people learn about other countries in the world. If you could travel to India, you would learn that it is an interesting country. Like the United States, India is filled with beautiful places and many groups of people who have different cultures.

People in Mumbai, India

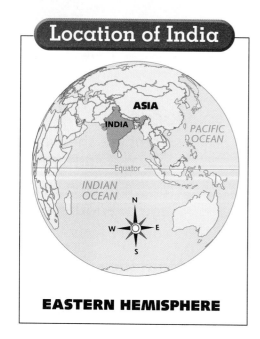

EASTERN HEMISPHERE

People and Places

The United States and India are located in very different parts of the Earth. The United States is on the continent of North America, in the Western Hemisphere. India is located on the other side of the world. It is on the continent of Asia, in the Eastern Hemisphere.

Both the United States and India are made up of states. There are 50 states in the United States. In India there are 25 states. In both places each state is different from the other states in some ways and like them in other ways.

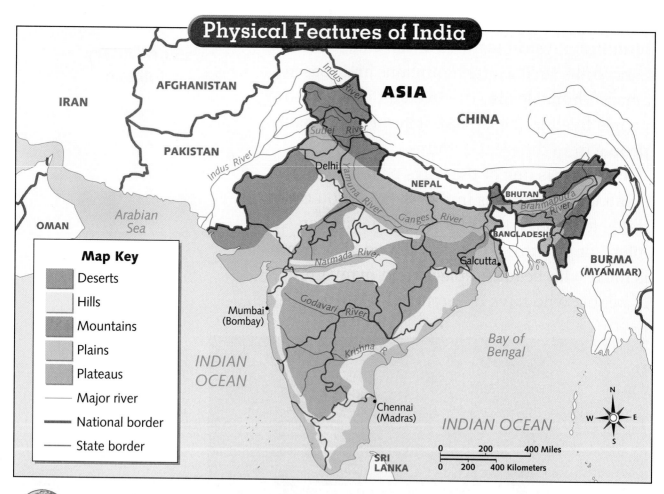

Physical Features of India

Map Key

- Deserts
- Hills
- Mountains
- Plains
- Plateaus
- — Major river
- — National border
- — State border

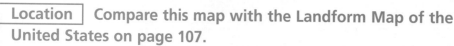

Location Compare this map with the Landform Map of the United States on page 107.

■ How are the two countries alike? How are they different?

Like the United States, India has many different landforms. There are mountains, hills, plains, and coasts. India also has many rivers flowing through it.

REVIEW **On which continent is India located?**

Many People, Many Languages

Many people live in India. The table on this page shows the five countries with the most people. You can use the table to compare the population of India with the population of the United States.

Population of Countries

COUNTRY	POPULATION
China	1,236,693,000
India	969,729,000
United States	267,661,000
Indonesia	204,323,000
Brazil	160,343,000

LEARNING FROM TABLES
Look at the table.
- Which country has more people, the United States or India?

Many cities in India are crowded.

The sign on this shop is in two different alphabets.

Like the United States, India has many different groups of people. People in each group have their own culture and may have their own language. One of the largest groups in India is the Hindu (HIN•doo) group. Most Hindus speak a language called Hindi (HIN•dee). But if you travel all over India, you can hear people speak many languages, including English.

Different languages are often written using different alphabets. So signs on shops and public buildings in India may be printed in three or more alphabets.

REVIEW **What is one of the largest groups of people in India?**

Children at an outdoor school in India

Literature

Like language, literature is an important part of any culture. One example of literature is the **folktale**, a traditional story that often teaches a lesson. "The Jackal's Tale" is an Indian folktale that teaches what can happen when someone pretends to be something he or she is not.

The Jackal's Tale

Once there was a clever jackal who always wanted to be something special. He tried hard to be noticed by the other animals in the forest, but nothing worked. Then one day he tripped and fell into a large bucket of blue powder. When he came out, his dull fur was a bright blue.

"At last!" the jackal thought to himself. "There is something different about me." But when he ran into the other animals, they looked at him in fear. They were frightened by the strange color of his fur and ran away.

The jackal called to them and said, "Do not be afraid. I was sent here to be your king." The other animals thought about what he said. They decided to welcome him. Not only that, they spoiled him. They brought him the best pieces of food to eat. They built a comfortable shelter where he could sleep in peace. Many days passed, and the jackal thought he was happy.

Then one night the jackal was awakened by the howls of a pack of jackals nearby. He suddenly felt very sad. He missed his old friends very much. Before he could think more about it, the blue jackal pointed his nose into the air and howled.

Then the other animals knew that the blue jackal was really just a jackal. He was not their king after all. They chased him back into the forest.

The lesson is that it is impossible to fool people for long. Sooner or later, your true colors will show through and people will know you as you really are!

REVIEW **What is the important lesson taught by "The Jackal's Tale"?**

Food, Clothing, and Music

In neighborhoods all over the United States, people of different cultures eat different kinds of food. This is also true in India. Many Indians eat foods made with curry. Curry is a mixture of spices. Some Indian cooks grind their own mixture of spices every day. They use the curry to flavor their foods.

People in India make many different kinds of bread, too. One kind, *chapati* (chuh•PAH•tee), is made from little balls of dough. Another kind of bread, *roti* (ROH•tee), is hollow. It is made by frying balls of dough in oil. The balls puff up like doughnuts.

All over India you can see people wearing different kinds of clothing. In some places in India, women and girls wear a long piece of cloth that is wrapped around the body. This is a kind of dress called a *sari* (SAR•ee). Often a piece of the same cloth is used to make a veil or a head covering. Saris are cool and comfortable, but it is not easy to run and play games in them.

Curry was used to make this dish of shrimp madras.

The small balls of *chapati* are pushed flat with the hands and then cooked on a griddle, a flat metal pan.

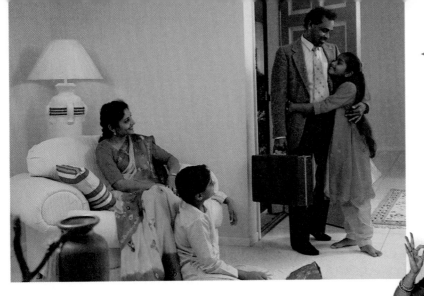

◀ In the cities, many Indian men wear suits and ties to work. The woman shown here is wearing a *sari* (SAR•ee).

Some adults and children wear loose cotton shirts and pants. Clothing for both boys and girls often has beautiful patterns and bright colors.

Music is another important part of India's many cultures. Indian musicians play mostly drums and instruments with strings. One stringed instrument is called a *sitar* (SIH•tar). It looks something like a guitar. At festivals Indian dancers perform to music. When they dance, they use their arms, hands, and fingers to tell stories.

REVIEW **What makes the people of India different from one another?**

▲ When Indian dancers perform, they wear colorful costumes.

The sitar was first played about 800 years ago. It is a stringed instrument made from a vegetable called a gourd. It can have as many as 19 strings.

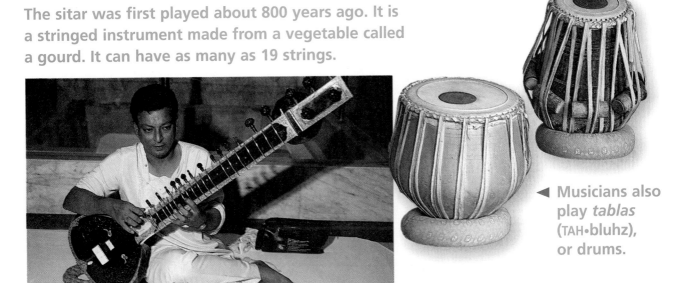

◀ Musicians also play *tablas* (TAH•bluhz), or drums.

The Belur Hindu
Temple in Karnataka
(kar•NAHT•uh•kuh), a state
in southwestern India

Religion

In India there are two main religions—Hinduism and Islam. About 776 million Indian people are Hindus. They follow Hinduism, one of the oldest religions in the world. Hindu temples can be found all over India.

About 116 million Indian people are Muslims. They follow the religion of Islam. Muslim mosques (MAHSKS), too, can be found all over India.

Although most people in India are either Muslim or Hindu, there are other religions as well. The table below shows how many people in India follow each religion. The table also shows how many people follow these religions in the United States.

LEARNING FROM TABLES
In which country do more people follow Hinduism?

Followers of Religions

RELIGION	INDIA	UNITED STATES
Hinduism	775,783,200	910,000
Islam	115,762,060	5,100,000
Christianity	23,273,496	225,135,000
Sikhism	19,394,580	190,000
Buddhism	6,788,103	780,000
Judaism	4,300	5,900,000

The Jama Mosque
in Delhi (DEH•lee),
India

People of many cultures live in the United States and in India. The languages and literature of the people are important parts of each culture. The foods they eat, the clothing they wear, the music they play, and the religion they follow are also important to the people of each culture.

REVIEW What are the two main religions in India?

HISTORY

The Taj Mahal

More than 300 years ago, about 20,000 workers built one of the world's most beautiful buildings, the Taj Mahal (TAHJ muh•HAHL). Shah Jahan, one of India's rulers, had the Taj Mahal built in memory of his wife. It is made of white marble and stands in a beautiful garden. The workers started building the Taj Mahal in 1632 and finished it 22 years later.

LESSON 5 REVIEW

Check Understanding

1 Remember the Facts What foods do people in India eat?

2 Recall the Main Idea In what ways are the United States and India alike? In what ways are they different?

Think Critically

3 Think More About It What is good about living in a country that has people of many cultures?

Show What You Know

Collage Activity
Choose a country you would like to know more about. Cut out magazine pictures or draw your own pictures that show the people, food, music, art, literature, and religions of that country. Share your collage with the class. Tell how the country's culture seems like cultures in the United States and how it seems different.

Use a Population

1. Why Learn This Skill?

Thousands of people may live in your community—or maybe just a few hundred live there. Like resources, population is not spread evenly around the Earth. More people live in some areas than in others. A population map shows areas where many people live and areas where few people live.

2. Understand the Process

Different areas have different population densities (DEN•suh•teez). **Population density** tells how many people live in an area of a certain size. The size is usually 1 square mile. A square mile is a square piece of land that is 1 mile long on each side.

Population density can affect the way people live. Suppose that an area had only two people living on each square mile of land. The population density would be two people per square mile. With so few people, there would be plenty of space. Suppose that another area had 5,000 people per square mile. With so many people living there, that area would be very crowded.

The map shown on page 455 is a population map of India. Use the map to answer the questions.

1. The map key shows four population densities. What color is used to show the lowest population density? What color shows the highest population density?

2. Find the city of Delhi on the map. Delhi, like India's other large cities, has a population density of more than 1,000 people per square mile. How do you think such a high population density affects the lives of people living in Delhi?

3. Now find the city of Calcutta. What is its population density?

4. Why do you think the population density is higher along the coastlines than in the center part of the country?

Map

3. Think and Apply

MAP SKILLS

In an encyclopedia or an atlas, find a population map of your state. What is the population density where you live? In which parts of your state is the population density the highest? In which parts is it the lowest? Share with family members the information you find.

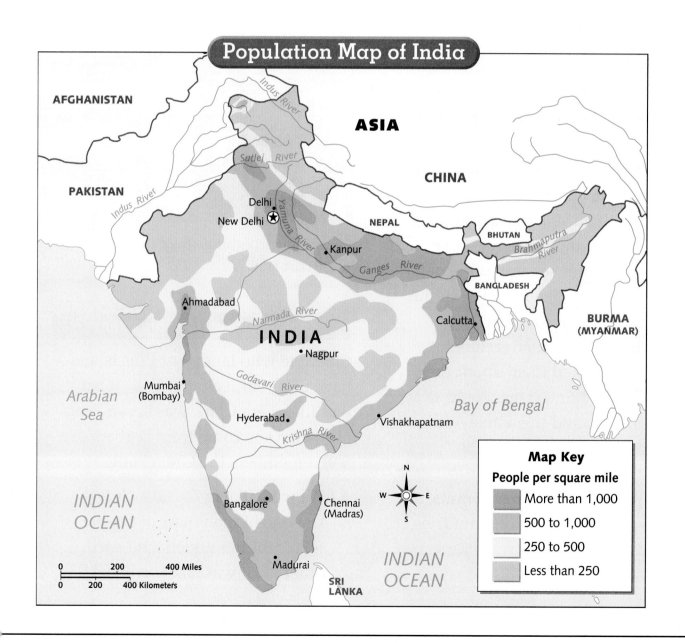

Population Map of India

AFGHANISTAN

ASIA

Indus River

CHINA

PAKISTAN

Sutlej River

Indus River

Delhi
New Delhi ✪

Yamuna River

NEPAL

BHUTAN

Brahmaputra River

• Kanpur

Ganges River

BANGLADESH

Ahmadabad •

Narmada River

Calcutta •

BURMA
(MYANMAR)

INDIA

• Nagpur

Mumbai •
(Bombay)

Godavari River

Arabian Sea

Hyderabad •

Bay of Bengal

Vishakhapatnam •

Krishna River

INDIAN OCEAN

Bangalore •

• Chennai
(Madras)

N
W · E
S

Madurai •

SRI
LANKA

INDIAN OCEAN

Map Key
People per square mile

More than 1,000

500 to 1,000

250 to 500

Less than 250

0   200   400 Miles
0   200   400 Kilometers

Islands of Tears OR

ELLIS ISLAND

In 1892 tiny Ellis Island in New York Harbor became the first stop in the United States for millions of immigrants. Newcomers were checked there before being allowed to live in this country.

Immigrants started in a baggage room and then walked up a long set of stairs. At the top of the stairs, they came to a huge room called the Great Hall. It spread out before them as far as they could see. Rows and rows of people stood in lines separated by metal pipes or wooden benches. In this room doctors examined the immigrants, and government workers asked them about their lives. The immigrants could hear people around them answering questions in more than 30 languages.

Ellis Island had restaurants, a hospital, a post office, laundries, and courtrooms. It was like a small city.

Immigrants climbing stairs to the Great Hall

One Memory of Ellis Island

People who landed at Ellis Island have different feelings about what it was like. Vera Clark was seven years old when she came from Barbados. She remembers the Great Hall.

66 We were like in cages . . . It was just one human mass of people who couldn't understand each other . . . it was just horrible. 99

Islands of Opportunity?

A Different Memory of Ellis Island

Other immigrants have different memories. Lillian Kaiz was also seven when she came from Russia. She remembers,

"I ate my first hot dog and my first banana there. . . . The first night they were celebrating Christmas. They had a movie. I had never seen one.**"**

Ellis Island Today

By 1954 fewer immigrants were passing through Ellis Island. The buildings began to fall apart, and it finally had to be closed. Today the buildings on Ellis Island have been rebuilt as an immigration museum. People can walk up the stairs to the Great Hall and imagine they hear the voices of their ancestors.

Ellis Island as it looks today

ANGEL ISLAND

Angel Island, in the middle of San Francisco Bay, opened in 1910. Like Ellis Island, Angel Island was a place where immigrants entered the United States. People arrived at these two immigration stations from different parts of the world. Angel Island received mostly Chinese immigrants. The United States, which the Chinese called Gold Mountain, was to them a symbol of opportunity.

Angel Island, however, became more like a prison for hundreds of Chinese immigrants. Before being allowed into the country, Chinese immigrants had to answer harder questions than the ones European immigrants answered at Ellis Island. Many immigrants waited months and months before finding out what would happen to them.

One Memory of Angel Island

The Chinese immigrants carved poems onto the wooden walls at Angel Island. The writings show how they felt while they waited to enter America. One man wrote these words about his experience.

66 Nights are long and the pillow cold. Why not just return home and learn to plow the fields? 99

▲ A view of the barracks where immigrants stayed

Chinese poetry ► carved into a barrack wall

▼ Immigrants on the steps of the administration building

A Different Memory of Angel Island

Other immigrants have happier memories. Mr. Wong was 12 when he came to Angel Island from China. He remembers,

66It was a beautiful island with beautiful scenery. Every time we ate, we had to go way down these stairs. Everything tasted good to me, because I never had those things before. **99**

Angel Island Today

The Angel Island station closed after a fire in 1940. Angel Island has since reopened as a state park. Many people have worked together to help make Angel Island a place where history is not forgotten. Visitors can look at the Chinese poems on the walls or enjoy the beauty of the island and think about what it meant for people to come to the United States.

Angel Island as it looks today

Compare Viewpoints

1. What is Vera Clark's memory of Ellis Island?

2. What is Mr. Wong's memory of Angel Island?

3. How are their viewpoints different?

4. Do you think their experiences affected their feelings about the United States? Explain.

Think and Apply

With a group, think of a place in your community that most of you have visited. How many students had a good time there? How many did not enjoy the place? Talk about why people can visit the same place but have different feelings about it.

FOCUS
How can culture and customs affect the people who live in a place?

Main Idea Find out how culture and customs affect the people of South Carolina.

Vocabulary
descendant
ethnic group
festival

The People of South Carolina

Today more than three million people live in South Carolina. Most were born here. Yet not everyone is a **descendant** (dih•SEN•duhnt), or the child or grandchild, of the early settlers. Many people have been moving to South Carolina from other places. Most of these new South Carolinians have come from other states. Some have come from other countries. Among these countries are Canada, Germany, India, Japan, Mexico, Nigeria, the Philippines, and the United Kingdom.

A Mix of Cultures

Newcomers to South Carolina belong to many ethnic (ETH•nik) groups. An **ethnic group** is a group made up of people from the same country, people of the same race, or people with the same way of life.

In their home this family celebrates both Japanese and American cultures.

Every ethnic group has its own culture. The culture of a group is made up of its customs and beliefs. Culture can be seen in the clothing people wear and heard in their language and music. It can be tasted in the foods they eat.

Each ethnic group has brought some of its culture to South Carolina. The mix of many cultures gives South Carolinians the chance to enjoy a richer life. It also explains why the people of South Carolina are different from one another in many ways.

REVIEW What are some things that make up a group's culture?

Top Ten Places of Birth of Foreign-Born Persons in South Carolina	
COUNTRY	NUMBER OF PEOPLE
Germany	6,224
United Kingdom	5,130
Philippines	3,429
Canada	3,218
India	2,307
Caribbean	2,243
Mexico	2,147
Korea	1,866
Japan	1,665
Vietnam	1,041

LEARNING FROM TABLES From which country do the greatest number of foreign-born people come?

▼ People of many ethnic groups gather at Shaw Air Force Base, in Sumter, to look at the airplanes during Shawfest.

Places of Worship

Charleston is sometimes called the Holy City because of its many places of worship. The oldest Christian church in the city is St. Michael's Episcopal Church. Charleston is the location of one of the oldest synagogues (SIN•uh•gahgz) in the United States, Beth Elohim (EL•oh•heem). A synagogue is a place where people of the Jewish religion worship. Charlestonians of the Muslim religion worship in mosques located in the city.

Many Religions

Religion is part of the culture of many groups. Religious beliefs affect the way people think about themselves and others. Religious traditions in South Carolina are as different as the state's people.

Christians make up the largest religious group in the state. The Southern Baptist Convention has the most members. Other Christian groups in South Carolina include Episcopalians, Presbyterians, Roman Catholics, Lutherans, Methodists, and African Methodist Episcopalians.

▼ Beth Elohim Synagogue

Besides Christians, South Carolina has Muslims, Jews, Buddhists, Hindus, and people of other or no religious groups. As more people have moved to South Carolina, the number of religious groups in the state has grown.

REVIEW **What is the largest religious group in South Carolina?**

▼ St. Michael's Episcopal Church

▲ Masjid Al-Jami Ar-Rasheed (mosque)

Common Customs

▼ The Spoleto Festival USA is held every spring in Charleston.

Each ethnic group in South Carolina has added to the way of life here. Do you and your family enjoy sitting on the front porch on hot summer nights? This custom was first brought to South Carolina by enslaved Africans. Porches were an important part of many houses in West Africa. Both places have a hot summer climate.

No matter where they came from, South Carolinians share many customs and ways of life. People in the state enjoy a large number of festivals. A **festival** is a celebration that takes place every year, usually at the same time of the year.

▼ At the Spoleto Festival USA, the music, dance, and folklore of many different cultures are celebrated.

Some festivals celebrate the cultural heritage of the different groups of people who live in South Carolina. Three of these are the Gullah Festival in Beaufort, the Edisto Indian Cultural Festival in Summerville, and the Hispanic Festival in Charleston. Yet other festivals and events, such as the Railroad Festival in Central and the Revolutionary War Battle Event at Cowpens, celebrate the state's historical heritage. Festivals and events help keep alive the special heritage of South Carolina.

REVIEW Why do people have festivals?

Near Rock Hill the Catawbas have celebrations where all South Carolinians can learn about their state's Native American heritage.

LESSON 6 REVIEW

Check Understanding

1 Remember the Facts What are some ways South Carolinians can share the heritage and history of different groups of people?

2 Recall the Main Idea How have the culture and customs of different groups of people affected your life?

Think Critically

3 Think More About It Why is it important for South Carolinians to learn about the heritage of the different groups of people in their state?

Show What You Know

Art Activity Imagine that you have been asked to help plan a festival to celebrate some part of your community's heritage. First decide what the festival will celebrate and what it will be called. Then design a poster for it, telling where and when it will be held. Add drawings or pictures to show what the festival celebrates. Hang your poster where other students can see it.

Folkways in South Carolina

In the last lesson you learned that South Carolina's many different groups of people contribute to the state's heritage. Read now to find out how people of different regions share their **folkways**, the ways a group of people think, feel, and act.

Sea Island Crafts

Along South Carolina's coast are many Sea Islands. Long ago, when these islands could only be reached by boat, the people who lived on them did not have much contact with others.

▼Sweetgrass baskets

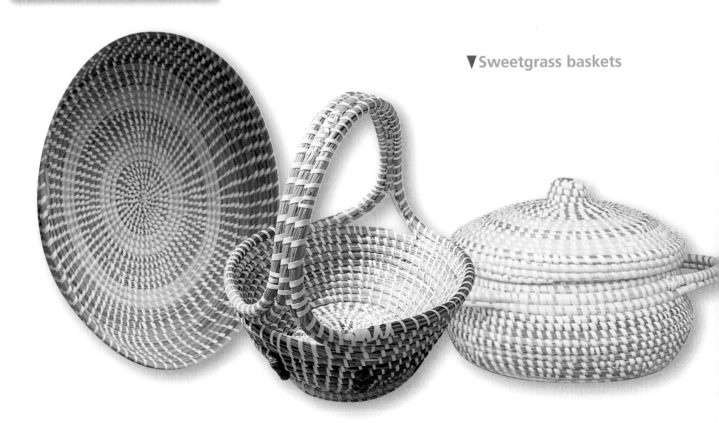

Many African-born people were brought to the Sea Islands to work as slaves. They brought with them the culture of their homeland. They also spoke their own language, called Gullah (GUH•luh), and practiced their own **crafts**, the making of items by hand.

Today tourists visit South Carolina's coastal communities and Sea Islands to watch African American folk artists make their famous sweetgrass baskets. These baskets were once made to carry everything from rice to children. Now the baskets are displayed in museums because they are an example of an original African craft. People buy the baskets because they are beautiful and because they tell something about Gullah culture.

REVIEW Why do people buy sweetgrass baskets?

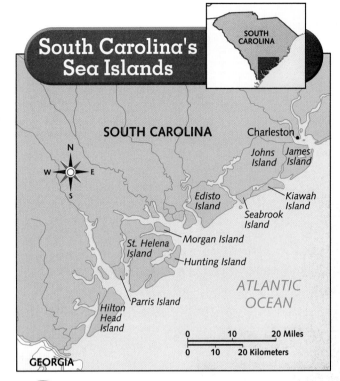

South Carolina's Sea Islands

SOUTH CAROLINA

Charleston

Johns Island   James Island

Edisto Island   Kiawah Island

Seabrook Island

St. Helena Island   Morgan Island

Hunting Island

ATLANTIC OCEAN

Parris Island

Hilton Head Island

GEORGIA

0   10   20 Miles
0   10   20 Kilometers

Regions This map shows the islands that form South Carolina's coast.

■ In which natural region are South Carolina's Sea Islands located?

HERITAGE

Basket Making

Sweetgrass basket making is an important part of South Carolina's African cultural heritage. This 300-year old art has been passed from parent to child to grandchild. However, the state's growth along the Sea Islands has destroyed much of the sweetgrass. So the Historic Charleston Foundation has donated land for growing sweetgrass. Students at Belle Hall Elementary in Mount Pleasant are helping too, by growing sweetgrass in their schoolyard.

South Carolina Folklore

People from all regions of South Carolina share their culture and traditions through folklore. **Folklore** is made up of the unwritten stories and sayings of a people. In South Carolina many stories have been handed down from generation to generation. They have been changed along the way, but they still show the traditions of the region they came from.

In the Low Country, people tell stories about Brer (BRAIR) Rabbit and Brer Fox. These characters have many adventures. They are tricksters who can think fast enough to trick those around them.

In the Up Country, Cherokee and Catawba Indians tell a tale about a possum who is tricked by a rabbit. A possum (short for *opossum*) is a furry animal with a pointed nose and long tail. Read now to find out why the possum's tail is bare.

Why Possum's Tail Is Bare

A long time ago, Possum had a bushy, beautiful tail. The other animals, especially Rabbit, were tired of hearing Possum brag about his tail. Rabbit told the other animals that they should have a dance to honor Possum's tail. The other animals agreed to the dance, but they did not know Rabbit was going to trick Possum. When Rabbit told Possum about the dance, he was excited.

On the day of the dance, Rabbit had Cricket, the haircutter, go to Possum's place to brush his tail. Possum bragged about his tail and did not notice that Cricket was really cutting off all the hair on his tail. Cricket kept the hair from falling off by wrapping the tail with a string. He told Possum not to pull off the string until just before his special dance.

That night at the dance, Possum pulled off the string, danced around, and bragged about his beautiful, bushy tail. All the animals began to laugh at Possum's long, pink tail with no hair. Ever since that time, all of Possum's children and grandchildren have had long, pink, hairless tails.

REVIEW What is the lesson taught by "Why Possum's Tail Is Bare"?

Cloggers at the Johnston Peach Festival in Johnston

Mountain Music and Dance

In the Up Country many people do a kind of dancing called clogging. Clogging is an old form of American folk dancing that grew from dances brought to the area by Irish, Scottish, and English settlers. It also comes from some Native American and African American dances.

Although the style of dancing is called clogging, dancers do not wear wooden clogs. They wear regular shoes with metal taps added to them.

HERITAGE

The Shag

A dance called "the shag" began in the 1930s on the shores of Myrtle Beach. The shag is done to beach music. Since the dance became such a well-known part of South Carolina's identity, it was named the state dance in 1984. Shag contests are held every year in Myrtle Beach and in other parts of the state.

These three bluegrass musicians are playing at the Come-See-Me Festival in Rock Hill.

South Carolina's folk dancing is done to a kind of music called bluegrass. Bluegrass music is a style of country music that began about 50 years ago. It is played by a string band that may include a banjo, fiddle, guitar, and mandolin. Bluegrass is heard in square dance music, religious songs, and ballads—songs that tell a story.

REVIEW What is clogging?

LESSON 7 REVIEW

Check Understanding

1. **Remember the Facts** What is bluegrass music?

2. **Recall the Main Idea** How do people in different regions of South Carolina share cultures and traditions?

Think Critically

3. **Explore Viewpoints** Why do you think people want to learn about arts and crafts that are made in traditional ways?

Show What You Know

Research Activity Pick a South Carolina craft that you would like to know more about. For example, you might choose basket making, quilting, or pottery making. Find out how the item is made and what resources are used. Also find out which groups of people make the item today and why. Share with classmates and family members what you learn.

An Old Tradition: The Blessing of the Fleet

▲ **People take part in the shrimp-eating contest.**

Mount Pleasant is a town on the coast of South Carolina near Charleston. Many people in the town work in the seafood industry. A lot of them work on shrimp boats.

Each year, the town holds a seafood festival. It is known as the Mount Pleasant Seafood Festival and Blessing of the Fleet. Several thousand people come to eat seafood.

When it is time for the parade of boats, the crowd moves down to the water. As each shrimp boat sails by, a blessing is offered for a good harvest in the year ahead. This tradition began long ago in ancient Greece.

After the blessing, the festival continues with clowns, puppets, and dancing to music. The festival is fun for everyone!

Think and Apply

The Seafood Festival and Blessing of the Fleet shows something about the culture of the people in Mount Pleasant. What traditions do you and your family follow that show something about your culture? Interview family members to find out about your family's traditions. Share your interview with classmates.

▼ A clown entertains the festival crowd.

HARCOURT BRACE

Visit the Internet at **http://www.hbschool.com** for additional resources.

▼ This shrimp boat is a part of the parade of boats about to be blessed.

VISUAL SUMMARY

Study the pictures and captions to help you review the events you read about in Unit 6.

Create a Mural Celebrate the different cultures of the world by making a class mural. Cover a bulletin board with paper. Then use art materials to create a mural that shows people from many cultures. Show different parts of each culture, such as food, clothing, art, musical instruments, and language. Add as many details as you can. Then invite other classes to see the mural.

1 People move from one community to another and from one country to another.

3 Language, customs, religion, food, literature, art, and music are important parts of a culture.

2 Large communities often have groups of people who share a culture.

4 People of many cultures can live together in one country, community, or neighborhood.

UNIT 6 REVIEW

Complete this graphic organizer by writing two supporting sentences for the main idea of each lesson. A copy of the organizer appears on Activity Book page 90.

Lesson 1
People move from one community to another and from one country to another.
1. _____
2. _____

Lesson 2
Large communities often have groups of people who share a culture.
1. _____
2. _____

The Many People of a Community

Lesson 4
People of many cultures can live together in one country, community, or neighborhood.
1. _____
2. _____

Lesson 3
Language, customs, food, literature, art, and music are important parts of a culture.
1. _____
2. _____

WRITE MORE ABOUT IT

Write a Story Write two paragraphs about your favorite holiday. In the first paragraph, tell why the holiday is special to you and why it is your favorite. In the second paragraph, explain some of the ways you and your family celebrate the holiday.

USE VOCABULARY

1 Choose five of the vocabulary words below. Use these words to tell a story about yourself or your community.

heritage   literature

holiday   opportunity

immigrant   tradition

CHECK UNDERSTANDING

2 What are three reasons people move from one country to another?

3 What makes up the culture of a group of people?

4 How do the different ways the New Year is celebrated in the United States show there are many cultures in this country?

THINK CRITICALLY

5 **Past to Present** How have immigrants who came to the United States in the past made a difference in the country today?

6 **Think More About It** Why is it important to learn about cultures that are different from yours?

7 **Personally Speaking** If you could live anywhere in the world, where would you live? Explain.

APPLY SKILLS

Understand Point of View

Look at this painting of the woman and her cat. Think about ways to understand the artist's point of view. Then answer the questions below.

© 1995, Board of Trustees, National Gallery of Art, Washington, D.C.

Woman with a Cat by Auguste Renoir

8 What is the woman doing?

9 What is the artist trying to tell you about this woman?

Use a Population Map

The map below gives you information about the population of some cities in California. Use the colors in the map key on the map to help you answer these questions.

⑩ What is the population density of the state's capital?

⑪ What are the population densities of San Francisco and Los Angeles?

⑫ Is the population density higher along California's eastern or western border? Why?

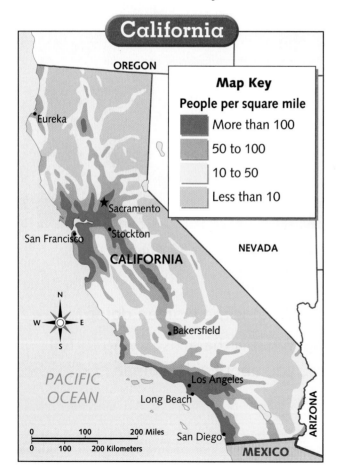

California

Map Key
People per square mile
More than 100
50 to 100
10 to 50
Less than 10

OREGON

Eureka

Sacramento ★

San Francisco

Stockton

CALIFORNIA

NEVADA

Bakersfield

PACIFIC OCEAN

Los Angeles

Long Beach

San Diego

ARIZONA

MEXICO

0   100   200 Miles
0   100   200 Kilometers

Follow a Sequence

Word clues can help you put events in the right order. Look for time-order words such as *next, then,* and *last*. On a sheet of paper, number these sentences in the right sequence.

⑬ _____ She went to high school in Baltimore, Maryland.

⑭ _____ Zora Neale Hurston was born in Florida.

⑮ _____ After college she began writing books.

⑯ _____ Then she went to college and became interested in African American traditions.

READ MORE ABOUT IT

Coming to America: The Story of Immigration by Betsy Maestro. Scholastic. This book explores the history of immigration and the many groups of people who have come to live in America.

HARCOURT BRACE

Visit the Internet at
http://www.hbschool.com
for additional resources.

REMEMBER

- Share your ideas.
- Cooperate with others to plan your work.
- Take responsibility for your work.
- Help one another.
- Show your group's work to the class.
- Discuss what you learned by working together.

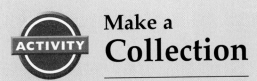

ACTIVITY

Make a Collection

Find and cut out pictures and articles about different cultures. Look for pictures of musical instruments, foods, clothing, and special customs and traditions. Work together to plan a scrapbook of your collection. You might organize your pictures by culture or by foods, clothing, and so on.

Unit Project Wrap-Up

Make an Immigration Station With your classmates, work in small groups to look at the information you have collected. Decide which maps, posters, time lines, calendars, and brochures you will put in your Immigration Station. Paste these items onto a display board. Title your display *Immigration Station*. Set up your board on a table in your classroom or school hallway. Then invite members of the community to see the Immigration Station.

For Your Reference

Contents

Discovering the History

BECOMING A HISTORIAN

Imagine that you have been asked to discover the history of your community. How should you begin? First, think of yourself as a historian. Historians are history detectives. Like detectives, historians look for facts about all kinds of things, from the biggest events to the smallest details. Historians make notes about each discovery. Then they put all of the information together to form a picture of what life was like in a community.

These third-grade students in Orlando, Florida, are about to become history detectives. They are going to look for clues about their community's history.

# of Your Community

Every community has its own history. Turn the page to find some of the ways you can discover the history of your community.

A historian's tools might include these items.

USE THE LIBRARY TO DISCOVER HISTORY

To discover the history of your community, start at the library. The library will have many reference works, or sources of facts. Ask a librarian to help you find what you need. Take notes when you find something useful at the library.

Reference works include books such as almanacs, atlases, dictionaries, and encyclopedias. They also include magazines and newspapers, which are known as periodicals. Reference materials are marked *R* or *REF* for *reference*. They are for use only in the library and may not be checked out. Many libraries also have electronic reference materials on CD-ROM and the Internet.

The library has many resources that you can use to do your research.

► HOW TO FIND NONFICTION BOOKS

Nonfiction books give facts about people, plants and animals, places, and events. In a library all nonfiction books are placed on the shelves in the order of their call numbers. You can find a book by looking up its call number in a card file or a computer catalog. To find this number, however, you need to know the book's title, author, or subject. Here are the cards for a book about the history of Orlando, Florida.

These students are learning to use a card catalog.

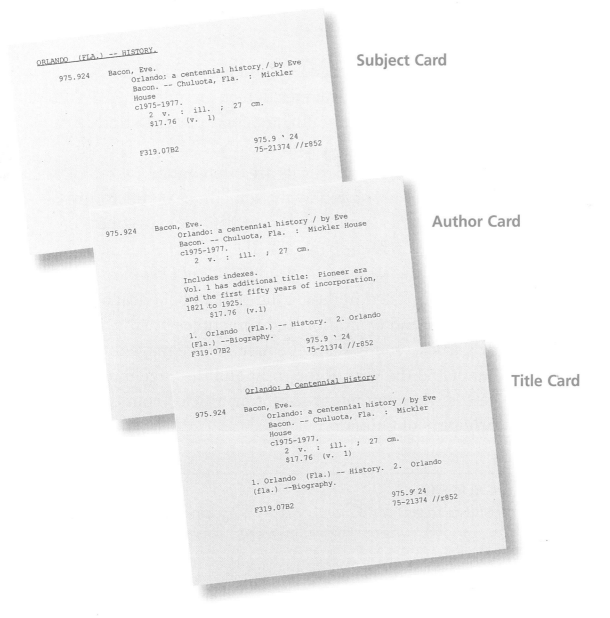

Subject Card

```
ORLANDO  (FLA.)  -- HISTORY.
      975.924    Bacon, Eve.
                   Orlando: a centennial history / by Eve
                 Bacon. -- Chuluota, Fla. :  Mickler
                 House
                 c1975-1977.
                     2  v.  :  ill.  ;  27  cm.
                       $17.76  (v.  1)

                                        975.9 ' 24
                                        75-21374 //r852
              F319.07B2
```

Author Card

```
      975.924    Bacon, Eve.
                   Orlando: a centennial history / by Eve
                 Bacon. -- Chuluota, Fla. :  Mickler House
                 c1975-1977.
                     2  v.  :  ill.  ;  27  cm.

                 Includes indexes.
                 Vol. 1 has additional title:  Pioneer era
                 and the first fifty years of incorporation,
                 1821 to 1925.
                       $17.76  (v.1)

                 1. Orlando  (Fla.)  -- History.  2. Orlando
                 (Fla.) --Biography.
                 F319.07B2              975.9 ' 24
                                        75-21374 //r852
```

Title Card

```
      Orlando: A Centennial History

      975.924    Bacon, Eve.
                   Orlando: a centennial history / by Eve
                 Bacon. -- Chuluota, Fla. :  Mickler
                 House
                 c1975-1977.
                     2  v.  :  ill.  ;  27  cm.
                       $17.76  (v.  1)

                 1. Orlando  (Fla.)  -- History.  2.  Orlando
                 (fla.) --Biography.
                                        975.9' 24
                                        75-21374 //r852
              F319.07B2
```

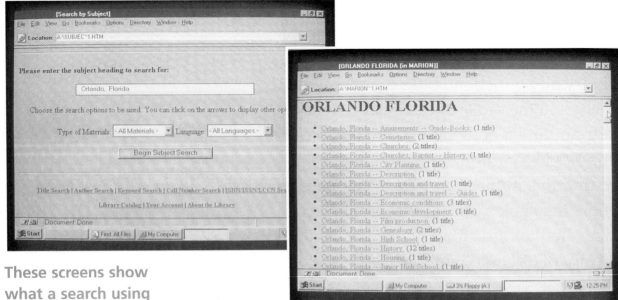

These screens show what a search using a computer catalog might look like.

▶ HOW TO FIND PERIODICALS

Libraries have a special section for periodicals. Newspapers and magazines, which are published every day, week, or month, are good places to find information about your community's history. The newest copies of periodicals are often out on racks. Older copies are stored away, sometimes on microfilm.

Most libraries have indexes, or lists, of magazine articles. You will probably use the *Children's Magazine Guide* and the *Readers' Guide to Periodical Literature*. Articles are listed in these guides in alphabetical order by subject and by author, and sometimes by title. For each article, you will see the name of the magazine, the month and the year of the copy, and the page numbers. Here is what you might see for an article about the early days of Orlando.

Heading
The topic you are researching

Title
The title of the article

ORLANDO
Historic Lake Davis, *Orlando History Magazine* 3 98: pp 18–23

Name
The name of the periodical

Date
The date of the periodical in which the article appears

Page Numbers
The pages on which the article appears

Ask a librarian to help you find an article that is stored on microfilm. He or she will get the microfilm, put it in a special machine, and help you use the machine to find the article. After you read the article, be sure to look at the advertisements and photographs around it. They can show you how people of that time dressed, communicated, and traveled.

◄ The librarian will help the students find an article that has been put on microfilm.

▼ When the roll of microfilm has been put in a special machine, the students can read the article.

INTERVIEW SOMEONE IN YOUR COMMUNITY

Asking people questions, or interviewing, is a good way to learn about the history of your community. There are many people you can interview. For example, if you want to know what life was like long ago, you can interview one of your grandparents or an older member of your community. If you want to know about your community's government or businesses, you can interview the mayor or a business leader. Here are some things you can do to get a good interview.

These students are interviewing a park manager about the history and geography of a community park.

Interview Questions

1. When did you move to Orlando?
2. Why did you and your family settle here?
3. What was school like?
4. How has the town changed from when you were young?
5. What did you and your friends do for fun?
6. Is there anything else you would like to share?

▶ **PLAN THE INTERVIEW**

- Make a list of the people you want to interview.
- Write to or call each person to ask for an interview. Tell the person who you are, why you would like to interview him or her, and what you want to talk about.
- Ask the person to set a time and place to meet.

▶ **BEFORE THE INTERVIEW**

- Read as much as you can about your topic. Also try to find out a little about the person you will be interviewing. That will help you as you talk with the person.
- Make a list of questions to ask.
- Be on time for the interview.

▶ **DURING THE INTERVIEW**

- Listen carefully. Do not interrupt the person.
- Take notes as you talk with the person. Write down the person's ideas and some of his or her exact words.
- If you want to use a tape recorder or a video camera, first ask the person if you may do so.

▶ **AFTER THE INTERVIEW**

- Before you leave, thank the person you interviewed.
- Follow up by writing a thank-you note.

It is helpful to make a list of your questions before an interview.

WRITE TO OR VISIT HISTORICAL SOCIETIES, MUSEUMS, AND HISTORIC SITES

To get more information about the history of your community, you can write to or visit historical societies, museums, and historic sites.

▶ HOW TO WRITE FOR INFORMATION

You can write a letter to ask for information about the history of your community. When you write, be sure to do these things.

- Write neatly or use a word processor.
- Tell who you are and why you are writing.
- Tell exactly what you want to know. For example, you might want to know how your community got its name or in what year it was started.

Piper Monson
123 Main Street
Hometown, FL 32839

April 26, 1999

Mrs. Marlene Miller
Orange Tree Historical Museum
456 Downtown Avenue
Hometown, FL 32803

Dear Mrs. Miller:

I am a third-grade student at Willow Elementary School. I am studying the history of Orlando. I would like to know the year our town was first settled. Also, how did our town get its name? Thank you for your help.

Sincerely,
Piper Monson

You might write letters to ask for information about your community's history.

The students learn about early printing equipment from a worker at a historical museum.

▶ HOW TO ASK QUESTIONS DURING A VISIT

If you have a chance to visit a museum or historic site, you can ask questions about your community's history. When you visit, be sure to do these things.

- Take along a list of questions you want to ask.
- Tell who you are and why you are visiting.
- Listen carefully, and take notes when your questions are answered.
- Take any folders or booklets of information the place has for visitors.
- Before you leave, thank the person who answered your questions.

An old newspaper is one kind of artifact you might see at a historical museum.

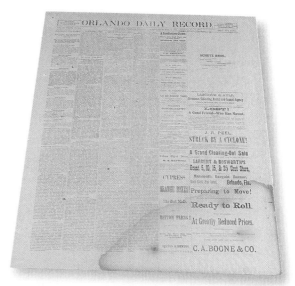

Many communities have monuments or historic markers. These tell about people or events important in the community's history.

FIND PHOTOGRAPHS AND MAPS OF YOUR COMMUNITY

Looking at photographs and maps from different years can help you see changes in your community. You can find photographs and maps at libraries, museums, and historic sites. Here are two photographs of Orlando. What changes do you see in the community?

Then

Orange Avenue and Church Street around 1900

Now

Orange Avenue and Church Street today

These maps show how the city of Orlando has grown. What things on the two maps have changed? What things have stayed the same?

Then

Orlando in 1884

Now

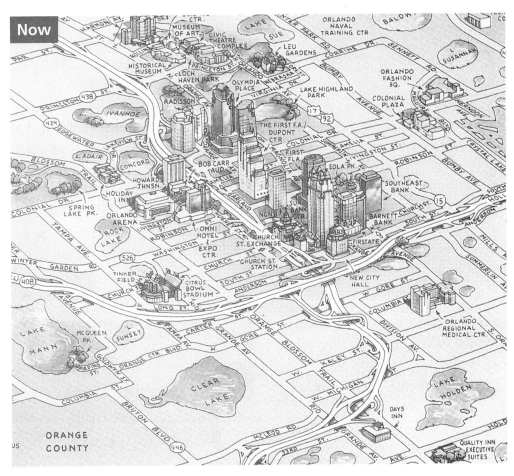

Orlando today

Learning About Your Community • **R13**

WRITE A REPORT

After you have gathered your facts and interviewed people, the next step is to show what you have learned. One way to do this is to write a report about the history of your community. Follow these steps when you write a report.

▶ GATHER AND ORGANIZE YOUR INFORMATION

- Gather all of your notes, articles, pictures, and other information. Set everything out in one place.
- Review your notes to make sure you have all the information you need.
- Organize your information. Make an outline that shows the order in which you want to present it.

You might decide to use a computer to write your report.

▶ DRAFT YOUR REPORT

- Write a draft of your report. Don't worry about mistakes here. You will fix them later.
- Present your ideas in a clear and interesting way.

▶ REVISE

- Check to make sure that you have followed the order of your outline. Move any sentences that seem out of place.
- Add any information you think is needed.
- Cut information that is not needed.
- If too many sentences follow the same pattern, rewrite some of them.

▶ PROOFREAD AND PUBLISH

- Check for errors. Use a dictionary to check spelling.
- Make sure nothing has been left out.
- Write your report neatly or use a word processor.

SHARE YOUR INFORMATION

In addition to writing a report, you can make maps, time lines, charts, or diagrams to share your information. You can also take photographs or cut pictures out of a magazine. Here are some of the things the student history detectives learned about Orlando.

IMPORTANT DATES IN ORLANDO'S EARLY HISTORY

1800 — 1850 — 1900

1835
Orlando Reeves
is killed near
Lake Eola

1843
Aaron Jernigan
is
first settler

1856
Orlando
becomes
county seat

1875
Orlando
becomes an
official
city

1885
Town Hall
is built

1894 – 1895
Great Freeze
kills most
fruit trees

Biographical Dictionary

The Biographical Dictionary lists many of the people introduced in this book. The page number tells where the main discussion of each person starts. See the Index for other page references.

A

Adams, John *(1735–1826)* A U.S. colonial leader and the second president of the U.S. He helped write the Declaration of Independence. He was the first vice president under George Washington. *p. 206*

Aiken, William *(1806–1831)* The head of the South Carolina Canal and Railroad Company. The town of Aiken, South Carolina, which began as a stopping point for the railroad, was named after him. *p. 152*

Aldrin, Edwin "Buzz" *(1930–)* An American astronaut who was the pilot of the first lunar lander, the *Eagle*. In 1969 he and astronaut Neil Armstrong were the first persons to set foot on the moon. *p. 373*

Ammann, Jacob *(1645–1730)* A Swiss religious leader whose followers became known as the Amish. *p. 266*

Anza, Juan Bautista de (AHN•sah) *(1735–after 1788)* A Spanish explorer who was the first European to cross the Colorado River into California. He crossed in 1774 with the help of the Yuma Indians. *p. 59*

Arledge, Buzz A musician who wrote the song "South Carolina on My Mind" with Hank Martin. The General Assembly picked their song to be an official state song in 1984. *p. 394*

Armstrong, Neil *(1930–)* An American astronaut who was commander of *Apollo 11*. In 1969 he and astronaut Edwin "Buzz" Aldrin were the first persons to set foot on the moon. *p. 373*

Ayers, Sara *(1919–)* A skilled Catawba potter from Columbia, South Carolina. She digs her own clay from riverbeds and makes her pottery the same way her ancestors did centuries ago. *p. 223*

Ayllón, Lucas Vásquez de *(1475?–1526)* A Spanish explorer who started the first European settlement in South Carolina in 1526. Ayllón and several others died of fever a few months later, and the rest left the settlement. *p. 224*

Aztec Indians People native to what is now Mexico. They built the city of Tenochtitlán in about 1325. *p. 193*

B

Banneker, Benjamin *(1731–1806)* An astronomer, mathematician, and farmer. He worked with Andrew Ellicott to survey the land for Washington, D.C. *p. 133*

Barton, Clara *(1821–1912)* The founder of the American Red Cross in 1882 and its first president. During the Civil War, she gathered and handed out supplies for the wounded. *p. 208*

Beal, Peter *(1985–)* A California boy who tells others about the importance of wearing bicycle helmets. He was hit by a car at age 11 and lived because his head was protected by a helmet. *p. 285*

Bell, Alexander Graham *(1847–1922)* An inventor and teacher born in Scotland. He came to America in 1871, opened a school for training teachers of the deaf in 1872, and invented the telephone in 1876. *p. 212*

Bethune, Mary McLeod *(1875–1955)* A South Carolina teacher who started a school for women in 1904. In 1923 it joined another school and became Bethune-Cookman College, in Daytona Beach, Florida. *p. 243*

Bolden, Charles F., Jr. *(1946–)* A former astronaut from Columbia, South Carolina. He served as pilot on the space shuttles *Columbia* and *Discovery*, and as mission commander on the shuttle *Atlantis*. *p. 245*

Brighouse, Sam *(1800s)* One of the founders of Vancouver, British Columbia. He, William Hailstone, and John Morton built a lumber mill there in 1865. *p. 67*

Burnett, E. C., III *(1942–)* A Justice of the South Carolina Supreme Court. Justice Burnett has served on this Supreme Court since 1995. *p. 387*

Burns, Robert *(1759–1796)* The Scottish poet who wrote "Auld Lang Syne," a song sung by many people on New Year's Eve. *p. 442*

Bush, George *(1924–)* The 41st president of the U.S. He also served as vice president under Ronald Reagan. *p. 363*

Carter, Jimmy *(1924–)* James Carter, the 39th president of the U.S. He arranged a peace treaty between Egypt and Israel in 1979. *p. 363*

Casper, John H. *(1943–)* An astronaut born in Greenville, South Carolina. He was selected to be an astronaut in 1984 and has flown aboard the space shuttles *Atlantis, Columbia,* and *Endeavour. p. 245*

Catawba Indians (kuh•TAW•buh) Native Americans whose first homeland was the area that is now Charlotte, North Carolina. *p. 179*

Catlin, George *(1796–1872)* An American artist and author who painted many pictures of Native Americans. *p. 188*

Charles II *(1630–1685)* The King of England from 1660 to 1685. South Carolina's first capital city, Charles Town, was named after him. *p. 142*

Chavez, Cesar *(1927–1993)* A farmworker and American leader who worked for fair treatment of all farmworkers. *p. 62*

Cherokee Indians A Native American group that was once one of the three largest tribes in South Carolina. Most were forced to move west in 1838–1839, and many now live in Oklahoma. *p. 223*

Chesnut, Mary Boykin Miller *(1823–1886)* A South Carolina writer whose book, *A Diary from Dixie,* is an important record of the Civil War. *p. 234*

Cheyenne Indians (shy•AN) North American Plains people. They lived in the Platte and Arkansas river areas during the 19th century, in what is now Minnesota and North and South Dakota. *p. 186*

Chouteau, René Auguste (shoo•TOH) *(1749–1829)* A fur trader and pioneer. With his French stepfather, he built a trading post on the Mississippi River in 1764. That post grew to become St. Louis. *p. 119*

Clark, William *(1770–1838)* An American explorer. In 1803, he and Meriwether Lewis led an expedition to the Pacific Coast and back. *p. 206*

Clinton, Bill *(1946–)* William Jefferson Clinton, the 42nd president of the U.S. He had been governor of Arkansas. *p. 363*

Coleman, Catherine G. *(1960–)* An astronaut born in Charleston, South Carolina. She was selected to be an astronaut in 1992 and has flown aboard the space shuttle *Columbia. p. 245*

Columbus, Christopher *(1451–1506)* Italian-born Spanish explorer who in 1492 sailed west from Spain and thought he had reached Asia, but he had actually reached islands near the Americas, lands that were unknown to Europeans. *p. 145*

Cortés, Hernando (kawr•TEZ) *(1485–1547)* A Spanish explorer who fought against the Aztecs. He captured the city of Tenochtitlán, which was rebuilt as Mexico City. *p. 195*

Costa, Lúcio *(1902–1998)* A French architect. His plan for Brasília, the new capital of Brazil, was chosen as the design for the city. *p. 140*

Culbertson, Frank L., Jr. *(1949–)* An astronaut born in Charleston, South Carolina. He was selected to be an astronaut in 1984 and has flown aboard the space shuttles *Atlantis* and *Discovery. p. 245*

Davis, Jefferson *(1808–1889)* A senator from Mississippi. He was president of the Confederate States of America during the Civil War. *p. 231*

de Klerk, Frederik W. *(1936–)* The president of South Africa from 1989 to 1994. He shared a Nobel Peace Prize with Nelson Mandela. *p. 380*

DeLarge, Robert *(1842–1874)* A former slave born in Aiken who served in South Carolina's state goverment and in the United States Congress from 1871–1873. *p. 236*

Dekanawida (deh•kahn•uh•WIH•duh) *(1500s)* A teacher and leader of the Iroquois Indians. He taught peace and made up a set of 13 laws. He also formed the League of Five Nations in 1570. *p. 348*

Douglass, Frederick *(1817–1895)* A leader and writer who was born in slavery in Maryland. He escaped in 1838 and helped in the fight against slavery. *p. 208*

Duke, Charles M., Jr. *(1935–)* A former astronaut who grew up in Lancaster, South Carolina. In 1972, he flew on *Apollo 16* and explored the moon's surface in a special car called a *lunar rover. p. 245*

Eads, James Buchanan *(1820–1887)* An American engineer. He built a triple-arched steel bridge over the Mississippi River at St. Louis, Missouri. *p. 122*

Edison, Thomas *(1847–1931)* An American inventor of more than 1,000 items. He is most famous for inventing the lightbulb, in 1879. *p. 213*

Ellicott, Andrew *(1754–1820)* An American surveyor. He worked with Benjamin Banneker to measure the land for Washington, D.C., and helped lay out the city. *p. 133*

Elliott, R. Brown *(1842–1884)* An editor and lawyer from South Carolina who from 1871–1874 was one of the first African Americans to serve in the United States Congress. *p. 236*

Farnsworth, Philo *(1906–1971)* An American engineer. In 1927 he invented the first television set. *p. 215*

Finney, Ernest, Jr. *(1931–)* The Chief Justice of the South Carolina Supreme Court. Justice Finney has served on this Supreme Court since 1985, and was elected Chief Justice in 1994. *p. 387*

Ford, Gerald *(1913–)* The 38th president of the U.S. He began serving as vice president in 1973 and became president in 1974 when Richard Nixon gave up his office. *p. 362*

Ford, Henry *(1863–1947)* An automobile engineer and manufacturer. He produced the first gasoline-powered automobile in 1893 and invented the Model T in 1908. *p. 215*

Franklin, Benjamin *(1706–1790)* A U.S. leader, writer, and scientist. He helped write the Declaration of Independence. *p. 206*

Gabrieleno Indians Native Americans who once lived near the Pacific Coast in southwestern California. *p. 192*

Gantt, Harvey *(1943–)* An architect and politician. He was the first African American to attend Clemson University in Clemson, South Carolina, and also the first African American mayor of Charlotte, North Carolina. *p. 243*

Grant, Ulysses S. *(1822–1885)* A general who led the Union army in the Civil War. In 1869, he was elected the 18th president of the United States. *p. 235*

Greenberg, Reuben *(1943–)* The Chief of Police of Charleston, South Carolina. Chief Greenberg was appointed by the mayor in 1982 and has received many awards for making Charleston a safer place. *p. 391*

Hailstone, William *(1800s)* One of the founders of Vancouver, British Columbia. He, Sam Brighouse, and John Morton built a lumber mill there in 1865. *p. 67*

Harlee, William *(1812–1897)* The head of the Wilmington and Manchester railroad line. He named the town of Florence, South Carolina, a stopping point on the railroad, after his daughter. *p. 150*

Hester, Sallie *(1835–?)* A young girl who kept a journal describing her trip by wagon train with her family to California. *p. 120*

Hiawatha (hy•uh•WAH•thuh) *(1500s)* A Mohawk medicine man who made a wampum belt that showed Dekanawida's 13 laws. He may have helped Dekanawida form the Iroquois League of Five Nations in 1570. *p. 349*

Hodges, Jim *(1956–)* The governor of South Carolina. Governor Hodges was elected to office in 1998. *p. 387*

Hollings, Ernest "Fritz" *(1922–)* A Senator from Charleston, South Carolina. He was also, at age 36, the youngest person elected governor of South Carolina in the 20th century. *p. 365*

Hoopa Indians Native Americans who lived along the Trinity River in the northwestern part of what is now California. *p. 186*

Hopi Indians (HOH•pee) Native Americans of northeastern Arizona. They lived the farthest west of the Pueblo Indians. *p. 197*

Hughes, Langston *(1902–1967)* An American writer who lived and worked in Harlem during the 1920s and 1930s. He wrote about the lives of African Americans. *p. 426*

Hurston, Zora Neale *(1903–1960)* An American writer who lived and worked in Harlem during the 1920s and 1930s. *p. 426*

Biographical Dictionary

Innes, John (*1700s*) An artist who painted a picture showing Captain George Vancouver near Vancouver Island. *p. 66*

Iowa Indians Native Americans who first lived in what is now Iowa. They later settled near where Cahokia once stood, in the area that is now St. Louis. *p. 119*

Iroquois Indians (IR•uh•kwoy) Native Americans who lived in upstate New York and the Lake Ontario area of Canada. They formed the League of Five Nations (Seneca, Oneida, Cayuga, Mohawk, and Onondaga) in 1570. *p. 348*

Jamison, Judith (*1944– *) A modern dancer and ballerina who is now the artistic director of a dance company in New York. *p. 428*

Jasper, William (*1750–1779*) A South Carolina sergeant during the American Revolution. He became a hero during the battle at Sullivan's Island when he replaced the flag that had been knocked down by English cannons. *p. 231*

Jefferson, Thomas (*1743–1826*) The 3rd president of the U.S. He wrote the first draft of the Declaration of Independence and presented it to Congress on July 2, 1776. *p. 206*

Johnson, Lyndon B. (*1908–1973*) The 36th president of the U.S. He was elected vice president in 1960 and became president after John F. Kennedy's death. *p. 362*

Johnson, Robert (*1676?–1735*) An early South Carolina governor. In 1730 he encouraged South Carolinians to settle further inland by giving away free land. *p. 148*

Karok Indians Native Americans who lived along the Klamath River in what is now northwestern California. They were neighbors of the Hoopa and Yurok Indians. *p. 189*

Keller, Helen (*1880–1968*) An American writer who lost her sight and hearing at 19 months of age. She was taught by Anne Sullivan. *p. 213*

Kennedy, John F. (*1917–1963*) The 35th president of the U.S. He was the youngest person ever to be elected president. *p. 362*

Key, Francis Scott (*1779–1843*) A lawyer and poet. In 1814 he wrote "The Star-Spangled Banner," the national anthem of the U.S. *p. 370*

King, Martin Luther, Jr. (*1929–1968*) A Baptist minister who used peaceful ways to try to make America's laws fair to everyone. A national holiday honoring him is celebrated every January. *p. 243*

Kwolek, Stephanie (*1923– *) Inventor of a fabric that is light, stiff, and stronger than steel. It is used in ropes and bulletproof vests. Her work has earned her a place in the National Inventor's Hall of Fame. *p. 303*

Latimer, Lewis (*1848–1928*) An American inventor who worked with Thomas Edison and helped the growth of early electrical power. One of his many inventions was a way to make lightbulbs glow longer. *p. 214*

L'Enfant, Pierre (lahn•FAHN) (*1754–1825*) A French-born American builder and city planner. He planned and designed Washington, D.C., the nation's capital. *p. 133*

Lee, Robert E. (*1807–1870*) A Confederate general who led one of the South's most successful groups of soldiers. His surrender to Ulysses S. Grant at Appomattox Court House, Virginia, ended the Civil War. *p. 235*

Lewis, Meriwether (*1774–1809*) An American explorer. In 1803 he and William Clark explored the land west of the Mississippi River. They made the first journey overland across North America to the Pacific Coast. *p. 206*

Lincoln, Abraham (*1809–1865*) The 16th president of the U.S. He was president during the Civil War. In 1863, he issued the Emancipation Proclamation, which made slavery against the law in the Confederate states. *p. 207*

Mandela, Nelson (*1918– *) A leader who became the first black president of South Africa. He shared a Nobel Peace Prize with Frederik W. de Klerk for fighting for equal rights for all people. *p. 385*

Biographical Dictionary • **R19**

Mankiller, Wilma *(1945–)* A Cherokee woman and community leader. In 1993 she became the chief of the Cherokee Nation in Oklahoma. *p. 243*

Marconi, Guglielmo *(mar•KOH•nee) (1874–1937)* The Italian inventor of the wireless telegraph. *p. 214*

Marion, Francis *(1732–1795)* A South Carolina general during the American Revolution. He was nicknamed the Swamp Fox because he and his men often hid in the swamps to attack the English by surprise. *p. 231*

Marshall, John *(1755–1835)* The fourth chief justice of the U.S. Supreme Court. *p. 366*

Martin, Hank A musician who wrote the song "South Carolina on My Mind" with Buzz Arledge. The General Assembly picked their song to be an official state song in 1984.

McNair, Ronald E. *(1950–1986)* An astronaut born in Lake City, South Carolina. He was killed in the space shuttle *Challenger* explosion on January 28, 1986. *p. 245*

Mitchell, Loften *(1919–)* An American writer who wrote about life in Harlem during the 1900s. *p. 425*

Moore, Darla *(1955–)* An entrepreneur and banker from Lake City, South Carolina. She was the first woman to have the business school of an important university named after her. *p. 316*

Moore, James E. *(1936–)* A Justice of the South Carolina Supreme Court. Justice Moore has served on this Supreme Court since 1991. *p. 387*

Morse, Samuel *(1791–1872)* An American artist and inventor. He invented a magnetic telegraph in 1835 and made up the Morse code for use with it in 1838. *p. 212*

Morton, John *(1800s)* One of the founders of Vancouver, British Columbia. He, William Hailstone, and Sam Brighouse built a lumber mill there in 1865. *p. 67*

Motte, Jacob *(1700–1770)* A plantation owner who settled across the harbor from Charleston. The town that developed around his plantation is now known as Mount Pleasant, South Carolina. *p. 150*

Moultrie, William *(1730–1805)* A South Carolina colonel during the American Revolution. Along with Colonel William Thompson, he led the victory against the English at Sullivan's Island on June 28, 1776. *p. 231*

Musqueam Indians *(MUHS•kwee•uhm)* A group believed to be the first people to live near what is now Vancouver, British Columbia, in Canada. *p. 66*

Navajo Indians *(NA•vuh•hoh)* Native Americans of northern Arizona and New Mexico. *p. 197*

Niemeyer, Oscar *(1907–)* An architect who helped plan the city of Brasília. His design work there includes the Metropolitan Cathedral and the President's Palace. *p. 141*

Nixon, Richard *(1913–1994)* The 37th president of the U.S. He gave up the office of president in 1974. *p. 362*

O'Connor, Sandra Day *(1930–)* An Arizona judge who became the first woman to serve on the U.S. Supreme Court. *p. 366*

Oliver, King *(1885–1938)* A musician whose real name was Joseph Oliver. He formed the Creole Jazz Band in 1922. *p. 427*

Osage Indians *(oh•SAYJ)* Native Americans who first lived in the Ohio River valley. They moved to settle along the Missouri River, near where Cahokia once stood, in the area that became St. Louis. *p. 119*

Penn, William *(1644–1718)* A colonist who was given a large area of land in North America by King Charles II. He called it Pennsylvania in honor of his father. *p. 204*

Pilgrims A group of English colonists who settled in Plymouth, Massachusetts, in 1620. *pp. 204, 350*

Pinckney, Charles *(1757–1824)* A leader who served in the South Carolina and United States governments. Many of his ideas were used in writing the Constitution of the United States, which he also signed. He was the cousin of Charles Cotesworth Pinckney. *p. 232*

Pinckney, Charles Cotesworth *(1746–1825)* A leader from South Carolina who served as an aide to General George Washington and signed the Constitution. He was the son of Eliza Lucas Pinckney and the cousin of Charles Pinckey. *p. 232*

Pinckney, Eliza Lucas *(1722?–1793)* A South Carolina farmer who grew the first successful indigo crop in the United States when she was seventeen. Indigo became one of the most important crops in early South Carolina. *p. 227*

Powhatan Indians (pow•uh•TAN) Native Americans who lived in the area that is now Virginia. They helped the settlers of Jamestown survive in their new homeland. *p. 204*

Quechan Indians (KECH•uhn) A group believed to be the first people to live near what is now Yuma, Arizona. They were part of the larger group of Yuma Indians, who also lived in southern California. *p. 58*

Rainey, Joseph M. *(1832–1887)* A political leader born in Georgetown, South Carolina, who was the first African American elected to the United States Congress. He served in Congress from 1869–1879. *p. 236*

Reagan, Ronald *(1911–)* The 40th president of the U.S. He served two terms in office. *p. 363*

Renoir, Auguste *(1841–1919)* A French artist known for his natural style of painting and his use of unmixed colors. *p. 477*

Ribaut, Jean *(1520?–1565)* A French explorer who started one of the first settlements in South Carolina, where Port Royal is today. During the colony's first winter, the settlers ran out of food and had to leave. *p. 225*

Rivera, Diego *(1886–1957)* A Mexican painter who was famous for his murals of Mexican history. He painted *Detroit Industry–North Wall* in 1933 and *The Great City of Tenochtitlán* in 1945. *pp. 194, 276*

Roosevelt, Franklin D. *(1882–1945)* The 32nd president of the United States, and the only president to be reelected three times. He helped the country get out of the Great Depression, and was an important leader in World War II. *p. 241*

Saarinen, Eero (SAR•uh•nuhn) *(1910–1961)* An architect who was born in Finland and later moved to the U.S. He designed the St. Louis Gateway Arch. *p. 124*

Shah Jahan *(1592–1666)* A ruler of India (1628–1658). He had the Taj Mahal built in memory of his wife. *p. 453*

Sherman, William T. *(1820–1891)* A general for the Union army in the Civil War. His march of destruction with 60,000 troops led to the defeat of the southern states. *p. 234*

Smalls, Robert *(1839–1915)* A slave from South Carolina who became a hero of the Union army in the Civil War. He gained control of the Confederate ship *The Planter*, gave it to the Union, and became a captain. *p. 237*

Smith, John *(1580–1631)* An English explorer who joined the colonists that settled in Virginia in 1607. He was elected leader of the colony. *p. 204*

Sullivan, Anne *(1866–1936)* The teacher of Helen Keller. She wrote, spoke, and worked for fair treatment of the deaf. *p. 213*

Tenenbaum, Inez Moore *(1951–)* A lawyer and the South Carolina State Superintendent of Education. She is in charge of all the public schools in the state. *p. 386*

Thompson, William *(1727–1796)* A South Carolina colonel during the American Revolution. Along with Colonel William Moultrie, he led the victory against the English at Sullivan's Island on June 28, 1776. *p. 231*

Thurmond, J. Strom *(1902–)* A Senator from Edgefield, South Carolina, who, in 1996, became the oldest person ever to serve in Congress. He also served as governor of South Carolina from 1947 to 1951. *p. 365*

Timrod, Henry *(1828–1867)* A poet from Charleston, South Carolina, who was called "the laureate [honored poet] of the Confederacy." His poem "Carolina!" was set to music and chosen as South Carolina's official state song in 1911. *p. 392*

Toal, Jean *(1943–)* A Justice of the South Carolina Supreme Court. Justice Toal has served on this Supreme Court since 1988. *p. 387*

Trumbull, John *(1756–1843)* An American soldier and painter whose work shows events and people of the Revolutionary War. His paintings include *The Declaration of Independence* and a portrait of George Washington. *pp. 131, 206*

Biographical Dictionary

Tutu, Desmond *(1931–)* A religious leader in South Africa. He won the Nobel Peace Prize in 1984. *p. 381*

Vancouver, George *(1757–1798)* A British sea captain who explored the Pacific Coast of North America. In 1792 he sailed around what is now Vancouver Island. *p. 67*

Waller, John, Jr. *(1937–)* A Justice of the South Carolina Supreme Court. Justice Waller has served on this Supreme Court since 1994. *p. 387*

Washington, George *(1732–1799)* The 1st U.S. president. He is known as the "Father of Our Country." He chose the location for the nation's capital city, Washington, D.C. He also led the U.S. in the revolution against Britain. *pp. 131, 206*

Winnemucca, Sarah (wih•nuh•MUH•kuh) *(1844–1891)* A Paiute woman who wrote a book calling for peaceful living between the Paiute Indians and the white people. *p. 345*

Wolf on the Hill *(late 1700s–?)* A chief of the Cheyenne Indians in the Great Plains region of the U.S. *p. 188*

Woodward, Henry *(1646?–1688)* A surgeon and explorer. He made contact with the Westo tribe and started South Carolina's trade with Native Americans. *p. 227*

Wright, Orville *(1871–1948)* An American who—with his brother, Wilbur—was the first to fly a motor-powered airplane. On December 17, 1903, the first flight was taken by Orville. Later that same day, Wilbur Wright flew the plane. *p. 216*

Wright, Wilbur *(1867–1912)* An American who—with his brother, Orville—flew the first motor-powered airplane near Kitty Hawk, North Carolina, in 1903. *p. 216*

Yamassee Indians A Native American group who were once one of the three largest tribes in South Carolina. *p. 223*

Young, Marilyn R. *(1934–)* The mayor of Yuma, Arizona, since 1993. *p. 52*

Yurok Indians Native Americans who lived along the Klamath River in what is now northwestern California. They were neighbors of the Hoopa and Karok Indian tribes. *p. 189*

Biographical Dictionary

Gazetteer

This Gazetteer is a geographical dictionary that will help you locate places discussed in this book. The page number tells where each place appears on a map.

Abbeville A city in western South Carolina; the county seat of Abbeville County. p. A14

Adirondack Mountains (ad•uh•RAHN•dak) A mountain range in northeastern New York. p. 348

Afghanistan A country in western Asia. p. 446

Africa The second-largest continent. p. 45

Aiken A city in western South Carolina; the county seat of Aiken County. p. A14

Alabama A state in the southeastern United States. p. 43

Alaska A state of the United States, in the northwestern corner of North America. p. 43

Albany The capital of New York. p. 137

Algeria A country in northwestern Africa. p. 381

Allendale A town in southwestern South Carolina; the county seat of Allendale County. p. A14

Amarillo A city in northwestern Texas. p. 181

Amazon River A river in South America; second-longest in the world. p. 139

Anderson A city in northwestern South Carolina; the county seat of Anderson County and home of Anderson College. p. A14

Annapolis The capital of Maryland. p. 137

Antarctica The continent surrounding the South Pole; covered by an ice cap. p. 45

Appalachian Mountains (a•puh•LAY•chuhn) A mountain range in the eastern United States that includes the Blue Ridge mountains. p. 107

Arctic Ocean The body of water north of the Arctic Circle. p. 45

Arizona A state in the southwestern United States. p. 43

Arkansas A state in the south central United States. p. 43

Ashley River A river in southeastern South Carolina that flows from Berkeley County southeast into Charleston Harbor, where it joins the Cooper River. p. A15

Asia The largest continent. p. 45

Atlanta The capital of Georgia. p. 137

Atlantic Ocean The ocean that separates North and South America from Europe and Africa. p. 45

Augusta The capital of Maine. p. 137

Aurora A city in Ohio. p. 98

Austin The capital of Texas. p. 137

Australia The smallest continent. p. 45

Baltimore A city on the Chesapeake Bay in Maryland. p. 425

Bamberg A town in southwestern South Carolina; the county seat of Bamberg County. p. A14

Barnwell A city in southwestern South Carolina; the county seat of Barnwell County. p. A14

Baton Rouge (BAT•uhn ROOZH) The capital of Louisiana. p. 137

Beaufort A city in southern coastal South Carolina, located on Port Royal Island; the county seat of Beaufort County. p. A14

Bell A city in Oklahoma. p. 343

Bennettsville A city in northeastern South Carolina; the county seat of Marlboro County. p. A14

Bhutan (boo•TAN) A kingdom on the northeastern border of India. p. 446

Billings A city on the Yellowstone River in south central Montana. p. 118

Bishopville A town in northeastern central South Carolina; the county seat of Lee County. p. A14

Bismarck The capital of North Dakota. p. 137

Blue Ridge region One of the six natural regions in South Carolina. p. A15

Boise The capital of Idaho. p. 137

Boston The capital of Massachusetts. p. 107

Brasília (bruh•ZIL•yuh) The capital of Brazil; designed by Lúcio Costa. p. 139

Brazil A country in South America; covers about half of the continent. p. 139

British Columbia A province on the Pacific coast of Canada. p. 67

Gazetteer • **R23**

Broad River A river in northern South Carolina that flows south and unites with the Saluda River near Columbia to form the Congaree River. p. A15

Bull Island An island off the northeastern coast of Charleston County, South Carolina. p. A15

Bulls Bay An inlet of the Atlantic Ocean on the northeastern coast of Charleston County, South Carolina, enclosed on the southwest by Bull Island. p. A15

Cahokia (kuh•HOH•kee•uh) An ancient village in Illinois; located where the Missouri River joins the Mississippi River. p. 118

Calcutta (kal•KUH•tuh) The capital of West Bengal, in eastern India. p. 446

California A state in the western United States. p. 43

Camden A city in north central South Carolina near the Wateree River; the county seat of Kershaw County. p. A14

Canada A country in North America. p. 43

Cape Island An island off the northeast coast of Charleston County, South Carolina, east of Bulls Bay. p. A15

Cape Romain National Wildlife Refuge A wildlife preserve that stretches along the coast of Charleston County in South Carolina. p. 147

Cape Town A seaport city in Cape Province in South Africa. p. 381

Caribbean Sea (kar•uh•BEE•uhn) A part of the Atlantic Ocean; the West Indies and Central and South America form its boundaries on three sides. p. 420

Carson City The capital of Nevada. p. 137

Casper A city in central Wyoming. p. 118

Cayce A city in Lexington County, South Carolina. p. 144

Central America Countries between North and South America, between Mexico and Colombia. p. 420

Chad A country in north central Africa. p. 381

Charleston A seaport city in southeastern South Carolina; the county seat of Charleston County. p. A14

Charleston Harbor A natural harbor on the east coast of Charleston County, South Carolina, at the mouths of the Ashley and Cooper rivers. p. A15

Charlotte The largest city in North Carolina. p. 185

Chattooga River A river that forms part of the border of northwestern South Carolina with Georgia; it flows southwest into the Tugaloo River. p. A15

Chennai A city in India on the Coromandel Coast; main port for southeastern India. p. 446

Chester A city in northern South Carolina; the county seat of Chester County. p. A14

Chesterfield A town in northeastern South Carolina; the county seat of Chesterfield County. p. A14

Cheyenne (shy•AN) The capital of Wyoming. p. 137

Chicago A city in northeastern Illinois. p. 107

China A country in eastern Asia. p. A3

Cincinnati A city in southwestern Ohio. p. 118

Clemson A city in Anderson and Pickens counties, South Carolina. p. A14

Cleveland The second-largest city in Ohio; located in the northern part of the state. p. 98

Coastal Plain A natural land region along the Atlantic coast of the United States. p. 107

Coastal Zone region One of the six natural regions in South Carolina. p. A15

Colorado A state in the western United States. p. 43

Colorado River A river in the southwestern United States. p. 59

Columbia The capital of South Carolina, located in the center of the state; the county seat of Richland County. p. A15

Columbus A city in western Georgia on the Chattahoochee River. p. 151

Columbus The capital of Ohio. p. 137

Concord The capital of New Hampshire. p. 137

Congaree River A river in central South Carolina formed where the Broad and Saluda rivers unite near Columbia; the Congaree unites with the Wateree River to form the Santee River. p. A15

Connecticut A state in the northeastern United States. p. 43

Conway A town in eastern South Carolina, on the Waccamaw River; the county seat of Horry County. p. A14

Cooper River A river in southern South Carolina; it flows south into Charleston Harbor. p. A15

Cuba An island in the West Indies. p. 107

Gazetteer

Dallas A city in northeastern Texas. p. 107

Darlington A city in northeastern South Carolina; the county seat of Darlington County. p. A14

Delaware A state in the eastern United States. p. 43

Delhi (DEL•ee) A city in northern India, on the banks of the Yamuna River. p. 446

Democratic Republic of the Congo A country in Africa. p. 381

Denver The capital of Colorado. p. 137

Des Moines (dih•MOYN) The capital of Iowa; the largest city in the state. p. 137

Detroit The largest city in Michigan. p. 425

Dillon A town in northeastern South Carolina; the county seat of Dillon County. p. A14

Dover The capital of Delaware. p. 137

Durham A city in northeastern North Carolina. p. 179

East Los Angeles A neighborhood in Los Angeles, California. p. 421

Eastern Cape A province in South Africa. p. 383

Eastern Hemisphere (HEM•uh•sfeer) The eastern half of the Earth. p. 46

Ecuador (EH•kwuh•dawr) A country in northwestern South America. p. A2

Edgefield A town in western South Carolina; the county seat of Edgefield County. p. A14

Edisto Island An island at the mouth of the Edisto River; it forms the southern tip of Charleston County, South Carolina. p. A15

Edisto River A river in southern South Carolina; it flows southeast from Edgefield County to the Atlantic Ocean. p. A15

Egypt A country in northeastern Africa; the Nile River, the longest river in the world, flows through Egypt. p. 381

El Paso A city in western Texas. p. 125

equator An imaginary line on the Earth; it is halfway between the poles. p. 45

Ethiopia (ee•thee•OH•pee•uh) A country in eastern Africa. p. 381

Europe The second-smallest continent. p. 45

Fall Line A line joining the waterfalls on numerous rivers in the eastern United States. p. 151

Florence A city in northeastern South Carolina; the county seat of Florence County. p. A14

Florida A state in the southeastern United States. p. 43

Folly Beach A beach off the coast of Charleston County, South Carolina. p. 147

Forest Acres A town in Richland County, South Carolina. p. 144

Fork Mountain A mountain in Oconee County, northwestern South Carolina, near the borders with North Carolina and Georgia. p. A15

Francis Marion National Forest A national forest in eastern South Carolina. p. 147

Frankfort The capital of Kentucky. p. 137

Free State A province in South Africa. p. 383

Gaffney A city in northern South Carolina; the county seat of Cherokee County and home of Limestone College. p. A14

Ganges River (GAN•jeez) A river in northern and northeastern India. p. 446

Georgetown A city and port of entry in eastern South Carolina, at the head of Winyah Bay; the county seat of Georgetown County. p. A14

Georgia A state in the southeastern United States. p. 43

Grand Strand A string of beaches along Long Bay, on the northern coast of South Carolina. p. A15

Great Basin An area of low, dry land in the western United States. p. 107

Great Lakes A chain of five lakes between the United States and Canada. p. 43

Great Pee Dee River A river that flows southeast from south central North Carolina through northeastern South Carolina to Winyah Bay. p. A15

Great Plains A large area of plains in the west central United States. p. 107

Greenland An island off the coast of northeastern North America. p. A4

Greensboro A city in north central North Carolina. p. 179

Greenville A city in eastern North Carolina. p. 179

Greenville A city in northwestern South Carolina; the county seat of Greenville county. p. A14

Greenwood A city in northwestern South Carolina; the county seat of Greenwood county. p. A14

Gulf of Mexico A body of water on the southeastern coast of North America. p. 43

Hampton A town in southwestern South Carolina; the county seat of Hampton County. p. A14

Harlem A neighborhood in New York City. p. 425

Harrisburg The capital of Pennsylvania. p. 137

Hartford The capital of Connecticut. p. 137

Hartwell Lake A lake in northwestern South Carolina into which the Tugaloo River flows. p. A15

Hawaii A state made up of a string of volcanic islands in the north central Pacific Ocean. p. 43

Helena The capital of Montana. p. 137

Hilton Head Island A town in Beaufort County, South Carolina, on an island in the Atlantic Ocean south of the mouth of the Broad River. p. A14

Honolulu The capital of Hawaii. p. 137

Hudson River A river in New York; begins in the Adirondack Mountains. p. 348

Hunting Island An island off the southeastern coast of South Carolina, between St. Helena Sound and Port Royal Sound. p. A15

Idaho A state in the northwestern United States. p. 43

Illinois A state in the central United States. p. 43

India A country in Asia. p. A3

Indian Ocean A body of water that is east of Africa, south of Asia, west of Australia, and north of Antarctica. p. 45

Indiana A state in the north central United States. p. 43

Indianapolis The capital of Indiana. p. 137

Indus River A river in Asia. p. 446

Inner Coastal Plain region One of the six natural regions in South Carolina. p. A15

Intracoastal Waterway A system of inland waterways in the eastern and southeastern United States. p. 147

Iowa A state in the north central United States. p. 43

Iran An Islamic country in southwestern Asia; formerly known as Persia. p. 446

J. Strom Thurmond Lake A reservoir on the border of Georgia with South Carolina; it was formed by the damming of the Savannah River. p. A15

Japan A country in the western Pacific Ocean, off the east coast of Asia. p. A3

Jefferson City The capital of Missouri. p. 137

Johannesburg A city in northeastern South Africa. p. 381

Juneau (JOO•noh) The capital of Alaska. p. 137

Kansas A state in the central United States. p. 43

Kansas City A city in Kansas. p. 425

Kentucky A state in the east central United States. p. 43

Kenya A country in eastern Africa; borders the Indian Ocean. p. 381

Kiawah Island An island in the Atlantic Ocean, part of Charleston County, South Carolina. p. 147

Kingstree A town in eastern South Carolina; the county seat of Williamsburg County. p. A14

Knoxville A city in Tennessee, on the Tennessee River. p. 107

Lake Greenwood A lake through which the Saluda River flows in northwestern South Carolina; it forms the border between Laurens and Greenwood counties. p. A15

Lake Keowee A lake in northwestern South Carolina; it forms the border between Oconee and Pickens counties and extends into Anderson County, connecting with Hartwell Lake. p. A15

Gazetteer

Lake Marion A human-made lake in east central South Carolina, formed by the damming of the Santee River; it is the largest lake in the state. p. A15

Lake Moultrie A human-made lake in Berkeley County, South Carolina; it is the second-largest lake in the state. p. A15

Lake Murray A human-made lake in central South Carolina; it is the third-largest lake in the state. p. A15

Lake Texcoco A dry lake near Mexico City; used to be the site of Tenochtitlán. p. 198

Lake Wylie A lake in York County, South Carolina; it forms part of the border with North Carolina. p. A15

Lancaster A city in northern South Carolina; the county seat of Lancaster County. p. A14

Lansing The capital of Michigan. p. 137

Laurens A city in northwestern South Carolina; the county seat of Laurens County. p. A14

Lesotho (luh•SOH•toh) A kingdom in southern Africa. p. 381

Lexington A town in central South Carolina; the county seat of Lexington County. p. A14

Little Pee Dee River A river that flows south from southern North Carolina through eastern South Carolina into the Great Pee Dee River near its mouth. p. A15

Little River A town in Horry County, South Carolina, at the northern tip of the Grand Strand. p. 77

Little Rock The capital of Arkansas. p. 137

London The capital of the United Kingdom. The Thames River flows through this city. p. 115

Long Bay A bay off the southern coast of North Carolina and the northeastern coast of South Carolina. p. A15

Long Beach A city in southwestern California. p. 130

Los Angeles A city in California. p. 125

Louisiana A state in the southeastern United States. p. 43

Louisville A city in north central Kentucky, on the Ohio River. p. 425

Macon A city in central Georgia on the Ocmulgee River. p. 151

Madagascar (mad•uh•GAS•ker) A country off the southeastern coast of Africa. p. 381

Madison The capital of Wisconsin. p. 137

Maine A state in the northeastern United States. p. 43

Manning A town in east central South Carolina; the county seat of Clarendon County. p. A14

Marion A town in eastern South Carolina; the county seat of Marion County. p. A14

Maryland A state in the eastern United States. p. 43

Massachusetts A state in the northeastern United States. p. 43

McCormick A town in western South Carolina; the county seat of McCormick County. p. A14

Memphis A city in southwestern Tennessee, on the Mississippi River. p. 118

Mexico A country in southern North America; borders on the Pacific Ocean and the Gulf of Mexico. p. 43

Mexico City The capital of Mexico. p. 198

Miami A city in southeastern Florida, on Biscayne Bay. p. 420

Michigan A state in the north central United States. p. 43

Minneapolis A city in southeastern Minnesota. p. 107

Minnesota A state in the northern United States. p. 43

Mississippi A state in the southern United States. p. 43

Mississippi River The longest river in the United States. p. 107

Missouri A state in the central United States. p. 43

Missouri River A river in the western United States; joins the Mississippi. p. 107

Moncks Corner A town in southeastern South Carolina; the county seat of Berkeley County. p. A14

Montana A state in the northwestern United States. p. 43

Montgomery The capital of Alabama. p. 137

Montpelier (mahnt•PEEL•yer) The capital of Vermont. p. 137

Mount Pleasant A town in Charleston County, South Carolina, east of the city of Charleston. p. A14

Mumbai The capital of Maharashtra, India. p. 446

Myrtle Beach A city in Horry County, South Carolina, on the Atlantic Ocean. p. A14

Nashville The capital of Tennessee. p. 137

Nebraska A state in the central United States. p. 43

Nepal (nuh•PAWL) A kingdom on the northeastern border of India. p. 446

Nevada A state in the western United States. p. 43

New Hampshire A state in the northeastern United States. p. 43

New Jersey A state in the northeastern United States. p. 43

New Mexico A state in the southwestern United States. p. 43

New Orleans A city in southeastern Louisiana. p. 107

New York A state in the northeastern United States. p. 43

New York City A city in New York. p. 125

Newberry A town in northwestern central South Carolina; the county seat of Newberry County. p. A14

Nigeria (ny•JIR•ee•uh) A country in western Africa. p. 381

North America The continent that includes the United States, Canada, and Mexico. p. 46

North Augusta A city in Aiken County, South Carolina, on the Savannah River across from Augusta, Georgia. p. A14

North Carolina A state in the southeastern United States. p. 43

North Charleston A city in Charleston County, South Carolina. p. 142

North Dakota A state in the northwestern United States. p. 43

North Korea A country on the eastern coast of Asia. p. A3

North Pole The northernmost place on the Earth; surrounded by the Arctic Ocean. p. 46

Northern Hemisphere The northern half of the Earth. p. 47

Oakland A city in California on the eastern side of San Francisco Bay. p. 130

Ohio A state in the north central United States; borders on Lake Erie. p. 43

Ohio River A river in the north central United States. p. 107

Oklahoma A state in the south central United States. p. 43

Oklahoma City The capital of Oklahoma; largest city in the state. p. 137

Olympia The capital of Washington. p. 137

Orangeburg A city in south central South Carolina; the county seat of Orangeburg County. p. A14

Oregon A state in the northwestern United States. p. 43

Orlando A city in central Florida. p. 107

Outer Coastal Plain region One of the six natural regions in South Carolina. p. A15

Pacific Ocean The body of water that extends from the western coasts of North and South America to Australia and the eastern coast of Asia. p. 45

Pakistan (PAK•ih•stan) A country in southern Asia. p. 446

Parris Island One of the Sea Islands in Beaufort County, South Carolina; it has been a U.S. Marine Corps training station since 1915. p. 147

Pennsylvania A state in the northeastern United States. p. 43

Philadelphia A city in southeastern Pennsylvania. p. 425

Philippines A country made up of islands off the southeastern coast of China. p. A3

Phoenix The capital of Arizona. p. 59

Pickens A town in northwestern South Carolina; the county seat of Pickens County. p. A14

Piedmont region One of the six natural regions in South Carolina. p. A15

Pierre (PIR) The capital of South Dakota, on the Missouri River. p. 137

Pittsburgh A city in southwestern Pennsylvania. p. 118

Platte River A river in the central United States; joins the Missouri River. p. 118

Port Royal A town on Port Royal Island in Beaufort County, South Carolina. p. 311

Port Royal Sound An inlet of the Atlantic Ocean between the islands of St. Helena and Hilton Head off the southeastern coast of South Carolina at the entrance to the Broad River. p. A15

Pretoria (prih•TOHR•ee•uh) The capital of South Africa. p. 381

Providence The capital of Rhode Island. p. 137

Raleigh (RAHL•ee) The capital of North Carolina. p. 137

Republic of the Congo A country in west central Africa. p. 381.

Rhode Island A state in the northeastern United States. p. 43

Richard B. Russell Lake A lake in northwestern South Carolina and northeastern Georgia, between Hartwell and J. Strom Thurmond lakes. p. A15

Richmond The capital of Virginia. p. 137

Ridgeland A town in southern South Carolina; the county seat of Jasper County. p. A14

Rio de Janeiro (REE•oh DAY zhun•NAIR•oh) A city in Brazil; famous for its beaches and mountains. p. 139

Rio Grande River A river in the southwestern United States. p. 98

Rock Hill A city in York County, South Carolina; home of Winthrop University. p. A14

Rocky Mountains A mountain range in western North America. p. 107

Sacramento The capital of California. p. 137

Salem The capital of Oregon. p. 137

Salt Lake City The capital of Utah. p. 137

Saluda A town in west central South Carolina; the county seat of Saluda County. p. A14

Saluda River A river in west central South Carolina that flows southeast from the Blue Ridge mountains through Lake Murray and comes together with the Broad River near Columbia to form the Congaree River. p. A15

San Francisco A large port city in California. p. 130

Sandhills region One of the six natural regions in South Carolina. p. A15

Santa Fe The capital of New Mexico. p. 137

Santee River A river in southeastern central South Carolina, formed where the Congaree and Wateree rivers meet. p. A15

Sassafras Mountain A mountain in Pickens County, South Carolina; it is the highest point in the state. p. A15

Savannah National Wildlife Refuge A wildlife preserve located between Hardeeville, South Carolina, and Port Wentworth, Georgia. p. 147

Savannah River A river that forms the border between South Carolina and Georgia. p. A15

Seabrook Island An island off the coast of Charleston County, South Carolina. p. 147

Seattle A large port city in western Washington. p. 125

South Africa A country in southern Africa. p. 381

South America A continent in the Western Hemisphere; includes most of Latin America. p. 45

South Carolina A state in the southeastern United States. pp. A14, A15

South Dakota A state in the northwestern United States. p. 45

South Island An island off the northern coast of South Carolina, south of Winyah Bay. p. A15

South Korea A country on the eastern coast of Asia. p. A3

South Pole The southernmost place on the Earth; located in west central Antarctica. p. 46

Southern Hemisphere The southern half of the Earth. p. 47

Spartanburg A city in northwestern South Carolina; the county seat of Spartanburg County and home of Converse College and Wofford College. p. A14

Springfield The capital of Illinois. p. 137

Sri Lanka An island in the Indian Ocean, south of India. p. 446

St. George A town in southeastern South Carolina; the county seat of Dorchester County. p. A14

St. Helena Island An island in Beaufort County, South Carolina. p. 147

St. Helena Sound An inlet on the northern coast of St. Helena Island, South Carolina. p. A15

St. Lawrence River A river in Canada that forms a border between Canada and New York. p. 348

St. Louis A large city in Missouri. p. 107

St. Matthews A town in central South Carolina; the county seat of Calhoun County. p. A14

St. Paul The capital of Minnesota. p. 137

Sudan (soo•DAN) A country in northeastern Africa. p. 381

Sumter A city in east central South Carolina; the county seat of Sumter County and home of Morris College. p. A14

Surfside Beach A town in Horry County, South Carolina, down the coast from Myrtle Beach. p. 147

Tahlequah (TA•luh•kwaw) A city in northeastern Oklahoma. p. 343

Tallahassee The capital of Florida. p. 137

Tanzania (tan•zuh•NEE•uh) A country in eastern Africa. p. 381

Tennessee A state in the southeast central United States. p. 43

Tennessee River A river in the southeastern United States. p. 118

Tenochtitlán (tay•nawch•teet•LAHN) The capital of the Aztec Empire; Mexico City is now in the same location. p. 193

Terlingua A ghost town in Texas. p. 181

Texas A state in the southern United States. p. 43

Thames River (TEMZ) A river that flows through London, England. p. 115

Togo A country in western Africa. p. 381

Topeka The capital of Kansas. p. 137

Trenton The capital of New Jersey. p. 137

Tucson (TOO•sahn) A city in Arizona. p. 59

Tugaloo River A river that forms part of the border between South Carolina and Georgia; unites with the Seneca River to form the Savannah River. p. A15

Tunisia (too•NEE•zhuh) A country in northern Africa. p. 381

Uganda (yoo•GAN•duh) A country in eastern Africa. p. 381

Union A city in north central South Carolina; the county seat of Union County. p. A14

Utah A state in the western United States. p. 43

Vancouver A city in Canada. p. 67

Vermont A state in the northeastern United States. p. 43

Vietnam A country in southeastern Asia. p. A3

Virginia A state in the eastern United States. p. 43

Walhalla A town in northwestern South Carolina; the county seat of Oconee County. p. A14

Walterboro A town in southern South Carolina; the county seat of Colleton County. p. A14

Washington A state in the northwestern United States. p. 43

Washington, D.C. The capital of the United States. p. 137

Wateree River A river in central South Carolina; joins the Congaree River to form the Santee River. p. A15

West Columbia A city in Lexington County, South Carolina, on the Congaree River. p. 144

West Virginia A state in the eastern United States. p. 43

Western Hemisphere The western half of the Earth. p. 46

Wichita A city in south central Kansas. p. 118

Winnsboro A town in north central South Carolina; the county seat of Fairfield County. p. A14

Winyah Bay An inlet of the Atlantic Ocean, off the southeastern coast of Georgetown County, South Carolina. p. A15

Wisconsin A state in the north central United States. p. 43

Wyoming A state in the northwestern United States. p. 43

Yellowstone River A river in the northwestern United States. p. 118

York A city in north central South Carolina; the county seat of York County. p. A14

Yuma A city in Arizona, along the Colorado River. p. 43

Zimbabwe (zim•BAHB•way) A country in south central Africa. p. 381

Glossary

This Glossary contains important social studies words and their definitions. Each word is respelled as it would be in a dictionary. When you see the ´ mark after a syllable, pronounce that syllable with more force than the other syllables. The page number at the end of the definition tells where to find the word in your book. The boldfaced letters in the examples that follow show how these letters are pronounced in the respellings after each glossary word.

add, āce, câre, pälm; end, ēqual; it, īce; odd, ōpen, ôrder; tŏok, pōol; up, bûrn; yōō as *u* in *fuse*; oil; pout; ə as *a* in *above*, *e* in *sicken*, *i* in *possible*, *o* in *melon*, *u* in *circus*; check; ring; thin; this; zh as in *vision*

advertisement (ad•vər•tīz´mənt) Information that a producer provides about products and services to help sell the item. *p. 283*

agriculture (ag´rə•kul•chər) The raising of crops and farm animals. *p. 130*

allegiance (ə•lē´jəns) Loyalty or devotion to something, such as the flag and what it stands for. *p. 371*

amendment (ə•mend´mənt) A change made to something that is already written. *p. 208*

ancestor (an´ses•tər) A member of a person's family who lived a long time ago, such as a great-great-grandparent. *p. 58*

anthem (an´thəm) A patriotic song. *p. 370*

archaeologist (är•kē•ol´ə•jist) A scientist who looks for artifacts and explains how they were used. *p. 197*

artifact (är´tə•fakt) An object that we find that was used by people in the past. *p. 197*

ballot (bal´ət) A piece of paper that lists all the possible choices in an election. *p. 354*

bar graph (bär graf) A graph with bars of different heights or lengths that show amounts of things. *p. 272*

barter (bär´tər) To trade one product or service for another. *p. 288*

basic needs (bā´sik nēdz´) Food, clothing, and shelter. *p. 266*

bay (bā) A body of water that is part of a sea or ocean and is partly enclosed by land. *p. 147*

biography (bī•o´grə•fē) The story of a real person's life. *p. 62*

border (bôr´dər) The lines that divide one state or country from another, such as a line on a map. *p. 136*

boundary (boun´drē) Another word for *border*. *p. 136*

branch (branch) A smaller river that flows into a larger one. *p. 118*

campaign (kam•pān´) A series of activities, including speeches, that will get voters to choose one candidate instead of another. *p. 354*

canal (kə•nal´) A waterway that is built by people. *p. 194*

candidate (kan´də•dāt) Someone who hopes to be elected for a job. *p. 353*

capital city (kap´ə•təl sit´ē) The city where the leaders of a country or state meet and work. *p. 131*

capitol (kap´ə•təl) The building where lawmakers meet. *p. 133*

cardinal directions (kär´də•nəl di•rek´shənz) The main directions: **N** means north, **S** means south, **E** means east, and **W** means west. *p. 49*

cargo (kär´gō) Products that are brought into a place by various vehicles. *p. 307*

causeway (kôz´wā) A road built on soil piled up in shallow water. *p. 194*

century (sen´chə•rē) A period of 100 years. *p. 177*

citizen (sit´ə•zən) A person who lives in a community. *p. 50*

Glossary

civil war (si´vəl wôr) A war in which two parts of one country fight each other. *p. 207*

climate (klī´mət) The kind of weather a place has in each season year after year. *p. 103*

coast (kōst) The land next to an ocean or a lake. *p. 102*

colony (ko´lə•nē) A settlement that is ruled by another country. *p. 205*

communication (kə•myōō•nə•kā´shən) The sharing of feelings, thoughts, and information. *p. 210*

communication links (kə•myōō•nə•kā´shən lingks) Machines that people who are far apart can use to communicate with one another. *p. 300*

compass rose (kum´pəs rōz) The symbol on a map that shows where the directions north, south, east, and west are. *p. 48*

competition (kom•pə•tish´ən) What happens when two or more companies produce and sell the same product. *p. 281*

compromise (kom´prə•mīz) To give up some of the things you want in order to resolve a disagreement. *p. 347*

conflict (kon´flikt) A disagreement. *p. 346*

conflict resolution (kon´flikt re•zə•lōō´shən) A way of solving disagreements among people or groups. *p. 346*

Congress (kong´gris) The elected representatives of the government that makes new laws for the nation. *p. 364*

consequence (kon´sə•kwens) Something that happens because of an action. *p. 51*

constitution (kon•stə•tōō´shən) A plan of government. *p. 206*

consumer (kən•sōō´mər) A person who buys a product or a service. *p. 280*

continent (kon´tə•nənt) One of the seven main land areas on the Earth. *p. 44*

cooperate (kō•op´ə•rāt) To work together to keep the community a safe and peaceful place. *p. 50*

council (koun´səl) A group of people who have been chosen by citizens to meet and solve problems. *p. 341*

county (koun´tē) A part of a state. *p. 134*

county seat (koun´tē sēt) A city or town where the leaders of the county meet. *p. 134*

craft (kraft) The making of items by hand. *p. 467*

crop (krop) A plant used by people for food or other needs. *p. 126*

crossroads (krôs´rōdz) A place where two routes cross. *p. 113*

culture (kul´chər) A people's way of life. *p. 65*

custom (kus´təm) A way of doing something. *p. 64*

cutaway diagram (kut´ə•wā dī´ə•gram) A drawing that shows both the inside and outside of an object at the same time. *p. 304*

decade (de´kād) A period of 10 years. *p. 177*

demand (di•mand´) The need or desire that people have for a product or a service. *p. 282*

descendant (di•sen´dənt) The child or grandchild of an ancestor. *p. 460*

desert (dez´ərt) A place with a very dry climate. *p. 104*

disaster (di•zas´tər) Something that happens that causes great harm to a community. *p. 182*

distance scale (dis´təns skāl) The scale on a map that tells the real distance. *p. 48*

distribute (dis•trib´yōōt) To send out. *p. 309*

education (ej•ōō•kā´shən) The learning you get when you go to school. *p. 386*

election (i•lek´shən) An event in which people vote to choose leaders or vote for or against new laws. *p. 351*

empire (em´pīr) The lands and peoples under the control of a powerful nation. *p. 195*

equal rights (ē´kwəl rīts) The same rights for all people. *p. 243*

Glossary

equator (i•kwā´tər) An imaginary line around the Earth halfway between the North Pole and the South Pole. *p. 46*

ethnic group (eth´nik gro͞op) A group of people from the same country, of the same race, or with a common way of life. *p. 460*

export (eks´pôrt) To send a product or resource from one country to be sold in another country. *p. 301*

fall line (fôl´ līn) The place where rivers drop from higher to lower land. *p. 151*

ferry (fer´ē) A boat that carries people and goods across a waterway. *p. 114*

festival (fes´tə•vəl) A celebration that takes place every year, usually at the same time of year. *p. 464*

flow chart (flō´ chärt) A group of pictures showing the steps that must be followed to make or do something. *p. 278*

folklore (fōk´lôr) The unwritten literature, stories, and sayings of a people. *p. 468*

folktale (fōk´tāl) A traditional story that often teaches a lesson. *p. 448*

folkways (fōk´wāz) The ways of thinking, feeling, or acting that are common to a group of people. *p. 466*

ford (fôrd) A shallow place in a waterway that can be crossed by walking, riding, or driving. *p. 114*

founders (foun´dərz) The people who start a community. *p. 66*

frontier (frun•tir´) The edge of a settled area. *p. 148*

fuel (fyo͞o´əl) A resource, such as oil, that can be burned for heat or energy. *p. 128*

gateway (gāt´wā) An entrance. *p. 120*

geography (jē•og´rə•fē) The study of the Earth's features. *p. 99*

ghost town (gōst´ toun) A deserted town with buildings but no people. *p. 129*

globe (glōb) A round model of the Earth. *p. 46*

government (guv´ərn•mənt) A group of elected citizens who make the rules for a community. *p. 50*

government services (guv´ərn•mənt sûr´vi•səz) Services that are provided for all the citizens of a community. *p. 342*

governor (guv´ər•nər) The elected leader of a state's government. *p. 357*

grid (grid) A set of lines the same distance apart that cross one another to form squares. *p. 296*

growing season (grō´ing sē´zən) The months in which crops can grow. *p. 127*

Gullah (gu´lə) A language made up of English and African words, spoken today by some of the people who live in South Carolina's Low Country and on the Sea Islands. *p. 228*

harbor (här´bər) A protected place where ships can stay safe from high waves and strong winds. *p. 109*

hemisphere (hem´ə•sfir) A half of the Earth. *p. 46*

heritage (her´ə•tij) The culture left to someone by his or her ancestors. *p. 426*

historical society (his•tôr´ə•kəl sə•sī´ə•tē) A group of people, usually volunteers, who have a special interest in the history of their community. *p. 220*

history (his´tə•rē) The story of what has happened in a place. *p. 58*

holiday (hol´ə•dā) A special day for remembering a person or an event that is important to the people in a community. *p. 438*

human resources (hyo͞o´mən rē´sôr•səz) The people who work for a company. *p. 276*

Glossary

human-made features (hyo͞o´mən•mād fē´chərz) The buildings, bridges, and roads that people have added to a place. *p. 105*

identity (ī•den´tə•tē) The sense of sameness people feel about something. *p. 378*

immigrant (im´ə•grənt) A person who comes to a country to live. *p. 419*

import (im´pôrt) To bring a product or resource into one country from another country. *p. 301*

independence (in•də•pen´dəns) Freedom from the rules of others. *p. 206*

industry (in´dəs•trē) All the companies that make the same product or provide the same service. *p. 277*

intermediate directions (in•tər•mē´dē•ət di•rek´shənz) The directions that are midway between two cardinal directions—northeast, southeast, southwest, and northwest. *p. 125*

international trade (in•tər•nash´ən•əl trād) Trade between people in different countries. *p. 299*

invention (in•ven´shən) Something that has been thought of and made for the first time. *p. 212*

judge (juj) A citizen who is chosen to work as a leader in the courts. *p. 53*

junction (jungk•shən) A place where rivers or roads meet. *p. 144*

jury (jo͝or´ē) A group of 6 to 12 citizens who sit in a courtroom and listen to what both sides have to say and then agree on a decision. *p. 358*

landform (land´fôrm) A natural feature, or shape, of the land. *p. 100*

law (lô) A rule that helps make a community a safe place to live. *p. 51*

legend (lej´ənd) A story that explains how something came to be. *p. 192*

lines of latitude (līnz uv la´tə•to͞od) A set of lines drawn on maps and globes that run east and west. *p. 310*

lines of longitude (līnz uv lon´jə•to͞od) A set of lines drawn on maps and globes that run north and south. *p. 310*

literature (lit´ər•ə•chər) The books, poetry, stories, and plays written by people to share ideas. *p. 426*

location (lō•kā´shən) The place where something is found. *p. 41*

lodge (loj) A home that is made of logs, earth, and grass. *p. 186*

majority rule (mə•jôr´ə•tē ro͞ol) The rule that if more than half make the same choice, they get their way. *p. 354*

manufacture (man•yə•fak´chər) To make goods. *p. 122*

map (map) A picture that shows the location of things or places. *p. 41*

map key (map´ kē) A section of a map that tells what the symbols on the map stand for. *p. 48*

marketing (mär´kət•ing) Planning how to sell a product to consumers. *p. 275*

mayor (mā´ər) The leader of a city or town government. *p. 52*

mediator (mē´dē•ā•tər) A person who works to help two sides settle a disagreement. *p. 347*

mineral (min´ər•əl) A resource, such as gold, that is found inside the Earth. *p. 128*

minority rights (mə•nôr´ə•tē rīts) The rights of those who did not vote for the winner to keep all their rights. *p. 354*

missionary (mish´ə•ner•ē) A person who is sent to tell others about his or her religious beliefs. *p. 60*

motto (mot´ō) A saying that people try to live by. *p. 378*

mountain range (moun´tən rānj) A large group or row of mountains. *p. 100*

N

natural resource (na´chər•əl rē´sôrs) Something found in nature that is useful to people. *p. 126*

nonrenewable resource (non•ri•noo´ə•bəl rē´sôrs) A resource that cannot be replaced, or made again, by nature or people. *p. 315*

O

ocean (ō´shən) A large body of salt water. *p. 45*

opportunity (op•ər•too´nə•tē) The chance to find a job, get an education, or have a better way of life. *p. 418*

opportunity cost (op•ər•too´nə•tē kôst) What you have to give up in order to have something else. *p. 286*

P

patriotism (pā´trē•ə•tiz•əm) The love that people have for their country. *p. 368*

peninsula (pə•nin´sə•lə) A piece of land that has water almost all the way around it. *p. 102*

petition (pə•tish´ən) A written request that people sign, calling for government action. *p. 340*

physical feature (fiz´i•kəl fē´chər) Something found in nature, such as weather, plant life, land, and water. *p. 99*

pictograph (pik´tə•graf) A graph that has small pictures that stand for numbers of things. *p. 272*

piedmont (pēd´mont) A name that means "foot of the mountain." The Piedmont of South Carolina is a region of rolling hills. *p. 78*

plain (plān) An area of land that is flat or nearly flat. *p. 101*

plantation (plan•tā´shən) A large farm. *p. 227*

plateau (pla•tō´) An area of high, flat land. *p. 101*

pledge (plej) A promise. *p. 371*

point of view (point uv vyoo´) The way a person feels about something. *p. 436*

pollution (pə•loo´shən) Anything that makes the air, land, or water unclean. *p. 199*

population (pop•yə•lā´shən) The number of people who live in a place. *p. 111*

population density (pop•yə•lā´shən den´sə•tē) The number of people who live in an area of a certain size. *p. 454*

port (pôrt) A place that has deep water, where ships can dock. *p. 108*

price (prīs) The amount of money needed to buy a product or service. *p. 281*

private property (prī´vət prop´ər•tē) Something that belongs to one person or a small group of people. *p. 357*

producer (prə•doo´sər) A person who makes a product. *p. 273*

product (prod´ukt) Something that people make or grow, often to sell. *p. 270*

profit (prä´•fət) The amount of money left after all the costs of running a business or making a product have been paid. *p. 313*

province (prov´ins) A division of a country with its own government. *p. 383*

public property (pub´lik prop´ər•tē) Something that belongs to all citizens. *p. 357*

rain forest (rān´ fôr´əst) A thick forest that has a wet climate. *p. 139*

rapids (rap´ədz) A part of a river where the water runs very fast, often over rocks. *p. 110*

raw materials (rô mə•tir´ē•əlz) The resources needed to make a product. *p. 274*

Reconstruction (rē•kən•strək´shən) A time of rebuilding the United States after the Civil War. *p. 236*

region (rē´jən) A place with at least one feature that makes it different from other places. *p. 75*

religion (ri•lij´ən) A set of beliefs about God or a set of gods. *p. 418*

renewable resource (ri•nōō´ə•bəl rē´sôrs) A resource that can be used again or made again by people or nature. *p. 313*

reservoir (rez´ər•vwär) A lake used for collecting and storing water. *p. 176*

resource (rē´sôrs) Something that people use to meet needs. *p. 55*

responsibility (ri•spon•sə•bil´ə•tē) A duty that citizens have. *p. 54*

revolution (rev•ə•lōō´shən) A fight for a change in government. *p. 205*

riverbank (riv´ər•bangk) The land beside a river. *p. 118*

route (rōōt) A path from one place to another. *p. 112*

rural (rŏor´əl) In the country; an area away from cities and towns. *p. 266*

S

satellite (sat´ə•līt) A spacecraft that is used to send radio, telephone, and television signals. *p. 216*

secede (si•sēd´) To withdraw from something, such as the states that left the Union at the time of the Civil War. *p. 233*

sequence (sē´kwens) The order in which things happen. *p. 444*

service (sûr´vis) Something one person does for another. *p. 269*

slave (slāv) A person who is owned by another person and works without pay. *p. 204*

solution (sə•lōō´shən) A way to solve a problem. *p. 202*

sound (sound) A long passage of water separating a mainland and an island. *p. 147*

state capital (stāt kap´ə•təl) A city where lawmakers meet to make laws for a state. *p. 134*

suburb (sub´ûrb) A community built near a city. *p. 215*

supply (sə•plī´) The amount of a product or service there is to be sold. *p. 282*

Supreme Court (sə•prēm´ kôrt) The most important court in the United States. *p. 366*

symbol (sim´bəl) A picture that is used to stand for something that is real on the Earth. A symbol may also stand for something that is not real, but that is an idea, such as Uncle Sam. *pp. 48, 374*

table (tā´bəl) A chart used to organize information. *p. 111*

tall tale (tôl tāl´) A story that tells about someone who does something impossible. *p. 429*

tax (taks) The money citizens pay to the government to run a city, state, or country. *p. 205*

technology (tek•nol´ə•jē) The use of machines, tools, and materials to communicate and make products faster and more easily. *p. 273*

tepee (tē´pē) An easily moved shelter made of poles covered with buffalo skins. *p. 187*

textile (teks´tīl) Woven cloth. *p. 238*

tidewater (tīd´wâ•tər) An area of water near the ocean where the waters rise and fall twice a day with the tide. *p. 76*

time line (tīm´ līn) A graphic organizer that shows when important events took place. *p. 63*

tourism (tŏor´iz•əm) The selling of products and services to tourists. *p. 316*

township (toun´ship) A planned community. *p. 229*

trade center (trād sen´tər) A community where buying and selling goods is the main work. *p. 110*

trade-off (trād´ôf) Giving up something you want in order to get something else. *p. 286*

tradition (trə•dish´ən) A custom, or way of doing something, that is passed on from parents to children. *p. 439*

transcontinental (trans•kon•tə•nen´təl) Extending from one side of a continent to the other. *p. 211*

transportation (trans•pər•tā´shən) Ways of moving things from one place to another. *p. 180*

valley (val´ē) The landform between ranges of hills or mountains. *p. 100*

volunteer (vol•ən•tir´) A person who chooses to work in a community without being paid. *p. 57*

vote (vōt) To say what you think a group should do. *p. 349*

wage (wāj) The money a worker is paid. *p. 276*

Glossary

Index

Page references for illustrations are set in italic type. An italic *m* indicates a map. Page references set in boldface type indicate the pages on which vocabulary words are defined.

Index

For permission to reprint copyrighted material, grateful acknowledgment is made to the following sources:

Atheneum Books for Young Readers, Simon & Schuster Children's Publishing Division: Aurora Means Dawn by Scott Russell Sanders, illustrated by Jill Kastner. Text copyright © 1989 by Scott Russell Sanders; illustrations copyright © 1989 by Jill Kastner.

Denny Music, Inc.: "South Carolina on My Mind" by Hank Martin and Buzz Arledge. Lyrics © copyright 1979 by Denny Music, Inc.

Dial Books for Young Readers, a division of Penguin Putnam Inc.: Cover illustration by Bernie Fuchs from *Carolina Shout!* by Alan Schroeder. Illustration copyright © 1995 by Bernie Fuchs.

Farrar, Straus & Giroux, Inc.: From *Saturday Sancocho* by Leyla Torres. Copyright © 1995 by Leyla Torres.

Free Spirit Publishing, Minneapolis, MN: "Honoring Her Ancestors," adapted from "Honoring Their Ancestors" in *Kids With Courage: True Stories About Young People Making a Difference* by Barbara A. Lewis, edited by Pamela Espeland. Text copyright © 1992 by Barbara A. Lewis.

Good Books: From *Reuben and the Fire* by Merle Good, illustrated by P. Buckley Moss. Text copyright © 1993 by Merle Good; illustrations copyright © 1993 by P. Buckley Moss.

Harcourt Brace & Company: Cover illustration from *The Buck Stops Here: The Presidents of the United States* by Alice Provensen. Copyright © 1997, 1990 by Alice Provensen.

Holiday House, Inc.: Cover illustration from *Stars & Stripes: Our National Flag* by Leonard Everett Fisher. Copyright © 1993 by Leonard Everett Fisher.

Henry Holt and Company, Inc.: Cover photographs from *All Around Town: The Photographs of Richard Samuel Roberts* by Dinah Johnson. Photographs copyright © 1998 by the Estate of Richard Samuel Roberts.

Houghton Mifflin Company: Grandfather's Journey by Allen Say. Copyright © 1993 by Allen Say.

Alfred A. Knopf, Inc.: From "Paul Bunyan" in *American Tall Tales* by Mary Pope Osborne, cover illustration by Michael McCurdy. Text copyright © 1991 by Mary Pope Osborne; cover illustration copyright © 1991 by Michael McCurdy.

Lothrop, Lee & Shepard Books, a division of William Morrow & Company, Inc.: Roxaboxen by Alice McLerran, illustrated by Barbara Cooney. Text copyright © 1991 by Alice McLerran; illustrations copyright © 1991 by Barbara Cooney. Cover illustration from *New Hope* by Henri Sorensen. Copyright © 1995 by Henri Sorensen.

Morrow Junior Books, a division of William Morrow & Company, Inc.: From *City Green* by DyAnne DiSalvo-Ryan. Copyright © 1994 by DyAnne DiSalvo-Ryan.

Pantheon Books, a division of Random House, Inc.: From *John Henry* by Ezra Jack Keats. Copyright © 1965 by Ezra Jack Keats.

Scholastic Inc.: Cover illustration by Susannah Ryan from *Coming To America: The Story of Immigration* by Betsy Maestro. Illustration copyright © 1996 by Susannah Ryan.

Scholastic Press, a division of Scholastic Inc.: Cover illustration by Ned Bittinger from *The Blue and the Gray* by Eve Bunting. Illustration copyright © 1996 by Ned Bittinger.

Simon & Schuster Books for Young Readers, an imprint of Simon & Schuster Children's Publishing Division: Cover illustration by Joyce Audy Zarins from *The Go-Around Dollar* by Barbara Johnston Adams. Illustration copyright © 1992 by Joyce Audy Zarins.

Viking Penguin, a division of Penguin Putnam Inc.: Shaker Lane by Alice and Martin Provensen. Copyright © 1987 by Alice Provensen.

PHOTO CREDITS:

Page Placement Key: (t)-top (c)-center (b)-bottom (l)-left (r)-right (fg)-foreground (bg)-background.

Contents: iii Timothy Fuller; iv Beverly Brosius/Harcourt Brace & Company; v Ron Kunzman/Harcourt Brace & Company; vi Weronica Ankarorn/Harcourt Brace & Company; vii Russell D. Curtis/Photo Researchers, Inc.; viii Michael Newman/Photo Edit.

Introduction: 20 Weronica Ankarorn.

Unit 1
Harcourt Brace & Company: 28 Victoria Bowen; 40, 72 Harcourt Brace & Company; 87 Sheri O'Neal.

Other: 24-25 Lawrence Migdale; 26 (t) Mark Lewis/Tony Stone Images; 26 (b) Aaron Haupt/Photo Researchers; 27 (tl), 27 (tr) Don Roper; 27 (bl) Chad Ehlers/International Stock Photography; 27 (br) Lawrence Migdale; 50 Bruce Ayres/Tony Stone Images; 51 52, 53 Timothy Fuller; 54 Lisa Quinones/Black Star; 55, 56 Timothy Fuller; 57 (t) Stephen McBrady/PhotoEdit; 57 (b) Timothy Fuller; 58 E.T. Corson-Clarissa Winsor Collection/Arizona Historical Society; 59 Timothy Fuller/Arizona State Museum, University of Arizona; 60 (t) Timothy Fuller; 60 (b) Courtesy: Yuma Territorial Prison State Historic Park, Arizona State Parks/Arizona Historical Society; 61 (t) Timothy Fuller; 61 (b) Yuma County Historical Society/Arizona Historical Society; 64 Richard Drew/Wide World Photos; 64 Timothy Fuller; 65 (t) Magaret Finefrock/Unicorn Stock Photos; 65 (b) Chad Ehlers/International Stock Photography; 66 Courtesy of the Native Sons of British Columbia and Simon Fraser University; 67 City of Vancouver Archives; 68 (t) Vancouver Public Library; 68 (b) Vancouver Public Library; 69 Greg Kinch/Black Star; 70 (t) Ed Gifford/Masterfile; 70 (bl) "Stamp reproduced courtesy of Canada Post Corporation"; 71 Stock Montage; 76 (t) A. J. Spillman; 76 (bl) Randy Wells/Tony Stone Images; 76 (br) Robert Clark; 76-77 (bg) Kevin Shields/New England Stock Photo; 77 Cheryl Callaman; 78 (t) Bill Terry; 78 (bl) J. Michael Krouskop/In-Stock Photography, Inc.; 78 (bc), 78 (br) Robert Clark Photography; 78-79 (bg) Randy Wells/The Stock Market; 79 Robert C. Clark Photography; 81 (b) James Magdanz.

Unit 2
Harcourt Brace & Company: 91 (tl) Beverly Brosius; 92 Sheri O'Neal; 103 (b) Beverly Brosius; 143 (t) Harcourt Brace & Company; 160 Sheri O'Neal; 161 Weronica Ankarorn.

Other: 88-89 Mark Segal/Tony Stone Images; 90 (t) Mark Segal/Panoramic Images; 90 (bl) Michael Collier/Stock Boston; 90 (br) David R. Frazier; 91 (tr) Yellow Dog Productions/The Image Bank; 91 (c) Stephen J. Krasemann/DRK; 91 (b) Jerry Whaley/Natural Selection Stock Photography; 99 Ranes Lynn/Photo Researchers; 100 (t) Jeff Foott/DRK Photo; 100 (c) Pat O'Hara/DRK; 100 (bl) David Muench Photography; 100 (br) Jerry Whaley/Natural Selection Stock Photography; 101 (tr) Stephen J. Krasemann/DRK; 101 (b) David Lissy/Natural Selection Stock Photography; 102 (t) Stephen J. Krasemann/DRK; 102 (c) David Muench Photography; 102 (b) David Muench Photography; 103 (t) Myrleen Ferguson Cate/Index Stock Photography; 104 Telegraph Colour Library/FPG International; 105 R.Mastroianni/Black Star; 108 Grant Heilman Photography; 110 Superstock; 114 (t) Nick Gunderson/Tony Stone Images; 114 (bl) Archive Photos/Popperfoto; 114 (br) R. Matassa/H. Armstrong Roberts; 117 William Iseminger; 118 The Detroit Institute of the Arts/Collection of the St. Louis Science Center; 119 (t) Jim Richardson/Westlight; 119 (c) Jim Richardson/Westlight; 119 (b) Missouri Historical Society; 120-121 (bg) Oregon Historical Society #97112; 120 (t) Oregon Historical Society #97120; 120 (b) Stephen F. Rich/Oregon Trail Regional Museum, Baker City, Oregon; 121 (t) Kansas State Historical Society, Topeka, Kansas; 121 (c) Oregon Historical Society, #097119; 121 (b) Oregon Historical Society #097118; 122 Culver Pictures; 123 Jim Blakeway/Panoramic Images; 124 International News Photos/UPI/Bettmann; 126 (l) AGStock USA; 126 (r) Holly Kuper/AGStock USA; 127 (t) Grant Heilman Photography; 127 (b) Dave Schaefer/The Picture Cube; 128 David L. Brown/The Picture Cube; 129 Tom Bean/DRK; 131 "Courtesy, Winterthur Museum"; 132 (t) The Granger Collection; 132 (b) Peter Gridley/FPG International; 133 (t) The Granger Collection; 133 (b) Schomburg Center for Research in Black Culture; 134 Maxine Cass; 135 Jeff Schultz/Alaska Stock Images; 138 Tony Stone Images; 140 Columbus Memorial Library at the Organization of American States; 141 (l) Jose Fuste Raga/The Stock Market; 141 (r) Tony Morrison/South American Pictures; 142-143 Colonial Williamsburg Foundation; 144 David R. Frazier; 145 (t) David R. Frazier; 145 (b) Scala/Art Resource, NY; 146 Michael J. Schimpf; 148 The Granger Collection, New York; 149 (t) Ron A. Rocz/Tradd Street Stock Photography; 149 (b) J. Faircloth/Transparencies; 150 (t) J. Faircloth/Transparencies, Inc.; 150 (c) From the collection of the Aiken County Historical Museum; 150 (b) Robert Clark Photography; 151 M. Krouskop/Tradd Street Stock Photography; 152 Michael Moore/Transparencies; 153 (l) Eric Horan/Liaison International; 153 (r) W. Metzen/H. Armstrong Roberts; 154-155 (bg) Robert Clark Photography; 154 Beach Sweep, River Sweep; 155 (t) Linda Blackwell; 155 (b) Beach Sweep, River Sweep.

Unit 3
Harcourt Brace & Company: 162-163 Richard Nowitz; 166 Weronica Ankarorn; 200 (b) Victoria Bowen; 212 (bc) Weronica Ankarorn; 218 (r) Terry D. Sinclair; 218 (l) Victoria Bowen; 219 (t) Ron Kunzman; 219 (b), 220 Ron Kunzman; 252, 253 Weronica Ankarorn.